The Changing School Scene: Challenge to Psychology
by Leah Gold Fein

Troubled Children: Their Families, Schools, and Treatments
by Leonore R. Love and Jaques W. Kaswan

Research Strategies in Psychotherapy
by Edward S. Bordin

The Volunteer Subject
by Robert Rosenthal and Ralph L. Rosnow

Innovations in Client-Centered Therapy
by David A. Wexler and Laura North Rice

The Rorschach: A Comprehensive System
by John E. Exner

D1602888

Theory and Practice in Behavior Therapy
by Aubrey J. Yates

Principles of Psychotherapy
by Irving B. Weiner

Psychoactive Drugs and Social Judgment: Theory and Research
edited by Kenneth Hammond and C. R. B. Joyce

Clinical Methods in Psychology
edited by Irving B. Weiner

Human Resources for Troubled Children
by Werner I. Halpern and Stanley Kissel

Hyperactivity
by Dorothea M. Ross and Sheila A. Ross

Heroin Addiction: Theory, Research, and Treatment
by Jerome J. Platt and Christina Labate

Children's Rights and the Mental Health Profession
edited by Gerald P. Koocher

The Role of the Father in Child Development
edited by Michael E. Lamb

Handbook of Behavioral Assessment
edited by Anthony R. Ciminero, Karen S. Calhoun, and Henry E. Adams

Counseling and Psychotherapy: A Behavioral Approach
by E. Lakin Phillips

Dimensions of Personality
edited by Harvey London and John E. Exner, Jr.

The Mental Health Industry: A Cultural Phenomenon
*by Peter A. Magaro, Robert Gripp, David McDowell,
and Ivan W. Miller III*

Nonverbal Communication: The State of the Art
by Robert G. Harper, Arthur N. Wiens, and Joseph D. Matarazzo

A Biodevelopmental Approach to Clinical Child Psychology: Cognitive
Controls and Cognitive Control Therapy
by Sebastiano Santostefano

Alcoholism and Treatment
by David J. Armor, J. Michael Polich, and Harriet B. Stambul

ALCOHOLISM AND TREATMENT

ALCOHOLISM AND TREATMENT

DAVID J. ARMOR
J. MICHAEL POLICH
HARRIET B. STAMBUL

A WILEY-INTERSCIENCE PUBLICATION

JOHN WILEY & SONS, New York • Chichester • Brisbane • Toronto

Published by John Wiley & Sons, Inc.

Copyright © 1978 by The Rand Corporation

The publication is designed to provide accurate and authoritative information in regard to the subject matter covered. It is sold with the understanding that the publisher is not engaged in rendering legal, accounting, or other professional service. If legal advice or other expert assistance is required, the services of a competent professional person should be sought.

From a Declaration of Principles jointly adopted by a Committee of the American Bar Association and a Committee of Publishers.

Library of Congress Cataloging in Publication Data:

Armor, David J.
  Alcoholism and treatment.
  "A Wiley-Interscience publication."
  Bibliography: p.
  1. Alcoholism—Treatment—United States.
2. Alcoholism—United States. I. Polich, J. Michael,
joint author. II. Stambul, Harriet B., joint author.
III. Title. [DNLM: 1. Alcoholism—Therapy. WM274
A733a]
HV5279.A75 1978   362.2'92   77-17421
ISBN 0-471-02558-5

Printed in the United States of America

10 9 8 7 6 5 4 3 2

Series Preface

This series of books is addressed to behavioral scientists interested in the nature of human personality. Its scope should prove pertinent to personality theorists and researchers as well as to clinicians concerned with applying an understanding of personality processes to the amelioration of emotional difficulties in living. To this end, the series provides a scholarly integration of theoretical formulations, empirical data, and practical recommendations.

Six major aspects of studying and learning about human personality can be designated: personality theory, personality structure and dynamics, personality development, personality assessment, personality change, and personality adjustment. In exploring these aspects of personality, the books in the series discuss a number of distinct but related subject areas: the nature and implications of various theories of personality; personality characteristics that account for consistencies and variations in human behavior; the emergence of personality processes in children and adolescents; the use of interviewing and testing procedures to evaluate individual differences in personality; effects to modify personality styles through psychotherapy, counseling, behavior therapy, and other methods of influence; and patterns of abnormal personality functioning that impair individual competence.

IRVING B. WEINER

Case Western Reserve University
Cleveland, Ohio

Preface

Alcoholism and Treatment is a scientific research study first published in 1976 as a Rand Corporation report.* Aside from minor editorial changes, the text of this book is virtually identical with that of the original report. The major addition is Appendix B, which documents some of the debate that followed the publication of the report.

This volume contains the findings of the first in a series of ongoing Rand alcoholism studies, supported by the National Institute on Alcohol Abuse and Alcoholism (Grant 2R01-AA-01203-04; Contract ADM-281-76-0006). These studies have the overall purpose of developing basic knowledge on the nature of alcoholism, alcohol abuse, and treatment. *Alcoholism and Treatment* was undertaken specifically to evaluate the effectiveness of the national system of alcoholism centers established by NIAAA in 1971. Our objective was to assess the nature of treatment outcomes, drawing on a large national data base of persons who had been treated at the NIAAA centers.

When first issued as a Rand report, this study sparked widespread public interest and debate, primarily because of the outcome ("remission") categories defined there. As described in detail in Chapter 4, these categories included long-term abstention, short-term abstention, and normal drinking. Much of the public discussion of the findings has centered around the inclusion of normal drinking as a form of remission; less attention has been given to other substantive findings and to important qualifications.

Accordingly, we wish to emphasize one principal point at the outset of this book. The outcomes presented here as research findings should *not* be viewed as recommendations for what individuals should do about their drinking behavior. In particular, *this study does not show that alcoholics may safely resume drinking*, nor does it suggest that any alcoholic should do so.

---

* David J. Armor, J. Michael Polich, and Harriet B. Stambul, *Alcoholism and Treatment* (Santa Monica, Calif.: The Rand Corporation, June 1976), R-1739-NIAAA.

Our caution derives from the existence of several uncertainties that have not yet been resolved by research. The question of how long an alcoholic will remain in remission is one important example. The term "remission," and not "recovery," was chosen precisely because the study spans only a relatively brief period of time, no more than 18 months after initial treatment. Whether any remission pattern might prove stable over a longer period remains an unanswered question. Added to this uncertainty are the methodological limitations posed by the conventional self-reporting measurements used in the study.

Many critical issues about alcoholism remain unresolved. While *Alcoholism and Treatment* provides no final answers, it raises questions that demonstrate the urgent need for further research. It is our hope that this book, and the continuing debate about the nature of alcoholism, will encourage the research effort needed to combat this important national health problem.

DAVID J. ARMOR
J. MICHAEL POLICH
HARRIET B. STAMBUL

Santa Monica, California
January, 1978

Acknowledgments

Beyond the generous sponsorship provided by NIAAA, this study would not have been possible without the actions and assistance of a great number of individuals and agencies. First recognition must go to Dr. Morris Chafetz, former director of NIAAA, who, with the assistance of Dr. Howard Blane of the University of Pittsburgh, conceived and promoted the concept of a comprehensive evaluation of NIAAA treatment centers. Further, this concept became a reality known as the Alcoholism Treatment Center Monitoring System only because of the painstaking labor of NIAAA's Program Development and Evaluation Branch and especially of Associate Director John Deering, Donald Patterson, and David Promisel. The Monitoring System was developed, tested, and installed by the Stanford Research Institute on contract to NIAAA, with important leadership provided by Leland Towle and later by Ann Mothershead. Leland Towle, Ann Mothershead, and Lee Ruggels of SRI were also responsible for the design and execution of the special 18-Month Followup Study, with further assistance provided by Rand on the analysis of treatment outcomes.

While the sources of data were crucial for this study, equally important were the many suggestions and comments provided during early stages of the research and on earlier drafts of this report. Special thanks to Leland Towle and David Promisel who have made numerous constructive suggestions for specific analyses that appear in this report. Formal reviews of earlier versions of the manuscript were made by Dr. Robert Moore, Mesa Vista Hospital, San Diego; Robin Room and Ronald Roizen, Social Research Group, Berkeley; and Drs. David Chu and Gus Haggstrom, Rand. A comprehensive critique was also received from Dr. Mary Pendery, Veterans Administration Hospital, San Diego.

Gratitude is extended to various groups and individuals who granted permission to use materials for Appendix B. Professors Lenin Baler, University of Michigan; Samuel Guze, Washington University; and Gerald Klerman, Harvard University, consented to publication of their reviews of the Rand report for NIAAA. The *Journal of Studies on Alcohol* as well as the individual authors consented to reprinting comments published in the January 1977 issue. The authors are Dr. Chad Emrick, Aurora Mental Health Center; Dr. Sheila Blume, Central Islip Mental Health Center; Dr. Allen Adinolfi, Boston Veterans Administration Hospital; and Ronald Roizen, University of California, Berkeley, School of Public Health.

The tedious task of typing several versions of the manuscript and its many tables was carried out by many Rand secretaries, including Linda Lazo-Lane, Marjorie Schubert, and Constance Smedley, but the bulk of the burden was handled admirably by Marcia Teeter.

Finally, and most important, considerable credit must go to the hundreds of treatment center staff members who had the primary responsibility for collecting the evaluation data on which this study is based.

D. J. A.
J. M. P.
H. B. S.

Contents

ALCOHOLISM AND TREATMENT

ONE

Introduction

Only twice in the 20th century has American alcohol consumption shown dramatic changes due to presumably natural causes. From about 1881 to 1900, consumption hovered around an annual per capita rate of about 2 gallons of absolute alcohol with only small fluctuations from year to year.[1] But at the turn of the century the rate began to rise rapidly; by 1915 it had reached 2.66 gallons, an increase of 33 percent. This translates to an equivalent per capita rate of about 2.2 ounces of hard liquor per day, or nearly two drinks per day for every man, woman, and child over age 15. Of course, this distribution was by no means uniform: some persons did not drink at all, and an even smaller group drank much larger amounts. Nonetheless the growing public controversy over the abuse of alcohol reached its peak in 1920 with our first national policy on alcohol use and abuse, Prohibition.

The second change occurred in the 1960s. Following the unsuccessful experiment with the Prohibition Amendment and its repeal in 1933, alcohol consumption rapidly reached a plateau at its turn-of-the-century level. From the World War II years to 1961, the rate held at a fairly constant level of about 2 gallons per year, seldom varying by more than a few hundredths of a gallon. In 1962, the rate began rising steadily and surpassed the pre-Prohibition high in 1971 with a rate of 2.68 gallons. And, perhaps not coincidentally, in 1970 the federal government implemented its second national policy on alcohol: Public Law 91-616, the Comprehensive Alcohol Abuse and Alcoholism Prevention, Treatment, and Rehabilitation Act, which had as its major thrust the creation of the National Institute on Alcohol Abuse and Alcoholism (NIAAA).

The formulation of national public policy rests ultimately on the perception of a national problem and a belief that a solution is at hand. Obviously, the extent to which these perceptions and beliefs are based on scientific methods and evidence varies greatly according to the nature of

---

[1] For persons aged 15 and over (Efron, Keller, and Gurioli, 1972). The convention of using age 15 as a cutoff point is justified in part by the observation that many persons have their first full drinks at this age.

1

the problem and the era of its recognition. In the case of Prohibition, the definition of the problem and its solution were based largely on religious convictions: Alcohol was debasing if not evil, and alcoholism was sinful behavior whose only answer was prohibition of alcohol by law. On the other hand, modern policy defines alcoholism as a health problem and, as with other health policies, depends heavily on the medical and behavioral sciences rather than the law for discovery of its causes and its cures. Thus Public Law 91-616 and the programs it authorized imply a set of assumptions about the nature of alcoholism as an illness, the causes of that illness, and the methods by which it can be remedied or alleviated. Unlike Prohibition policy, modern health programs such as those promoted by NIAAA can often be evaluated to generate further understanding about the causes of and remedies for the illness.

This study constitutes an evaluation of a major component of NIAAA policy, namely its comprehensive alcoholism treatment centers. Using data gathered by NIAAA as part of an ongoing monitoring system of its treatment programs, the study aims to extend our knowledge of alcoholism and its remedies by evaluating the success of these centers.

TREATMENT EVALUATION AND ETIOLOGY

In accordance with its Congressional mandate, NIAAA has invested much of its resources in a series of treatment and rehabilitation programs for the alcoholic population, the largest of these being the Comprehensive Alcoholism Treatment Center Program. Initiated to demonstrate the efficacy of a comprehensive, multiple-service approach to treatment, this program now funds 44 treatment centers (ATCs) throughout the country offering services that include detoxification, hospitalization, rehabilitation, and residential and outpatient treatment.

Clearly, the large investment of public funds into a comprehensive treatment program designed to alleviate a health problem calls for an equally comprehensive evaluation of its effectiveness. But a treatment evaluation can be more than simply a statement of which treatment works best. A given treatment program necessarily makes certain assumptions about the nature of the illness, its causes, and its remedy; the programs sponsored by NIAAA are no exception. Moreover, since there is no final consensus among professionals in the field about the ultimate causes of alcoholism or its most effective remedies, there are various kinds of treatment programs, each reflecting somewhat different assumptions about the nature of alcoholism. Therefore, by comparing the efficacy of different programs, treatment evaluation can also contribute to our understanding of alcoholism.

In the NIAAA treatment programs, the opportunities for etiological insights are especially enhanced by the diversity of treatments represented, the heterogeneity of clients in treatment, and the availability of campable data on alcoholics not in treatment and on alcohol use in the general population. These data allow investigation of the factors that distinguish the alcoholic in treatment from the normal drinker not in treatment, and treatment regimens that produce differing degrees of success. It is possible to compare, for example, not only the overall effectiveness of inpatient versus outpatient care but also their effectiveness for subgroups of clients representing differing levels of impairment and varying social backgrounds. Moreover, the outcomes of individuals who enter treatment can be compared with those who make contact with the center but do not enter treatment. Such comparisons offer a preliminary investigation of the issue of "natural" remission and its implications about the nature of alcoholism and its treatment.

Rarely, in the long history of alcoholism, has there been an opportunity to conduct a large-scale study of alcoholism and its treatment such as that offered by the current NIAAA programs and the evaluation data collected by them.

NIAAA EVALUATION DATA

The common belief that some treatments work better than others, especially for certain types of clients, rests more on clinical experience than on systematic research findings. Two problems have limited current research. First, there has tended to be a bifurcation of research between studies of alcohol consumption or problem drinking among general populations on the one hand and studies of treatment effects or etiology among alcoholics who enter some type of clinic or treatment program on the other. Thus, systematic comparisons between treated and untreated alcoholics or problem drinkers are seldom available within the same study. Consequently, it has been difficult to generalize about client characteristics that may be of prognostic value.

A second, more important, problem is that most treatment evaluation studies are conducted within only one or two treatment centers. Client populations are therefore relatively homogeneous and the treatment modes few in number. The most comprehensive evaluation study to date (Gerard and Saenger, 1966) covered only nine treatment centers in one part of the country and investigated outpatient care exclusively. The limited scope of existing research is understandable, given the great cost of national comparative studies and the limited federal funds available for alcoholism research until NIAAA was established in 1970.

It was therefore a welcome event when NIAAA implemented a series of comprehensive monitoring systems and evaluation projects for its treatment, prevention, and education programs. Because these systems and projects were designed to use compatible measurements of both drinking behavior and social characteristics, comparative analyses of both treated and untreated alcoholics or problem drinkers of various types can be conducted on a scale far larger than has been possible to date. These systems and projects have generated a vast comparative data resource that should prove to be of considerable value to research in alcoholism and its treatment.

This study will use three of these data resources in order to conduct a comprehensive evaluation of treatment programs and the etiological models implied by them. These include data generated by the ATC Monitoring System, the special ATC Followup Study, and the Public Education Campaign surveys.

The ATC Monitoring System

The largest monitoring system used by NIAAA is that designed for the comprehensive alcoholism treatment centers (ATCs). In full operation since September 1972, this system contains a broad set of client, treatment, and outcome data on nearly 30,000 clients who have entered treatment at the 44 comprehensive treatment centers throughout the country.[2]

The data are collected by the treatment-center staff, with a variety of instruments.[3] Contact and intake forms include information on demographic variables, social background, drinking history, behavioral and social impairment, and consumption. In order to assess treatment outcomes, those characteristics that can change over time, such as social stability and drinking behavior, are reassessed by means of a followup form 6 months after intake. Finally, for every client in treatment, an individual service report is completed each month, indicating the days of various types of inpatient care and the number of visits for various types of outpatient care.

The data are collected but not processed by the ATCs. Instead, completed forms are sent to a central contractor for editing, validating, and

---

[2] The original ATC Monitoring System was developed and implemented by the Stanford Research Institute on contract to NIAAA (Towle et al., 1973).

[3] See Appendix D for the ATC Monitoring System data-collection forms.

updating a series of master files.[4] The contractor not only maintains these data bases but also processes them routinely to produce a series of monitoring reports that are sent to both NIAAA and individual ATCs. These routine reports can be used by NIAAA and the ATCs to evaluate a series of management and treatment outcome issues. The data base can also be used by researchers studying more specific questions, such as the present evaluation of treatment.

The ATC 18-Month Followup Study

The ATC Monitoring System has two characteristics that limit generalizations about treatment effectiveness. First, the outcome evaluation occurs at 6 months following intake. This means that only relatively short-term outcomes can be evaluated. Second, the 6-month followup is routinely administered only to those clients who are easily accessible to the ATC; this results in 6-month followup reports on only about 25 percent of the clients who enter treatment.

The special ATC 18-Month Followup Study largely solves both of these problems for a selected number of ATCs.[5] A large sample of clients was drawn from 8 representative ATCs, and these clients were interviewed approximately 1½ years from intake. The data gathered included information compatible with the regular 6-month followup report. Completed interviews were obtained on nearly two-thirds of those clients in the original sample that had formally entered treatment. The special ATC Followup Study therefore represents a potential replication of the results from the 6-month analysis but on a smaller, longer term, more complete set of data.

Public Education Campaign Surveys

The ATC Monitoring System and the special ATC Followup Study yield data only on alcoholics in treatment. Thus, in order to select those client characteristics that have etiological or prognostic value for a treatment evaluation, it is necessary to compare the treated alcoholic population with both the general population and the untreated alcoholic or problem-drinker population. Such comparative analyses are rare in treatment evaluation research because comparable measures on both treated and untreated groups are seldom available.

[4] Informatics, Inc., on contract to NIAAA.
[5] The study was designed and supervised by Stanford Research Institute; the data were collected by the ATCs (Ruggels et al., 1975).

A partial remedy is available through a third NIAAA evaluation effort. In connection with its national public education campaign, NIAAA commissioned a series of national surveys to evaluate the impact of the campaign on the public's awareness of and attitudes toward alcoholism, including an assessment of the public's own drinking behavior and drinking problems. During the period from August 1972 to January 1974, four national surveys were conducted by Louis Harris and Associates, yielding a total of over 6000 respondents. Although the surveys were commissioned primarily to study the impact of the education campaign during that period, a considerable amount of information was collected on the respondents' social background and drinking behavior, comparable to that collected in the ATC Monitoring System. This information and the large number of respondents make it possible to define and select subpopulations of both normal and problem drinkers. Since the survey data were collected during the same period as the ATC data base, it is possible to compare the characteristics of a large national sample of alcoholics in treatment with those of the general population and of a national subpopulation of problem drinkers not in treatment.

PLAN OF THE STUDY

The major goal of this study is to provide a broad evaluation of alcoholism treatment and its etiological implications by investigating alcoholics in treatment as well as alcoholics and problem drinkers not in treatment. This goal will be pursued through several distinct stages.

The first step is to formulate an appropriate model within which to test hypotheses about treatment effects and their relationship to various etiological conceptions of alcoholism. This model must define and include both the major types of alcoholic clients and the methods of treatment that are believed to be the most effective for each client type. Accordingly, in Chapter 2, we present a review of the relevant literature, examining both theory and evidence bearing upon the definition and etiology of alcoholism, as well as the correlates of treatment success. The etiological review is important for identifying potential treatment modalities and prognostic factors that may not have been revealed by existing research on treatment effectiveness. The assumption here is that those factors known to be associated with the onset of alcoholism may well be important prognostic factors for treatment success, whether or not treatment evaluation studies have examined them. The conclusion of Chapter 2 proposes an "input-output" model for evaluating treatment effects.

One of the critical issues in the formulation of an input-output model is the identification of those client characterisics deemed most important for differential treatment success. While the literature review assists us in this search, we put these literature suggesions to an empirical test in Chapter 3 via a comparative analysis of the national surveys and the data base from the ATC Monitoring System. Differences among the general population, the problem-drinking subgroup of the general population, and the ATC intake population indicate client characteristics that have potential etiological roles and hence potential prognostic significance in the treatment of alcoholism.

The input-output model, developed in Chapters 2 and 3, will be explored in Chapters 4 and 5, using the ATC Monitoring System 6-month followup and the ATC 18-Month Followup Study. In Chapter 4, we present the basic changes in client outcomes from admission to 6 and 18 months after intake, respectively. Changes are examined for a number of different criteria of treatment success; we also propose a definition of remission that will be used throughout the remaining analyses in the report. In addition, we discuss the relationships between client characteristics and outcomes, and present a special analysis of relapse rates for a group of clients having both 6- and 18-month followup reports.

The specific effects of treatment are considered in Chapter 5. First, we examine the effects of treatment over and above "natural" remissions, using groups of clients in treatment compared with groups of clients who contacted the center but did not stay for treatment. Within the latter group, comparisons will be made beween those who sought help from AA and those who did not. Second, we analyze specific treatment regimens used with clients, the effectiveness of different settings such as inpatient and outpatient care, and the effects of different therapies such as individual psychotherapy, group counseling, and drug treatment. Third, we address the important issue of whether certain types of treatment are more successful when coupled with certain types of clients having differing prognostic characteristics.

In the concluding chapter, we summarize the findings about treatment effects, placing particular emphasis on their etiological implications. We will attempt to describe a general model of the cause and treatment of alcoholism consistent with our empirical findings.

TWO

Perspectives on Alcoholism and Treatment

While national alcohol consumption has increased in recent years, excessive drinking in amounts considered symptomatic of alcoholism is confined to a relatively small proportion of the total population.[1] Nonetheless, this small proportion yields a group of alcohol abusers and alcoholics estimated by NIAAA to number some 9 million Americans with an associated annual cost of $25 billion (NIAAA, 1974). In the context of such disquieting statistics, consider some of the major findings of the most recent "state of the art" report to Congress on alcoholism treatment and research (NIAAA, 1974). The report states, for example, that the mechanisms of alcohol intoxication and addiction remain "outstanding fundamental questions" requiring intensive research. While alcoholism is treatable, the findings continue, "different treatments are required by different individuals" with the precise relationships hopefully to be determined by "valid studies or clinical experience." Regarding identification, the report finds that the "current lack of parameters with regard to comparatively safe versus unsafe drinking patterns provides an inefficient and inadequate clinical basis for the diagnosis of alcoholism." Finally, the report maintains that while the incidence of alcoholism remains high in the population, and the practice of drinking has become almost universal among youth, currently only a "small portion of the alcoholic population is receiving the required treatment" (NIAAA, 1974, p. xi).

Clearly, basic questions as to the nature and treatment of alcoholism remain unanswered. This fact is not accounted for by any dearth of research on the topic, but rather by the sheer complexity of the issues. Indeed, the literature on alcoholism is vast. The present chapter will review those aspects of the literature that bear upon the development of an empirical model for evaluating alcoholism treatment effectiveness. Since it is our position that treatment evaluation research can have broader implications than simply a specification of what seems to work in treating alcoholism, the review will include etiological theories and their treatment implications, as well as empirical studies of variables in the treatment process. Although

[1] See Appendix A for different methods of estimating this proportion.

8

different treatment interventions vary in the extent to which they explicitly derive from a theory of etiology, it is arguable that most clinical approaches rest on certain assumptions about the nature of the disorder they seek to ameliorate. In this sense, evaluation research has relevance to underlying theoretical models about the nature and causes of alcoholism.

Following a brief consideration of the definition of alcoholism, this chapter presents three major categories of etiological models evaluated in light of current empirical research. The second part of this chapter examines treatment approaches to alcoholism, including their relationship to etiological models and their efficacy, as well as the contribution of client characteristics to the outcome of treatment. Finally, an input-output model for evaluating alcoholism treatment that seeks to integrate client, treatment, and outcome factors is proposed, and a number of hypotheses and research questions to be investigated in the subsequent empirical analyses are outlined.

THE PROBLEM OF DEFINITION

The complex nature of alcoholism is reflected in the controversy, ambiguity, and confusion that surround its definition in the literature (see Bowman and Jellinek, 1941; Keller, 1960; Keller and McCormick, 1968; Cahalan, 1970). The problem of how to define alcoholism constitutes more than an inconvenience or semantic debate. Rather, its definition has significant consequences for research, treatment, and public policy. Epidemiological studies, for example, hinge on the criterion used for nose counting; treatment is limited to those individuals diagnosed as alcoholics according to the prevailing medical definition; theory and research on etiology are influenced to the extent that the definition of the "effect" in question determines the search for relevant causal links; and public policy toward treatment and prevention is influenced by the scope of the defined problem.

The most heated controversy in recent years has centered around the conception of alcoholism as a physical disease entity. Jellinek's (1952) distinction of alcohol addiction as a specific diagnostic category, and his elaboration of the natural history or developmental course of the addiction process, exemplified the disease model. Although several writers (e.g., Hoff, 1968; Room, 1970) have seriously questioned the validity of Jellinek's theoretical progression of malign symptoms, most leading authorities have retained elements of the disease concept. The World Health Organization's (1952) official definition reads in part, "Alcoholics are those excessive drinkers whose dependence on alcohol has attained such a degree that it shows a noticeable mental disturbance or an interference with their bodily and mental health." Keller's (1962, p. 316) definition also refers to alcoholism as a disease: *"Alcoholism* is a chronic disease manifested by repeated implicative drinking so as to cause injury to the drinker's health or to his social or economic functioning."

A number of benefits have derived from defining alcoholism as a disease. By removing the stigma of moral turpitude, the disease conception of alcoholism has made it possible to provide medical and psychological treatment in place of punitive measures. By effecting changes in public attitudes, the disease definition has led to a proliferation of treatment facilities and support of valuable research. Notwithstanding these important gains and the well-intentioned motives of those who have advocated the medical model, the disease conception of alcoholism has been a mixed blessing. As Cahalan has noted, ". . . the net effect of efforts to establish alcoholism as a disease has led to a popularization of the concept of alcoholism as constituting an either-or, all-or-nothing disease entity—with adverse inhibiting effects on research and treatment" (1970, p. 3).

According to the critics, the major difficulty with the disease model results from placing alcoholism within the medical tradition of either-or differential diagnosis. Overemphasis on the medical model, it is maintained, leads to the probably erroneous assumption that alcoholism is essentially a singular entity analogous to tuberculosis or diabetes. Scott has argued that "asserting that alcoholism is a disease runs the risk of obscuring the probable truth that it may be a symptom of a number of quite separate conditions" (1968, p. 221).

Several further criticisms have been leveled against the disease concept. The medical model of alcoholism places causation "inside-the-man," thereby taking inadequate account of sociocultural factors that may play a causal role. Furthermore, the disease model directs the responsibility for treatment toward medical practitioners who perpetuate the doctor-patient relationship, encouraging the latter to assume a passive role (Scott, 1968). Other authors have held that the "sick role" has, in some cases, made alcoholics worse, not better (Roman and Trice, 1967; Roman, 1968). The disease concept has had the deleterious effect, it is argued, of creating a self-fulfilling prophecy. Problem drinkers are frightened away from early treatment by the dictum "once an alcoholic, always an alcoholic" (Reinert, 1968).

The utility of the medical model for treatment has been questioned by many, including Mulford (1970). "Alcoholism," he maintains, "has not been defined in terms that tell a physician what to do about it." And further, "medically oriented clinicians have not shown that they are any better prepared to exorcise 'alcoholism' than the morally oriented clergy and courts were to exorcise the 'demon' " (p. 5). Jellinek also recognized the serious limitations of taking the disease concept too literally, as is evident in his later writings: "If the formation *of the nature of alcoholism as an illness* rigidly claims that alcohol addiction or any other species of alcoholism is purely a medical problem, any preventive attempt may be seriously impaired. The usefulness of the idea that alcoholism is a medical and public health problem depends, to a large extent, upon the recognition of social and economic factors in the etiology of all species of alcoholism" (1960, p. 158). Chafetz (1966a) has supported the opposition to unidimensional concepts of alcoholism: "We . . . must conclude that alcoholic excesses, alcoholic problems, alcoholism, or any label you care to affix is produced by complex, multidimensional factors, and that, in fact, there is no such thing as *an alcoholic . . .*" (emphasis added, p. 810).

As has been recognized with other complex disorders of human behavior (e.g., schizophrenia), the existence of various definitions suggests the multidimensional nature of the problem and the necessity of multiple indicators for its diagnosis and measurement. In the case of alcoholism, the multiple criteria position is well illustrated by the guidelines for diagnosis compiled by the criteria committee of the National Council on Alcoholism (1972). Criteria recognized in the evaluation of alcoholism are assembled according to type—"physiological and clinical" and "behavioral, psychological and attitudinal"—and weighted for diagnostic significance.

These diagnostic guidelines reflect the fact that, despite controversy over its precise definition, there is a general consensus in the literature and among practitioners as to the basic characteristics and manifestations of alcoholism once it is established. Most descriptions of alcoholism use one or more of the following dimensions of the disorder:

1. Large quantities of alcohol consumed over a period of years.
2. Physiological manifestations of ethanol addiction.
3. Abnormal, chronic loss of control over drinking, shown by inability to stop or refrain.
4. Chronic damage to physical health or social standing, resulting from sustained alcohol abuse.

It is worthwhile to consider the implications of these dimensions for the construction of a multidimensional operational definition of alcoholism. While excessive drinking constitutes the sine qua non of the disorder (Keller, 1962), without further quantification terms such as "excessive" or "large quantities" provide little utility and invite extreme subjectivity of judgment. Thus, an adequate operationalization of the first criterion rests on well-constructed measures of quantity of ethanol consumed, frequency of consumption, and the patterning of drinking behavior (e.g., chronic vs. spree).

The second and third criteria invoke the concept of physiological addiction to and/or psychological dependence on the drug ethanol. In operational terms, addiction is manifested by a withdrawal syndrome when alcohol intake is interrupted or decreased. Clinically, the symptoms include gross tremor, hallucinosis, withdrawal seizures, and delirium tremens. Physiological dependence is also evidenced by tolerance to the effects of alcohol as reflected in high blood alcohol levels (e.g., >150 mg) without gross evidence of intoxication and in a high consumption index. According to the National Council's criteria guidelines, clear clinical evidence of physiological addiction constitutes a sufficient condition for a "classical, definite, obligatory" diagnosis of alcoholism (1972, p. 251).

The fourth criterion specifically concerns alcohol-related physical and/or social impairment. The physical complications of alcohol abuse, especially liver cirrhosis, have been well documented and are detectable through medical examination. Indices of social impairment include loss of employment, marital instability or dissolution, loss of family and friends, alienation from the community, etc. It should be noted that such social impairment factors may be causal in nature as well as resultant from the excessive use of alcohol.

In summary, the ambiguity and dissent that marks the definition of alcoholism parallels the complex and multidimensional nature of the disorder. Researchers, therefore, are well advised to utilize multiple indicators of alcoholism, including both direct and precise measurement of consumption and drinking-related behaviors and symptoms.

ETIOLOGY OF ALCOHOLISM

As with its definition, theories of the etiology of alcoholism are numerous and diverse. In contradistinction to other addictive substances (e.g., heroin), alcohol is commonly used and normatively sanctioned in most Western cultures. The task of the theorist thus lies in delineating those conditions that cause only some drinkers to become alcoholics. Despite numerous attempts to accomplish this task, there is a scarcity of well-established facts regarding the etiology of alcoholism, and no single theory has proven adequate to explain the complex syndrome. Indeed, attempts to specify a single causative factor of alcoholism may well be unrealistic and counterproductive, a point to which we shall return later.

Naturally, the impetus to continued etiological research is the implicit assumption that with an understanding of the cause comes the knowledge of how to treat, cure, and ultimately prevent the condition. In the case of so complex a disorder as alcoholism, however, the relationship between etiology and treatment is not always clear-cut. Some etiological models point to causal factors that seem amenable to treatment, and so the treatment is aimed at modifying or removing the causal conditions. In other models, the causal variables have the status of "givens" that, at least with present knowledge, are viewed as immutable. In this case treatment is not directed at the etiological factors but aims instead to control the disorder through modification of other than causal conditions. A more detailed discussion of the relationship between specific models and treatment interventions follows the review below of three major categories of etiological theories: (1) physiological and biological models, (2) psychological models, and (3) sociocultural models.

Physiological and Biological Models

Several decades ago, a prevalent conception concerning the etiology of alcoholism held that the circumstance of intoxication was itself a necessary and sufficient condition for instituting a vicious spiral toward ever-increasing drinking, craving, and pathology (e.g., Emerson, 1934). This position was predicated on the potent addictive properties of the drug ethanol. While physiological addiction to beverage alcohol does occur, marked by increased tissue tolerance, withdrawal symptoms, subjective craving, and loss of control of consumption, the strength of a strict physiological addiction model of alcoholism has been questioned by a number of authorities. Jellinek (1960) has commented on the low incidence of alcohol addiction relative to that for users of heroin and morphine. He concluded that psychological and cultural factors, in addition to physiological conditioning, must be significant. Ausubel (1958) has also characterized alcohol as a relatively inefficient addictive drug as compared with opiate substances, due to its shortcomings as a "genuine euphoriant." Nonetheless, after several years of hard drinking, stubborn addiction to ethanol results. What the strict addiction model lacks is a specification of factors that account for the persistence of excessive consumption before actual tissue adaptation occurs.

More recent models have described a range of biochemical, physiological, and neurophysiological parameters to suggest possible mechanisms of alcohol addiction. Essentially, theories in this category portray individuals who, by virtue of some organismic defect, are constitutionally predisposed to develop alcoholism. Alcoholic behavior is viewed as resulting from a medical condition (i.e., alcoholism) which, in turn, arises from an underlying biological malfunction.

Empirical investigations have been aimed at detecting biological and/or physiological differences between alcoholics and nonalcoholics that may provide clues for understanding the pathogenesis of the disorder. This research, however, has depended heavily on physical measurements of individuals already under treatment for alcoholism. Thus, while a substantial body of literature has been generated that documents differences between alcoholics and "normals," considerable ambiguity surrounds the causal status of the pathological conditions, since they may just as well be consequences as antecedents of alcohol abuse.

Genetotrophic Theory. Advanced by R. J. Williams (1947; 1959), genetotrophic theory postulates that alcoholism results from an inherited metabolic defect that causes the need for certain dietary substances in excess amounts to those provided in the ordinary diet. Since alcohol has caloric value, ingestion is thought to temporarily alleviate the symptoms of the dietary deficiency but not to provide necessary nutriments. When increasing alcohol consumption comes to replace necessary food consumption, the dietary deficiency is aggravated and a craving for alcohol to satisfy the abnormal metabolic needs is perpetuated. While Williams' hypothesis enjoyed substantial popularity and eventuated in the field of megavitamin therapy, it remains unproven and has been met with criticism on theoretical and empirical grounds (Lester, 1960; Popham, 1953).

Other theorists have also advanced explanations whereby the action of alcohol as a food results in the development of alcoholism in susceptible individuals with physiological deficiencies (e.g., Mardones, 1951; Lester, 1960; Randolph, 1956; Karolus, 1961). Again, supportive empirical evidence for such theories is lacking. Moreover, no unique metabolic pathways for alcohol as a nutrient distinct from other food substances have been discovered.

Endocrine Theories. A second major biochemical-physiological approach hypothesizes that endocrine dysfunction is causal in the development of alcoholism (Gross, 1945; Lovell and Tintera, 1951; Smith, 1949). Hypoglycemia caused by pituitary-adrenocortical deficiency is believed to cause unpleasant emotional symptoms that constitute a stimulus to drinking. Alcohol is thought to relieve the hypoglycemia temporarily by elevating the blood sugar, but the chronic hypoglycemic condition is ultimately intensified by the alcohol, inducing dependence on increasing amounts to obtain relief. Although some empirical association between alcoholism and hypothyroidism has been reported (Richter, 1956), no strong evidence for the causality of endocrine dysfunction has been obtained.

"Normalizing" Effect of Alcohol in Alcoholics. In addition to the more formalized causal models presented above, a host of empirical studies exist that document physiological, biochemical, and neurophysiological parameters that differentiate alcoholics from nonalcoholic control samples. Kissin (1974) has reviewed a number of such studies and reported that in most instances alcohol ingestion by alcoholics has a normalizing effect. Thus, in a "dry" state, alcoholics' indices differ significantly from those of nonalcoholic controls; following their ingestion of alcohol, the alcoholics' indices change in the direction of greater normality. The normalizing effect of alcohol on alcoholics has been demonstrated by both objective laboratory tests and subjective self-reports (e.g., feeling more normal). The amelioration in alcoholics of aberrant physiological states through alcohol ingestion suggests a possible explanation for the pathogenesis of alcoholism: if the physiological or biological differences between alcoholics and normals could be demonstrated to antedate the onset of alcohol abuse, one could argue that alcohol has a unique functional value for the incipient alcoholic that it does not have for normals.

Notwithstanding their tentative theoretical status, empirical physiological differences constitute what Kissin has termed a "form of abnormality" from which "a spectrum of the pathology of alcoholism can be delineated" (1974, p. 4). One such difference, reported by Petrie (1967), is that alcoholics tend to experience intense sensory stimuli more acutely than nonalcoholics. Petrie hypothesized that a neurophysiological overreactivity in alcoholics accounted for the contrast from normals and that the functional value of alcohol to alcoholics may therefore lie in reduction of the intensity of painful stimuli (external and internal) and the subsequent lessening of suffering. Other physiological and biochemical parameters that differentiate alcoholics from normals include resting electroencephalograph (EEG) alpha wave activity (Naitoh and Docter, 1968), sleep patterns (Johnson, 1971), physiological responsivity, including salivary flow, glucose tolerance, and water balance (Kissin et al., 1959), and urinary VMA excretion (Kissin et al., 1973). In all of these instances, the alcoholic group evidenced aberrant conditions that were changed in the direction of greater normalcy following the ingestion of alcohol. Nonetheless, the paramount unanswered question remains: Are the physiological abnormalities associated with alcoholism antecedent to the condition and thereby causative in nature, or do such conditions arise as a consequence of prolonged and excessive drinking, thus constituting physiological dependence phenomena? Until there is conclusive evidence to demonstrate the proper causal sequence, the physiological normalizing model of addiction remains a speculative proposal.

Genetic Models. It has long been recognized that alcoholism is a familial disorder in the sense that prevalence rates of alcoholism are far higher among relatives of alcoholics than among the general population (Goodwin and Guze, 1974). Since a familial disease is not necessarily hereditary, the inevitable issue arises as to whether genetic mechanisms can be discerned in the transmission of alcoholism. In a recent review article on heredity and alcoholism Goodwin and Guze (1974) describe several strategies that have been developed to investigate the nature-nurture question. Researchers have documented familial incidence of alcoholism (e.g., Winokur et al., 1970), associations between alcoholism and known inherited characteristics or "genetic markers" (e.g., Cruz-Coke, 1964; Camps and Dodd, 1967), preference for alcoholism in genetic strains of mice (Rodgers, 1966; McClearn and Rodgers, 1959; 1961), and the incidence of alcoholism among adoptees with a known biological parent from whom they were separately reared (Goodwin et al., 1973; Schuckit et al., 1972).

Unfortunately the number of confounding variables in most heredity studies mitigates the validity of their results. The most promising evidence for the role of genetic mechanisms comes from the recent, carefully controlled adoption studies of Goodwin and his associates (1973) and Schuckit et al. (1972). These studies indicate that where children have been separated from their biological parents at birth or shortly thereafter, the presence of alcoholism in the biological parents is of far greater predictive significance than the presence of the disorder in the adoptive parents in determining the development of alcoholism in the offspring. While suggestive, such evidence should not be interpreted as conclusive proof for the genetic inheritance of alcoholism. Goodwin and Guze conclude with the caveat that the genetic predisposition argument remains "more probable than proven and certainly may not apply to all alcoholics" (1974, p. 42). Moreover, despite attempts to control for bias in research designs, the adoption studies are still open to alternative explanations that invoke nongenetic factors. For example, selectivity may have operated in the adoption process itself, resulting in placement of the offspring of alcoholics with so-called less desirable adoptive parents. Or, a "family skeleton" phenomenon may be operating wherein adopted children have knowledge of the alcoholism present in their natural family's history and feel that they are "doomed" to similar circumstances, thus producing the dreaded condition as a self-fulfilling prophecy.

While the heredity studies suggest the presence of genetic factors in alcoholism, they do not provide any clues as to how the predisposition is transmitted. Nor do they specify exactly how much of the variance in the development of alcoholism can be accounted for strictly on the basis of hereditary factors. Pattison (1974) has argued that, on intuitive grounds, alcoholism seems far too complex a behavior pattern to be explained solely by genetic determinants or biological defects. Individuals may only inherit what Jellinek (1945, p. 105) characterized as a "breeding ground" for alcoholism in which sociocultural factors play a large intervening role. In the absence of clear empirical data, the precise role of physiological, biological, and genetic variables as determinants of alcoholism remains unknown.

Psychological Models

Most psychological theories of etiology are based on the assumption that alcoholics share certain traits or personality structures that are thought to be of causal significance in the development of their disorder. The thrust of such theories is a search for the so-called "alcoholic personality" that constitutes a psychological vulnerability to develop alcoholism.

Psychodynamic Models. According to psychodynamic explanations, alcoholism results from one or more unconscious conflicts or tendencies of which the individual is unaware and for the expression of which excessive alcohol consumption has functional value. Freud (trans. 1955) and other early psychoanalytic writers traced the origins of alcoholism to traumatic early childhood experience caused by defects in the parent-child relationship. In the psychoanalytic view, overgratification or frustration of a child's earliest needs by the parent leads to the development of an inadequate personality fixated at the oral stage. As an adult, the so-called oral personality is believed to lack self-control, show passive-dependent traits, possess self-destructive impulses, and to use the mouth as a primary means of gratification. Alcohol consumption is seen as one form of such gratification, and alcoholism as a manifest and pathologic expression of orality.

Retrospective case studies of alcoholics have provided some evidence of early childhood experience consistent with the psychoanalytic model. Knight (1938) and Wall and Allen (1944) reported case histories of male alcoholics that included overprotective and overindulgent mothers and severe fathers. It is hypothesized that such familial constellations led to the development of personalities marked by passivity and conflicted masculine strivings. Wood and Duffy (1966) studied 69 alcoholic women and reported that most recalled dominant and emotionally distant mothers and warm but alcoholic fathers. Whereas such retrospective accounts are suggestive of etiological factors, they are also subject to errors of memory and intentional distortion. The studies cited above also lack appropriate nonalcoholic control groups with whom childhood background factors of alcoholics could be compared.

Several longitudinal studies have also examined childhood behavior and environmental conditions as they relate to adult onset of alcoholism. In general, such studies have found an association between adult drinking problems and pathological family backgrounds and early antisocial behavior, including lack of control, aggressiveness, and impulsivity (Jones, 1968; Lisansky-Gomberg, 1968; McCord et al., 1960; Robins, 1966).

McCord et al. (1960) studied characteristics of boys prior to determining which among them subsequently developed alcoholism. Several family background factors were associated with the manifestation of the disorder, including high incidence of broken homes, nonaffectionate parents, and parental relationships characterized by dominant mothers and openly antagonistic fathers. The authors concluded that the majority of future alcoholics suffered from both rejection and role confusion. Robins (1966) and Robins et al. (1962) studied 524 patients of a child guidance clinic over a 30-year followup period. Examination of 15 percent of the former patients who became alcoholics indicated that parental inadequacy and antisocial behavior in childhood were most strongly associated with the subsequent development of alcoholism. Other childhood factors reported to be associated with alcoholism include early parental loss through death or divorce (Hilgard and Newman, 1963) and later or last ordinal birth positions in the family (Sampson, 1965; Barry et al., 1969).

It should be noted that while the disruptive experiences of early childhood may increase susceptibility to the development of alcoholism, they are not specific to an alcoholic disorder but probably increase the likelihood of various types of psychopathology. Moreover, childhood factors have not been demonstrated to bear strong enough degrees of association to account for substantial proportions of the variance in alcoholism incidence.

A relatively new formulation of the motivation for excessive drinking is derived from the psychoanalytic approach. According to this new hypothesis, the functional significance of alcohol lies in its ability to maintain and enhance regression and denial in individuals whose personalities function at an immature level of development (Barry, 1974). This formulation focuses on the tendency of alcoholics (while intoxicated) to express impulsively their dominant mood or emotion while simultaneously suppressing incompatible motives, a behavioral mode presumed to be regressive. Some empirical studies have shown a tendency for alcoholics to express denial of real aversive consequences in experimental learning situations (Wallgren and Barry, 1974; Weingartner and Faillace, 1971) and to lack perseverance of achievement motivation (a "mature" motive) as assessed by Rorschach responses (Southerland et al., 1950).

Since the regression and denial hypothesis is a relatively new formulation, it has not yet received adequate empirical study. It does seem problematic, however, as a specific explanation for alcoholism. While it is true that alcoholism is a pathological condition characterized by immature functioning, regression and denial are also associated with several other forms of psychiatric illness, most particularly with character disorders and sociopathic personalities. Moreover, the disinhibiting effects of alcohol that facilitate the overt expression of regressive behavioral modes are commonly observed among drinkers who have not lost control of their consumption. Thus, it remains to be demonstrated that alcoholics as a group differ systematically with respect to level of personality development from other categories of mental disturbance, and that the disinhibiting effects of alcohol leading to regressive behavior are quantitatively or qualitatively different for alcoholics than for so-called normal drinkers.

A second psychodynamic formulation holds that alcoholism results from enhanced feelings of self-esteem and prowess that the ingestion of beverage alcohol provides. In this view, alcoholics are individuals who suffer from pervasive feelings of inferiority and powerlessness coupled with unusually strong inhibitions against the expression of hostile or aggressive impulses. For such individuals, the exaggerated aura of competence and the disinhibition of impulses provided by alcohol have special value. A recent version of this striving-for-power theme has been presented by McClelland and his associates (1972), who believe that alcoholism results from frustrated ambitions and a consequent "fall from status." The alcoholic is pictured as having an enhanced need for power but inadequate personality resources to achieve his goals. In the face of frustrated ambitions, the alcoholic resorts to drinking to achieve a euphoric sense of power and achievement, as well as a release from tension. Since alcohol abuse interferes with realistic coping behavior, the individual's problems continue to mount, and ever-increasing consumption of alcohol results. The thesis of McClelland et al. highlights the "lethal" aspects of being male in a culture that places great value on masculine power and achievement.

McClelland's team has reported a series of studies to demonstrate the disinhibiting effects of alcohol. Changes in the fantasies of normal male drinkers after ingestion of alcohol were measured by means of the Thematic Apperception Test (TAT). A consistent disinhibitory effect of alcohol was found manifested by an increase in power themes contained in the TAT stories of intoxicated subjects. It is important to note, however, that the subjects tested by McClelland's team were normal drinkers. It may be that alcoholics represent a special population of drinkers to whom the results of the TAT study do not generalize validly. Although the increase in power fantasies resulting from heavy drinking was greater for those subjects who chose to drink larger amounts in experimental drinking situations (McClelland et al., 1972), a study by Cutter et al. (1973), using a sample of alcoholics, yielded negative results. Some evidence for the power-fantasy motive comes from Stein et al. (1968), who reported a tendency for alcoholics to state that drinking helped them to feel superior. The striving for power formulation, then, remains an interesting but as yet inconclusively supported hypothesis.

A final psychodynamic approach to the etiology of alcoholism focuses on the intrapsychic conflict between intense dependency needs and parallel strivings for autonomy and independence thought to characterize the alcoholic's personality structure. Drinking presumably provides reinforcement for the opposite motives simultaneosuly. Overt dependency is exhibited behaviorally through sociability and sentimentality, and through explicit dependence on beverage alcohol. At the same time, alcohol permits disinhibition of impulses, giving rise to feelings of independence and strength. Finally, the sedative property of ethanol is thought to diminish the effect of logical inconsistencies and enables denial of the dynamic conflict (Barry, 1974). Blane (1968) has reported various expressions of overtly dependent and counterdependent behavior in an alcoholic sample, based primarily on clinical case studies.

It should be noted that the struggle between dependency needs and autonomous strivings does not in itself constitute a symptom of pathology. Indeed, many theories of psychological development invoke this struggle as an inevitable and ultimately beneficial aspect of human experience (Freud, trans. 1955; Sullivan, 1953; Erikson, 1950). The validity of the dependency-conflict model as an etiological explanation for alcoholism rests on a demonstration that alcoholics have intense, unusual, and unresolved dependency and autonomy needs as compared with nonalcoholics. There does not, however, appear to be clear empirical support for such a position. What is available empirically is largely inferential data suggesting that an underlying dynamic struggle may be present. For example, the presence of exaggerated "counterdependent" behavior (i.e., hostility, aggressiveness, etc.) is held to be an indication that intense conflict over dependency needs exists (McCord et al., 1960; Robins, 1966; Blane and Chafetz, 1971). The rather tenuous nature of such evidence seems obvious. Other authors have presented data showing high scores on measures of "overt masculinity" and low scores on "covert masculinity" associated with heavy drinking among adolescent boys (Harrington, 1970; Zucker, 1968). Similarly, an association between inconsistencies in feminine role preference (presumably indicating conflict over dependency-autonomy needs) and alcoholism in women has been documented (Parker, 1972; Wilsnack, 1972).

Notwithstanding the rather indirect nature of the evidence for an underlying dependency conflict in alcoholics, it is not clear that such a dynamic, if present, would differentially predict the development of alcoholism. Dependency-need conflicts have also been invoked in causal models of schizophrenia and several neurotic disorders (Coleman, 1972).

Personality Traits. Personality-trait theorists have sought to find a consistent set of characteristics that correlate with the development of alcoholism. A large number of studies have generally failed, however, to identify any specific personality traits that clearly differentiate alcoholics from other deviant groups or from persons judged to be "normal" (Sutherland et al., 1950; Syme, 1957). While most writers agree that no unique, premorbid alcoholic personality has been discovered (Syme, 1957; Armstrong, 1958; Rosen, 1960), there exists some empirical evidence to suggest that alcoholics show a cluster of personality traits once their drinking patterns have been established. Included in this cluster are low stress tolerance (Lisansky, 1960), dependency (Blane, 1968), perceptual dependence (Witkin et al., 1959), negative self-image, and feelings of isolation, insecurity, and depression (Irwin, 1968; Weingold et al., 1968; Wood and Duffy, 1966). In their recent national survey of problem drinking among American men, Cahalan and Room (1974) reported intrapunitiveness, impulsivity, and tolerance of deviant behavior other than drinking to be personality trait correlates of problem drinkers. Interestingly, however, personality variables were demonstrated to be the major determinants of tangible aversive consequences from drinking, while sociocultural variables were better predictors of actual heavy consumption.

The most serious limitation of the personality-trait approach is that measurements are most often made on populations of alcoholics. Thus the inevitable problem of interpretation arises as to whether such traits preceded the alcoholic behavior and therefore may be viewed as etiological factors, or whether the cluster of traits is a consequence of the addiction that already exists. The best evidence for the causal status of trait variables in the development of alcoholism is to be found in longitudinal studies of personality that are rare in the literature. Jones (1968) reported on the personality characteristics of 6 cases out of 66 boys studied during childhood who subsequently manifested "problem drinking." The 6 boys were reportedly uncontrolled, impulsive, and rebellious during childhood. The very small sample size, however, reduces the usefulness of these results.

One empirically studied explanation for excessive drinking invokes the particularly rewarding sedative effect of alcohol for highly anxious individuals. There is empirical support for the positions that some alcoholics manifest high anxiety levels and that ethanol has depressant, sedative pharmaceutic properties (Wallgren and Barry, 1970; Barry, 1974; Vogel-Sprott, 1972). Furthermore, studies have demonstrated that the precipitating occasion for the onset of drinking episodes in alcoholics is often the occurrence of heightened anxiety (Belfer et al., 1971; Brun-Gulbrandsen and Irgens-Jensen, 1967).

Although it may well be that alcoholics suffer from relatively high levels of anxiety that they learn can be dissipated rapidly by the ingestion of alcohol, there has been inadequate empirical demonstration that anxiety is more prevalent among alcoholics than among other groups of disturbed individuals for whom alcohol has not become a major coping device (e.g., anxiety neurotics, phobic personalities, etc.).

Behavioral Learning Model. A third psychological model of alcoholism derives from the field of experimental learning psychology. The key feature of this approach is a focus on observable behavior (i.e., alcoholic drinking) and on those environmental conditions that serve to elicit and/or maintain excessive consumption. Alcoholism is viewed as a conditioned behavioral response that can be "unlearned" through the appropriate modification of environmental stimuli and reinforcement situations.

The simplest behavioral theory of alcoholism invokes the Pavlovian or classical conditioning model. Alcoholic behavior is seen as caused and maintained by the simple association of alcohol ingestion with positive, rewarding experience. Accordingly, modification of alcoholism should occur through changing the stimulus value of alcohol from positive to negative by pairing drinking with aversive consequences.

With the advent of operant conditioning theories and the emergence of behavior modification as a unified system of psychotherapy in the early 1960s, behavioral models of alcoholism became more complicated. In such models alcoholism, now recognized as a highly complex behavior, is broken down into its separate behavioral components. Each component behavior in turn is viewed as subject to modification through one or a variety of techniques. The major causal assumption of most behavioral models is that alcoholics begin and continue drinking because alcohol ingestion is followed by a reduction in anxiety, psychological stress, or tension. The corollary of this hypothesis is that intervention must seek either to change the situations that induce psychological stress (environmental modification) or to modify the individual's maladaptive response to stressful situations.

Bandura (1969) has elaborated a two-stage, operant conditioning process that he maintains is the mechanism by which excessive drinking is acquired and maintained. According to this conditioning model, the positive value of alcohol derives initially from the central nervous system depressant and anesthetic properties of the drug. Thus, individuals who are subjected to stressful situations may obtain relief from stress through the ingestion of alcohol due to its pharmaceutic effects. In conditioning terms, the behavior of drinking is reinforced by the reduction of unpleasant experience that follows from it. Repeated experiences in which anxiety, stress, or other aversive stimuli are reduced by drinking alcohol lead to a progressive strengthening of the drinking habit. Once habitually established, the excessive use of alcohol begins to have consequent aversive effects on the individual (e.g., loss of job, arousal of guilt) that in turn set up renewed stimulus conditions for continued drinking. Eventually, with prolonged heavy alcohol usage, alterations in the metabolic system occur, constituting physiological addiction. Once addiction occurs, the second stage of the conditioning mechanism is reached. In this stage, metabolic alterations produce aversive physiological reactions if alcohol is withdrawn, consisting of tremulousness, nausea, vomiting, marked weakness, diarrhea, fever, hypertension, excessive perspiration, and insomnia. Thus, after the individual has become physiologically addicted, the disstressing withdrawal symptoms themselves become the stimulus conditions for alcohol consumption. In second-stage conditioning, drinking is reinforced automatically and continually through the termination of withdrawal symptoms that it provides. Although Chafetz and Demone (1962) have argued that the devastating social and physical consequences of chronic drinking far outweigh its temporary-relief value, Bandura maintains that behavior is more powerfully controlled by its immediate than its delayed consequences: ". . . it is precisely for this reason that persons may persistently engage in immediately reinforcing, but potentially self-destructive, behavior" (1969, p. 530).

Some support for the tension-reduction hypothesis has been obtained from laboratory studies of alcohol self-selection by animals under conditions of stress (Cicero et al., 1968; Clark and Polish, 1960; Wright et al., 1971) and of the effects of alcohol on animals subjected to stressful situations (Conger, 1951; Freed, 1968; Masserman and Yum, 1946; Smart, 1965). However, the theoretical reliance on tension and its reduction as the sole causal factor controlling alcoholic behavior does not seem warranted by the empirical evidence. In a recent extensive review of experimental literature on tension reduction, Cappell and Herman (1972) concluded that the evidence for alcohol as a tension reducer is equivocal at best and, in fact, largely negative.

A number of behavior theorists, including Bandura, have recognized that a broad range of factors other than tension reduction may have etiological significance in the development of alcoholism. For example, social reinforcement (e.g., peer approval), modeling, or imitative learning (e.g., of parental drinking styles) and situational cues (e.g., cocktail parties, bars) may serve to trigger and/or maintain excessive drinking. Recent broad-spectrum behavioral approaches to alcoholism (e.g., Hunt and Azrin, 1973; Sobell and Sobell, 1972) have operated on the assumption that although behavior is controlled by certain classes of stimulus and reinforcement events, the specific antecedents and reinforcers of excessive drinking may well be highly variable from individual to individual. Careful functional analysis of the precise stimulus-response-reinforcement relationships in each individual case is therefore held to be prerequisite to an understanding of etiology and the formulation of treatment plans and goals.

Sociocultural Models

The models of etiology thus far considered invoke internal determinants such as physiological malfunctions, psychological traits, conditioned associations, or habituated responses, as the critical antecedent variables in the development of alcoholism. The viability of any one such model as an adequate explanation of alcoholism becomes doubtful when the strong empirical relationships between sociocultural variables and the incidence of alcohol use and alcoholism are considered.

In their conclusions of the first national probability sampling of American drinking practices, Cahalan, Cisin, and Crossley (1969, p. 200) state that "whether a person drinks at all is primarily a sociological and anthropological variable rather than a psychological one." McCord et al. (1960), in their study of the backgrounds of male alcoholics, found that differences between boys who became alcoholics as adults and those who did not were primarily cultural; alcoholism was demonstrated to be related more to ethnic and social background variables than to physiological or psychological differences. And while they acknowledge the importance of social, psychological, and personality variables, Cahalan and Room (1974) report that problem drinking among males can be predicted quite well by using only the traditional demographic variables of age, socioeconomic status (SES), urbanization, ethnic origin, and religion.

Most theories that fall under the present classification recognize the significant causal role of factors other than sociocultural variables (e.g., psychological, physiological) in the process of alcohol addiction. Nonetheless, since patterns of drinking behavior in America have been shown to vary as a function of class status, religious affiliation, sex, age, racial and ethnic background, and urban versus rural residence (Cahalan, 1970; Cahalan and Room, 1974), the contribution of sociocultural variables to the etiology of alcoholism merits consideration.

Culture and Socialization. Ethnic and subcultural differences in the use of alcohol suggest the importance of prealcoholic social learning factors in the development of alcoholism. At a general level, cultural norms define the reinforcement contingencies associated with the use of alcohol (Bandura, 1969). That is, the "appropriate" use of intoxicants, attitudes toward alcohol, mores regulating drinking practices, and environmental support for drinking are largely determined by cultural setting. Children are socialized into culturally prescribed beliefs, attitudes, and practices regarding the use and consumption level of alcohol. Thus, exceedingly low rates of alcoholism among Jews, Mormons, and Moslems, for example, can be accounted for on the basis of cultural proscriptions against the use (in the case of Mormons and Moslems) or abuse (as for Jews) of alcoholic beverages. Similarly, some data have shown that the Irish surpass all ethnic groups in chronic alcoholism (Chafetz and Demone, 1962), a possibility that could be explained largely by the cultural support for excessive consumption of alcohol.

Cultural Stress Factors. In addition to regulating whether and how alcohol will be used, cultural factors also contribute to the degree of stress that members of a given society are likely to be subjected. Horton's (1943) early study on social stress in 56 primitive societies revealed that the insecurity or anxiety level of the culture was positively correlated with the amount of alcohol consumed, due allowance having been made for the availability of alcohol. Bales (1946) outlined three major contributing factors in determining the incidence of alcoholism in a given society: (1) the degree of stress and inner tension produced by the culture; (2) the attitudes toward drinking fostered by the culture; and (3) the degree to which the culture provides substitute means of satisfaction and coping with anxiety.

Familial Patterns. Sociocultural factors also operate by structuring familial patterns that in turn provide role-modeling and social learning experiences for children. In a study of 20 adolescent alcoholics, Mackay (1961) reported that a large number of his subjects had alcoholic fathers and that, in attempting to cope with their own problems of feeling rejected, inadequate, and depressed, the adolescents imitated the dominant parental mode of adjustment (i.e., excessive alcohol consumption). Other studies of the family backgrounds of alcoholics have revealed an unusually high incidence of familial alcoholism (Fort and Porterfield, 1961; Lemere et al., 1942; Wall, 1936). While such data may suggest a genetic interpretation, it appears that the pattern of familial drinking and the range of circumstances in which such drinking occurs are modeled by offspring, suggesting a strong social learning component.

Instability and Crisis. Social factors may also contribute to conditions of environmental stress that precipitate the onset of heavy consumption. Alcoholism has been reported to develop during "crisis periods," when significant changes in an individual's life situation or social role lead to instability, confusion, and stress (Coleman, 1972). Curlee (1969), for example, found that women alcoholics who began excessive drinking in their late thirties and early forties related the onset of drinking problems to changes in their roles as wife or mother, such as menopause, loss of husband, children leaving home, etc. Other instances of crisis include loss of employment, death of a spouse, and marital instability. Often during such periods of heightened stress, an individual's normal coping methods prove inadequate and he resorts to more extreme means of alleviating the stress including, in some cases, heavy consumption of alcohol.

The extremely high rate of divorce and separation among alcoholics as compared with nonalcoholics has been widely reported in the literature. Several writers have interpreted this unusually high rate as resulting from disabling psychological factors in the alcoholic's personality. Barry (1974) has characterized the social behavior of the alcoholic as alternating between cycles of sociability and alienation, a pattern that makes the maintenance of marital relationships difficult. Other theorists have attributed the high marital failure rate to the alcoholic's poor choice of a spouse, arising out of dependency needs (Armstrong, 1958) or fantasies of vicariously acquiring power (McClelland et al., 1972). Notwithstanding psychological factors, it is reasonable to expect that the presence of alcoholism in a marital partner would in itself constitute sufficiently aversive conditions for divorce or separation to occur. On the other hand, the causal relationship between alcoholism and marital instability may in fact be reversed. Thus, the occurrence of marital tension and discord may constitute a crisis situation that results in the onset of heavy alcohol consumption and eventual alcoholism.

A cyclical relationship exists between social instability and alcoholism. Heavy consumption of alcohol may occur in response to changes in one's social environment that create aversive stress; this excessive drinking in turn results in further deterioration of social adjustment, creating even greater stress and perpetuating the alcoholic process.

The Multivariate Approach

The foregoing discussion has been organized around three broad classes of causal variables. As we have seen, no explanation that invokes a single class of etiological factors seems adequate to account for what is most likely an "overdetermined" disorder with multiple causes and a complex developmental course. Some theorists have suggested a multifaceted approach to the study of alcoholism causes that would incorporate two or more elements from the broad areas of psychology, physiology, and sociology.

One such model has been summarized by Plaut as follows:

> A tentative model may be developed for understanding the causes of problem drinking, even though the precise roles of the various factors have not yet been determined. An individual who (1) responds to beverage alcohol in a certain way, perhaps physiologically determined, by experiencing intense relief and relaxation, and who (2) has certain personality characteristics, such as difficulty in dealing with and overcoming depression, frustration, and anxiety, and who (3) is a member of a culture in which there is both pressure to drink and culturally induced guilt and confusion regarding what kinds of drinking behavior are appropriate, is more likely to develop trouble than will most other persons. An intermingling of certain factors may be necessary for the development of problem drinking, and the relative importance of the differential causal factors no doubt varies from one individual to another (1967, p. 49).

Trice (1956) anticipated the interactionist position by saying that "the time is long overdue when researchers in the alcohol field will look upon alcoholism as a *process*, not a single-factor, one-way cause and effect result" (p. 40). Jellinek (1952) concluded that the insistence on an alcoholic personality, isolated from environmental influences, was probably not tenable: "Apart from psychological and possibly physical liabilities, there must be a constellation of social and economic factors which facilitate the development of addictive and nonaddictive alcoholism in a susceptible person" (p. 679).

It has now become apparent to most theorists and researchers in the field that a great range of sociological, cultural, and psychological variables can be invoked to account for variance in problem drinking and alcoholism. The full range of such factors and their possible interactive effects with one another and with various clinical interventions must be considered in any comprehensive model of causation, treatment, and cure.

APPROACHES TO TREATMENT

Underlying Models

In theory, a model for the treatment of alcoholism implies a certain concept of etiology, specifies methods of intervention, and defines expectable outcomes and therapeutic goals. In practice, these relationships are not always clear. Nonetheless, certain assumptions about the nature of alcoholism underlie most clinical approaches. Therefore, the results of treatment-evaluation research may provide at least inferential evidence for the validity of the underlying models on which treatments are based. In this context, a brief exploration of the relationship between the major etiological models and approaches to treatment seems warranted.

Despite their as yet unconfirmed status, physiological and biological models of alcoholism continue to attract wide attention from both professional scientific and lay public circles. Pattison (1974) has suggested that ideological factors rather than scientific concern account for the continued focus on physiological theories. Because these theories generally posit an underlying biological defect as the cause of alcoholism, they are consistent with the disease model, justify medical interventions, provide an effective defensive rationale for those who suffer from the condition (e.g., "I have an illness"), and hold out the promise of a potential medical cure. The critical assumption of physiological models is that the alcoholic has a physical condition that renders him chronically ill and forever vulnerable to alcohol. By definition, the biological condition that causes alcoholism cannot, with present knowledge, be cured; at best, the alcoholic can be rehabilitated and the alcoholism controlled. A widely held belief among treatment professionals who assume that alcoholism is an irreversible medical condition is that total abstinence is the only legitimate goal of therapy. This position is predicated on the belief that loss of control is the defining feature of the alcoholic's chronic condition, so that even one drink is thought to lead inexorably to alcoholic behavior.

The most radical departure, in both theory and practice, from the assumptions of the physiological models is the behavior modification approach of establishing controlled drinking as a goal for at least some alcoholics (e.g., Sobell and Sobell, 1972, 1973). Since excessive consumption is viewed as learned behavior rather than an irreversible process, controlled drinking is seen as a reasonable and viable endpoint of an appropriate behavior modification program.

The more traditional operant conditioning models (e.g., Bandura, 1969) focus on the tension-reduction value of alcohol ingestion. Treatments deriving from this view seek to change the functional value of drinking behavior from positive to negative, and to teach alternative modes of coping behavior in response to anxiety-inducing situations. The two-stage conditioning model further implies that intervention must first be directed at breaking the addiction cycle (second stage) and only thereafter at changing the drinking response to situational cues.

According to the psychodynamic and trait models, excessive alcohol consumption is a manifest symptom of underlying pathology. Treatment, therefore, is not aimed solely at the symptomatic behavior but rather seeks to uncover the intrapsychic conflicts and to achieve an ultimate cure by altering the patient's basic personality structure. Even though abstinence is generally viewed as a necessary condition for sustained therapeutic involvement, the model predicts that the attainment of abstinence in the absence of solving the deeper psychological problems that led initially to excessive drinking may result in decompensated functioning in other life areas ("symptom substitution") or alcoholic relapse.

The treatment implications of sociocultural models are somewhat less clear than for the other etiological theories. Many demographic or social background variables reported to account for substantial variance in drinking behavior are not amenable to therapeutic change. Nonetheless, intervention is indicated at the level of changing social variables that are thought to be causal or supportive of alcoholism. Thus, "sociotherapies" include programs aimed at rehabilitation of the severely socially impaired alcoholic. Halfway house settings, milieu therapy, job counseling, and alterations in fundamental social contexts are treatment modes derived from sociocultural models.

In principle, the preferred therapeutic technique used by a given facility or clinical practitioner reflects adherence to one of the general etiological models. In practice, treatment delivery for alcoholism tends to be based on one of two common policies (NIAAA, 1974). In some treatment centers, a single modality is available (e.g., disulfiram, traditional insight therapy, etc.) and is uniformly implemented with each patient seeking help. When the patient "fits" the treatment, he is helped; if the fit between patient and therapy is not met, the effort is presumably in vain. Other treatment centers employ an opposite strategy: patients are exposed to a wide variety of treatments in what the NIAAA report characterizes as a "salad-like mixture" (p. 145). This latter approach to treatment seems to derive from the vague notion that "something" may work, in which case a certain subset of patients will be helped. In both treatment philosophies, there is considerable waste of resources, both human and monetary. Thus, the necessity arises for the development of a research model whereby the appropriate treatment or combination of treatments can be systematically matched to the individual alcoholic patient. Before proposing such a model, we will consider the current range of treatment settings and therapeutic techniques available to the alcoholic population.

Treatment Setting

While there is a wide array of treatment facilities and programs for alcoholism, the settings in which treatment is delivered can be grouped roughly into three types: inpatient, intermediate, and outpatient care.

Inpatient Care Setting. Inpatient treatment of alcoholism may take place in a variety of facilities, including general hospitals, state mental hospitals, and private hospitals or sanitariums. Despite these variations, most inpatient programs share a number of common features. The hospitalized alcoholic is removed, for the duration of his stay, from the immediate environment that presumably created the stress leading to and/or supporting his excessive drinking. In the highly structured hospital setting, the inpatient is thus protected from the external social conditions associated with alcohol use. Moreover, the nonavailability of alcohol in the restrictive hospital setting aids sobriety efforts, since no present temptation exists. Inpatient settings generally offer a range of treatment modalities, including didactic instruction about alcoholism, group and/or individual therapy, and supportive drug treatment. Moreover, many modern hospitals have adopted the concept of "milieu" therapy, in which the inpatient ward becomes a therapeutic community governing itself, planning activities, and supporting its members. Finally, an important feature of the inpatient setting is the medical model on which it is based. Consistent with this model, alcoholics who enter an inpatient setting are viewed as "patients" and may adopt a relatively passive role, attributing primary responsibility for their treatment and recovery to the medical personnel in residence.

Intermediate Care Setting. The intermediate care facility, a major development of the last decade, provides a transitional setting for severely impaired individuals in their movement from inpatient care back to community life. Intermediate care facilities for the alcoholic consist mainly of "halfway houses," although a graded series of quarterway to three-quarterway houses exist to provide varying levels of support in the resocialization process (Maters, 1972; Rubington, 1970). Intermediate care differs in several respects from both inpatient and outpatient settings. First, halfway houses are generally nonprofessionally staffed. While adjunctive professional personnel are available for needed medical care, the therapeutic mode of the halfway house lies in the provision of an overall milieu of supportive communal living. Recovering alcoholics in this setting are thought to experience the emotional warmth and support of a reconstituted family. Moreover, the setting provides its residents with adequate food, shelter, vocational guidance, and a structured environment. In turn, the halfway house requires continued abstinence by its residents. Like the inpatient setting, the intermediate care facility represents a social environment totally removed from that in which the alcoholic previously experienced stress, alienation, and often social support for his drinking (e.g., skid row). By its very nature, the halfway house is generally seen as a facility most suitable for those alcoholics who have experienced rather gross social and often physical deterioration as a result of lengthy alcoholic histories but for whom rehabilitation and return to a productive role in the community are possible.

Outpatient Care Setting. In an outpatient setting, alcoholics usually receive from one to several hours of treatment weekly in facilities ranging from hospital outpatient clinics through community agencies to offices of private practitioners. The key feature of the outpatient setting is that while in treatment the recovering alcoholic is subject to the same environmental situation, with its accompanying stress and demands and its abundant availability of alcohol, in which the maladaptive drinking began. Thus, the outpatient alcoholic may experience greater difficulty in maintaining abstinence than those alcoholics treated in structured and restricted settings. On the other hand, the outpatient setting affords the client access to possible environmental supports for his abstinence efforts (e.g., a supportive sponse, an intact family, concerned employer, etc.). Also, since the client in an outpatient setting is exposed concurrently to environmental stress, therapy can focus on the development of alternative means of coping with aversive conditions.

In practice, a large proportion of alcoholic patients experience more than one treatment setting, Inpatient care, for example, is frequently provided during the detoxification period and for some time thereafter, following which the client may move to an intermediate care facility or back home with continued treatment on an outpatient basis.

Treatment Process

In addition to variations in setting, current approaches to the treatment of alcoholism encompass a range of therapeutic philosophies and techniques. It should be noted that the approaches are not necessarily mutually exclusive; often a combination of approaches is used for the same alcoholic client. Moreover, most can take place within more than one type of treatment setting.

Psychotherapy and Counseling. Psychotherapeutic approaches to treatment derive from psychological models in which alcoholism is viewed as symptomatic of underlying pathology, such as unconscious conflicts, repressed inpulses, fixations, etc. Generally, one of two therapeutic orientations is used in the treatment of alcoholics. The more traditional approach is insight-oriented psychotherapy in which the patient, through extensive verbal interaction with the therapist, is presumably helped to achieve insight into the psychological causes of his/her alcoholic behavior. Included in this first category are Freudian psychoanalysis, Rogerian client-centered therapy, and Transactional Analysis. However, because insight-oriented therapy requires lengthy, consistent, and intensive contact with a psychotherapist, in practice counseling and psychotherapy with alcoholics are more commonly oriented toward a "here and now" perspective in which directive approaches are used, together with confrontation techniques aimed at solving the immediate problem (i.e., drinking) rather than at the achievement of insight.

Counseling and psychotherapy may be conducted in either individual or group contexts, although group contexts are often preferred because more patients receive help with less expenditure of staff time. Important components of successful therapy are believed to include a positive patient-therapist relationship, strong motivation on the part of the patient to change his/her behavior, and at least average intellectual and verbal patient abilities. Group therapy and counseling is also thought to depend on cohesive group functioning, mutual trust, willingness of group members to share feelings and provide emotional support, and on the development of strong group norms prohibiting the further use of alcohol.

Drug Treatments. A wide range of pharmaceutic agents has been employed in the treatment of alcoholism. In most cases, drugs are used as adjuncts to other therapeutic modalities. The most commonly used drugs in the treatment of alcoholism are the aversively protective agents, among which disulfiram (Antabuse) receives widest use in the United States. Individuals who have ingested disulfiram and who subsequently consume even very small amounts of alcohol experience severe discomfort characterized by headache, flushing of the head and neck, rise in blood pressure, faintness, and nausea. Disulfiram is generally used as an adjunct to outpatient treatment to prevent the patient's resumption of drinking and to keep him/her available for therapeutic intervention. The efficacy of disulfiram treatment is obviously dependent on the patient's willingness to continue taking the medication.

A second class of drugs includes tranquilizers, antidepressants, and antipsychotic compounds. Among the most widely used are chlordiazepoxide, diazepam, meprobamate, imipramine, promazine, haloperidal, and lithium (Mottin, 1973). The implicit assumption behind the use of such agents is a drive-reduction theory (Baekeland et al., 1975). According to this view, alcoholics are believed to suffer from various dysphoric symptoms, including anxiety, depression and, if physically addicted, symptoms of withdrawal. Alcohol is seen as a form of self-medication because it reduces the symptoms. Therefore, it is hypothesized, drugs that reduce the symptoms should consequently reduce the desire, need, or drive to consume alcohol.

A final group of drugs that has been tried in alcoholism treatment comprises the hallucinogenic agents, primarily lysergic acid diehylamide (LSD). Such drugs are thought to disrupt the self-destructive alcoholic cycle by facilitating traumatic cathartic experiences and deep personal insight.

Some writers have suggested that an important aspect of drug therapy, and a partial explanation for its effectiveness, lies in the psychodynamic nature of the relationship involved in giving and receiving medication (Pattison, 1974). Thus, drug therapy provides some alcoholics with a concrete sense of receiving treatment but enables them to maintain a relatively low-intensity emotional interaction with medical personnel. These factors in turn are thought to facilitate the development of a positive therapeutic relationship from which beneficial outcomes may be derived. In this view, the drug (independent of its pharmacological effect) is an important symbol in a kind of transactional treatment program.

Behavior Modification Techniques. The behavior modification approach seeks a twofold goal: (1) to eliminate excessive alcohol consumption as a dominant response to stress and other aversive situations; and (2) to establish alternative, adaptive modes of coping behavior (Bandura, 1969). A number of conditioning techniques have been tried in the treatment of alcoholism. It should be noted, however, that in most instances the conditioning techniques that have been used serve primarily to accomplish only the first part of the goal, that of eliminating the alcohol-drinking response, and thus constitute only a partial treatment.

Conditioned aversion therapy has received the most attention as a behavior modification technique for treating alcoholism. This approach is a classical conditioning paradigm in which the habituated alcohol-drinking response is paired with an extremely aversive stimulus. Aversion has been produced in a number of ways. Typically, after detoxication, an emetic substance such as emetine hydrochloride is injected intramuscularly into the client. Just prior to the extreme nausea that results from the injection, the client is asked to smell, taste, and look at an alcoholic beverage, thereby causing the stimulus qualities of alcohol to become associated with severe vomiting and retching (Franks, 1966). Other methods include the use of electroshock (Vogler et al., 1970), verbally induced aversions (Anant, 1967), and succinylcholine, a chemical substance that induces temporary paralysis and respiratory arrest in an injected subject.

Bandura (1969) has stressed the imperative that alcoholics treated by aversive conditioning must subsequently be provided with alternative behavioral competencies for securing gratification while sober if abstinence is to be maintained. Narrol (1967) reports the use of positive reinforcement principles to promote vocational activities in chronic hospital-ized alcoholics. Desensitization by reciprocal inhibition, a technique devel-oped by Wolpe (1958), in which the relaxation response is conditioned to formerly stressful situations, has been used with alcoholics by Kraft and Al-Issa (1967). This technique, in theory, desensitizes the client to stress-ful, interpersonal, and other environmental situations that typically pro-voke the alcoholic-drinking response.

The most recent trend in behavior modification therapy for alcoholism has been the attempt to teach controlled drinking as an alternative to alco-holic consumption. The approach is, of course, highly controversial, since the specification of controlled drinking as a treatment goal is in direct con-tradiction to the traditional "loss of control" model of alcoholism. The most thoroughly researched and followed-up program in this category is the "individualized behavior therapy for alcoholics" developed by Sobell and Sobell (1972), 1973). Essentially, this approach permits the patient to select his/her own treatment goal: either abstinence or moderate, con-trolled drinking. The choice is subject to review by the treatment staff. An individually tailored, stimulus-control program is then developed for each patient aimed, in the controlled-drinking case, at modifying behaviors that differ from those that are characteristic of social drinkers (e.g., gulping or ordering straight drinks are punished behaviors). In addition, the approach includes training the patient to identify the setting events for his excessive drinking and to devise and perform acceptable alternative behaviors. Patients also learn assertion techniques and behavioral repertoires that assist them in turning down proffered drinks and in ordering half-sized mixed cocktails.

Family Therapy. A notable advance in the treatment of alcoholism has been the recognition that, in many cases, family interaction factors play a significant role in the chronic drinking problems of a family member. Familial factors (e.g., marital disharmony) often contribute to the pre-cipitating stress conditions leading to excessive drinking. Moreover, the alcoholism of a family member exacts a harsh toll on the emotional, social, and economic adjustment of the rest of the family, thereby often eliciting hostility and resentment.

Family therapy, an outgrowth of group-therapy techniques, treats the familial system in which an alcoholic client is embedded. In this context, drinking is examined with respect not only to the individual alcoholic's needs but also to the functions it serves in maintaining a pathological fam-ily system. Family members are helped to develop and integrate more adaptive coping behaviors that support the alcoholic in his/her attempts to attain sobriety. Advances in family-treatment theory and techniques have led to the inclusion of family members in many alcoholism programs, either through direct family therapy or adjunctive treatments of family members (e.g., therapy groups for wives of alcoholics, etc.).

Alcoholics Anonymous. Founded in 1935, Alcoholics Anonymous (AA) is the oldest and best established self-help organization for alcoholism. While its membership would probably resist the categorization of AA as a formal treatment method, participation in AA groups on a voluntary or often compulsory basis is an integral part of many inpatient and outpatient treatment programs. AA adopts what is essentially a spiritual approach to changing alcoholic behavior. Its precepts (so-called 12 steps) involve the alcoholic's admission that he/she is an alcoholic and that his/her drinking is out of his control, his admission of his wrongs and willingness to make amends, his submission to God as he understands him, and his promise to carry AA's message to other alcoholics. Two fundamental AA assumptions have been highly influential among both professional therapists and the lay public. First, AA maintains that "once an alcoholic, always an alcoholic"; i.e., an individual can never be "cured" of alcoholism but can learn through fundamental spiritual change and social support to control the disorder. The corollary to this position is that the recovered alcoholic may never again consume even negligible amounts of alcohol. While lifetime abstinence is the long-range goal, the decision to remain abstinent is encouraged on a day-at-a-time basis. Despite its very substantial membership and lengthy history, surprisingly little is known about the effectiveness of AA in a systematic way because the group has consistently avoided rigorous scientific study.

EVALUATION OF TREATMENT

Outcome Measures

A review of treatment efficacy is immediately complicated by the usage of different operational measures of outcome across evaluation studies. The lack of consistency makes comparative analyses of data from different studies problematic. Moreover, it raises the much debated question of what constitutes recovery from alcoholism. Among the most prominently used indicators of posttreatment change are abstinence, consumption level, frequency of drinking, behavioral impairment (related to drinking), employment status, and marital status. Attrition rate (i.e., rate of dropout from therapy) and/or degree of acceptance of treatment have also been used as outcome measures. The abstinence criterion has been the most widely used measure of treatment success. However, considerable controversy has arisen over the use of abstinence as a singular outcome criterion (e.g., Pattison, 1966). Gerard et al. (1962) have presented empirical data contradicting the assumption that the achievement of abstinence will necessarily result in the amelioration of the alcoholic's related life problems. In the Gerard study, a sizable number of totally abstinent alcoholics were rated as overtly disturbed. A second line of empirical evidence that mitigates the usefulness of the abstinence criterion is the reported ability of a subset of treated alcoholics to resume controlled "normal" drinking and still maintain stability in other areas of adjustment (Davies, 1962; Kendell, 1968; Pattison, 1966).

In reaction to the reliance on abstinence as a sole criterion of success, some writers have advocated multidimensional measurement of treatment outcome (e.g., Foster et al., 1972). This position holds that although a major purpose of treatment is the modification of the target problem behavior (in this case, excessive consumption of alcohol), the efficacy of a given method of treatment can best be evaluated in terms of its total consequences. In chronic alcoholism, the multiple-outcome argument has considerable appeal, since the disorder has profoundly disruptive effects on social, marital, occupational, and other areas of functioning. According to a multidimensional approach, treatment success would presumably be evaluated by such measures, in addition to abstinence, as job and social adjustment, emotional stability, interpersonal involvement, and marital adjustment.

In emphasizing the value of multiple-outcome criteria, some researchers have made the error of discounting the relevance of the alcohol consumption criterion. Success has thus been claimed for some therapies on the basis of inferred psychological changes even though the intended objective (i.e., to halt excessive drinking) has not been achieved. An ordering of outcome criteria would seem desirable. Although complete social and psychological recovery of clients is probably the ultimate goal of most treatment programs, the primary objective remains the elimination of excessive alcohol use and the gross signs of behavioral impairment that result from it. It is quite possible that other indicators of treatment outcome (e.g., social adjustment, marital status, income level) are not immediately affected by intervention techniques that reduce consumption level and resultant behavioral impairment.

Methodological Problems

Four other factors complicate the interpretation of treatment-evaluation research. First, many evaluation studies are conducted within the context of ongoing treatment centers that, as a matter of policy, do not deny treatment to any individual requesting help. The establishment of untreated control groups in research designs is, therefore, problematic. Second, in some treatment centers, de facto selectivity biases operate in the assignment of clients to therapist and/or treatment technique. That is, clinical practitioners often have preferences for certain types of clients with whom they believe they have the best chances for success, and clients are selected accordingly. This results in an obvious lack of randomization of client types across treatment conditions and greatly increases the probability of spurious effects. Third, in practice, most treatment programs include a wide variety of therapeutic activities, so that a singular technique of treatment administered in isolation from other methods is a rare occurrence. Thus, multiple treatments used in various combinations create a serious confounding of conditions for the purposes of evaluation research. Fourth, a commonplace difficulty is the unavailability of certain clients at the time of followup measurement, thereby creating a "subject mortality" bias in the results.

Reported rates of successful treatment for alcoholism vary widely in the literature. Emrick (1974), in an analysis of 265 evaluation studies of psychologically oriented treatments for alcoholism, found a two-thirds improvement rate, with half of those improved achieving abstinence for varying periods of time. Other reports of treatment success range from 30 to 75 percent, depending on the type of therapy and outcome measure used. In their excellent critique of evaluation research in the alcoholism field, Hill and Blane (1967) maintain that abstinence or improvement rates, taking methodological problems into account, are probably less than 50 percent.

Effects of Treatment

Psychotherapy. Many studies have sought to demonstrate the positive results of traditional individual psychotherapy for alcoholism, but there is little empirical evidence for its efficacy. Hill and Blane (1967) have pointed out that, with few exceptions, the serious defects in experimental design and inadequate methods of obtaining followup data have invalidated the conclusions of most studies claiming high rates of success with psychotherapeutic methods. Voegtlin and Lemere (1942) surveyed reports of psychoanalytic therapy with alcoholics. Not only is psychoanalysis lengthy and extremely expensive, but the technique often arouses intense anxiety to which many alcoholics react by resorting to their habituated, anxiety-reduction response of drinking. Moore and Ramseur (1960) evaluated a program in which veterans were treated with intensive psychoanalytically oriented, individual psychotherapy and reported a 30 percent improvement rate after 3½ years. This rate is particularly unimpressive when compared with very similar outcomes for patients who received only custodial state hospital treatment (Cowen, 1954; Selzer and Holloway, 1957). Differences in sample characteristics among these studies, however, mitigate the validity of cross-study comparisons. In a controlled study, Levinson and Sereny (1969) examined an experimental 6-week program in which half the patients received insight-oriented therapy, group therapy, didactic lectures, and occupation and recreational therapy. Controls received only occupational and recreational therapy. One-year followup data indicated no between-group differences. It is possible, however, that the treatment length was too short to achieve positive effects from psychotherapy. A final example comes from a survey of members of the Southern California Psychiatric Association (Hayman, 1956). Among those psychiatrists who treated alcoholics (mostly with psychoanalytically oriented individual psychotherapy), over one-half reported no success with any alcoholic patients; of those who did succeed, it was limited to 10 percent of their cases.

A critical factor in the success of psychotherapy is believed to be the quality of the therapist-client relationship. Chafetz et al. (1962; 1964) have presented data showing that establishing an early therapeutic relationship through a psychotherapeutic interview with alcoholics shortly after admission to the emergency ward greatly increased the probability of continued client visits. Milmore et al. (1967) studied attributes of the therapist's voice as a factor in therapy. Successful outcomes were correlated with voices that connoted a low degree of anger, kindliness, and sympathetic concern as rated by observers.

Evidence for the effectiveness of group therapy with alcoholics, despite its widespread use, is similarly marginal. A number of clinical practitioners have claimed successful results through the use of group therapy techniques although valid empirical support for these claims is generally unavailable. Some studies have shown changes in psychological test measures following group therapy in hospital settings (Ends and Page, 1957, 1959; Mindlin and Belden, 1965). Wolff (1968), however, reported nonsignificant differences in group therapy versus control-group abstinence rates at a 6-month followup.[2] Gerard and Saenger (1966) reported that group therapy seemed to be related to continuance in treatment (but not necessarily improvement) among a sample of outpatient-clinic alcoholics. In

---

[2] It should be noted that Wolff advances his results to demonstrate the efficacy of group therapy. Baekeland et al. (1975) recalculated Wolff's data and found no significant differences.

sum, it would appear that the empirical data to support the effectiveness of group therapy as "almost an article of dogma" (Baekeland et al. 1975, p. 265) is lacking.

Family therapy has also been reported as a successful intervention for alcoholism by a number of clinicians (e.g., Corder et al., 1972; Esser, 1970; Smith, 1969). Again, however, few empirical evaluations of family therapy methods are reported. One controlled study (Corder et al., 1972) does bear out the relative advantage of including wives of alcoholics in a comprehensive treatment program. In this study, the controls received the usual 4-week program of group therapy, lectures, and recreational and occupational therapy. In addition to the usual program, experimental subjects also received an intensive 4-day workshop with wives and husbands. At the 7-month followup, the latter group was significantly more abstinent. However, subject selection biases may contribute to the reported differences.

Drug Therapy. In a recent comprehensive review, Mottin (1973) concluded that very little empirical evidence exists for the efficacy of most pharmacological interventions in the treatment of alcoholism. Retrospectively, it appears that many of the early claims for therapeutic success of particular drug treatments were largely due to placebo effects.

Among the drug treatments used as "substitute" compounds for the pharmaceutic properties of alcohol, only the positive effects of chlordiazepoxide (Librium) have been demonstrated empirically (Hoff, 1961; Ditman, 1961; Kissin and Gross, 1968; Kissin and Platz, 1968). Benar and Ditman (1964, 1967) concluded in their review that tranquilizers and phenothiazines have little therapeutic value in the treatment of alcoholism, although Kline (1973) has recently reported some success with lithium. Gerard and Saenger (1966) reported lower rates of improvement among outpatients who were administered tranquilizers. It is possible, however, that the group for whom tranquilizers were prescribed were more severely impaired initially. Barbiturates, paraldehyde, and other drugs with potential cross-dependencies for alcoholics are contraindicated, since addiction may develop and the resultant incapacity and withdrawal from such drugs may be even worse than for alcohol. Double-blind studies comparing antidepressant compounds (e.g., imipramine and amitriptylline) and placebos have not supported claims for the therapeutic value of the drugs (Ditman, 1961; Kissin and Gross, 1968).

Brief chemical intervention in the form of LSD ingestion has been touted as a successful breakthrough in the treatment of alcoholism (Smith, 1958; Chwelos et al., 1959; Jensen, 1962; O'Reilly and Funk, 1964). However, methodological critiques of the studies on which such claims were based cast doubt upon the validity of the results (Smart and Storm,

1964). Most studies lacked control groups and probably used unrepresentative samples of alcoholics. More recent studies that have employed experimental designs have failed to yield significant results in support of the long-term therapeutic effectiveness of LSD (Smart et al., 1966, 1967; Johnson, 1969; Van Dusen et al., 1967). Self-reports of alcoholics after LSD sessions provide some anecdotal evidence for at least short-term efficacy of the drug (Ditman et al., 1962; Sarett et al., 1966). In general, it appears that any therapeutic gains that result from LSD treatment are limited to only a few months' duration (Ludwig et al., 1969; Hollister et al., 1969).

Ditman (1967) has commented that in the face of generally disparate empirical results, the continued prescription of ineffectual drug treatments reflects many physicians' stubborn adherence to the medical model of alcoholism. In contrast to most "substitute" drug treatments, however, the use of the aversively protective agent disulfiram (Antabuse) has met with some degree of therapeutic success. In Wallerstein's (1956, 1957) study, Antabuse yielded the highest improvement rate at followup (53 percent) as compared with three other treatments. Gerard and Saenger (1966) found a higher percentage of improvement among 50 disulfiram-treated patients than among 495 treated without disulfiram. It is possible, however, that the patients treated with disulfiram differed systematically from other clients at intake. Hoff (1961) attributed the superior outcome of a large number of disulfiram-treated patients, as compared with a smaller group not given the drug, to the lower incidence in dropout rate among the former group. Other studies have reported abstinence rates of about 50 percent among disulfiram-treated alcoholics, suggesting that disulfiram therapy may be equal in efficacy to more costly and time-consuming psychotherapeutic methods with some clients (Borne et al., 1966; Bowman et al., 1951; Brown and Knoblock, 1951).

The efficacy of the disulfiram regimen has not, however, received unqualified support. The indiscriminate prescription of Antabuse to all clients in a treatment facility has not yielded positive results (Gerrein et al., 1973; Glasscote et al., 1967). It has been suggested that disulfiram works best when it serves as a "chemical fence" or positive ego reinforcer to clients whose motivation to stop drinking is strong (Lundwall and Baekeland, 1971; Baekeland et al., 1971). Jacobsen (1950) has emphasized that the duration and degree of abstinence attained with disulfiram treatment is contingent on the duration and regularity with which the medication is used. Since the aversive effect of disulfiram does not become conditioned to alcohol psychologically but depends instead on the physical interaction with alcohol, many alcoholics reportedly go on sprees following cessation of the drug-taking regimen. Several clinician-researchers who use disulfiram have, therefore, emphasized the necessity of adjunctive supportive psychotherapy.

A number of side effects result from prolonged usage or excessive dosages of disulfiram, including drowsiness, nausea, headache, unpleasant body odor, gastrointestinal disturbance and, occasionally, decreased sexual potency (Child et al., 1951; Martensen-Larsen, 1953). Because of its side effects and pharmaceutic properties, disulfiram is contraindicated in the treatment of alcoholics who suffer from cardiovascular disorders, cirrhosis, nephritis, diabetes, epilepsy, advanced arteriosclerosis, or who may be pregnant. The effectiveness of metronidazole (Flagyl), another aversively protective drug with fewer negative side effects and limitations of usage, has not been supported empirically (Linton and Hain, 1967; Egan and Goetz, 1968; Penick et al., 1969).

Behavior Therapy. Most empirical assessments of the effects of behavior therapy have focused on the aversion-conditioning paradigm. Reported abstinence rates obtained by aversion therapy range from as low as 30 percent (Edlin et al., 1945) to highs of 80 or 90 percent (Miller, 1959; Anant, 1967; Kant, 1945). The variation in reported outcomes is largely attributable to variations in followup periods. Some 40 to 60 percent of alcoholics who receive aversive conditioning resume excessive drinking after a period of abstinence (usually between 6 and 12 months after treatment) unless the technique is supplemented with other therapeutic programs (Bandura, 1969). The rather high remission rate following short-term aversion therapy is not surprising in light of the experimental learning principles on which conditioning treatments are based. That is, aversive conditioning, in theory, creates a reduction in the positive value of intoxicants by producing an aversive association to drinking. However, unless new responses to strenuous situations such as anxiety or depression are developed in the alcoholic, eventually the strength of the conditioned association will dissipate and relapse will occur. In this sense, aversion therapy constitutes only a partial treatment for alcoholism. Voegtlin et al. (1942) reported that, in the absence of alternative therapy, willingness of alcoholics to return for periodic reconditioning sessions within the first year was related to better long-term improvement. It is possible that sustained contact with treatment personnel, rather than the booster treatments themselves, was responsible for the improvement.

Among the stimuli used in aversive conditioning, emetic substances are probably superior choices. Electric shock has not been proved effective (Blake, 1965, 1967; Hsu, 1965), and the extremely traumatic effects of succinylcholine (apnea induction) do not seem warranted (Sanderson et al., 1963; Laverty, 1966; Farrar et al., 1968).

As Bandura (1969) has noted, the lack of controlled experimentation with adequate sample sizes in evaluation studies of aversion therapy makes it impossible to determine the degree to which outcomes are differently affected by the number of conditioning sessions, clients' resources for alternative response modes to stress, environmental contingencies, or nature of the aversive stimulus.

The more recent, broad-spectrum, behavior therapy approaches have gone beyond simple extinction of the drinking response through aversive conditioning. These programs have sought to shape alternative behaviors by using operant reinforcement procedures. Hunt and Azrin (1973) used a treatment strategy in which a maximally reinforcing natural environment was engineered for the alcoholic client. A wide variety of reinforcements was available contingent on abstinence, whereas temporary withdrawal of reinforcements was contingent on drinking. The results of this so-called "community-reinforcement" approach yielded highly significant differences between the behaviorally treated group and a control group who received conventional mental hospital treatment, favoring the former. Lovibond and Cady (1970) reported a 77 percent success rate of patients who were considerably or completely improved through the use of an operant conditioning program that punished heavy but not moderate drinking. However, a number of uncontrolled factors in their study suggest the need for a careful replication of their procedure.

In the largest scale controlled-drinking study to date, Sobell and Sobell (1972, 1973) reported 80 percent and 75 percent success rates (abstinent or controlled drinking) for their abstinent-goal and controlled-drinking-goal groups, respectively, at a 1-year followup. These figures contrast sharply with the 33 percent and 26 percent improvement rates of the control groups treated with conventional approaches. In summary, the broad-spectrum behavioral approach that adopts controlled drinking as an acceptable goal or index of recovery seems quite effective relative to more traditional interventions. The approach is, however, only in its early stages of development, and further empirical investigation is required before conclusive statements about its relative effectiveness can be made.

Treatment Comparisons. Emrick (1975) reviewed 384 studies of psychologically oriented treatment of alcoholism to assess the relative effectiveness of different treatment approaches. Of these, only 72 studies used random assignment or matched treatment groups, thereby permitting assessment of treatment differences unconfounded by patient characteristics. In all, only 5 studies were found that presented significant long-term differences (i.e., longer than 6 months) between treatment groups. Ends and Page (1957) compared four treatment groups and found client-centered and psychoanalytic groups to be superior to a learning-theory group and social discussion group. Pittman and Tate (1972) and Vogler et al. (1971) reported significantly better functioning among patients in groups who received some form of aftercare than among those for whom followup treatment was not available. Tomsovic and Edwards (1973) found superior outcomes for their lysergide group compared with a no-lysergide control. Finally, as stated previously, Sobell and Sobell (1972, 1973) reported superior outcomes for behavior therapy with controlled drinking groups than for conventionally treated inpatient controls.

Emrick has argued persuasively that even in these five cases of differential treatment effects, the results may be due to some elements in the treatment environment that "harm alcoholics by eliciting thoughts and feelings of disappointment, abuse, neglect or rejection" (1975, p. 94). That is, "control"-group alcoholics may have actually felt rejected by not being permitted to receive the experimental treatment. The resultant aversive state they experinced may have been an antecedent to further drinking. The differential effects, therefore, may be due more to the relatively harmful effects of the "control treatment" than to the beneficial effects of the intervention under study. The fact that the great majority of studies show very moderate or insignificant differences among treatment modalities (Emrick, 1975; Wallgren and Barry, 1970) suggests that all approaches seem about equally helpful. Moreover, Emrick's extensive review indicates that treatment of any kind generally seems to have beneficial effects on patient functioning.

Treatment Setting. Systematic comparisons of treatment settings (i.e., inpatient, outpatient, intermediate) are rare in the literature and, when available, are often ridden with methodological problems of patient selection biases and treatment confoundings. Baekeland et al. (1975) reviewed separately the outcomes of inpatient and outpatient treatments. These authors did not find strong evidence to support the view that either setting is generally preferable. One of the few controlled studies that randomly assigned patients to either 2 months' inpatient or outpatient care, reported nonsignificant between-group differences at 6 and 10 months (Edwards and Guthrie, 1966). Studies of differential setting effects, however, have not adequately explored the issue of establishing which types of patients might need, and therefore benefit from, specific treatment settings.

Amount of Treatment. In general, treatment length has been found to be positively related to outcome in outpatient treatment studies (Fox and Smith, 1959; Gerard and Saenger, 1966; Kissin et al., 1968; Ritson, 1969). The evidence for inpatient treatment outcome in relation to length of treatment is equivocal. Some investigators have reported a better prognosis following relatively longer hospitalization (Ellis and Krupinski, 1964; Moore and Ramseur, 1960; Rathod et al., 1966), whereas others have failed to find length of stay predictive of outcome (Ritson, 1969; Willems et al., 1973). In both inpatient and outpatient studies, however, length of stay has been confounded by such factors as motivation, social background, and other prognostic variables, making conclusions rather tenuous.

Baekeland et al. (1975) approached the issue by examining the relationship between treatment length and outcome in studies rather than in individuals. Reporting on results of 24 inpatient and 7 outpatient studies, these authors concluded, on the basis of rather tentative findings, that treatment length is more strongly related to abstinence than to other indices of improvement that may depend more on environmental factors.

Client Factors in Treatment Outcome

An array of factors have been reported to favor good outcome in alcoholism treatment. Given the relative absence of strong evidence for differential treatment effects in the literature, Baekeland et al. have even raised the question of "whether we should applaud the treatment programs or the patients they treat" (1975, p. 262).

Social stability in the form of steady employment, residency, and familial relationships, has been consistently reported as a positive prognostic factor in both inpatient (Bowen and Androes, 1968; Dubourg, 1969; Gillis and Keet, 1969; Kish and Hermann, 1971; Pokorny et al., 1968; Rosenblatt et al., 1971) and outpatient treatment (Baekeland et al., 1973; Gerard and Saenger, 1966; Goldfried, 1969; Mayer and Myerson, 1971; Kissin et al., 1971). Socioeconomic status (SES) (related to social stability itself) has also been found to relate to successful outcome (Gillis and Keet, 1969; Mindlin, 1960; Trice et al., 1969).

A special subset of clients, the skid row alcoholics or public inebriates, represents a class of social characteristics that has consistently been related to poor prognosis and treatment failure. The skid row alcoholic is impoverished both in personal and social resources and typifies the low end of the social stability continuum. Moreover, the skid row drinker can be viewed as a member of a deviate subculture in which negative values are attached to norms and demands of the dominant culture. In the skid row milieu, powerful influences operate to maintain the alcoholism of its residents (Pittman and Gordo, 1958). These special characteristics of the skid row alcoholic's environment suggest the need for treatment intervention at the level of residential care and provision of an alternative total social milieu.

Since social stability indices relate to treatment outcome, it is reasonable to expect history or duration of alcoholism to have negative prognostic significance due to the progressive social deterioration that parallels the alcoholism process. There have been some studies that suggest the effectiveness of early treatment, i.e., intervention before the severe social and physical impairment of prolonged alcoholism has developed. Pfeffer and Berger (1957) attributed the very high success rate (92 percent) of a group of alcoholics voluntarily treated in an industrial alcoholism program to the relatively early stage of the disorder manifested in the sample. Fox and Smith (1959) reported a tendency for superior outcome among younger alcoholics in their sample who, by inference, have shorter histories of alcoholism and less advanced symptomatology.

There is, however, contradictory evidence on this point. Many studies report a positive correlation between percentage of abstinence and age (Voegtlin and Broz, 1949; Wolff and Holland, 1964; Kissin and Platz, 1968; Winship, 1957). Therapeutic success has also been correlated with duration of excessive drinking and enlarged liver, but negatively correlated with extreme pathology such as delirium tremens (Rathod et al., 1966; Voegtlin and Broz, 1949). Other studies have shown spontaneous abatement of alcoholism with advancing age (Lemere, 1953; Drew, 1968).

Some therapeutic philosophies hold that an alcoholic must "hit bottom" before he/she can be helped. Only then does the alcoholic presumably drop his defensive denial and become open to therapeutic intervention. Moore and Murphy (1961) found that the degree of diminution of denial among alcoholics in their study was positively related to improvement. The hitting bottom argument is consistent with results showing greater improvement with advanced age and longer drinking history. However, conflicting empirical results on the relationship between age or duration of alcoholism and therapeutic outcome suggest the need for further research to clarify this issue.

Because of the far higher ratio of men to women who are heavy drinkers and alcoholics (Cahalan, 1970), most of the empirical research reported in the literature has been based on samples of predominantly male patients. In recent years, however, increasing attention has been given to the sex of the client as a potentially important variable in the etiology and treatment of alcoholism. Some writers have claimed that alcoholism in women shows a more rapid and severe development than it does among men (Wallgren and Barry, 1970). However, other researchers have failed to find consistent differences between the sexes in the pattern of alcoholism development (Wanberg, 1969; Wanberg and Horn, 1970). Studies that have examined sex as a prognostic variable have been contradictory. Superior outcome by women was reported by Voegtlin and Broz (1949) and by Fox and Smith (1959), whereas Pemberton (1967) found greater therapeutic success with men in his sample.

Two studies have suggested that differential variables may be associated with recovery in male and female alcoholics. Davis (1966) studied 45 female and 86 male alcoholics and reported marked differences between the sexes in the factors related to therapeutic outcome. The women, although more unstable than men, showed greater improvement at followup, using degree of sobriety as a dependent measure. Prognostic factors correlated with sobriety in women were voluntary commitment, dependency, and marital difficulty. In men, sobriety was correlated with number of previous admissions, effect of the alcoholism problem on the family, divorce, and dread of marital rejection. Bateman and Petersen (1972) reported 6 out of 28 tested variables to be correlated with total abstinence at followup in their male sample: age (45 or older), full-time employment after treatment, at least 1 week abstinence prior to treatment, a previous history of regular attendance at AA meetings, and a deceased mother, or less than monthly contact with mother if living. Of the variables correlated with abstinence in men, only the age factor and full-time employment after treatment were significant in the female sample. Other variables correlated with abstinence in women (but not in men) were less-than-high-school education, low-status occupations, employment at time of intake, lower social status, IQ of 110 or more on the Army Beta, average ethanol consumption of more than 4 ounces daily in year preceding intake, and first drink at age 19 or younger. While the large number of tested variables and significant correlations in this study raise the possibility that many associations are spurious, the fact that only two variables had prognostic value for both sexes suggests that sex may be an important variable in predicting treatment outcome.

While psychological variables have received considerable attention as etiological factors in alcoholism, their status as prognostic factors in treatment remains unclear. Some writers (e.g., Selzer, 1967) have speculated that the presumed personality traits of alcoholics (e.g., dependent, hostile, depressed, manipulative, etc.) constitute a serious impediment to successful psychotherapy. What little evidence exists on prognostic psychological variables, however, does not support this contention.

Dependency has been studied as a predictive variable and, in general, has been found to correlate positively with good treatment outcome. Blane and Meyers (1963) found that overtly dependent alcoholics, as opposed to counterdependent types, were more likely to continue in treatment. This relationship has also been found by Tarnower and Toole (1968). In addition to continuation in treatment, superior therapeutic outcome has been reported for alcoholics who are relatively more passive psychologically or socially isolated, and emotionally disturbed (Muzekari, 1965; Pokorny et al., 1968). Wallerstein (1957) found improvement to relate to passive-dependent character structure across four different treatment modalities. Blane and Meyers (1964) interpret their finding of greater improvement with lower SES patients to be due to the beneficial effects of greater dependency induced by the relatively large discrepancy in status levels between therapists and patients.

Other psychological variables reported to have prognostic significance include relatively superior intellectual and emotional functioning (Mindlin, 1959; Rossi et al., 1963), moderate levels of self-punitive "conscience structure" (Walton et al., 1966), high affiliative needs, and group dependence (Trice and Roman, 1970). The most consistently poor prognostic indicator has been evidence of a sociopathic personality structure (Muzekari, 1965; Pokorny et al., 1968; Ritson, 1971).

Finally, the concept of client motivation is frequently invoked by theorists as an important prognostic factor in treatment outcome. Several attitudinal surveys have demonstrated that professionals and laymen alike tend to view the alcoholic as an individual who "chooses" to drink and therefore entraps himself in his own alcoholism (Linsky, 1970; Pattison et al., 1968; Sterne and Pittman, 1965). Paradoxically, this intention is attributed to alcoholics even though the traditional defining characteristic of the disorder is an inability to control drinking behavior. Nonetheless, the attribution that alcoholism is a "self-chosen" disease may lead to the assumption that unless he deliberately chooses treatment and evidences a high level of motivation to change the alcoholic will not profit from therapy.

A number of studies have reported motivation to be related to good treatment outcome (Gerard and Saenger, 1966; Baekeland et al., 1973; Goldfried, 1969; Mayer and Myerson, 1971). Aharan et al. (1967), however, found no measure of motivation used in their study to predict treatment outcome. Pittman and Sterne (1965) have aptly criticized the ambiguity and circular usage of the term "motivation" in the treatment literature. Often, there is no clear operational or conceptual definition provided and there is a general failure to distinguish between extrinsic motivation (social pressure to seek treatment; coercion) and intrinsic motivation (Baekeland et al., 1975). Finally, the motivation of a client is often seen as synonymous with positive and accepting attitudes toward the therapist and treatment. It would seem a profitable research endeavor to assess the prognostic value of motivation in its various meanings by careful conceptualization of the term and proper operationalization of its components.

Client Therapy Interactions

Bowman and Jellinek (1941) theorized that no one therapeutic modality can be successful with all patients who exhibit a drinking problem. Their view suggested the need for studies in which large, heterogeneous, randomly designed samples are exposed to a variety of therapeutic techniques to determine possible client-therapy interactions. Unfortunately, very few researchers have adopted such a strategy.

The most direct examination of patient-treatment match to date has been done by Kissin and his coworkers (Kissin et al., 1968, 1970, 1971). By using a design that combined random assignment to treatment with a variable of allowing or not allowing patients to reassign themselves, it was found that treatment acceptors had better outcomes than treatment rejectors. The number of treatment alternatives made available was also positively related to better outcome. In general, psychotherapy was the choice of the most "socially and psychologically intact" clients, rehabilitation of the least, and drug therapy of those in between (Kissin et al., 1970).

On the basis of empirical data comparing successes and failures in three treatment groups, Kissin et al. (1968) found the following interactive relationships: those alcoholics who were most socially and psychologically competent benefited most from psychotherapy; those who were socially competent but less competent psychologically, from drug therapy; and those socially incompetent but highly competent psychologically, from an inpatient rehabilitation ward program. Social and psychological competence were ascertained by examination of social stability and other background variables (e.g., SES) and by performance on a number of standard psychological tests.

Pattison et al. (1969) have suggested that degree of improvement of patients in various treatment settings may be contingent on the extent of fit between the patient's rehabilitation needs and the methods, facilities, and goals of the therapeutic program. Gerard and Saenger (1966) have provided data suggesting that outpatient treatment is probably best suited to socially stable alcoholics. Intermediate care, as discussed earlier, seems particularly suited to the needs of socially deprived alcoholics who require a total social alternative to their deviate subcultures. Certain hospital settings that emphasize a biochemical etiology of alcoholism may provide the appropriate medical rationalization enabling relatively high-status alcoholics to receive treatment and maintain their status (Pattison et al., 1969).

A number of other psychological variables have been cited as indicators of differential treatment preference. Blane and Meyers (1963) and Blane (1968) have suggested that a therapeutic emphasis on sympathy, support, and permissiveness may be particularly suitable for overtly dependent alcoholics, whereas more directive, authoritarian techniques may work best with "counterdependent" alcoholics. Trice (1957) reported "susceptibility" to AA to be related to affiliative needs and extroversion. Vogel (1960, 1961) reported that aversive-conditioning techniques were most effective with introverted, solitary drinkers. Aversion therapy has also been reported to be most successful with alcoholics whose habituation has developed through prolonged, heavy social drinking and who possess sufficient personal resources to derive adequate gratifivation from sober behavior (Thimann, 1949; Voegtlin and Broz, 1949). Favorable prognostic factors in disulfiram therapy have been reported to be older age (Serény and Fryatt, 1966; Baekeland et al., 1971), social stability (Proctor and Tooley, 1950; Rudfeld, 1958), and good motivation (Baekeland et al., 1971; Rudfeld, 1958). Significant depression is seen to have negative prognostic significance in disulfiram therapy (Baekeland et al., 1971; Winship, 1957). Finally, high anxiety levels appear to contraindicate self-confrontation therapy (Shaeffer et al., 1971) and traditional psychoanalysis (Wallgren and Barry, 1970).

AN INPUT-OUTPUT MODEL FOR TREATMENT

It is obvious from the preceding review that no single theory has yet encompassed the myriad of etiological, prognostic, and therapeutic variables that have been put forth in the literature as important for understanding and treating alcoholism. While it would be premature for us to suggest such a theory, it is nonetheless helpful to have a framework that will give structure to our empirical analysis. For this purpose we propose an "input-output" model. This model is not to be seen as a theory of alcoholism and its remedy, but rather as a means of organizing and testing relationships among outcomes, client characteristics, and treatment characteristics.

The input-output model diagramed in Figure 1 is useful for several reasons. First, it classifies important etiological and prognostic input factors into two conceptually distinct categories: client inputs and treatment inputs. *Client inputs* are client characteristics present at intake to treatment that may be considered by a center in making assignments to treatment modalities. These client characteristics are essentially "given" conditions over which a treatment center has little control prior to the onset of treatment. *Treatment inputs* are center characteristics representing the policy of a treatment center as to the type and amount of treatment. The model allows a summarization of the most important observed empirical relations between treatment outcomes and client or treatment inputs (represented by the single-pointed arrows). It also highlights the "interaction" between

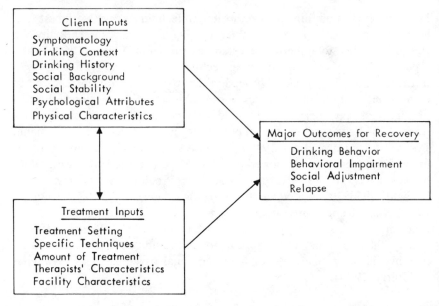

Figure 1   An input-output model for treatment evaluation.

client and treatment characteristics that might affect outcomes (represented by the double-pointed arrow). This permits examination of the possibility that certain client characteristics interact with different treatment modalities so that successful outcome depends on "matching" the appropriate treatment to the type of alcoholic client.

While the input-output model is not itself a causal theory or a remedy theory for alcoholism, it does allow us to test some of the research questions and hypotheses that are generated from the etiological and prognostic perspectives reviewed in earlier sections of this chapter. We will present these hypotheses as we review the various components of the model.

Outcomes for Recovery

The output side of the input-output model consists of treatment outcomes, and in particular those outcomes that can be used to define recovery from alcoholism. Defining recovery is not a simple matter, especially when there is no rigorous and accepted definition of alcoholism in the first place. But even if there were agreement on a certain level or pattern of drinking or impairment that defined alcoholism, one would not necessarily have a definition of recovery. As shown in our review, the main reason is that there is no consensus on how an alcoholic, once recovered, can remain free of alcoholic drinking. The proponents of physiological predisposition and addiction models, including adherents of the AA philosophy, generally argue that abstention is the only proper definition of recovery since, for a true alcoholic, even a small amount of alcohol will cause a "loss of control" and an inability to stop drinking. But proponents of other schools of thought have argued that once psychological causes of alcoholism are removed, or once reconditioning has occurred, the alcoholic can return to social, nonalcoholic drinking. Finally, from other perspectives, particularly those derived from sociocultural models, alcoholism is intimately related to social factors such as job and family stability; these perspectives often emphasize recovery in terms of social adjustment rather than drinking behaviors per se.

Lacking final definitions of recovery, we will adopt several strategies. First, we will use the multiple-outcome approach by examining several outcomes that indicate alcoholic behavior, depending on one's theoretical perspective. These include abstention, level of alcohol consumption for nonabstainers, and behavioral impairment resulting directly from alcohol use (e.g., withdrawal symptoms, symptomatic drinking, missing work due to drinking). We will also examine social adjustment criteria, such as job and marital stability, although we feel that from a theoretical standpoint stability factors should be viewed as client inputs rather than treatment outcomes. An alcoholic who stops drinking but does not have a job is a stronger candidate for being considered recovered than is an alcoholic who finds a job but does not stop excessive drinking—at least if the illness is alcoholism rather than unemployment. There are many conditions leading to marital or job instability other than alcohol abuse, and many alcohol abusers never have serious marital or employment problems. If a treatment evaluation is to have etiological relevance, it is our position that while social adjustment cannot be ignored, major emphasis must be placed on drinking-related behaviors as treatment outcomes.

Our second strategy will be to develop a single definition of remission based on a series of drinking and impairment behaviors that seem to us reasonable in the light of existing research. While we provide detailed information about our definition in Chapter 4, suffice it to say that our definition includes both abstainers and clients who drink at "normal" levels but do not show signs of alcoholic behavioral impairment. Given the controversy about whether alcoholics can ever drink again without returning to excessive alcoholic drinking, one of our major research questions concerns the frequency with which clients in our followup samples return to drinking behaviors that can be described as normal.

Finally, a single followup study is limited to assessing the rate of improvement at only one point in time. The existence of two followup reports for a subgroup of clients—one at 6 months and one at 18 months—allows us to conduct a unique investigation of relapse rates. A client who relapses is one who is in remission at one followup point (by our definition) but who exhibits alcoholic drinking and symptoms at a later followup point. Thus, relapse rates are an important outcome criterion because they establish the rate of stable remission as opposed to remission at a single point in time.

These various definitions of treatment outcomes allow us to investigate the following research questions with our data:

- Is alcoholism "treatable?" That is, can alcoholics be helped by a formal treatment program to achieve remission rates exceeding those of alcoholics who are not in treatment?
- What is the typical remission pattern of alcoholics, particularly with regard to the proportion abstaining versus the proportion returning to some form of normal drinking, and with regard to the impovement in social adjustment as contrasted with improvement in drinking behavior?
- Do alcoholics who return to some form of drinking have a higher likelihood of relapse than those who adopt a personal policy of abstention?

Client Inputs

Client inputs are those characteristics of a client that are initial given conditions at intake to treatment. We have selected client characteristics according to two different criteria, as emphasized in our review of existing research on the etiology and treatment of alcoholism. First, some client characteristics are implicated in the etiology of alcoholism (depending on the theory) and hence may either aid or hamper the treatment process; examples might be family alcoholism, dependent personality traits, or job and marital instability. Other factors are not necessarily involved in etiology per se but are nonetheless prognostic for recovery; examples might be degree of alcoholic impairment itself, drinking context (to the extent that context is a consequence for alcoholism rather than vice versa), and motivation for recovery.

Symptomatology. This category of client inputs refers to the type and severity of alcoholism symptoms manifested at intake. Relevant variables in this class include pattern of alcoholism, consumption level, alcohol-related physical impairment, and alcohol-related behavioral impairment.

Drinking Context. The context of drinking includes alcohol-related environmental conditions, such as drinking behavior of household or family members, drinking behavior of friends or associates, and location of drinking, such as bars or taverns.

Drinking History. Included in this category are variables related to the genesis of alcoholism and to treatment history. Examples are age when drinking started, presence of alcoholism or heavy drinking in the family when growing up, number of times previously treated, and so forth.

Social Background. This category includes the set of sociological variables reported to account for a large amount of the variance in national drinking patterns, such as age, sex, ethnicity, religion, geographical region, income and educational level, and status of occupation. In general, these background variables can be seen to have antedated the onset of alcoholism.

Social Stability. This category reflects the relative social stability of the client at the time of intake to treatment. Defining variables in this class are marital status, employment status, number of jobs in the year prior to intake, years of residence in current community, and status of current residence (e.g., own home, group quarters, rented private residence, etc.). Unlike social background, these characteristics are frequently so intertwined with alcoholic behavior itself that it is hard to decide which behavior came first.

Psychological Variables. This category includes the range of personality and background factors invoked by psychological theories of alcoholism (e.g., dependence, need for power, orality, etc.). In addition, psychological prognostic variables include the client's assessed and self-reported motivation for treatment, attitudes toward alcohol, and personal prognosis for recovery. Variables of familial psychological functioning may also have prognostic significance.

Physiological Characteristics. Physiological predisposition theories posit certain physical characteristics that may be involved in the genesis of alcoholism and hence in successful treatment. These might include tissue tolerance to alcohol, metabolic factors causing high alcohol elimination rates, and so forth. While these characteristics are rarely measured in treatment-evaluation studies, an investigator should be aware of their potential importance when interpreting treatment outcomes.

Research Questions. The NIAAA data we are using in this study do not include measurements for all clients inputs that have potential importance for treatment success; in particular, there are no measurements for physiological characteristics and very few psychological measurements. Yet we can address a number of specific research questions involving drinking behaviors and social characteristics at intake to treatment, as follows:

- Do alcoholics differ significantly from the normal population in terms of social characteristics?
- Are social factors that typify the NIAAA alcoholic population also related to heavy or problem drinking in the normal population, or do alcoholics seen in these clinical settings comprise a different population altogether?
- Do these social characteristics that differentiate the alcoholic from the general population also have a prognostic role in treatment success?
- Does the symptomatology or seriousness of the alcoholism at intake have prognostic importance for treatment success above and beyond the importance of social background factors?

Treatment Inputs

Treatment inputs differ conceptually from client inputs insofar as they are under the control of the treatment center and staff. While we have already reviewed some of the major variations in treatment techniques, we need to emphasize those treatment inputs that will receive special attention in our analysis of the NIAAA data.

Treatment Setting. Treatment setting refers to the environment within which treatment takes place and in particular to the distinction between inpatient and outpatient care. Inpatient care can be broken down further into full hospitalization settings as distinct from rehabilitation or intermediate settings, such as halfway houses or recovery homes. Combinations of treatment settings can also be distinguished, such as hospital plus outpatient care or intermediate plus outpatient care.

Treatment Processes. Processes refer to specific treatment techniques practiced within a particular setting, such as individual psychotherapy, group counseling, drug treatment, and aversive conditioning.

Amount of Treatment. This category includes measures of the amount of services received by a client in one or a combination of settings. It can also include measures of the duration and pattern of treatment, such as length of total contact with a treatment center.

Therapist Characteristics. The therapist's characteristics may have potential relevance to the treatment outcome. Therapists can be differentiated on a professional/nonprofessional dimension. Within these broad categories, finer distinctions can be made on the basis of level or type of professional training (e.g., Ph.D., M.A., M.D.) and alcoholism history of lay counselors (e.g., recovered alcoholics versus "paraprofessionals" with no alcoholism history). Other therapist variables include attitudes toward alcoholism and alcoholic clients, personality characteristics (e.g., warmth, authoritarianism, etc.), and general quality of the therapeutic relationship.

Facility Characteristics. There are a number of potentially important characteristics of a treatment facility as a whole that are not reducible to specific treatment or therapist characteristics. These might include financial resources, the number of different treatment options available, staff-client ratio, proportion of treatment staff with professional training, and general facility characteristics such as age, attractiveness, location, and so forth. Some of these characteristics can be measured explicitly, but it is also possible to treat the whole center as an input by comparing between-center differences in recovery rates.

Research Questions. The major research questions we wish to address regarding treatment inputs are as follows:

- Does the effectiveness of treatment differ according to treatment settings and to specific treatment techniques within settings?
- Does the effectiveness of treatment differ according to the amount and duration of treatment? Are alcoholics who enter treatment at a regular treament center more likely to recover than those who do not enter treatment or who seek non-ATC help, such as AA?
- Do treatment centers themselves have varying rates of success apart from the different types of clients they treat and the different treatment settings they offer?

Client-Treatment Interactions

Client-treatment interaction means that certain types of treatment might be best for certain types of clients. Obviously, the possible combinations among all the client and treatment inputs in Figure 1 are far too numerous to examine even with a large set of data. Rather, we will examine certain "optimal" combinations that are prominent in the treatment field today, particularly among NIAAA's treatment programs. These can be formulated as a set of hypotheses about those treatment modalities believed to yield the greatest success for particular types of clients. Among the client-treatment interactions that will be examined in our evaluation, the following five research questions will receive special attention:

- Is full hospitalization best for more severely impaired alcoholics, regarding both consumption and physical impairment, for whom total abstention is necessary either permanently or until alcohol dependence is broken?
- Is intermediate care (e.g., halfway houses or recovery homes) crucial for alcoholics who are socially impaired due to job and/or marital instability, and who consequently need social rehabilitation as well as elimination of alcohol abuse?
- Is outpatient care optimal for more socially stable clients with relatively less alcohol impairment, where abstention may be a less common goal than reduced consumption?
- Is individual psychotherapy more effective for better educated, middle-class clients; and is individual or group counseling—often similar to AA meetings—more workable with less educated, lower-class clients?
- Is Antabuse therapy best for clients who require or want abstention but who are in outpatient status and cannot control their impulses to drink?

Clearly, these questions do not exhaust the range of possible investigations into alcoholism treatment, nor are they the only questions that can be addressed with the NIAAA data. But they are among the most important research and policy questions being raised in the alcoholism field today, and the answers available from the unique, large-scale data bases assembled by NIAAA are likely to have an important impact on future research and policy directions.

THREE

Social Correlates of Alcoholism and Problem Drinking

The input-output model described in Chapter 2 included those social characteristics bearing on both the etiology of alcoholism and the probable success of treatment, according to the current literature. It is contended, however, that existing studies contain various shortcomings which limit generalizations about the importance of such factors for either etiology or treatment. Using new data, this chapter provides an empirical analysis of the role of social characteristics in distinguishing both problem drinkers and the treated alcoholic population. When taken together with the treatment evaluation in succeeding chapters, the resulting combination provides new information about the importance of social factors in the etiology and treatment of alcoholism.

There have been two major approaches for identifying potential etiological factors in alcoholism research. The first, more classic approach compares the characteristics of alcoholics in treatment or clinical settings with those of the general population. The other and more recent approach has been through general population surveys within which a heavy or problem-drinking subpopulation is formed and compared with the remaining population (Cahalan and Room, 1974). Both approaches are valuable, but taken separately they can lead to different conclusions about potential etiological factors. The first approach is limited by not knowing the factors that lead alcoholics into treatment or clinical settings; i.e., those alcoholics are not necessarily representative of all alcoholics. The second approach is often limited by having a sample of problem drinkers who are less severely impaired than most alcoholics. Sample sizes in general population surveys are generally too small to permit a stringent definition of problem drinking; if the general population includes 5 percent alcoholics, then a sample of 1500 persons would yield only 75 alcoholics (assuming complete representativeness). In order to get sufficient numbers for analysis, survey approaches often rely on larger numbers of drinkers with milder symptoms.

The NIAAA evaluation data can solve some of these problems. First, the pooled Harris national surveys yield a substantial sample size of over 6000 adults. This number is large enough to include a sizable subsample of problem drinkers, using a more restrictive definition of problem drinking than has been possible in previous efforts with smaller samples. Second, the Alcoholism Treatment Center (ATC) population of treated alcoholics and the national surveys have compatible measures of drinking behavior and social characteristics. Thus the characteristics of both a treated-alcoholic population and a highly impaired problem-drinking population can be compared simultaneously with those of a general population. Those factors that have potential etiological significance should be consistently different for the problem-drinking population as well as for the treated-alcoholic population when compared with the general population. Inconsistent differences may yield information about those characteristics that differentiate treated- from untreated-alcoholic populations. These latter characteristics are less likely candidates for etiological significance, although they may have prognostic value.

Another problem with a simple comparison between treated alcoholics and the general population is that it is usually not possible to investigate the importance of certain factors by controlling for other factors via multiple-regression techniques. This problem does not arise in a general population survey with a problem-drinking subpopulation, since regression analysis can be done with a dependent variable indicating the existence or absence of problem drinking. Therefore, if our problem-drinking population appears to resemble an untreated-alcoholic population, regression analyses can be carried out using the national surveys—with problem drinking as a dependent variable—to give a more rigorous test of the suggestions from the comparisons of alcoholic and general populations.

THE DATA

The ATC data base used for the comparative analysis in this chapter consists of approximately 14,000 non-DWI (Driving While Intoxicated) clients admitted to treatment at 44 NIAAA-supported ATCs throughout the country from September 1972 to April 1974.[1] Although there is no guarantee that this is a representative sample of all alcoholics in treatment, to our knowledge it is the only current national data base of treated alcoholics, and it is definitely the only national data base in which the social and drinking measures are comparable to those of the national

---

[1] DWI clients are generally in treatment under court order and differ considerably from alcoholic populations under regular treatment.

cross-sectional survey data. More detailed descriptions of this data base are found elsewhere (Towle, 1973; NIAAA, 1974).

The Harris survey data used for defining the general population and its problem-drinking subpopulation were collected in four waves between August 1972 and January 1974. Each wave was an independent, national probability sample of approximately 1500 persons aged 18 and over; more detailed descriptions of the survey techniques can be found elsewhere (Harris and Associates, 1973, 1974). The analysis in this chapter pools all four of these independent surveys to produce a sample size of approximately 6300 adults.

Parts of these analyses and discussions employ various terms to describe nondrinking, consumption, problem-drinking, and behavioral impairment groups. The following are precise definitions for such terms:

Abstainers: A subgroup of the national survey data base who say they are abstainers (i.e., drink one drink per year or less) and who report no drinking within the past month (N = 2200).

Drinkers: A subgroup of the national survey data base who report *some* drinking within the past 30 days (N = 3660); it includes those persons who described themselves as abstainers but who nonetheless drank during this period.

Daily consumption: Defined only for drinkers (N = 3660); it is an index that estimates the ounces of absolute alcohol consumed in the past 30 days expressed in ounces per day.[2]

Problem drinkers: A subgroup (N = 242) of the Harris survey data base who report daily consumption of over 1.5 ounces of absolute alcohol *and* who are above the median on an index of symptoms of problem drinking or alcoholism (e.g., morning drinking, drinking to feel better, drinking more than 2 or 3 drinks at one sitting, drinking alone).

Impairment: An index varying from 0 to 30, indicating gross behavioral impairment resulting from alcohol consumption; items include withdrawal symptoms, blackouts, missing meals while drinking, and missing work due to drinking. This measure is available only for a single national survey.

Treated alcoholics: All non-DWI clients at the comprehensive ATCs supported by NIAAA.

---

[2] See Chapter 4 and Appendix A for more information on the consumption, problem-drinking, and impairment indices.

In addition to these variables, our analyses also involve a set of social characteristics used in various comparisons. The criteria for inclusion in this set are previous research indicating an etiological or prognostic significance, and the existence of comparable measures in both the ATC and national survey data bases (with two exceptions). The set is as follows:

Past family drinking: A dichotomous variable scored as "yes" (or 1) if any member of the immediate family was a frequent or heavy drinker while the respondent was growing up, and "no" (or 0) otherwise.

Present household drinking: A dichotomous variable scored as "yes" if any member of the respondent's current household is a frequent or heavy drinker (persons living alone coded as missing data).

Drinks at bars: A dichotomous variable scored as "yes" if respondent drinks mostly at bars or equally at bars and at home or at other social gatherings. Not coded for abstainers and not available for the ATC population.

Age of first drink: Self-explanatory. Not coded for abstainers and not available for the ATC population.

Employment: A variable indicating regular employment, unemployment, or not in the work force for the head of household only. Work force excludes housewives, retirees, and students. For the correlation and regression analyses, it is dichotomized by excluding those not in the work force.

Marital status: Distinguishes among those married, those single, and those separated or divorced. For correlation and regression analyses, it is dichotomized into those married and those not married.

Sex: Self-explanatory.

Age: Self-explanatory.

Region: Dichotomized into South and North, according to census definitions, where South includes Texas, Oklahoma, Arkansas, Louisiana, Kentucky, Tennessee, Alabama, Mississippi, Virginia, West Virginia, Maryland, North Carolina, South Carolina, Georgia, and Florida. The North includes all remaining states.

Religion: Distinguishes among Protestant, Catholic, and no religious preference. For the correlation and regression analyses, the variable is dichoto-mized by eliminating the "no religion" category.

Race: Distinction is made between white, black, and Spanish-American, but it is dichotomized in the correlation and regression analyses by elim-inating a small group of Spanish-Americans.

Social class: An index made from an average of three variables—income, occupational status, and education—scored in equivalent ranges. In some cases the three components are presented separately.

We recognize that this list does not include all social characteristics that have been cited in one source or another as important etiological or prog-nostic factors in alcoholism and, moreover, that it does not include the many psychological or attitudinal variables that have been cited in at least one treatment evaluation or etiological study. In some cases, these omis-sions are intentional; this is especially true for those variables dealing with attitudes toward alcohol use itself. It is by no means clear that a tolerant attitude toward alcohol use is substantively different from alcohol use itself, and therefore it might be legitimately questioned as an independently defined variable. Other omissions are due to unavailability in the data being used. This is the case for potentially important personality traits, such as dependence or passivity, although the significance of these and other psychological variables is not fully established by existing research. With these exceptions, the social variables included here are a fair repre-sentation of those social correlates of alcoholism that have received exten-sive documentation in the literature and that are conceptually distinct from drinking or problem-drinking behavior itself.

CORRELATES OF ALCOHOLISM VS. PROBLEM DRINKING

The first question in this investigation is the extent to which problem drink-ers resemble ATC alcoholics, and how both groups differ from the general population. These comparisons are examined separately for males and females.

Males

Table 1 shows that, compared with the general population and the alco-holic population, male problem drinkers have an intermediate position on average daily consumption and behavioral impairment. In the general

Table 1.   Comparisons of the General, Problem-Drinking, and Alcoholic Male Populations

Characteristics	General Population	Problem Drinkers[a]	ATC Alcoholics[b]
Consumption (oz/day)[c]	.91	4.4	8.4
Impairment	1.2[d]	3.6[d]	13.3
Abstainers[e] (%)	26	—	—
Unemployed (work force) (%)	4	12	60
Marital			
Single(%)	20	37	18
Separated/divorced (ever married) (%)	5	17	54
Median age	43	33	45
Black or Spanish-American (%)	12	17	25
Religion			
Protestant (%)	58	43	69
Catholic (%)	28	36	24
None (%)	6	15	5
South (%)	28	18	48
Blue collar occupation (%)	60	54	79
Median annual household income ($)	10,000	10,500	5500
Median education (years)	11.5	11.8	10.6
Past family drinking (%)	32	54	48
Present household drinking (%)	12	32	17
(N)	(3104)	(184)	(11,536)

[a] A subgroup of the general population.
[b] Excluding DWI clients.
[c] Absolute alcohol; for nonabstainers only.
[d] One survey only; N = 52 for problem drinkers.
[e] Drink once a year or less.

population, men who drink consume a daily average of .91 ounce of absolute alcohol, compared with 4.4 ounces for the problem drinker and 8.4 ounces for the alcoholic. It is known that general population surveys underestimate total consumption by about one-half, and the NIAAA national surveys are no exception; thus, the true figures for the general population and problem drinkers might be considerably higher (see Appendix A). Nonetheless, the relative ranking of the three groups on the consumption and behavioral impairment index is what one would expect if problem drinkers, as defined here, were a somewhat less-impaired, untreated-alcoholic population.

While the groups show expected relationships for their own drinking behavior, the situation is mixed with respect to potential etiological social factors. The most important finding consistent with existing research concerns the two stability measures, employment and marital status. The general population work force has a 4 percent unemployment rate, whereas for problem drinkers unemployment is 12 percent and for alcoholics a remarkable 60 percent. Thus, the problem drinker is 3 times and the alcoholic 15 times more likely to be unemployed than the average male. Similar ratios are observed for separation or divorce, with rates of 5 percent, 17 percent, and 54 percent, respectively. It is encouraging that the two social characteristics most frequently cited in the literature reveal the largest difference between the alcoholic and the general population and, moreover, that the problem drinker shows an intermediate position on both. Naturally, we do not know for sure whether those factors helped cause the alcoholism and problem drinking or are consequences of them.

In other respects the problem drinker is not in an intermediate position. One such variable that may help to explain other relationships is age. The alcoholic population is slightly older than the general adult population (45 compared with 43), but the problem drinker is much younger than either, having a median age of 33. Thus the problem-drinking group is half a generation younger than the alcoholic group, and this may explain why a number of social characteristics—especially socioeconomic status—show the pattern they do. For example, problem drinkers are more white collar, have more education, and earn more money than the average person, whereas the alcoholic is lower on all counts. Of course, unlike the other characteristics, the large difference in income for alcoholics is mostly explained by the extremely high rate of unemployment. But the education and occupational status differences—which are smaller—most likely occurred before the onset of alcoholism and may be explained in part by the fact that at any point in time a younger cohort will be more educated and more white collar than an older one. The difference in education and occupation between the alcoholic and general populations suggests that alcoholics in the NIAAA treatment centers have a lower social class position than the average person.

The age differences might also explain the variations in consumption and impairment levels. The problem drinker may be a younger version of the alcoholic population, a prealcoholic group that has not yet reached the consumption or impairment levels of chronic alcoholics.

Problem drinkers are more likely than alcoholics to report frequent drinking in their homes while growing up or in their current household (for those not living alone). The difference for past family drinking is not large, being only 6 percent, but the relatively large difference for current household drinking—32 percent for problem drinkers and only 17 percent for alcoholics—suggests a possible determinant of being in treatment as opposed to being an alcoholic. Persons who drink heavily but whose spouse or other significant family members do not drink—perhaps because of moral convictions—may be more pressured to seek out treatment, either voluntarily or involuntarily.

A similar cultural explanation may account for some of the differences for religion and region. Treated alcoholics are more likely to be Protestant and more likely to be from the South than the general population, whereas problem drinkers are less likely to be Protestant and from the South. As we shall see in the next section, these two factors are major explanations of abstention rates and are consistent with other information about cultural and value orientations concerning the use of alcohol. It could well be that Catholics and Northerners are more likely to become heavy drinkers but that cultural or moral intolerance is more likely to lead heavy drinkers into treatment centers if they are from Protestant families or live in the South (or both).

The differences for ethnicity are similar to those for employment and marital status, where the alcoholic is more likely to be black or Spanish-American than the general population and the problem drinker is in an intermediate position. Yet the differences are not large; ethnicity does not appear to be as strong a correlate of either alcoholism or problem drinking as several other social variables.

The fact that the alcoholic population is more Southern than the general population raises the possibility that some of the other differences we observe in Table 1—especially socioeconomic differences—are due to a Southern bias. To check this possibility, we recalculated all statistics for the ATC alcoholics and weighted the Northerners more heavily to produce a proper regional distribution matching the general population. None of the statistics in Table 1 varied by more than a percentage point or two. It is interesting that the NIAAA treatment centers tend to be concentrated in the South although problem drinking appears to be more concentrated in the North. This does not necessarily represent a regional bias, however, since NIAAA evaluates treatment-center grant applications regardless of regional location. There may, in fact, be more treatment centers in the South on a per capita basis, a situation that would be consistent with a stronger cultural intolerance of drinking and alcohol abuse.

Females

The comparisons for the female population shown in Table 2 reflect some of the patterns observed for males, but there are some important differences. Note that ATC female alcoholics consume far less alcohol than males (4.5 oz/day compared with 8.4 for males), but their impairment is about the same. This suggests that females can experience alcoholic symptoms to the same degree as males, with considerably less alcohol.

Table 2.   Comparisons of the General, Problem-Drinking, and Alcoholic Female Populations

Characteristics	General Population	Problem Drinkers[a]	ATC Alcoholics[b]
Consumption (oz/day)[c]	.44[c]	5.0	4.5
Impairment	.9[d]	4.3[d]	12.0
Abstainers[e] (%)	44	—	—
Unemployed (work force)[f] (%)	13	30	45
Marital			
Single (%)	10	17	9
Separated/divorced (ever married) (%)	7	12	44
Median age	39	40	44
Black or Spanish-American (%)	12	14	18
Religion			
Protestant (%)	62	49	71
Catholic (%)	28	37	24
None (%)	3	10	4
South (%)	28	17	38
Blue collar occupation (%)	56	29	54
Median income ($)	9250	10,000	5200
Median education (years)	11.8	12.0	11.2
Past family drinking (%)	33	46	53
Present household drinking (%)	17	63	35
(N)	(3160)	(41)	(2598)

[a] A subgroup of the general population.
[b] Excluding DWI clients.
[c] Absolute alcohol; for nonabstainers only.
[d] One survey only; N=52 for problem drinkers.
[e] Drink once a year or less.
[f] Heads of household only.

With the exception of the drinking variables, the differences in social characteristics seem to be less intense; this is especially true for age, occupation, and education. The results for stability factors are almost identical to those for males; the same is true for the cultural factors of region and religion. Socioeconomic factors have the same pattern but weaker relationships. It is interesting that the male to female ratio for problem drinkers is almost identical to that for treated alcoholics—4.5 to 1 and 4.4 to 1, respectively.

For females, the effect of age is different from that for males. The male problem drinker tends to be considerably younger than the general-population male, whereas the average female problem drinker is 1 year older than the general-population female. This is consistent with findings by Cahalan and Room (1974) that problem drinking tends to be fairly concentrated among males under 25 but not among younger females. Females tend to increase their drinking after marriage, whereas males show the opposite pattern.

The most striking difference between men and women occurs in the present-household-drinking characteristic (which in almost all cases describes spouses). For women, 63 percent of the problem drinkers report that someone in their immediate household is a frequent or heavy drinker compared with 35 percent for female alcoholics. For men, the comparable figures are 32 and 17 percent, respectively. The suggestion is strong that spouses' drinking plays a stronger causal role for females than for males.

Summary

The comparison of alcoholics in treatment, problem drinkers not in treatment, and the general population yields some confirmations and some discrepancies from the current research on etiological and prognostic social factors in alcoholism. On the positive side, the strongest and most consistent correlates of alcoholism appear to be social instability in the form of employment and marital status. Socioeconomic factors tend to be more weakly associated with alcoholism and problem drinking, and they show inconsistent results for the two groups. The suggestion is that lower social class may be a moderate determinant of entering treatment, but that higher social class may be a weak determinant of problem drinking or alcoholism. The large age difference may be causing some of the social class differences, since a younger population is known to have higher educational and occupational status.

The reversals between alcoholics and problem drinkers for the factors of social class, religion, region, and drinking context may indicate cultural or environmental predisposition toward alcohol that acts in opposite directions for alcoholism on the one hand and for entering treatment on the other. Alcoholism may be more likely to arise in the families and regions that are *tolerant* of alcohol use; but when it does arise, those families or regions that are *intolerant* of alcohol are more likely to seek or provide treatment for the problem.

Our task now is to test these suggestions, in part, by a more formal prediction analysis that will enable us to examine the importance of a given factor while controlling for the effects of other concomitant variables.

PREDICTING DRINKING BEHAVIOR IN THE GENERAL POPULATION

The preceding discussion suggests that there are systematic social differences between problem drinkers and the general population. However, since these differences are not always consistent between the problem drinker and the treated alcoholic, the question is raised as to whether a given difference is really etiological in nature or whether it is "spuriously" caused by other differences between the problem-drinker group and the general population. For example, the problem drinker is younger than the general population, yet the treated-alcoholic population is older. Since this may make social class differences between problem drinkers and the general population appear more important etiologically than they are, we should examine the association of each social factor with problem drinking while controlling for other factors. The appropriate method for this task is multiple regression analysis.

In conducting the prediction analysis, we must stress that we are not establishing a final causal or etiological model for problem drinking or other drinking behaviors. First, we are using cross-sectional data that do not allow empirical decisions about time order; hence variables we include as "predictors" of problem drinking based on current theories of alcoholism may in fact be consequences (e.g., marital instability). Second, there may be causal sequences within the predictor variables that cannot be determined with these data; for example, marital instability may cause drinking in bars, which in turn causes problem drinking. Our strategy is to enter all variables into a single equation for the purpose of deciding which factor appears to have the most direct impact on drinking behavior, and to control for other variables without regard to other possible causal patterns among the predictors. While this analysis will not generate rigorous causal inferences, the results should suggest potentially important etiological and prognostic social background factors in the treatment of alcoholism.

Selection of Drinking Behaviors

For a number of reasons we wish to broaden the analysis to predict other drinking behavior besides problem drinking. First, it is by no means clear that our definition of problem drinking is the only way to define alcohol abuse. The early stages of alcoholism may involve heavy drinking without the symptoms identified in our symptomatic drinking or impairment indices. Thus a complete analysis should study the correlates of consumption itself, not simply problem drinking.[3] Second, preliminary analyses suggested that a model for predicting *any* drinking (versus abstention) was different from the best model for predicting consumption level among drinkers. Therefore our prediction analysis will employ three dependent variables:

---

[3] Studies by Cahalan and Room (1974) have suggested that consumption and problem drinking have different predictors.

abstention, consumption level among drinkers, and problem drinking among drinkers.

A preliminary judgment about the importance of distinguishing these three drinking behaviors can be made from the data assembled in Table 3. We have categorized all of the potential social correlates and for each category we present the percent of abstainers, the nonabstainers' mean consumption (in ounces of absolute alcohol per day), and the percent of problem drinkers. Some very clear differences are evident among the three drinking behaviors, particularly between abstaining and consumption among nonabstainers. If the correlates are to have the same relationship, then we would expect those characteristics associated with lower rates of abstention to be associated with higher rates of consumption among non-abstainers. This is the case for some predictors: the unmarried, the male, the Northerner, the Catholic, and those from drinking environments (both past and present) are less likely to abstain and, if they drink, are likely to drink more heavily than their counterparts. But the opposite is true for other factors. The unemployed, older persons, and black respondents are *more* likely to abstain as well as to drink more heavily if they do not abstain. Social class shows a different pattern: lower-class persons are far likelier to abstain than upper-class individuals, while *both* upper- and lower-class respondents among the nonabstainers are more likely to drink at heavier levels than middle-class persons.

In contrast to abstention, the correlates show a similar pattern for consumption level and problem drinking. Only one characteristic, age, shows a different relationship: the older a drinker is, the more likely he is to drink heavily *but* the less likely he is to have a drinking problem.

It would be futile to try to explain these various relationships and anomalies given only the results in Table 3. The fact is that these variables are defined for different populations which vary in age composition, sex composition, and so forth. Moreover it is well-known that such variables as religion, social class, ethnicity, age, and employment are all interrelated and, given the differing populations, it is impossible to make judgments about potential causal significance based on simple two-variable correlations. A multiple regression analysis is necessary before making final interpretations.

Predicting Abstention

Multiple regression analysis has the advantage of allowing an estimate of the magnitude of an effect while simultaneously controlling for other factors. Since we are dealing with groups that differ in social composition and have intercorrelations among these social characteristics, a multiple regression analysis will allow us to determine the potential causal significance of

Table 3. Social Correlates of Abstention, Consumption, and Problem Drinking

Characteristics	Percent of Abstainers	Nonabstainers' Mean Consumption (oz/day)	Nonabstainers' Percent of Problem Drinkers
Employment (work force)			
Unemployed	42	1.20	16
Employed	25	.78	9
Marital status			
Not married[a]	24	1.06	15
Married	35	.58	6
Sex			
Male	26	.91	12
Female	44	.44	4
Age			
Under 30	23	.66	9
30 to 50	31	.72	9
Over 50	49	.77	7
Region			
North	28	.73	9
South	54	.63	8
Religion[b]			
Catholic	22	.72	9
Protestant	42	.65	7
Race[c]			
Black	43	1.26	16
White	34	.68	8
Social class			
Lower	52	.74	10
Middle	34	.65	7
Upper	21	.74	9
Past family drinking			
Yes	28	.87	12
No	38	.63	6
Present household drinking			
Yes	19	1.15	16
No	38	.54	6
Drinks at bars			
Yes	—	1.10	18
No	—	.62	9
Age at first drink			
Under 16	—	.95	14
16 to 19	—	.62	7
Over 19	—	.58	5
(N)	(6282)	(3660)	(2621)[d]

[a] Includes single, separated, and divorced.
[b] Other religion or no religion excluded.
[c] Excludes Spanish-American.
[d] The number of drinkers is smaller for this analysis because one survey did not assess problem drinking symptoms.

each social factor while taking into account these varying compositions and correlations.

The regression results for predicting abstention are shown in Table 4.[4] The left-hand column shows the raw product-moment correlation, and the standardized regression coefficient is shown in the right-hand column. The standardized coefficient is interpreted as the amount of change in abstention rate (in fractions of a standard deviation) due to a one standard deviation increase in the given social factor, with all other factors held constant. The variance explained is 22 percent; the five largest coefficients are in boldface.

Two of the anomalies in Table 3 are resolved by the regression analysis: the sign of the regression coefficient for unemployment and race is opposite to that of the raw correlation, indicating that when other factors are controlled, blacks and the unemployed are less likely to abstain (although the coefficients are not large). But the coefficients for both age and social class retain the same sign as the original correlations.

It is clear from the regression results that the important predictors of abstention, when other factors are controlled, are mainly demographic

Table 4.   Prediction of Abstention

Predictor	Raw Correlation	Standardized Regression Coefficient[a]
Demographic		
Sex (male)	−.18	**−.22**
Age	.22	**.17**
Region (North)	−.25	**−.18**
Race (Black)	.05	−.04
Religion (Catholic)	−.19	**−.14**
Social class	−.18	**−.25**
Stability		
Unemployed	.13	−.10
Unmarried	−.09	.01
Drinking-related		
Past family drinking	−.10	−.03
Current household drinking	−.14	.10
Variance explained (R^2)		22% (N=6282)

[a] All coefficients are significant at less than the .001 level.

[4] All correlations and regressions were computed by the "missing observation" method, in which each correlation uses only the pairs that had observations. In no case did excluded cases exceed 10 percent, with the exception of unemployment, which is based on 80 percent of the sample.

and cultural factors. Abstainers are more likely to be female, older, of lower social class, Protestant, and Southern; drinkers are more likely to be male, younger, of higher social class, Catholic, and Northern. Some of these results are in good accord with the history of alcohol intolerance in our country. Protestants stood at the center of the Prohibition Movement, especially in the rural Midwest and South. Moreover, women had a strong voice in the Movement. But as newer generations with more tolerance toward alcohol have replaced older generations, the belief in abstention has waned. Today abstention remains as a cultural feature specific to certain areas and social groups. The influence of the Baptist religion among the poor and older persons in the South comes to mind as a unifying illustration for these relationships.

Given the relatively higher rate of abstention for women compared with men, there is the possibility that the prediction models differ within the sexes. To test this possibility, regressions were run separately for men and women. The relationships were nearly identical with those in Table 4, including the variance explained (17 percent and 22 percent, respectively). Thus, for men and women separately, the strongest predictors of abstention are age, social class, and the cultural factors of religion and region.

Predicting Consumption and Problem Drinking

Before presenting the regression results for alcohol consumption and problem drinking, we want to point out two important aspects of our analyses for these criteria. First, both analyses are carried out on the nonabstaining subgroup of the general population; abstainers are not a "low" or "0" end of either the consumption measure or the drinking-problem dichotomy. The justification for this is that the prediction models for abstention, consumption level, and problem drinking are all different, and any attempt to combine them would obscure important differences in predictor relationships. Second, all analyses of the consumption variable are done using a semilog model; i.e., the log of consumption is used as the dependent variable instead of raw consumption. This choice was motivated in part by the highly skewed distribution of alcohol consumption. More importantly, substantially better "fit" to the data was obtained using the semilog model.[5]

---

[5] Thus, the regression equation is of the form $C = e^{\alpha + \Sigma \beta x}$, where C is consumption and the x are social predictors. There have been some arguments recently that alcohol consumption in some countries follows a log normal distribution (i.e., the log of consumption is normally distributed; Ledermann, 1956; de Lint and Schmidt, 1971). Without debating the merit of these arguments, it is certainly true that the alcohol consumption measure in the Harris survey data closely approximates a log normal distribution (see Appendix A).

The regression results for consumption and problem drinking are presented in Table 5. The largest regression coefficients for each analysis are in boldface. Considering first the results for consumption, it is interesting that neither of the cultural factors that were important for abstention—religion and region—figure strongly as predictors. Social class and sex do show a consistent relationship, but age shows an opposite relationship: The older drinkers are more likely to abstain; if they do drink, they drink at heavier levels, when all other variables are held constant. The two drinking-related variables of age at first drink and household drinking also have moderate relationships. Thus the heavier drinker—as opposed to the problem drinker —tends to be male, older, of higher social class, to begin drinking at an earlier age than most, and to have someone in his present household who drinks frequently or heavily. The heavier drinker also tends to be unmarried and to drink at bars. The total variance explained by all the social factors is 20 percent, a figure comparable to that for abstention, although

Table 5. Prediction of Consumption and Problem Drinking for Nonabstainers

	Log Consumption		Problem Drinking	
Predictor	Raw Correlation	Standardized Regression Coefficient	Raw Correlation	Standardized Regression Coefficient
Demographic				
Sex (male)	.26	**.26**	.14	**.17**
Age	.00	**.13**	−.04	.04*
Region (North)	.05	.04**	.01	.01 ns[a]
Race (black)	.05	.09	.07	.07
Religion (Catholic)	.05	.06	.04	.04*
Social class	.12	**.17**	−.01	.05*
Stability				
Unemployed	−.03	.07	.07	**.12**
Unmarried	.15	.12	.14	**.08**
Drinking history				
Past family drinking	.09	.04**	.10	.05*
Age at first drink	−.17	**.13**	−.10	−.06**
Drinking context				
Present household drinking	.19	**.19**	.14	**.15**
Drinks at bars	.18	.12	.16	**.11**
Variance explained (R^2)		20%		10%
(N)		(3660)		(2621)

[a] ns = not significant.
* = $p < .05$.
** = $p < .01$.
All other coefficients have $p < .001$.

the ranking of the predictors is quite different. The reversal for age suggests a curvilinear association: older persons are more likely to abstain on the whole; but among persons who drink the older person drinks more. It is interesting to speculate whether part of the reason for this is an adaptation to alcohol. Perhaps as people get older they either learn to abstain from alcohol or become more dependent on it.

It is equally interesting that the best predictors for problem drinking and consumption are different. Most important, neither age nor social class appears to be an important predictor for problem drinking. Instead, the stability factors of employment and marital status, and the drinking context factors of present household drinking and drinking at bars, are the strongest predictors of problem drinking. Thus the problem drinker is more likely to be male, unemployed, to have someone in the household drinking frequently, to drink at bars, and to be unmarried. The variance explained is only 10 percent, but there are some technical reasons for this that will be clarified presently.

Since the treated-alcoholic population discussed in later chapters is largely male, and since considerably fewer females are found in the problem-drinking population, it is of interest to examine the regression results for males only presented in Table 6. The model for consumption is quite similar to the overall model; the heavier drinker is more likely to be older, black, to have someone drinking frequently in his household, to drink at bars, and to be unmarried. Higher social class and a younger age at first drink are also related to heavier drinking, and the variance explained drops to 16 percent (largely due to the loss of the sex effect).

But the important results occur for problem drinking. For males, the region, religion, and social class effects drop to near zero. Although the age and race effects are strengthened somewhat, they remain weak. The four strongest predictors are the two stability measures and the two drinking context variables. Thus, for males in the Harris sample, neither cultural nor socioeconomic factors play a significant role in predicting problem drinking; stability and drinking context factors are the most important. The variance explained actually increases to 11 percent even though sex— a strong correlate of problem drinking—was eliminated. The findings for drinking context are particularly consistent with the recent findings of Cahalan and Room (1974).

Again we must stress that we are using the terms "predictive" or "potential cause" with the full knowledge that the causal orderings of variables being analyzed are not fully established, particularly in the case of the drinking context and the stability variables. It could well be that a person develops into an alcoholic or a problem drinker and only then suffers sta-

Table 6.   Prediction of Consumption and Problem Drinking for Males

	Log Consumption		Problem Drinking	
Predictor	Raw Correlation	Standardized Regression Coefficient	Raw Correlation	Standardized Regression Coefficient
Demographic				
Age	−.03	**.15**	−.07	.08
Region (North)	.06	.05	.03	.01 ns[a]
Race (black)	.08	**.14**	.08	.08
Religion (Catholic)	.09	.10	.05	.04 ns
Social class	.10	.13	.00	.03 ns
Stability				
Unemployed	.04	.03 ns	.12	**.10**
Unmarried	.17	**.14**	.17	**.12**
Drinking history				
Past family drinking	.14	.07	.13	.07**
Age at first drink	−.14	−.13	−.11	**−.09**
Drinking context				
Present household drinking	.24	**.18**	.18	**.14**
Drinks at bars	.21	**.16**	.19	**.15**
Variance explained (R^2)		16%		11%
(N)		(2119)		(1556)

[a]ns = not significant.
* $= p < .05$.
** $= p < .01$.
All others coefficients have $p < .001$.

bility problems or seeks out a more compatible drinking context. The cross-sectional data we are analyzing cannot decide this issue.

A final comment is needed on the issue of the variance explained by the problem-drinking correlates in Tables 5 and 6. The variance explained for problem drinking is substantially less than that found by some recent studies, particularly those of Cahalan and Room (1974). Part of the reason for this may be the dependent variable. They used a multiscored variable, whereas we use a dichotomy that yields only 9 percent problem drinkers (12 percent for males). A dichotomous variable with such an extreme split generally constrains the correlations and reduces the explained variance (this is probably why the male-only model explained slightly more variance than the combined male-female model). But additional factors may be other studies' inclusion of nondrinkers as a low end of the drinking continuum and the inclusion of various attitudinal and behavioral factors that are treated as independent variables but are difficult to distinguish from the dependent variable.[6] On the other hand, although the Harris population is larger, there are not nearly so many social and psychological variables available for the regressions as in the Cahalan and Room surveys. The lower variance explained might be due to omission of critical variables.

IMPLICATIONS FOR ALCOHOLISM TREATMENT EVALUATION

It is clear that the relationships among different types of drinking behavior and alcoholism are more complex than has been fully documented to date. The decision to drink, the amount of drinking for drinkers, the development of problem drinking or alcoholism among heavier drinkers, and the decision to enter treatment all appear to have differing patterns of social correlates. What are the implications for the use of social characteristics as prognostic factors in treatment evaluation?

It will be helpful if we first summarize our findings. Perhaps the easiest way to do this is to differentiate the various groups we have analyzed according to their tendencies to have certain characteristics as verified by

Abstainers tend to be:	*While drinkers tend to be:*
Protestants	Catholic
Southern	Northern
Older	Younger
Low SES	Higher SES

Light drinkers tend to be:	*While heavier drinkers tend to be:*
Married	Unmarried
Younger	Older
In a nondrinking context	In a drinking context
White	Black
Lower SES	Higher SES

Problem drinkers tend to be:	*Alcoholics tend to be:*
Unemployed	Unemployed
Unmarried	Unmarried
In a drinking context	Southern
	Lower SES
	Protestant

[6] This problem might be especially troublesome in the Cahalan and Room study (1974) in which a drinking context variable—one that produced the strongest relationships with problem drinking—included the frequency with which drinks are served when friends are visiting. This is difficult to distinguish from the respondent's own drinking frequency.

the regression analyses and the comparisons in Table 1.[7] The results for males are on page 75.

Thus, the decision to drink at all is influenced heavily by cultural factors of region and religion, as well as by age and SES; but cultural factors are not important determinants of other drinking behaviors until we consider alcoholics in treatment. We conclude, then, that the decision to drink is influenced more by basic values than by specific social contexts.

Among drinkers, marital status, age, drinking context, race, and SES tend to predict heavier as opposed to lighter drinking. Age works in an opposite direction to that for abstention. Younger persons are more likely to be drinkers, and are more likely to be lighter drinkers once other variables are controlled. This fits the interpretation that, all else being equal, drinkers will tend to consume more as they get older, possibly due to the addictive properties of alcohol. Aside from the age and race factors, however, heavier drinking tends to be associated with life style and normative factors such as drinking context, marital status, and social class.

Unlike heavier drinking, problem drinking is associated almost entirely with immediate social situational factors such as drinking context (spouse drinking and drinking at bars), marital status, and unemployment. Thus, cultural, demographic, and social class factors do not seem to play an important role in differentiating the male problem drinker from the normal population. Of course, none of the factors associated with problem drinking—drinking context and stability—can be established with certainty as existing prior to the onset of problem drinking. Yet there are solid theoretical reasons to suspect that family and job instability may be the precursors to problem drinking. They could be the source of psychological crises and anxieties from which a drinker seeks relief and sedation by heavy and symptomatic drinking. Unfortunately, at present no adequate longitudinal data exist to help settle the issue.

Although the results for treated alcoholics are not based on regression analyses, the trends, as shown in Table 1, are suggestive. For the treated alcoholic unemployment and marital status are two of the strongest correlates. But treated alcoholics also resemble abstainers in that they are more likely to be Southern, Protestant, and of lower SES than the general population. This appears at first to be an anomaly. But it could very well be that the existence of those cultural and life style conditions that lead to

---

[7] The treated alcoholic-general population differences cannot be verified by regression analysis. It would not be appropriate to combine the Harris problem-drinking group with the ATC group for the purpose of regression to predict treated versus untreated status, since they were drawn from different populations. Moreover, it is not clear that the problem-drinking group is really representative of untreated alcoholics.

abstention are the same ones that place more pressure on an alcoholic to seek treatment. Thus, while more drinking and heavy drinking arise in the North among Catholics, and in the higher SES levels, those heavy drinkers who become alcoholics are more likely to be in treatment if they are Southern, Protestant, and have lower SES levels. The explanation for religion may involve values; the explanation for region may be due to values as well as opportunity, if it can be shown that there are more treatment programs in the South on a per capita basis. The explanation for social class may involve pressures that are exerted in job settings rather than the family. It is considerably easier for persons in many middle-class occupations to drink more without social pressure than it is for working-class persons. Some of this is due to a greater ability to adapt a work schedule around drinking habits (as for self-employed professional, business, or sales persons); some has to do with norms of the job itself, as in the case of occupations that involve extensive entertainment.

The implications for treatment rest on the fact that, although the treated alcoholic tends to be different from the general or problem-drinking population in certain characteristics, there is some variation within the group regarding these same characteristics. Thus, treated alcoholics are not completely homogeneous with regard to important social characteristics that might be associated with a better treatment prognosis.

The five major factors differentiating treated alcoholics from the general population are candidates for prognostic significance but for varying reasons. The stability characteristics of unemployment or marital status are important because of their contribution to either the cause of alcoholism or its maintenance. It is therefore reasonable to predict that the more stable clients among the treated-alcoholic population (married or employed) are more likely to have successful treatment.

The factors of religion, region, and social class may be important prognostic factors but, as the earlier analyses suggest, not for etiological reasons. It is reasonable to hypothesize that those alcoholics who experience more social pressure for treatment—arising from cultural values, life style, job setting, or other environmental sources—have a better prognosis. This would lead to an expectation that alcoholics from the South, from Protestant backgrounds, and in working-class occupations (controlling for stability) will experience more successful treatment. The prediction for social class is contrary to that made in most treatment evaluations; the difference hinges on the proper interpretation of the social class differences between the treated alcoholic and the general population. Most studies have identified it as an etiological variable, but comparisons among treated alcoholics and heavy or problem drinkers suggest that it is more likely to be a determinant of entering treatment rather than alcoholism per se.

FOUR

Patterns Of Remission

Chapter 3 shows that persons who enter the NIAAA Alcoholism Treatment Centers have severe alcohol problems, much more severe than most problem drinkers in the general population. To aid efforts at recovery, the treatment centers offer numerous treatment programs that vary greatly in the type of service, length and intensity of treatment setting, cost and, possibly, in effectiveness. In this chapter and in Chapter 5 we assess the effectiveness of this treatment process by examining the changes in clients' alcoholic symptoms at two followup points after treatment is started.

The first task is to establish criteria by which the success of treatment can be judged. Obviously, the ultimate criterion is recovery from alcoholism. But the continuing disagreement over a definition of alcoholism, documented in Chapter 2, and the method by which recovery is attained leaves us with no single, universally accepted definition of recovery. Moreover, the concept of recovery implies a relatively stable and permanent state of symptom remission, so that a final determination of recovery status —regardless of its defining attributes—may require followup periods longer than those available from the NIAAA followup studies. Accordingly, the primary purpose of this chapter is to examine patterns of symptom remission and to establish a criterion of remission that can be used for evaluating the success of treatment.

We pursue a definition of remission by offering several analytical strategies. First, we examine changes in alcohol consumption, behavioral impairment, and social adjustment as separate criteria measures. This establishes the degree of improvement in a number of dimensions considered relevant to the alcoholism syndrome. Second, we examine the interrelationships among the separate criteria as they change over time. These interrelations lead to a definition of remission based on both consumption and impairment behaviors. This definition is used throughout the analyses in this chapter and in Chapter 5.

The main reason for the continuing controversy over definitions of recovery and remission stems from two conceptions about the nature of the addictive process: one stresses the necessity of total abstention, and the other the possibility of a return to normal or controlled drinking. With our two followup reports we can address a key issue in this debate: Which mode of remission, abstention or normal drinking, is least likely to lead to relapse and a return to alcoholic behavior? This question will be answered by examining relapse rates at 18 months for clients with the different remission modes at 6 months.

Finally, the issue of remission raises the further question of different types of alcoholics according to the severity of their addiction and according to potential prognostic and etiological factors documented in Chapters 2 and 3. An examination of the influence of client characteristics on remission rates concludes this chapter and sets the stage for the more detailed analysis of differential treatment effects in Chapter 5.

THE ANALYSIS DESIGN

The sources of data for this assessment of effectiveness are the NIAAA Monitoring System and a special NIAAA Followup Study, hence the basic design of the analysis derives both its advantages and its limitations from these data collection efforts. The most prominent advantage of this analysis over others is the scope and variety of treatments, clients, and treatment agencies for which data are available. Because of the large number of clients who have passed through the system, extensive analyses of many variations in treatments and client backgrounds may be undertaken with more adequate statistical controls than is usually possible in such studies. Moreover, the existence of a special 18-month followup on one sample of clients and a 6-month followup from the ATC Monitoring System on another larger sample of clients offers the unique opportunity of conducting both a short-term and a relatively long-term evaluation of treatment effectiveness.

As with all studies of this type, there are constraints as well. A brief description of the data collection procedures employed in the Monitoring System and in the Followup Study will provide a basis for understanding the limitations of this analysis.

The Monitoring System and 6-Month Followup

A schematic representation of the treatment process and the Monitoring System data collection points is diagramed in Figure 2. When a client decides to enter a program offered at one of NIAAA's 44 ATCs, he is formally admitted in a procedure called *intake*. At this point, the center

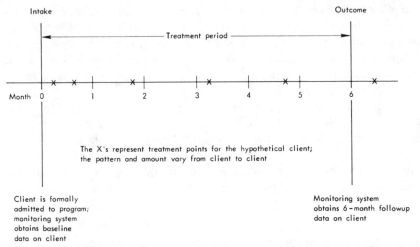

Figure 2.   Treatment process for a hypothetical client.

administers a Client Intake Form[1] that collects a variety of information pertaining to the client's alcoholism, social background, current social and economic situation, and drinking history. As shown in Figure 2, the client then receives a pattern of treatment services, which may vary from a few days of hospital care to an extended period of care encompassing hospital treatment, halfway house, and outpatient therapy. During each month of the treatment period, the center files a Client Services Report for every client, describing the types and amounts of treatment administered during that month.

At a point approximately 6 months after intake to the program, the center is required to obtain followup information about each client, using a Client Followup Form, whether or not the client is still in treatment. At that time, the center contacts the client and administers a followup interview. This interview represents a conceptual posttreatment measurement, although some clients actually continue in treatment beyond the 6-month point.[2] The Client Followup Form repeats all information in the Client Intake Form that is subject to change; hence it is possible to examine not only alcoholic behavior at followup but also changes in alcoholic and other behaviors between intake and followup.

Unfortunately, the routine 6-month followup report is not completed

---

[1] Data collection forms used are reproduced in Appendix D.

[2] In fact, centers frequently performed the followup interviews between 5 and 8 months after intake, so that the outcome measures really pertain to a point that is only approximately 6 months past intake.

for all clients. For a variety of reasons, one involving the high mobility of some ATC clients and another limited ATC resources, 6-month followups are generally completed for only one-fourth to one-third of clients who were official intakes. For the 6-month followup sample used in this report, completed followup reports are available on 2371 male clients out of approximately 11,500 male non-DWI (Driving While Intoxicated) clients admitted to treatment between October 1972 and September 1973. This introduces a potential bias in the 6-month followup sample, thereby hampering inferences to the full intake population. We shall address this problem explicitly in a later section.

The 18-Month Followup Study

The data for the 18-month followup sample arise from a special study undertaken for NIAAA expressly to respond to concerns about the low completion rates for the routine 6-month reports from the Monitoring System.[3] In the 18-month study, clients were sampled in a stratified design based on length of the time in treatment to ensure that dropouts as well as continuing clients would be represented. Clients were sampled from a pool of 8 ATCs (out of 44 possible), using the population of clients who were intakes between January and April 1973.[4] At a point about 18 months after intake (August through October 1974), the selected clients were interviewed by specially trained interviewers hired by the ATCs.

Interviews were completed for 1340 clients, representing an overall response rate of 62 percent. Of this sample, approximately 600 were male non-DWI intakes, the main target for our analysis; the response rate for this group was also 62 percent. The Followup Study also included interviews with approximately 400 clients who had made contact with the ATC but were not admitted to treatment and hence did not have intake information from the Monitoring System. This comparison group of "untreated" alcoholics will be used in some of the analyses in Chapter 5.

The 18-month followup interview was conducted with a modified version of the Client Intake and Client Followup forms; modifications were required in order to collect information about other treatment services received since leaving the ATC. But for the critical information concerning treatment outcomes and client characteristics, the 18-month form used the standardized definitions from the Monitoring System form (see Appendix D).

[3] The 18-month study was carried out by the Stanford Research Institute under NIAAA contract ADM-41-74-0008. For a comprehensive summary of the study design and its findings, see Ruggels et al. (1975).

[4] The ATCs were not randomly sampled but were drawn so as to represent a cross-section of the 44 ATCs in the Monitoring System.

Analysis Limitations

While the Monitoring System and 18-Month Followup Study yield two sets of data with unusually broad scope and rich potential, they are also accompanied by several limitations and restrictions that must be borne in mind. First, the findings here cannot necessarily be generalized to the total population of treated alcoholics in the United States. Not only are we restricted to the population of alcoholics entering treatment at NIAAA centers, which are not necessarily representative of all treatment centers, but we have further restricted our analyses to male, non-DWI clients.

The reasons for restricting our analysis to male non-DWI clients are illustrated in part in Table 7, which shows that both female and DWI clients have quite different alcohol consumption characteristics at both intake and followup; the difference is especially marked for the DWI group.[5] Other characteristics yield similar differences; in many respects, the DWI population does not appear to be alcoholic in the way we would define that term. At the very least, a meaningful study would require separate investigation for each group. Unfortunately, there are insufficient cases in the female and DWI groups to support the extensive and detailed analysis we wish to conduct here. Given that the DWI group may not be

Table 7.   Differences in Daily Alcohol Consumption of Male, Female, and DWI[a] Clients

Group	Daily Alcohol Consumption[b]	
	6-Month Followup	18-Month Followup
Male non-DWI		
Intake	7.7	8.1
Followup	2.1	2.5
(N)	(2339)	(597)
Female non-DWI		
Intake	5.0	4.5
Followup	1.8	1.3
(N)	(658)	(158)
DWI		
Intake	2.3	1.7
Followup	.8	.9
(N)	(876)	(175)

[a] A DWI is a client whose treatment is related to a driving-while-intoxicated incident.
[b] Mean ounces of ethanol per day for last 30 days (QF).

[5] More information on the daily alcohol consumption measure will be provided in a later section.

truly alcoholic, and the substantial evidence that alcoholism is much more prevalent among men, we do not feel these exclusions represent serious limitations.

A second and potentially more serious limitation stems from the response rates in the two followup samples. The fact that the 6-month followup sample and the 18-month followup sample represent only 21 percent and 62 percent of their full intake populations can mean that they are not fully representative of these populations. Such losses of clients are not unusual in followup studies, particularly for the routine Monitoring System where resources for followup expenses are scarce. Treatment centers must concentrate their efforts on those clients who remain in treatment and available to the center. Even when a special study is undertaken to locate and interview clients, as in the special 18-month followup, there are often insuperable obstacles to locating persons among such a transient, disadvantaged population. Of the 38 percent not interviewed in the 18-Month Followup Study, 70 percent could not be located; only 12 percent refused to be interviewed (Ruggels et al., 1975). Hence any bias introduced in the followup samples is more likely to be associated with mobility than noncooperation.

Fortunately, the existence of complete intake data on all clients enables us to offer more precise estimates about sample bias. Table 8 presents a

Table 8. Client Characteristics Measured at Intake for the 6-Month Followup, 18-Month Followup, and Full Intake Samples

Characteristics at Intake[a]	6-Month Followup Sample	Followup 18-Month Sample	Full Intake Sample
Daily consumption (oz)[b]	7.7	8.1	8.4
Days drank last month			
Behavioral impairment	12.4	12.7	13.3
Percent prior treatment	44	40	43
Percent ever in AA	58	54	56
Percent unemployed	54	57	60
Percent separated/divorced	39	38	44
Percent in group quarters	13	14	18
Percent nonwhite	17	25	25
Percent without HS diploma	52	48	53
Age	47	46	45
Income last year ($)	5800	6300	5500
Years in community	12.7	11.2	10.2
(N)	(2371)	(600)	(11,505)

[a] Means where not otherwise indicated.
[b] Ounces of ethanol (absolute alcohol).

number of client characteristics measured at intake for the 6-month and 18-month followup samples compared with the full 1972-1973 intake population. As we shall see in later sections, these characteristics include those most strongly related to client outcomes at followup. First, despite the fact that the 6-month sample represents less than one-fourth of the full male non-DWI population, it has no important biases at intake. It is especially fortunate that the differences are smallest for drinking behaviors. Mean daily alcohol consumption is 7.7 for the 6-month sample compared with 8.4 for all intakes; differences are even smaller for behavioral impairment and average days client drank in the last month.[6] Somewhat larger differences are observed for some of the social background characteristics, but even here the largest differences are only 7 percent for percent nonwhite and 6 percent for percent unemployed. All the differences are in the same direction, tending to make the 6-month followup sample slightly less impaired with respect to some social and drinking characteristics.

The 6-month followup sample represents all 44 ATCs, whereas the 18-month sample represents only 8 ATCs. Nonetheless, the higher response rate for the 18-month study yields a better match with the full intake sample on most characteristics. In this case the drinking behaviors are nearly identical, and most social characteristics are quite similar. The largest differences occur for percent divorced/separated and annual income, but even here the differences are only 6 percent and $800, respectively.

It is reasonable to conclude that the two followup samples are not seriously biased according to the most important alcoholic symptoms and social behaviors measured at intake. Of course, the two samples may still yield biased measures for various outcome criteria, with those clients followed up having higher remission rates. We cannot settle this issue definitively with our data, but we can test the effect of nonresponse indirectly by comparing outcome results for the 6-month and 18-month followups. Since the latter has a response rate three times higher than the former, any serious bias due to nonresponse should result in less favorable outcomes for the 18-month followup. The extent to which the findings of the followup studies converge is the degree of confidence we can have that the followup samples are not seriously biased with respect to remission rates. (See also the ATC response rate analysis in Chapter 5).

Finally, all large-scale surveys and data collection efforts have some inherent restrictions regarding the manner in which information is collected. The Monitoring System and the 18-Month Followup Study use

[6] Standard deviations are 8.2 for consumption and 7.8 for impairment for the intake sample.

standardized interview forms that necessarily rely on the client for accurate self-reports and on ATC staff for honest recording of these self-reports. There are undoubtedly occasions when pressures on both the client and the ATC staff are sufficient to cause distortion of the true picture, intentional or not, sometimes to legitimatize the client's sickness and sometimes to enhance his remission. As to the extent and seriousness of such distortions, there is no complete, definitive answer. While we know such situations occur, we do not feel that they have serious impact on most of the results and conclusions presented in this report. The basis for this belief rests on some special reliability and validity studies of certain self-reported information, most of which is presented in Appendix A, as well as on the natural variations observed for many of these measures throughout this report. Although the standardized interview technique is not comparable to clinical observation and may not be totally complete and accurate for every client, the summary statistics presented for groups of clients appear to be quite stable and valid. In any event it is not possible to conduct evaluation studies of this magnitude without the restrictions inherent in a standardized interview instrument. The losses in accuracy for individual clients must be weighed against gains in scope, comparability, and generalizability of the results.

BASIC OUTCOME RESULTS

Although the research and literature on alcoholism have not yet generated a single precise definition of alcoholism, it is reasonable to assume that it is indicated by the excessive use of alcohol and that it is associated with various types of behavioral and social impairment arising from that excessive consumption. Accordingly, remission from alcoholism can be defined in numerous ways, depending on one's relative stress on drinking behavior per se or its physical, psychological, or social consequences. Moreover, within each of these domains there is no specific point, either qualitative or quantitative, at which alcoholism either occurs or abates. Each is a many-faceted dimension along which one can slide in either improving or deteriorating directions.

In the face of these definitional problems, one reasonable course is to present outcome results for a number of criteria that can be considered relevant to remission from alcoholism. While the results for different criteria are similar, as we shall see, the multiple criteria approach has the advantage of allowing for an assessment of remission from a number of different definitional perspectives. The criteria we employ are amount and pattern of alcohol consumption (including abstention), behavioral impairment due to the use of alcohol, and several indicators of social adjustment.

Alcohol Consumption

Since alcoholism starts from excessive use of alcohol, it seems logical to give prominence to consumption as a component for recovery. One of the most important consumption indices used in the ATC Monitoring System is known as the Quantity-Frequency (QF) index, which expresses alcohol consumption in average ounces of ethanol (absolute alcohol) per day. We shall refer to this index as "daily consumption" throughout this chapter.

The index is derived from self-reports of the number of days on which beer, wine, or liquor were drunk during the last 30 days (frequency), using separate reports for each beverage, and the amount of each beverage consumed on a typical day of drinking (quantity). The product of the quantity and frequency reports, appropriately coded to reflect alcoholic content, are then summed across the three beverages to yield average ethanol consumed per day last month.[7] The fact that different beverages contain different proportions of alcohol necessitates an index of ethanol use, rather than of number of drinks, in order to establish a common base of measurement.

The changes in daily consumption from intake to followup are shown in Table 9 for the two male, non-DWI followup samples. The distribution of

Table 9.   Changes in Daily Alcohol Consumption

Abstention or Consumption Level Last 30 Days	6-Month Followup Sample		18-Month Followup Sample		General Male Popula-
	Consumption at Intake (%)	Consumption at Followup (%)	Consumption at Intake (%)	Consumption at Followup (%)	
Abstained					
Last 6 months	3	17	1	24	26[a]
Last month only	8	37	8	21	8
Consumption					
0-1 oz/day	11	19	10	23	48
1-3 oz/day	14	9	15	13	13
3-5 oz/day	12	5	13	4	2
5-7 oz/day	10	3	9	4	2[b]
7-10 oz/day	13	3	14	4	
10-12 oz/day	5	2	5	1	
Over 12 oz/day	23	5	25	7	
Total	100	100	100	100	100
Mean	7.7	2.1	8.1	2.5	.62
(N)	(2339)		(597)		(3104)

[a] One drink or less per year.
[b] Over 5 oz/day.

[7] See Appendix A for more details on how the index is derived.

consumption for the general male population (from the Harris surveys) is also shown for comparative purposes. There is little doubt that both followup samples are very heavy users of alcohol at intake, at least in comparison to the average male. Slightly over half report consumption of more than 5 oz/day the month before starting treatment; this is equivalent to three-fourths of a pint or more of hard liquor per day. This is contrasted with the general male population where only 2 percent report consumption levels this high.[8] We note further that about one-fourth of both samples report consumption at intake of more than 12 oz/day, which is equivalent to about a fifth of hard liquor per day. While persons consuming more than 12 oz/day are clearly alcoholic, the lower 5 oz/day criterion is sometimes used when alcoholism is defined solely by consumption (de Lint and Schmidt, 1971).

Not all clients report extremely heavy consumption, however. About 20 percent report short-term abstention during the past month or consumption of less than 1 oz/day; another group of 26 to 28 percent report a daily consumption of 1 to 5 ounces. We cannot assume, of course, that none of these clients is an alcoholic. Alcohol can have extremely diverse effects on different persons; moderate amounts can be innocuous for most persons but can cause serious impairment in others. This is especially true for some long-term alcoholics for whom even small amounts of alcohol produce intoxicating effects. Also, institutionalization prior to intake can explain some of the light drinking, particularly the short-term abstention. Some alcoholics in our samples enter treatment after treatment in a regular hospital for a medical complication, and in certain cases they have been in jail for extended periods. In either case alcohol use would necessarily be restricted. Finally, some alcoholics who are abstaining or drinking lightly start treatment because they feel their control is beginning to weaken.

In spite of the high levels of consumption at intake, both samples show substantial improvement at followup. Only 27 percent of the 6-month sample are drinking more than 1 oz/day at followup, with 13 percent drinking more than 5 oz/day. The 18-month sample shows similar results; only 32 percent are drinking more than 1 oz/day, with 16 percent drinking more than 5 oz/day. Given the levels of consumption at intake, these figures represent a relative rate of improvement greater than 70 percent for both samples. These improvement rates are clearly impressive, not only in degree, but also for the close agreement between two samples followed up at quite different intervals.

---

[8] We have reason to believe that the general population figures are underestimates, perhaps by a factor of 2. Among males there should be about 4 percent who consume more than 5 oz/day (see Appendix A).

It must be stressed, however, that long-term abstention—defined here as not drinking for 6 months or more—is relatively infrequent in both samples. Only 17 percent report long-term abstention at 6 months, and only 24 percent do so for the 18-month followup. Another 37 percent of the 6-month sample report abstention for the past 30 days (but some drinking in the past 1 to 5 months), but this drops to 21 percent for the 18-month sample. It would appear, then, that clients abstaining for 1 month at 6-month followup will move either toward permanent abstention or toward more drinking. On the other hand, since there is only a small increase during the 6- to 18-month period among those drinking more than 5 oz/day, it is possible that for some nonabstaining clients the increasing consumption represents a return to some sort of "normal" or moderate drinking rather than a relapse to excessive drinking. We use the term "normal" here to describe drinking levels similar to those reported by males in the general population; that is, a majority of males who drink report drinking between 0 and 1 oz/day last month. Thus alcoholics who maintain consumption in this range could be described as normal drinkers.

The fact that about half of the treated alcoholic population reports either periodic drinking or daily consumption of less than 1 ounce raises two critical questions. First, are the low average consumption figures masking heavier, binge-type drinking? Average-consumption indices have been criticized as being insensitive to alcoholics who may drink very large amounts but do so infrequently; a person who drinks 2 quarts of hard liquor but only 1 day a month will have a daily consumption average of about 1 ounce. Second, although the consumption of small amounts of alcohol may be normal in the general population, is it possible that those same levels represent merely a temporary way-station for some alcoholics headed for a full relapse? If so, it may be unreasonable to consider small amounts of drinking as "normal" for alcoholics. We will address both of these questions in subsequent sections in this chapter.

Behavioral Impairment

As we pointed out in Chapter 2, alcoholism is rarely defined by consumption alone unless the amount becomes extremely large, such as a fifth of hard liquor per day. The alcoholic generally exhibits other symptoms that reflect damage or impaired functioning due to the use of alcohol. Moreover, some specialists would hold that the true alcoholic must have certain physical or behavioral symptoms indicating physical dependence or addiction.

Whereas neither the Monitoring System nor the 18-Month Followup Study has measured all of the impairment criteria used in the diagnosis of alcoholism, such as the criteria recently established by the National Council on Alcoholism (1972), information is collected on the frequency of occurrence of the following 12 signs of behavioral impairment or dependence on alcohol in the past 30 days:

1. Tremors ("shakes")
2. Alcoholic blackouts (loss of memory)
3. Missing meals due to drinking
4. Drinking on awakening
5. Being drunk
6. Missing work days due to drinking
7. Difficulty in sleeping
8. Quarreling with others while drinking
9. Drinking on the job
10. Continuous drinking
11. Drinking alone
12. Time between drinking sessions

Most of these items are coded on a 0 to 3 frequency scale, where 0 means that it did not occur at all in the past 30 days and 3 means that it happened very often (5 or more times for some items and 10 or more times for others). A behavioral impairment index is formed by averaging the 12 frequency codes and multiplying by 10. The index can thus range from a low score of 0 to a high score of 30. (See Appendix A for more details about constructing the index.)

In some cases it will be useful to distinguish among clients who appear to be definite alcoholics, in the sense of physical addiction to alcohol versus clients who are alcohol abusers but perhaps not physically addicted per se. The clearest sign of physical addiction is the gross withdrawal syndrome, delirium tremens, but this is not a necessary condition for physical addiction and is not assessable in the Monitoring System. Instead, we must choose symptoms from the list above. We have taken three different approaches. First, we have given special emphasis to the "tremors" symptom; this is the only impairment item in our data that is part of the alcoholic withdrawal syndrome. Second, we have used a subset of the 12 items to define a "serious symptoms" category. Placement in this category requires frequent episodes (frequency codes 2 and 3) of at least 3 of the first 6 items in the list: tremors, blackouts, missing meals, morning drinking, being drunk, and missing work. Third, we have developed a definition for "definite" alcoholism that combines these various criteria into an overall index. A client is considered *definitely alcoholic* if he meets any one of the following 3 criteria in the past 30 days: (1) drinking more than 12 ounces of ethanol on typical drinking days; (2) experiencing episodes of tremors; or (3) falling into the category of "serious symptoms" as described above. Within the constraints of the available data, this definition parallels the criteria established by the National Council on Alcoholism for the diagnosis of alcoholism (1972).

The changes in behavioral impairment between intake and followup, shown in Table 10 for both followup samples, are similar in magnitude to those observed for the consumption index.[9] While 80 percent of the 6-month sample and 84 percent of the 18-month sample show substantial levels of impairment at intake (an index score of 6 or higher), only 30 percent and 31 percent, respectively, are substantially impaired at followup. This rep-

Table 10.   Changes in Behavioral Impairment[a]

Abstention or Impairment Level, Last 30 Days	Behavioral Impairment (%)			
	6-Month Followup Sample		18-Month Followup Sample	
	Intake	Followup	Intake	Followup
Abstained				
Last 6 months	3	17	1	24
Last month only	8	37	8	21
Impairment Score				
1-5	9	16	7	24
6-10	19	10	19	12
10-15	23	8	27	10
15-20	20	6	20	7
Over 20	18	6	18	2
Mean	12.4	4.3	12.7	4.0
Percent reporting tremors	60	21	64	18
Percent with serious symptoms[b]	48	14	52	13
Percent "definitely" alcoholic[c]	71	26	74	24
(N)	(2337)		(596)	

[a] See text for description; range = 0 − 30.
[b] Frequent episodes of at least 3 of the following 6 symptoms: tremors, blackouts, missing meals, morning drinking, being drunk, missing work.
[c] Meeting one of the following criteria in the past 30 days: (1) drinking more than 12 ounces of ethanol on a typical drinking day; (2) one or more episodes of tremors; (3) experiencing symptoms as defined in note b.

[9] Those clients who reported abstention in the past 30 days were not asked the impairment questions; therefore, by definition, the percentage of abstainers are identical to those for the daily consumption index.

resents a relative improvement rate of about 63 percent. Scoring abstainers as 0, mean impairment falls from 12.7 at intake to 4.0 at 18 months, a relative improvement of 69 percent. Thus the improvements in behavioral impairment are comparable to the improvements in consumption.

Substantial improvements are also observed for the indicators of severe impairment. About 64 percent of the 18-month sample report some tremors at intake compared with 18 percent at followup; serious symptoms decline from 52 percent to 13 percent; signs of definite alcoholism fall from 74 percent at intake to 24 percent at followup. Similar changes occur for the short-term followups. The importance of the high proportion of definite alcoholics at intake cannot be overemphasized. The ATC male non-DWI population is not comprised primarily of problem drinkers or merely of excessive users; on the contrary, nearly three-fourths of both samples meet a fairly strict definition of alcoholic behavior at entry to treatment.

Social Adjustment

As we documented in Chapter 3, many ATC alcoholics suffer from a number of social disabilities beyond alcohol impairment, particularly disabilities arising from instability in both job and marriage. In this respect they resemble many other chronic alcoholic populations in the research literature. As a group, the ATC alcoholics are much more likely to be divorced or separated and unemployed than the general population or even a subpopulation of problem drinkers. Although it is not clear whether these social difficulties precede alcoholic behavior or are consequences of it, most treatment programs aim to provide relief with such special services as family counseling and vocational rehabilitation and with such special settings as the halfway house or recovery home.

Changes in marital and job stability indicators are shown in Table 11. Despite the dramatic changes in drinking behavior, there is almost no change at all in marital status. In fact, the correlation between being divorced or separated at intake and at followup is .9, indicating very little turnover.[10] Whatever the role of marital instability in the genesis of alcoholism for these clients, successful reduction of consumption and behavioral impairment does not appear contingent upon restoration of a successful marriage within the 18-month period covered by the longer term followup.

---

[10] Stable percentages for a group as a whole can mask substantial change for individuals, with equal numbers entering as well as leaving married status. In such cases of high turnover, however, the correlation would be relatively low (see Appendix A).

Table 11.   Changes in Social Adjustment

Social Adjustment Indicator	6-Month Followup Sample		18-Month Followup Sample	
	Intake	Followup	Intake	Followup
Separated/divorced (%)	39	39	38	39
Unemployed[a] (%)	54	37	57	43
Days worked last month[a]	8.7	12.4	7.9	11.4
Income last month ($)	([b])	([b])	265	424
(N)	(2371)		(600)	

[a] For those in labor force only; 2195 clients in the 6-month survey and 544 clients in the 18-month survey are in the labor force (i.e., not retired or students).
[b] Not available.

The picture for job stability indicators is considerably different from that for marital status. While unemployment remains relatively high at followup, there is a decline from 54 percent to 37 percent for the 6-month followup and from 57 percent to 43 percent for the 18-month followup. These declines represent relative improvement rates of 25 percent and 31 percent, respectively. Similarly, the average number of days worked increase by about 4 days for both groups; and for the 18-month group, monthly income increases by about $160 per client (including clients not in the work force). Allowing normal wage increases of about 15 percent, this represents a real change of $120, or a relative improvement rate of about 45 percent.

While the improved job stability is significant, the fact that few clients change their marital status and that many remain unemployed will come as a disappointment to some, particularly in view of the substantial changes in drinking behavior. On the other hand, it is reasonable to posit that an improvement in drinking behavior is a necessary first step toward improved social adjustment, and that the ATCs appear to be making important strides in this respect. Broader social outcomes may be largely beyond the control of an ATC, at least in the short run. But it is also possible that social adjustment requires a longer period than changes in drinking behavior, and that an 18-month followup will not capture the full range of improvement.

ESTABLISHING A REMISSION CRITERION

The high rates of improvement across many outcome measures affirm that alcoholism is being treated in NIAAA centers with considerable success, if we consider outcomes for clients taken as a group. For several reasons, however, we cannot use any of these outcome measures alone as a definition of remission for individual clients.

First, the daily consumption index is a summary measure of the volume of drinking and can be misleading for those clients who only occasionally engage in excessive drinking. Second, since alcoholism is generally indicated by the joint occurrence of excessive alcohol consumption and behavioral consequences, definitions of remission must necessarily deal with combinations of both consumption and impairment characteristics. Finally, the fact that many improved clients are still drinking at what appear to be moderate levels raises the difficult problem of defining "normal" drinking for alcoholics.

We deal with all of these issues in this section and propose a definition of remission that seems consistent with our data and with other concepts in the field. This definition can then be used as the main outcome criterion for our more extensive analysis of relapse, client effects, and specific treatment effects.

Typical Quantity of Alcohol Consumed

The daily consumption index measures the total volume of alcohol consumed in a 30-day period expressed as a daily average. Although this can be a useful summary statistic, it has the potential limitation of combining clients who drink small or moderate amounts of ethanol daily with those who drink very large—and possibly damaging—amounts of alcohol infrequently. That is, a daily consumption index score of 1 oz/day for the past 30 days can be obtained by drinking one sizable (2¼ ounce) dry martini every day, or by drinking 1 quart of gin on two consecutive days but nothing on the other 28 days. Since infrequent but concentrated heavy drinking is likely to be more damaging than daily light drinking, alcoholics drinking in this fashion should not be considered in remission. Obviously, if there are many such alcoholics in our samples at followup, then the changes in daily consumption shown in Table 9 could give a misleading picture of improvement.

Information about the extent of concentrated or binge drinking in both the 18-month followup sample and the general population is provided in Table 12. For the alcoholic population, we give the percentage distribution of the quantity of alcohol consumed on a typical drinking day last month within each category of daily consumption (e.g., 0 to 1 oz/day, 1 to 3 oz/day); this is the quantity side of the Quantity-Frequency index of daily consumption.[11] Binge drinkers should show up on the lower left-hand part

---

[11] See Appendix A for more details.

Table 12.   Percentage Distribution of Consumption on Typical Drinking Days, by Daily Consumption Last Month, 18-Month Followup

Quantity Consumed on a Typical Drinking Day Last Month	Daily Consumption Last Month							General Male Population[a] (%)
	Abstained	0-1 oz	1-3 oz	3-5 oz	5-7 oz	Over 7 oz	Total (%)	
Abstained	100						45	34
0-1 oz		22					5	14
1-3 oz		52	32				16	32
3-5 oz		9	14	46			6	10
5-7 oz		2	16	4	57		5	4
7-10 oz		7	25	23	19	15	8	3
Over 10 oz		9	13	27	24	85	16	2
Total	100	100	100	100	100	100	100	100
(N)	(268)	(134)	(77)	(22)	(21)	(75)	(597)	(3104)

[a] The mean is 3.1 for those males who drink.

of the table. As we can see, however, 74 percent of the clients whose daily consumption is in the 0 to 1 range drank 3 ounces or less on typical drinking days; only 16 percent drank more than 5 ounces on typical drinking days. In addition, 46 percent of those whose daily consumption ranges from 1 to 3 ounces drank less than 5 ounces on drinking days. Thus, although there are some clients with low daily averages who drink large quantities on drinking days, most clients do not follow the binge pattern. Also note that the modal quantity of consumption among drinkers in the general population is 1 to 3 ounces/day, and a sizable proportion falls into the 3 to 5 ounces/day range.

It might be helpful to add some content to these figures by describing the categories used in the interview to determine quantity and frequency of consumption. The relation between typical quantity of ethanol consumed and the actual beverage amounts is as follows:

Typical Quantity	Beer	Wine	Liquor
0-1 oz	1-2 cans	1-2 glasses[a]	1-3 shots
1-3 oz	3-6 cans	3-5 glasses	4-6 shots
3-5 oz	8 cans (3 qt)	6 glasses to 1 fifth	7-10 shots
5-7 oz	4 qt	(no category)	11-14 shots
7 oz+	5 qt+	2 fifths+	1 pt+

[a] A 4-oz wine glass.

For example, a person could fall into the 1 to 3 ounces/day category if he drank 3 to 6 cans of beer, 3 to 5 glasses of wine, or 4 to 6 shots of liquor on a typical day of drinking.

The real problem, of course, is deciding which of these categories constitute safe or normal drinking and which constitute excessive drinking. The literature is not helpful here, even if we restrict our concern to physiological effects rather than behavioral impairment. There is simply no specifiable amount of alcohol short of lethal doses that could be considered dangerous for all persons. We must, therefore, seek other ways of defining normal drinking. One approach might be to examine the pattern of drinking in the general male population (see Tables 9 and 12) as a basis for establishing norms. For example, we find that for men the modal daily consumption is 0 to 1 ounce and the modal quantity is 1 to 3 ounces, although fairly large numbers have a daily consumption of 1 to 3 ounces and typical amounts of 3 to 5 ounces (13 percent and 10 percent, respectively). But the percentages drop off rapidly for daily consumptions of more than 3 ounces and for typical quantities exceeding 5 ounces. Therefore, based strictly on an assessment of drinking patterns in the general population, we might set upper limits for normal drinking at 3 oz/day for daily consumption and 5 ounces for typical quantities.

The difficulty with this approach, of course, is that alcoholics are not a normal population when it comes to alcohol consumption. In particular, consumption of what might be a normal amount for the average male might cause serious damage to the average alcoholic. A more reasonable approach would be to investigate the effect of varying consumption levels on behavioral impairment.

Impairment and Consumption

Definitions of both alcoholism and remission must take into account the joint relationship between consumption and impairment. Some persons can drink relatively large amounts of alcohol with little impairment, whereas others experience substantial impairment from relatively small amounts. The task here is to assess their relationship and to establish useful levels of consumption and impairment for distinguishing remissions from nonremissions among persons who have exhibited alcoholic symptoms in the past.

The overall relationship between the behavioral impairment index and three consumption characteristics is shown by the product-moment correlations in Table 13. The first set of correlations shows drinking behaviors at entry to treatment; the second set shows the same indicators measured at the 18-month followup.[12] It is interesting that, in spite of its summary nature, the daily consumption index has higher correlations with impair-

---

[12] In the followup study, abstainers were not asked the impairment questions and are excluded from these correlations.

Table 13.   Correlations Among Behavioral Impairment Index and Three Consumption Indicators for the 18-Month Sample

Consumption Indicator	Behavior Last Month		
	Behavioral Impairment Index	Daily Consumption Index	Typical Quantity Index
At intake[a]			
Behavioral impairment	1.00		
Daily consumption[b]	69	1.00	
Typical quantity[b]	.49	.81	1.00
Days drank	.65	.57	.42
At followup (excluding abstainers)[c]			
Behavioral impairment	1.00		
Daily consumption	.68	1.00	
Typical quantity	.67	.73	1.00
Days drank	.42	.55	.27

[a] N's range from 595 to 599.
[b] Categorized according to the dividing points in Table 12.
[c] N's range from 326 to 329; see fn 12.

ment at both intake and followup than with either typical quantity or number of drinking days. In spite of the criticisms of typical volume measures for general populations, in our data the daily consumption index appears to be more consistently related to behavioral consequences of alcohol than either the frequency or the quantity of consumption alone. These correlations also establish a reasonable level of internal consistency and validity for the various indices of drinking behavior. Correlations of .6 to .7 between different aspects of drinking behavior suggest a fairly substantial degree of measurement reliability. We would also expect that the correlation would be lowest between typical quantity consumed and number of days the individual drank, since some alcoholics are binge drinkers who drink large quantities infrequently.

Although the substantial correlations between most of the consumption indicators and the impairment index confirm the expected causal link between them, the correlations are not so high as to preclude patterns of high consumption–low impairment or low consumption–high impairment. Accordingly, we need a more detailed examination of behavioral impairment within various levels of consumption.

Table 14 shows the percentage of clients reporting tremors at the 18-month followup, based on various levels of both daily consumption and quantity consumed on a typical drinking day. We have focused on the tremors symptom here because, as pointed out earlier, this is the only

Table 14. Percentage of Clients with Tremors at 18-Month Followup, by Quantity Consumed on a Typical Drinking Day and Daily Consumption

Quantity Consumed on a Typical Drinking Day	Daily Consumption Last Month						Total Percent
	Abstaining	0-1 oz	1-3 oz	3-5 oz	5-7 oz	Over 7 oz	
Abstaining	0						
0-1 oz		8					8
1-3 oz		4	18				8
3-5 oz		8	17	50			23
5-7 oz		50[a]	30	33[a]	45		39
7-10 oz		22	40	80	33[a]	30	38
Over 10 oz		50	56	20	83	67	61
Total percent		12	30	48	50	62	

[a] Under five cases. See Table 12 for Ns.

behavioral symptom measured in the followup studies that is part of the alcoholic withdrawal syndrome. Thus, Table 14 allows us to examine the relationship between consumption levels and the symptom in our data most closely associated with physical dependence on alcohol at followup.

First, when daily consumption exceeds 3 ounces, the proportion with tremors is generally substantial even when consumption on a typical drinking day is only 3 to 5 ounces. On the other hand, when typical quantity exceeds 5 ounces, the proportion with tremors is high even when daily consumption is in the range of 0 to 3 ounces. In other words, signs of physical addiction appear frequently for this sample of alcoholics whenever daily consumption exceeds 3 ounces *or* when typical amounts exceed 5 ounces. Other measures of impairment give similar results, although we generally find that crossing the 3 oz/day point for daily consumption causes a bigger impairment difference than crossing the 5 oz/day point for typical quantity.

Our data indicate that most alcoholics consuming amounts of alcohol within the "normal" ranges found in general populations do not have substantial levels of impairment. Accordingly, it appears reasonable to define normal consumption for alcoholics as amounts under 5 ounces on any drinking day, provided the daily average does not exceed 3 ounces. Of course, those clients who do experience serious impairment at these moderate consumption levels should not be considered remissions, but we discuss this issue explicitly in the next section. Interestingly, the cutoff point of 3 oz/day for daily ethanol consumption is below the limit of 8 oz/day of 86-proof spirits (3.4 ounces of ethanol) cited in a recent summary of expert opinion about damaging amounts of alcohol (Fisher, 1975).

It must be stressed that this definition of normal drinking refers to the consumption of alcohol and to the statistical frequency with which a restricted number of impairment characteristics are observed. Some chronic alcoholics may have such severe medical complications that even small amounts of alcohol would be dangerous and would not be considered normal for those persons. Obviously, our definition of normal drinking is not intended to replace clinical diagnosis and prescription; rather it classifies groups of alcoholics according to the best information available in this study.

A Definition of Remission

The documented relationships between alcohol consumption and impairment enable a preliminary definition of remission that can be used throughout the remainder of this report. At the outset, it should be stressed that our definition of remission is based strictly on drinking behaviors; social adjustment indicators such as marital status or employment are excluded. Our rationale is a desire to keep the definition of remission conceptually close to the condition of alcoholism per se, a condition we view as a physical and psychological dependence on alcohol. While alcoholism may cause or be caused by social instability, the two are sufficiently distinct, both analytically and empirically, to justify separate consideration. Thus, we are concerned here with a definition of what should be called alcoholic remission rather than social rehabilitation

Given the drinking behavior information available in these studies, we propose a definition of remission at a given followup that has three possible patterns based on the client's drinking over the period preceding that followup. These patterns are: abstained for 6 months, abstained for 1 month; and normal drinking.

Abstained for 6 Months: This pattern denotes relatively long-term abstention. A client falls into this category if he reports no drinking at all for 6 months or more prior to the followup interview.

Abstained for 1 Month: The 1-month abstainers are clients who report no drinking in the past 30 days but some drinking in the past 1 to 5 months prior to the followup.

Normal Drinking: Clients who report drinking in the last 30 days at followup can fall into this category only if they satisfy the normal drinking criteria described in the previous section and if they do not have serious levels of impairment. More specifically, the recovered alcoholic who is classified as a normal drinker must meet *all* of the following criteria:

1. Daily consumption of less than 3 ounces of ethanol.
2. Typical quantities on drinking days less than 5 ounces.

3. No tremors reported.
4. No serious symptoms.[13]

Nonremissions: Clients who do not fit into any of these three categories are considered nonremissions regardless of other drinking and impairment characteristics.

These definitions reflect the inherent limitations of the available data as well as the necessary arbitrariness of drawing boundaries. We do not have complete clinical reports on each client, information that is rarely available in evaluation studies of this type. We are thus required to draw boundaries based on a more restricted (but more standardized) set of variables. Thus, we are certain that some clients—perhaps even some of the abstainers—are misclassified as remissions when they are in fact nonremissions and some remissions may be misclassified as nonremissions. There are likely to be as many errors in one direction as the other, so that the aggregate recovery rate is probably accurate. In any event, all large-scale evaluation studies face these problems: lines must be drawn, definitions formulated, and persons classified to derive any conclusions that can be generalized to other populations.

We are also aware that the inclusion of a normal drinking category in a definition of remission is not conventional in all quarters although, as was reported in Chapter 2, the recent research literature contains a large number of studies claiming to have observed normal or moderate drinking among some treated alcoholics. We certainly recognize that many professionals believe that permanent abstention is the only solution for alcoholism; no doubt for many alcoholics—including some of those in the present study—it is the best solution. But one must also deal with the empirical finding in this and many other followup studies of treated alcoholics that permanent abstention is adopted by only a small proportion, while many others report drinking at levels similar to those observed in the general population. There seems no choice but to entertain the possibility that some alcoholics return to a pattern of drinking without necessarily exhibiting alcoholic symptoms.

In proposing this definition of remission, we must emphasize two further qualifying conditions. First, these outcome patterns depend on self-reports of abstention and consumption levels. Our analysis of the validity of self-reports presented in Appendix A suggests that whereas the large

---

[13] Serious symptoms are frequent episodes of three or more of the following: blackouts, missing work, morning drinking, missing meals, and being drunk. "Frequent" means three or more episodes of blackouts or missing work in the past month, or five or more episodes of the other symptoms.

majority of both normal and alcoholic populations probably give truthful answers, the group most likely to distort—by underestimation—appears to be the heavier drinkers, although even here distortion seems to be a minority phenomenon. Unfortunately, none of the validity analyses apply directly to the more detailed consumption questions used in the ATC Monitoring System. Second, our definition of remission applies only to behavior in the period prior to a single followup point. Accordingly, a given remission pattern should not be interpreted as a *permanent* state. It is quite possible for alcoholics to move in and out of one remission pattern or another or from remission to nonremission status over an extended period of time. The extent to which this occurs for our sample, especially for those in the normal drinking category, will be discussed explicitly in a subsequent section dealing with relapse.

Remission Results

A summary of remission rates for the two followup samples is shown in Table 15 along with some key drinking characteristics for the remission and nonremission groups. Similar to our findings for other outcome cri-

Table 15. Remission Rates for the 6-Month and 18-Month Followup Samples

| Remission Status | Percent | Drinking Behavior Last Month | | | Impairment Last Month | | |
		Daily Consump-tion (oz)	Typical Quan-tity (oz)	Days Drank	Tremors (%)	Serious Symp-toms[a]	Definite Alcohol-ism (%)
6-Month Followup							
Remissions	68						
Abstained 6 months	*18*	0	0	0	0	0	0
Abstained 1 month	*38*	0	0	0	0	0	0
Normal drinking[b]	*12*	0.5	1.9	7	0	0	0
Nonremissions	32	6.7	12.1	14	69	44	83
(N)	(2250)						
18-Month Followup							
Remissions	67						
Abstained 6 months	*24*	0	0	0	0	0	0
Abstained 1 month	*21*	0	0	0	0	0	0
Normal drinking[b]	*22*	0.7[c]	2.1[d]	10	0	0	0
Nonremissions	33	7.1	13.1	17	54	39	84
(N)	(597)						

[a] See Table 10, note *b*.
[b] Clients who drank last month but who met all four of the following criteria: (1) daily consumption less than 3 oz/day; (2) quantity on typical drinking days less than 5 oz; (3) no tremors reported; and (4) no serious symptoms (see note 13).
[c] Range = 0.1 to 2.4; three cases over 2.0.
[d] Range = 0.9 to 4.4; five cases over 4.0.

teria, remission rates are nearly identical for both followup periods: 68 percent at 6 months and 67 percent at 18 months. However, we note that the distribution across patterns of remission is not as stable; in particular, 1-month abstention declines, whereas normal drinking and, to a lesser extent, long-term abstention increase. As pointed out earlier, 1-month abstention appears to be a less stable remission pattern, with some clients returning to normal drinking and others adopting permanent abstention.

From Table 15 we can also compare the drinking behaviors of the normal drinkers with those of nonremissions. The typical normal drinker at 18 months reports a daily consumption of .7 ounce and an average of 10 drinking days last month, or 1 day out of 3. Not surprisingly, then, the mean typical quantity is 2.1 ounces, which would be equivalent to about 4 cans of beer, 4 glasses of wine, or 4 shots of liquor on drinking days. Of course, some clients drink more than this and others less, but only five normal drinking clients report typical amounts exceeding 4 ounces at the 18-month followup period. In contrast, the nonremissions have drinking characteristics very much like those of the entire sample at entry to treatment. We note in particular that 83 percent of nonremissions at 6 months and 84 percent of nonremissions at 18 months have symptoms indicating definite alcoholism.

Finally, the remission rates of 68 percent and 67 percent compare quite favorably with the improvement rates shown in earlier tables for individual outcome criteria, so that for groups of clients the degree of success or improvement does not vary from one criterion to another. We will use the remission criterion throughout most of the remaining analyses in this report, but it must be emphasized that results for the more detailed analysis of client and treatment effects do not vary from one criterion to the other.[14]

RELAPSE

The results described thus far have depended on followup reports taken as single observation points or "snapshots" of the two client samples. However, the particular properties of alcoholism could render a single followup report misleading. Specifically, it could be argued that some alcoholics follow cyclical patterns in which they fluctuate between stages of alcoholic drinking, abstention, and normal drinking. If this were true, then one might find many persons in remission at one followup period but not in

---

[14] See also Ruggels et al. (1975).

remission at a later one. This is particularly worrisome if normal drinking and short-term abstention are included as models of remission; it is entirely possible that normal or periodic drinking is simply a temporary stage for an alcoholic on his way back to a full relapse. If so, then we would expect such drinkers to have a higher relapse rate than abstainers.

The solution to these problems requires "relapse" as another outcome criterion. A relapse criterion addresses the question of the stability of remission at different followup periods rather than the proportion of clients in remission at a single followup period. Although we cannot address this question for the entire 18-month followup sample, we can make a preliminary assessment of relapse using a subsample of clients in the 18-month sample that received 6-month followup interviews as part of the regular ATC monitoring system. For this subsample, relapse will be assessed by comparing remission status at 6 months with remission status at 18 months following intake.

Since the 6-month followups are generally completed on a fairly small portion of intakes, only about one-third of the intake clients in the 18-month Followup Study have 6-month followup reports. Before embarking upon this assessment, we should settle the crucial issue of the extent of bias, if any, in the subsample used for the relapse analysis.

Comparisons of some of the more important client characteristics between the relapse sample and the full 18-month sample of male non-DWIs are shown in Table 16. For drinking characteristics at intake, the relapse sample is nearly identical to the full sample; for social background characteristics there are some differences, but even here they are not large. The relapse sample shows somewhat less marital disruption (30 percent compared with 38 percent) and has somewhat fewer low-SES clients (44 percent compared with 50 percent). As might be expected, the 18-month followup characteristics show larger differences. The subgroup that has both followup reports tends to have more remissions (76 percent compared with 67 percent), although the distribution is nearly identical among the three patterns of remission. Note that the percent of normal drinkers is about the same in both samples (25 and 22 percent).

We conclude that the sample to be used for the relapse analysis has a slightly higher proportion of clients who are in remission and who are socially stable than the full 18-month followup sample, and hence the absolute relapse rates may be slightly biased. Our primary focus will, therefore, be on the comparison of relapse rates for different types or groups of clients within the relapse sample rather than on absolute relapse rates for the sample as a whole. Aside from the issue of sample bias, the small proportion of clients with two followup reports renders our findings for relapse necessarily tentative.

Table 16.   Comparison of the Relapse Sample[a] **with the 18-Month Followup Sample**

Characteristics	Relapse Sample	18-Month Followup Sample
At Intake		
Daily consumption (oz.)	8.2	8.1
Typical quantity consumed (oz.)	11.6	11.9
Behavioral impairment	13.0	12.7
Percent definitely alcoholic	74	74
Percent divorced/separated	30	38
Percent unemployed	52	57
Percent low SES	44	50
Age	46	45
At 18-Month Followup		
Daily consumption (oz)	1.9	2.5
Typical quantity consumed (oz)	3.6	4.8
Behavioral impairment	3.2	4.0
Percent remissions	76	67
Abstained 6 months	27	24
Abstained 1 month only	23	21
Normal drinking	25	22
Percent unemployed	37	42
(N)	(225)	(597)

[a] Male non-DWI clients with both 6-month and 18-month followup reports.

Aggregate Relapse Rates for ATCs

There are two levels at which one can examine relapse rates. The first level consists of "aggregate" relapse rates that reveal the extent to which remission rates at 6 months resemble those at 18 months for all clients as a whole or for subgroups of clients, such as those within an individual ATC. This level of relapse analysis is useful for determining whether the remission rate found in an earlier followup is a good predictor of the remission rate in a later followup for some grouping of clients. The second level focuses on individual relapse rates, or the extent to which clients change from remission to nonremission status in two successive followup. Obviously, it is possible to have a high rate of aggregate stability with a low rate of individual stability, provided equal numbers of clients both enter and leave a given state.

Aggregate relapse rates can be used to determine the validity of the 6-month followup reports for individual ATCs, as shown in Table 17. The bottom of the table shows that the overall remission rate for clients with both reports is quite stable, declining from 77 percent to 76 percent over the 1-year period. As was shown in Table 15, however, the pattern of

Table 17.   Remission Rates for Clients with 6-Month and 18-Month Followups, Classified by ATC

ATC	6-Month Followup (%)	18-Month Followup (%)	(N)
A	61	61	(18)
B	79	79	(39)
C	76	69	(29)
D	82	68	(22)
E	87	79	(63)
F	83	92	(12)
G	70	90	(10)
H	54	77	(26)
Total Remissions	77	76	(219)
Abstained 6 months	*18*	*27*	
Abstained 1 month	*45*	*23*	
Normal drinking	*14*	*26*	

remission has shifted substantially, with a decrease in 1-month abstention and an increase in both 6-month abstention and normal drinking.

There is also remarkable stability in the remission rates for individual ATCs, even though the number of clients is quite small in many instances. Most differences are 10 percent or less, with only two centers showing differences of 20 percent. There is no particular pattern of change; some ATCs show an increase in remission rate and others a decrease. Therefore it is likely that most of the variations are due to the statistical instability inherent in the small numbers of clients.

These results, together with the earlier 6-month and 18-month comparisons, allow us to conclude that the 6-month followup report is a relatively valid indicator of remission over a longer run. This holds especially for the client population as a whole, and it is probably true for most ATCs, provided sufficient numbers of clients are available.

Individual Relapse

The stable rate of remission for the sample as a whole across two followup reports 1 year apart still does not reveal the degree of individual stability between the two periods. For example, our sample could have 75 percent remission rates at the two followup periods even though 25 percent went from remission status at 6 months to nonremission status at 18 months, and another 25 percent switched from nonremission to remission status. Hence only 50 percent would actually be in a "stable" remission state. What is needed is a tabulation of relapse for individual clients. Aside from the question of stability, such a tabulation can also answer the critical question of which remission pattern, if any, is more likely to result in relapse.

Individual relapse rates are shown in Table 18. Although there is some instability over time, very little of it is a result of relapse. Of those clients in remission at 6 months, more than 80 percent are in remission at 18 months for all three patterns of remission. This represents a "stable" group of remissions accounting for 63 percent of the total sample. Half of the instability arises from clients who are not in remission at 6 months but are in remission at 18 months; this represents about 13 percent of the sample. The other half stems from relapse. The nonremissions at 6 months who are still nonremissions at 18 months constitute 10 percent of the total sample. Thus the stable clients, in remission or not, represent 73 percent of the total sample.[15] Also, long-term abstention at both followups occurs for only 10 percent of the total sample. This means that if we used long-term abstention as our only definition of remission, we would have to conclude that only a very small proportion of our sample shows stable remission.

The more important information in Table 18 concerns the relapse rates for differing patterns of remission at 6 months, particularly the comparison

Table 18.   Relapse Rates at 18 Months: Full Sample

	Percentage Distribution of 18-Month Status				
	Remission Status at 6 Months				
Remission Status at 18 Months	Abstained 6 Months	Abstained 1 Month Only	Normal Drinking	Nonremission	Total
Abstained 6 months	53 ⎫	32 ⎫	10 ⎫	8 ⎫	27
Abstained 1 month only	15 ⎬ 83	19 ⎬ 81	27 ⎬ 87	35 ⎬ 57	23
Normal drinking	15 ⎭	29 ⎭	50 ⎭	14 ⎭	26
Nonremission (relapse)	17	19	13	43	24
(N)	(40)	(99)	(30)	(51)	(220)

In remission at both followups	63%
In remission at 6 months; not in remission at 18 months	14%
Not in remission at 6 months; in remission at 18 months	13%
Not in remission at both followups	10%
Abstaining 6 months at both followups	10%

[15] It should be pointed out that reliability of measurement also affects the proportions in the unstable cells and is certainly a factor in the present case. A two-category variable with reliability of .8 would yield a turnover table in which 10 percent of the sample should fall into the unstable cells because of error alone.

between normal drinking and long-term abstention. If total abstention is a more effective path to recovery than moderate drinking, or if normal drinking is only a way station for alcoholics returning to alcoholic drinking, then we would expect normal drinkers to have a higher relapse rate than long-term abstainers. The table shows, however, normal drinkers have a slightly lower rate of relapse than either of the two abstaining groups, although the difference is not large.

It might be fairly argued that the issue of abstention versus normal drinking is relevant only to the definite alcoholic, i.e., to the alcoholic who is physically addicted to alcohol and thus cannot have a drink without loss of control. According to this view, excessive users who are not true alcoholics might be able to return to normal drinking, but the true alcoholic cannot do so without a loss of control and, eventually, a full relapse. This view is prominent in physiological theories of alcoholism and in AA philosophy. Accordingly, since the followup sample includes some clients not definitely alcoholic at intake, the relapse analysis needs to be repeated excluding this group.

Relapse rates for definitely alcoholic clients, as that group has been defined, are shown in Table 19. Although there are some differences for this group as compared with the full sample, none of the differences are major. The normal drinkers among definite alcoholics are slightly more likely to be nonremissions at 18 months than the full sample (16 percent

Table 19. Relapse Rates for Clients Definitely Alcoholic at Intake

	Percentage Distribution of 18-month Status				
	Remission Status at 6 Months				
	Abstained 6 Months	1 Month Only Abstained	Normal Drinking	Nonremission	Total
Abstained 6 months	48 ⎫	33 ⎫	10 ⎫	8 ⎫	27
Abstained 1 month only	19 ⎬ 83	25 ⎬ 78	37 ⎬ 84	40 ⎬ 55	29
Normal drinking	16 ⎭	20 ⎭	37 ⎭	8 ⎭	19
Nonremission (relapse)	16	22	16	45	26
(N)	(31)	(73)	(19)	(38)	(161)

In remission at both followups 61%

In remission at 6 months; not in remission at 18 months 16%

Not in remission at 6 months; in remission at 18 months 12%

Not in remission at both followups 11%

Abstaining 6 months at both followups 9%

compared with 13 percent), but long-term abstainers in this group also have an identical relapse rate (16 percent). Interestingly, the 1-month abstainers have the highest relapse rate of all (22 percent), although even here the difference is not large. Short-term abstainers apparently include more alcoholics who are fluctuating between abstention and alcoholic drinking.

Note also that the stability of remission for this severely impaired group is quite similar to that for the full relapse sample. About 61 percent are in remission at both followups, and only 16 percent of those in remission at 6 months have experienced relapse at 18 months. Again, a relatively small group, 9 percent, report long-term abstention at both followups. It seems clear that for this group, as well as for the full relapse sample, most of the instability stems from shifts from one remission pattern to another rather than from changes from remission to nonremission status.

We cannot overemphasize the significance of these findings. Based on the relapse rates for a subsample of clients with followup reports a year apart, it appears that some alcoholics do return to normal drinking with no greater likelihood of relapse than alcoholics who choose permanent abstention. While the evidence here is by no means final, it supports a definition of remission that allows for drinking in normal or moderate amounts. Even though total abstention by definition is a more certain method for avoiding harmful consequences of alcohol, there is no guarantee that those who adopt a total abstention policy will adhere to it forever. Empirically, our data suggest that totally abstaining clients are just as likely to return to alcoholism as those who choose to drink at normal levels. Moreover, long-term abstention—defined as abstaining 6 months at both followups—is a relatively rare event, occurring in only 10 percent of the sample.

Instability is not confined to the 6 month abstainers. Only 7 percent of the full sample and 4 percent of the definite alcoholics are normal drinkers at both followups, and the outcome is similar for 1 month abstainers. The dominant theme of these results is that alcoholics fluctuate, not between remission and nonremission, but between the three remission states of short-term abstention, long-term abstention, and normal drinking.

While the relapse data are intriguing, we emphasize that they are based on only a small subsample of the full 18-month followup study and apply to only a 1-year interval. Before a final conclusion can be drawn about the stability of remission and the likelihood of relapse for normal drinkers compared with abstainers, it will be necessary to obtain two-wave followup data on a larger and more complete sample and, ideally, one that is followed for a period longer than 18 months.

EFFECTS OF CLIENT CHARACTERISTICS

So far we have treated the followup samples largely as single, undifferentiated groups. In spite of the fact that alcoholics as a group are easily differentiated from the general population according to drinking behavior and social background, there is considerable within-group variability. And given the etiological or prognostic significance attached to many of these client characteristics by an extensive research literature, we would not expect treatment results to be uniform for all types of clients.

In this section we will examine the effect of client characteristics at entry to treatment on subsequent remission. The prognostic factors to be investigated include the severity of alcoholism as well as drinking history and social background. As such, this analysis will help set the stage for a subsequent analysis of the success of different treatment modalities for certain types of clients.

Severity of Alcoholism

As with many illnesses, it is reasonable to posit that the more severe the alcoholic symptoms the less likely a full recovery. The severe, chronic alcoholic is addicted to such an extent that cessation of consumption is accompanied by considerable physical and psychological distress, sometimes including severe withdrawal symptoms. The less impaired alcoholic, on the other hand, may give up or reduce alcohol consumption with only moderate discomfort.

The effect of severe alcoholic symptoms on remission is shown in Table 20. Remission rates are given for clients with definite alcoholism symptoms as contrasted with those having less severe symptoms, many of whom may be excessive users but not true alcoholics. The level of impairment at intake has an impact on chances for remission, with less impaired clients much more likely to experience remission than definite alcoholics. Since most of the alcoholics in these two samples have definite alcoholism symptoms, the remission rate of this group is not much lower than the remission rate for the samples as a whole.

There are some further differences between the two groups in the pattern of remissions, especially in the 18-month followup. We find that the difference in remission rate is almost entirely accounted for by a higher proportion of normal drinkers among the less-impaired clients (36 percent compared with 16 percent), so that the percent abstaining is almost identical for both groups. At first glance it might appear that normal drinking is less successful for the definite alcoholic than for the less impaired alcoholic. Recall, however, that the relapse analysis suggests that treatment

Table 20. Effect of Severe Alcoholic Symptoms on Remission

Remission Status	Remission Rates (%)	
	Definite Alcoholism at Intake	Less Definite Symptoms at Intake
6-Month Followup		
Remissions	63	81
Abstained 6 months	*15*	*27*
Abstained 1 month	*39*	*36*
Normal drinking	*10*	*18*
Nonremissions	37	19
(N)	(1605)	(644)
18-Month Followup		
Remissions	62	80
Abstained 6 months	*23*	*28*
Abstained 1 month	23	*16*
Normal drinking	16	*36*
Nonremissions	38	20
(N)	(435)	(156)

failure occurs relatively uniformly across the three patterns of remission at 6 months. That is, of the 38 percent nonremissions at 18 months who were in remission at 6 months, approximately equal proportions derive from the three remission patterns. Accordingly, the lower rate of normal drinking by definite alcoholics at 18 months cannot be explained by failure to maintain stable, normal drinking started at an earlier period. Actually, only 10 percent of the definite alcoholics are drinking normally at 6 months. A better explanation is that definite alcoholics are less likely to adopt or accept a solution of normal drinking, either because of advice they receive during treatment or because they reject such a course for their own reasons.

It should be noted that the relationships between remission and other alcoholic drinking characteristics, such as daily consumption, typical quantity consumed, and the overall behavioral impairment index, although not shown in separate tables, yield results similar to those for definite alcoholism. In general, the more serious the symptoms the less likely the improvement across a broad set of criteria.

Client Background

A number of other client characteristics deemed important for treatment prognosis can be grouped loosely under the categories of drinking history and social background. There is a common belief among many practitioners that the chronic alcoholic with a long history of alcoholism is harder to treat and is less likely to improve than clients with a recent history, who are experiencing their first treatment episode, although the research literature to date is equivocal. Similarly, those clients with certain social characteristics—higher SES, greater job and marital stability, nondrinking contexts, and so forth—are generally expected to have a greater chance of recovery because of their more supportive environments. As was indicated in Chapter 3, the prognostic role of SES was unclear, since higher SES is associated with heavier drinking and lower SES with being in treatment.

The relationships between the most important drinking history and social background characteristics available in our data are shown in Table 21 as they affect remission rates. For drinking history, the expected relationships do occur, but they are not very strong for either followup study. In fact, years of heavy drinking have a slight nonlinear relationship, with short-history and long-history clients having slightly better chances of remission than those with histories in the middle range. But even here the differences are too small to justify major emphasis.

Among the social background characteristics, only stability and SES have a substantial impact on remission rates.[16] Both stability and SES have large effects on remission and, for the 18-month followup, the effects are nearly as large as those observed for the severity of alcoholism (17 percent and 16 percent, respectively). On the other hand, the effects for age, race, father's drinking, and spouse's drinking are much smaller, although they are in the expected direction.

We conclude that for these two samples most drinking history and social background factors are not strongly predictive of treatment success. The two exceptions are social stability and SES, where those with greater social stability and higher SES are more likely to be in remission.

Interactions of Severity of Alcoholism and Background Characteristics

The various drinking and social characteristics we have examined are not independent; i.e., unstable clients are likely to have a lower SES, definitely alcoholic clients are likely to be more unstable, and so forth. Are some of

---

[16] The stability index measures residential, job, and marital stability. The "low stability" clients are those who live in group quarters (regardless of marital and job status) or those who are both divorced or separated and unemployed (provided they are in the work force); the "high stability" clients are all others. The SES index is a measure of social class, computed as the average of income, education, and occupational status variables (each coded on 13-point ordinal scales) and dichotomized at the median value of the full-intake population.

Table 21.   Effects of Client Characteristics at Intake on Remission Rates at Followup

Characteristics at Intake	Remission Rates (%)			
	6-Month Followup	(N)	18-Month Followup	(N)
Drinking Behavior				
Prior treatment	63 } 8[a]	(914)	61 } 9	(240)
No prior treatment	71	(1190)	70	(356)
Ever attended AA	65 } 7	(1264)	64 } 6	(322)
Never attended AA	72	(935)	70	(272)
Under 10 years heavy drinking	70	(938)	71	(251)
10-20 years heavy drinking	63	(683)	62	(178)
Over 20 years heavy drinking	70	(628)	65	(160)
Social Background				
Low stability[b]	63 } 9	(860)	56 } 17	(239)
High stability	72	(1315)	75	(346)
Low SES[b]	62 } 12	(1064)	58 } 16	(267)
High SES	74	(1201)	74	(328)
Under 35	69	(423)	65	(126)
36–50	67	(923)	64	(229)
Over 50	69	(901)	70	(236)
White	70 } 6	(1701)	70 } 11	(429)
Nonwhite	64	(358)	59	(140)
Father heavey drinker[c]	66 } 4	(641)	68 } 0	(169)
Father not heavy drinker	70	(1337)	68	(358)
Spouse heavy drinker[d]	76 } 4	(81)	64 } 12	(14)
Spouse not heavy drinker	72	(854)	76	(226)

[a] Percentage difference.
[b] See footnote 16 for description.
[c] For those living with father while growing up.
[d] For those currently married.

these effects explained by only one or two of the other effects? A more formal analysis of the joint effects of both client and treatment characteristics will be pursued in Chapter 5. At present, we are interested in whether the effects of the three strongest client characteristics—severity of alcoholism, stability, and SES—have independent effects on remission or whether some are largely redundant.

It is clear from Table 22 that the effects of these three client input variables are not redundant, although there are some interactions and all three do not have equally strong effects on remission. The remission rates

Table 22.   Effects of Client Alcoholic Status, Stability, and SES on Remission Rates at 18-Month Followup

| | Remission Rates (%) | | | | |
| | Unstable | | Stable | | |
Alcoholic Status	Low SES	High SES	Low SES	High SES	Percent
Definite alcoholism symptoms	51	56	60	76	62
(N)	(113)	(79)	(85)	(152)	(421)
Less definite symptoms	69	59	74	90	80
(N)	(26)	(17)	(35)	(74)	(156)
Total percent	55	56	64	81	
(N)	(139)	(96)	(120)	(226)	

are generally low for the unstable clients, regardless of social class; even definite alcoholism does not make a consistent difference, although it does have a fairly strong effect for low SES clients. Interestingly, the unstable clients with less definite alcoholism symptoms tend to do better if they have lower SES, although there are only 17 clients in one of the cells. This suggests, however, that high SES is not always strongly related to good prognosis.

Stable clients have generally better prognosis than unstable ones, but in this case SES makes a substantial additional contribution regardless of the severity of alcoholism. Also, the severity of alcoholism has a fairly uniform effect for all other categories. The joint effect of all three characteristics is therefore quite substantial: stable, high SES clients with less definite symptoms of alcoholism have a remission rate of 90 percent, whereas unstable, low SES clients who are definitely alcoholic have a rate of 51 percent. Yet it appears that stability and severity of alcoholism are more important than SES in predicting favorable remission rates. The important question now is whether these variations in remission rates for different types of clients are affected by different types of treatment.

FIVE

The Effectiveness of Treatment

The fact that most clients are in remission and have continued in remission as long as 18 months certainly suggests that treatment has produced substantial effects. However, a number of issues must be resolved before definite conclusions can be drawn about effectiveness. For example, a major issue concerns the degree to which remission can be attributed to treatment received from the ATC, as opposed to other influences, such as "natural remission" or help received from non-ATC sources. Another important issue concerns the effectiveness of differing *types* of treatment. Despite the high overall remission rates, it is possible that some treatments are especially effective, whereas others make a relatively poor showing. In this chapter we discuss these issues and attempt to sort out and evaluate the relative impact of various treatment and client factors.

The available data, including both the 6-month and the 18-month followup, allow tests of a number of specific hypotheses concerning treatment effectiveness. First, the 18-month sample includes a large group of clients who made only a few contacts with a treatment center and who received little or no actual treatment. These "untreated" clients can be compared with treated clients to produce an assessment of the benefits of treatment itself, separating out spontaneous remission. In addition, both followup samples provide information about the amount of treatment given to a client and the length of time (duration) over which treatment was given. This information will allow an estimate of the benefits that may be associated with greater or lesser amounts of treatment and the penalties that may be attached to dropping out of treatment prematurely.

Second, the treatment records of the ATC Monitoring System contain detailed information about the types and combinations of treatments provided to each client. These types will be examined according to the broad setting of treatment (hospital, intermediate, or outpatient) and according to the more specific therapy (individual counseling, drug therapy, and the like). Analysis of these types will make it possible to determine whether

113

any particular treatment, or perhaps a combination of treatments, offers an advantage in effectiveness.

Third, the presence of heterogeneous client populations among the treatment centers offers an unusual opportunity to examine the interplay of client characteristics with treatments. Given the evidence of client effects in both the literature and the results of Chapter 4, it is evident that a thorough analysis of treatments must take these client factors into account. Our data are well suited to this purpose, allowing special tests of the importance of client-treatment interactions, i.e., tests to locate which treatments (if any) appear to produce especially high remisson rates for certain types of clients. As noted in Chapter 2, both theoretical models and existing therapy programs assume that certain treatment types (e.g., halfway-house care) are best suited to certain types of clients (in this instance, unstable or disadvantaged clients). The analysis of client-treatment interactions will show whether such combinations are crucial to treatment success.

These results are of obvious importance in the planning and operation of treatment programs, but there are further implications as well. The analyses presented here represent an implicit test of several broad theories concerning the nature of alcoholism. Most prominent models in the research literature emphasize differentially the importance of physiological, psychological, or sociocultural factors in the genesis and maintenance of alcoholism. Some of these models provide the rationales for various aspects of the treatment process. If one of these models is more appropriate than the others, the mode of treatment based on it should be more effective in combating the disorder, and should thus lead to higher remission rates. By testing this hypothesis, the evaluation of treatment effectiveness can also shed some light upon the theories that offer conflicting explanations of alcoholism phenomena.

COMPARING TREATED AND UNTREATED CLIENTS

A necessary first step in establishing the effectiveness of treatment is to show that persons who received treatment fared better than similar persons who did not. In a laboratory setting, this might be accomplished by an experiment in which a group of treated clients is compared with an untreated, but otherwise equivalent, group. Obviously, in these functioning treatment agencies it would be neither feasible nor desirable to withhold treatment from a randomly selected control group. Instead, we must search out, after the fact, a group of alcoholics who receive little or no treatment, and delineate them by a careful definition of nontreatment.

Defining Groups of "Treated and "Untreated" ATC Clients

There is one source of data on untreated alcoholics at these ATCs: the set of clients who contacted the treatment centers but who, for some reason, never formally entered treatment. Although there is no ironclad guarantee that these clients are equivalent to those who entered treatment, they can be used as a baseline for preliminary comparisons. Normally, only minimal demographic information is collected on such clients. Because they do not enter a formal treatment program, neither intake nor 6-month followup information on them is included in the Monitoring System. The 18-Month Followup Study, however, was specifically designed to include such clients by designating two untreated groups as sampling strata. The first group, designated "single contact," includes clients who made only one visit to a treatment center and who received no further treatment. The second group, designated "preintake," consists of clients who made contact and received minimal services (usually detoxication), but who then left the center and never resumed contact. Both groups were interviewed at 18 months after first contact.

The untreated clients are compared with treated clients in Table 23, which shows the amount of service provided by the ATC to various groups. One omission has been made from the untreated groups: those persons who said in the followup interview that they had never had a

Table 23.   Amount of ATC Service Recorded for Treated and Untreated Clients

	Untreated Clients[a]		Treated Clients		
Service Recorded	Single Contact	Preintake	Low Amount of Treatment[b]	High Amount of Treatment	All Treated Clients[c]
Percent with inatient care	3	51	70	66	72
Median inpatient days[d]	2	3	10	29	14
Percent with outpatient care	37	40	67	61	70
Median outpatient visits[d]	1	1	2	15	5
(N)	(153)	(139)	(184)	(275)	(600)

[a] Excluding those who reported that they had never had a problem with frequent or heavy drinking.
[b] Low amount of treatment is defined as 1 week or less of hospital care, 3 weeks or less of intermediate care, or 5 visits or less of outpatient care. For inpatient-outpatient combinations, a client must be below the limits on both types to qualify as "low." High amount of treatment is similarly defined as amounts above these limits.
[c] Includes clients in low- and high-treatment categories, plus clients in inpatient-outpatient combinations who were not classified as either low or high because they had a low amount of one type but a high amount of the other type.
[d] Among clients receiving this type of treatment.

problem with frequent or heavy drinking have been excluded (about 13 percent). This was done in order to eliminate nonalcoholics, since we know that in some hospital settings a client may be contacted by an ATC and recorded as a single contact, even though it may subsequently be found that alcoholism is not involved. Among the treated groups, a further subdivision has been made according to amount of service provided to the client. Clients who received less than a typical amount of a certain type of treatment (split as close to the median as practicable) are classified as "low" in amount of treatment, and those who received greater amounts are classified as "high." Some clients received more than one type of treatment and could not be unambiguously classified as low or high for each type; these clients are not tabulated separately, but are included along with the low and high groups in the total of all treated clients.

It should be clear from Table 23 that both the untreated groups received minimal amounts of service from the ATC. Among the single-contact group, for example, only a handful of persons received any inpatient care. About half of the preintake group received some very limited inpatient treatment, averaging about 3 days; most of it is detoxification with no further treatment. Similarly, outpatient service is recorded only for a minority of the untreated groups, and that service which is recorded is limited to one outpatient visit. This visit for the untreated clients reflects a procedure in which some ATCs file a Client Service Report recording the initial contact as a single outpatient visit, although treatment is carried no further.

Table 23 also shows that treated clients can vary greatly in the amount of treatment they receive. Those we have classified as low in treatment show very modest amounts of treatment: an average of 10 inpatient days and about 2 outpatient visits. For practical purposes, clients with this small amount of treatment might well be considered untreated and, as we shall see shortly, they do not appear to have received great benefits from their treatment. In contrast, those who are classified as high in treatment have usually completed about 1 month's worth of total inpatient care, and about 15 outpatient visits—which would be almost 4 months of care at a rate of 1 visit per week.

Remission Rates of Treated and Untreated Clients

These differences in amount of treatment are of crucial importance in evaluating the effectiveness of treatment. As shown in Table 24, the differing amounts of treatment are reflected in substantially different outcomes. At 18 months, about 67 percent of the treated clients are in remission, compared with only 53 percent of those making a single contact with the

Table 24.   Remission Rates for Treated and Untreated Alcoholics, 18-Month Followup

	Remission Rates (%)				
	Untreated Alcoholics		Treated Alcoholics		
Remission Status	Single Contact	Preintake	Low Amount of Treatment	High Amount of Treatment	All Treated Clients
Remissions	53	54	58	73	67
Abstained 6 months	*11*	*15*	*22*	*26*	*24*
Abstained 1 month	*13*	*13*	*16*	*21*	*21*
Normal drinking	*29*	*27*	*20*	*26*	*22*
Nonremissions	47	46	42	27	33
Daily consumption (oz)	3.3	3.0	2.9	2.2	*2.5*
(N)	(105)	(136)	(184)	(272)	(596)

treatment center. Moreover, the remission rate of treated clients varies substantially according to the amount of treatment received. Among clients with high amounts of treatment the remission rate climbs to 73 percent, but among those with low amounts the remission rate is only slightly better than for untreated alcoholics. Similarly, if the daily consumption rates are examined, it is clear that the untreated groups are similar to the low-amount treated group—each drinking an average of about 3 oz/day—whereas the high-amount treated group has a considerably lower consumption rate.

It is also interesting to note the drinking and abstention patterns exhibited by remissions among these groups. As amount of treatment increases, both the proportion of long-term abstainers and the proportion of 1-month abstainers increase, while the proportion of normal drinkers varies only slightly. In each group, the long-term abstainers are only a small minority —about one-quarter or fewer. Regardless of treatment, a substantial group of clients manifests a remission pattern that involves drinking small amounts of alcohol, rather than permanent and total abstention.

Before these comparisons can be accepted at face value it is essential to consider factors other than the treatment that might have caused these differences. An obvious potential problem is the possibility that the groups shown here may have differed initially on some important characteristics; for example, the "single contacts" could have had more serious drinking problems that led to lower remission rates. Because we have no data on the initial drinking practices of the untreated clients, we are unable to dismiss this possibility completely. However, we do have measures of their social background and surroundings (measured from the followup interview), and based on these characteristics the untreated clients are very similar to the treated clients. In fact, the results shown in Table 24 changed only slightly when we performed statistical adjustments for background differences among the groups (including years of heavy drinking, previous treatment, social stability, socioeconomic status, age, and race). Thus it seems that the different remission rates for treated and untreated clients do not reflect different backgrounds. It is still possible that the untreated clients differed in some other way, but we doubt it, considering the nearly identical backgrounds of the two groups.

A second caveat should be entered when discussing the remission rates of untreated clients. These clients all voluntarily contacted an alcoholism treatment center, and hence there is good reason to suspect that they are different from the ordinary "untreated alcoholic." It seems that they have recognized they have a drinking problem serious enough to require professional help. Furthermore, they may well be more motivated to control their drinking than alcoholics who do not volunteer. It is therefore quite likely that the untreated group has already been selected—probably self-selected—in such a way that the group's remission rates are abnormally high, compared with the "natural" remission rate. Indeed, the high remission rates for the single-contact group suggest that perhaps the crucial ingredient in treatment success is not really treatment at all but rather the person's decision to seek and remain in treatment. These ideas are necessarily speculative because data to confirm them are lacking. But we do *not* claim that our untreated group's remission rates reflect the experience of the average alcoholic person in the population; they *do* reflect the outcomes to be expected from persons who contact a treatment program.

Despite these qualifications, it seems safe to conclude that there is a substantial difference between clients who receive treatment and those who do not. The main differences are between those who receive adequate *amounts* of treatment (what we have called statistically "high" amounts) and others. Among clients receiving such amounts of treatment, the remission rates average 73 percent—about 20 percent higher than for clients with no treatment. For the clients receiving only small amounts of treatment, however, there is hardly any noticeable payoff; their remission rates are only slightly higher than those among untreated alcoholics.

AA and Other Treatment

Many of the clients of these treatment centers were also involved in other programs that aid the alcoholic. Some treatment facilities hold Alcoholics Anonymous meetings on the premises or otherwise encourage clients to participate in non-ATC activities designed to facilitate recovery. In addition, some clients may have abandoned ATC treatment but have sought help later from another treatment agency. The existence of such treatment programs presents an additional problem for our analysis: some of our treatment effects could be due to help received from these other sources. To investigate this possibility, we have classified clients according to their participation in such programs, as shown in Table 25, separating out AA programs because they constitute the most frequently cited source of non-ATC treatment.

Generally, these remission rates depend not only on the presence or amount of ATC treatment but also on the nature of the client's other treatment. The highest remission rates appear among those client groups that received only ATC treatment or AA treatment. In either case, the amount of ATC treatment makes a substantial difference (up to 30 percent) in the client's chances for remission. On the other hand, if a client received some other additional treatment (not from the ATC or from AA), his chances are much poorer and his prognosis does not improve notably even if he receives high amounts of ATC treatment. Although we have no definitive data on this point, it may be that the poor prognosis for those with "other" treatment reflects the fact that they are chronic failures in treatment. That is, it is likely that these clients received other treatment precisely because they failed or withdrew from ATC treatment, so that they are a highly selected group with especially severe and chronic problems. AA treatment alone, on the other hand, would not be a reliable indicator of chronicity since many ATCs include AA meetings and activities as an adjunct to formal treatment.

Because of the importance of Alcoholics Anonymous, it is worthwhile to examine the apparent effects of AA in more detail. Table 26 shows outcomes according to regularity of AA attendance and amount of ATC

Table 25. Effects of Other Treatment in Past Year on Remission Rates of Alcoholics Treated and Untreated by ATCs

	Remission Rates (%)			
	Alcoholics Untreated by ATC		Alcoholics Treated by ATC	
Other (Non-ATC) Treatment	Single Contact	Preintake	Low Amount of Treatment	High Amount of Treatment
None	53	56	58	83
(N)	(97)	(79)	(95)	(112)
AA Only	56	56	63	72
(N)	(27)	(32)	(51)	(116)
Other Treatment	54	48	50	55
N	(26)	(25)	(38)	(44)

Table 26. Effects of AA Attendance and Amount of ATC Treatment on Remission Rates

	Remission Rates (%)		
ATC Treatment	No AA Attendance in Past Year	Irregular AA Attendance	Regular AA Attendance
None or			
Low Amount			
Remissions	55	55	71
Abstained 6 months	*16*	*12*	*36*
Abstained 1 month	8	*15*	*35*
Normal drinking	*31*	*28*	*0*
Nonremissions	45	45	29
(N)	(268)	(82)	(28)
High Amount			
Remissions	83	62	84
Abstained 6 months	*28*	*20*	*48*
Abstained 1 month	*14*	*24*	*26*
Normal drinking	*41*	*18*	*10*
Nonremissions	17	38	16
(N)	(112)	(66)	(50)

treatment. The regular AA participants have been distinguished from irregular participants because it was expected that irregular attendance, as a sign of less motivation, might result in low recovery rates. Regular AA participation, on the other hand, was expected to produce high remission. These expectations are generally upheld by the data in Table 26.

The crucial comparisons in this table are those between regular AA participants and nonparticipants. When these two groups are compared, it is clear that the effects of AA depend on the level of treatment received from the ATC. If the client received little or no ATC treatment, AA can make a substantial difference, raising the remission rate from 55 to 71 percent. If the client received a substantial amount of ATC treatment, AA makes almost no difference, changing the remission rate from 83 to 84 percent. Thus, in the absence of any other treatment, AA achieves a substantial positive effect; but if other treatment is available the impact of AA on general remission rates is minimal.

It must be remembered that the AA philosophy advocates a very specific type of goal: total abstention. If attention is directed to this outcome only, regular AA participation appears to make a substantial and consistent difference. Regardless of amount of ATC treatment, the regular AA participant is about 20 percent more likely to be a long-term abstainer than is a non-AA client. The AA clients also include more short-term abstainers among their number than do other groups, although the short-term abstainers have not really achieved success according to strict AA doctrine. In general, the main impact of AA is not to increase remission rates, but rather to shift the pattern of remission in the direction of abstention. It appears that for the minority of clients who choose to attend AA regularly (only about 13 percent of the clients in Table 26), this AA approach is successful.

However, these effects of AA should not be allowed to obscure the greater effects of treatment by the treatment centers. The treatment center effects can be seen by comparing the high-amount groups with the untreated or low-amount groups, with AA participation controlled. Without AA, the client who receives a high amount of ATC treatment gains a 28 percent increase in chances for remission, an effect much larger than any of the effects for AA. Since most clients do not attend AA even irregularly, this effect has even more practical significance. Moreover, even if the client attends AA regularly, ATC treatment is able to make a further contribution to his or her remission chances, increasing them from 71 percent to 84 percent. Overall, it seems that the treatment centers produce the most favorable outcomes, though regular attendance at AA also plays a significant role.

COMPARING TREATMENT CENTERS

Persons familiar with treatment practices often comment on the wide variations in kind of care provided by different centers. It is asserted that there are "good" and "bad" treatment programs or that some are more effective than others. In addition to aspects of the treatment program, there are obvious variations among centers in the nature of the client populations, the cultural milieu of communities, and in many other factors that might lead to higher remission rates. There are thus many a priori reasons to expect substantial differences in outcomes among treatment centers.

The actual differences in outcomes among the 8 treatment centers at the 18-month followup are shown in Table 27. Although there are variations among centers for some criteria, we are struck by the overall uniformity of results that is displayed. With one exception (treatment center A), the total remission rates are very close together, varying at most from 63 percent to 81 percent. If attention is focused on the more restrictive criterion of long-term abstention, the results are even more uniform. No center has more than 36 percent of its clients abstaining over the period of 6 months or more, or fewer than 17 percent. Long-term abstainers are a minority at all treatment centers, even among clients in remission, and the size of that minority does not vary appreciably among centers.

Table 27. Differences in Remission Rates Among Treatment Centers at 18-Month Followup

Treatment Center	Percent Remissions			Total Percent Remissions	Percent Non-remissions	(N)
	Abstained 6 Months	Abstained Last Month	Normal Drinking			
A	17	15	17	49	51	(113)
B	22	13	46	81	19	(78)
C	25	21	19	65	35	(57)
D	36	15	20	72	28	(39)
E	24	30	15	70	30	(148)
F	29	31	14	74	26	(42)
G	28	14	38	79	21	(29)
H	27	20	18	63	37	(90)

Summary of Treatment Center Effects on Remission

	Percent of Variance Explained[a]
Treatment center (not controlling for client factors)	3.2
Client factors[b]	6.6
Treatment center (after controlling for client factors)	1.9

[a] Sum of squares due to a factor as a percentage of total sum of squares for remission in a one-way analysis of covariance (8 treatment centers).
[b] Definite alcoholism symptoms at intake, stability, socioeconomic status, years of heavy drinking, previous treatment, age, and race used as covariates.

The results for individual treatment centers do not alter our original conclusions that about two-thirds of all clients are in remission, and that behavior patterns involving some drinking are common among these improved clients. While there are some differences among centers, the variations are minor ones that do not change this picture. One reason why we regard these differences as minor is explained in the summary statistics at the bottom of Table 27. When the effects of treatment center classification on remission are considered in an analysis of variance model, only 3.2 percent of the total variance in remission is accounted for by the treatment center. Moreover, even part of this small effect is actually due to the centers having slightly different types of clients entering their programs (e.g., treatment center A has a high proportion of Black clients). Since the center has no control over the type of client in the community, it seems appropriate to control for client background in evaluating the differences among centers. When this is done (as shown in the summary of Table 27), the apparent effect of the treatment center is further reduced and is not even statistically significant at the .05 level. Therefore it seems clear that although there are some notable differences among treatment cnters, the remission chances of a client do not generally depend on the particular center where he receives treatment.

These results are confined to the 18-month followup sample, which has a large number of clients per treatment center. A similar analysis using the 6-month data on all 44 centers is not feasible because of the small number of cases available for any particular center, although the patterns are similar among those centers that do have large samples. However, the breadth of the 6-month sample, covering so many more treatment centers with greater variations in programs than in the 18-month sample, made it possible to carry out a different type of analysis. For each center in the 6-month sample, several attributes of the center were recorded: (1) *client caseload per staff member*, the number of clients treated per full-time equivalent staff member during the third quarter of 1973; (2) *professionalization of staff*, the proportion of staff members who possessed a graduate degree in a treatment-relevant field; and (3) *breadth of treatment program,* a typology representing the configuration of services (hospital, intermediate, outpatient) at the center. These measures were then correlated with the treatment center's remission rate.

These attributes of the treatment center are often thought to be measures of the quality of care or the amount of available resources for treatment. Hence, one would expect at least modest correlations between such measures and the center's overall outcomes. However, the correlations were actually all very near zero (the highest being .02). Again, this suggests that there is no strong relation between the overall characteristics of a treatment center and the remission of the average client. It should be noted that these measures are aggregate figures, i.e., global measures of the center's features; they do not necessarily reflect the program or staff to which a particular client was exposed. Nevertheless, the fact that they are unrelated to overall remission rates reinforces the conclusion that the location or nature of a treatment center, as an aggregate, is not an important determinant of remission.

Finally, some investigators have emphasized the role of differential interview completion rates as a factor affecting differential remission rates in followup studies. That is, clients not in remission may be more difficult to locate or less cooperative, and therefore followup studies with high noncompletion rates may have spuriously high remission rates. Since each ATC conducted its own 18-month followup study, and since followup completion rates varied from one ATC to another, such biases might produce some variation in remission rates, particularly that for center A. Even though the variations in the other centers are minor, a strong association between remission and noncompletion rates could have important implications for our conclusions.

Table 28 shows the rank order of remission rates and noncompletion

Table 28. Remission Rates and Noncompletion Rates for 18-Month ATC Samples

Treatment Center	Percent Remissions	Percent Noncompleted Interviews	Rank Order of Remissions	Rank Order of Noncompletion
B	81	21	1	7
G	79	30	2	6
F	74	32	3	4
D	72	64	4	1
E	70	52	5	3
C	65	56	6	2
H	63	31	7	5
A	49	16	8	8

Rank order correlation $= -0.7$

rates for the 18-month ATC samples. While center A has the lowest remission rate and the lowest noncompletion rate, centers B and G have the second and third lowest noncompletion rates but the first and second highest remission rates. Overall, the rank order correlation is nearly zero. Therefore, differential followup completion rates are not an explanation of the relatively small amount of variation in remission rates among ATCs.

THE SETTING OF TREATMENT

Given that treatment administered in sufficient amounts seems to make a significant impact—a 20 to 30 percent increase in remission rates compared with nontreatment—it is natural to inquire about the possible effects of different types of treatment. At NIAAA treatment centers, these types cover a wide variety of treatment services, ranging from informal peer counseling to emergency medical care. The very number of treatment modalities complicates the task of defining clear categories of treatment that can be measured across all clients and all centers. In this section we describe the broad categories that have been developed and present the basic outcomes for each category.

Treatment Setting Categories

A distinctive feature of the NIAAA treatment centers is their comprehensive array of treatment settings and therapies. A typical center offers treatments in all three major settings: hospital, intermediate, and outpatient. This feature allows the center to follow up an emergency detoxification treatment, for example, with an extended term of halfway-house care or outpatient therapy sessions. At the same time, the availability of different treatments in the same location is intended to enable the center to better match the type of treatment to the client's needs. The type and amount of such treatments given to each client are recorded in the regular monthly reports filed by the treatment center as part of the Monitoring System. Our data on treatments are drawn from these reports.

The particular types of treatment recorded in the Monitoring System fall into 10 major categories, which may be grouped according to the setting in which treatment is given, as follows:

Hospital Setting:
Inpatient hospital, traditional 24-hour/day service, based on a medical model but often including psychotherapy as well.

Partial hospitalization, day care in a hospital setting (not 24 hour/day), allowing the patient to go home or to work at appropriate times.

Detoxification, a short "drying out" period for patients with serious toxic symptoms (e.g., delirium tremens), usually custodial in nature but occasionally including emergency medical measures.

Intermediate Setting:
Halfway house, a total-milieu facility providing living quarters and ancillary services (job counseling, psychotherapy, etc.) for patients in need of extended care but not requiring hospital treatment.

Quarterway house, a facility similar to a halfway house, but offering more intensive, often physical, care under more structured conditions.

Residential care, a facility providing living quarters but little or no other therapy.

Outpatient Setting:
Individual counseling, treatment sessions given by a paraprofessional (i.e., someone without a graduate degree in psychology, medicine, social work, or a similar relevant field).

Individual therapy, treatment sessions given by a professional (someone who holds a relevant graduate degree).

Group counseling, group sessions given by a paraprofessional.

Group therapy, group sessions given by a professional.

Ideally, a treatment evaluation would examine each of these individual treatments. However, the very nature of the comprehensive treatment center, which encourages multiple treatments for each client, makes such an analysis impossible. Most clients have received not one but a combination of treatments. Furthermore, the number of unique combinations is very large, and the number of clients in each combination is very small. For some outpatient treatments, where a sensible analysis of specific treatments can be made, detailed comparisons will be presented later. But for an overall comparison of treatments, a broader classification of treatment types is required. Therefore we have grouped clients according to the combinations of treatment settings they have experienced.

Given the three settings of treatment (hospital, intermediate, and outpatient), one can form seven possible combinations. These combinations will be grouped into five broad categories that together provide a complete, nonoverlapping classification of clients, as shown in Table 29. In this classification, the combination of intermediate care with hospital care is treated as if it involved intermediate care only. On the average, the term of hospital care is quite short, whereas intermediate care extends over a much longer period. It would be expected then, that when a client received both types of care, the bulk of it in both duration and effect would be intermediate care. In fact, analysis showed that clients who received both types of treatment were very similar in background and in outcome to those who received intermediate care only. Thus these categories may be combined safely without fear of concealing important distinctions between them. Moreover, combining them in this way increases the sample sizes, makes inferences more sound, and reduces the complexity of analysis.

Obviously, these treatment categories are only an approximation of the actual differences among differing approaches to alcoholism treatment. Obviously, these categories neglect many important factors: the psychological or medical orientation of the therapist, the underlying philosophy of treatment, the actual procedures followed, the actual experiences of the client, and much more. Despite their broad nature, however, they represent the major differences among treatment modalities that are available in the ATC programs. It seems likely that if great differences in success do

Table 29.   Client Treatments Classified by Treatment Setting

Treatment Setting Category Code	Treatments Received by Client	Duration of Treatment in Months[a]	(N)
H	Hospital care alone	1	(141)
I	Intermediate care alone or		
	Intermediate care and hospital care	8	(265)
O	Outpatient care alone	7	(820)
HO	Hospital care and outpatient care	7	(661)
IO	Intermediate care and outpatient care or		
	Intermediate, outpatient, and hospital care	8	(448)

[a] Months between intake and last treatment (median), all 44 ATCs.

exist between treatments those variances ought to appear between such grossly disparate categories as hospital and outpatient treatment. It must be remembered that these treatment centers are striving to offer a wide variety of treatment settings precisely because it is assumed that different types of clients require different treatments for successful recovery. Given the potentially large cost differences among these settings, it is worth investigating whether this rationale appears to be supported by the data on the clients' outcomes.

Outcomes of Treatment Settings

The results of treatment within each of the five treatment settings are shown in Table 30. While there are some minor variations among the settings, the major implication of this table is that clients in all settings experienced high remission rates. Despite the gross differences in the nature of treatment involved, no treatment varies from the overall remission rate by more than 11 percent. This stability is even more striking when one reflects that it is replicated in both sets of data based on quite different sampling and measurement procedures and conducted at different followup points.

Furthermore, the nature of drinking behavior (long-term abstention, 1-month abstention, or normal drinking) also appears relatively invariant

Table 30.   Remission Rates of Clients in Five Treatment Settings

	Treatment Setting					
Remission Status	H	I	O	HO	IO	All Settings
6-Month Followup						
Percent remissions	70	78	70	62	67	68
Abstained 6 months	*14*	*19*	*21*	*14*	*17*	*18*
Abstained 1 month	*48*	*49*	*34*	*36*	*40*	*38*
Normal drinking	*8*	*10*	*15*	*12*	*10*	*12*
Percent nonremissions	30	22	30	38	33	32
Daily consumption (oz)	2.9	1.9	1.5	2.6	2.4	2.1
(N)	(133)	(251)	(797)	(627)	(426)	(2234)
18-Month Followup						
Percent remissions	78	56	69	74	61	67
Abstained 6 months	*29*	*15*	*26*	*26*	*25*	*24*
Abstained 1 month	*25*	*30*	*15*	*25*	*16*	*21*
Normal drinking	*24*	*12*	*29*	*23*	*20*	*22*
Percent nonremissions	22	44	31	26	39	33
Daily consumption (oz)	1.6	4.1	1.8	2.0	2.8	2.5
(N)	(59)	(108)	(157)	(126)	(134)	(584)

across treatment settings. While there is a shift toward normal drinking between the 6-month followup and the 18-month followup, this shift occurs in all settings. No single treatment appears to produce a disproportionate number of abstainers or normal drinkers. It is also notable that if long-term abstention were used as a criterion of remission, no treatment setting could be considered much better than another, although only about one-fourth of these clients could be considered in remission by that definition.

The largest difference among treatment settings concerns the comparison between intermediate care and other settings. The differences, however, work in opposite directions: at the 6-month followup, intermediate-care clients show higher remission rates than others, but at the 18-month follow-up they show lower rates. This inconsistency between the 6- and 18-month followups suggests caution in interpreting the intermediate-care effects, but there are several other caveats that should be expressed. First, the disadvantage for the intermediate-care group at 18 months is reduced and becomes statistically insignificant when controls for client background and initial drinking are instituted, as will be shown shortly. This is due mainly to the fact that hafway houses tend to receive clients with special disabilities (such as marital instability or joblessness); for proper interpretation of the *treatment effects*, these special attributes of the intermediate client must be taken into account.

We are more inclined to accept at face value the favorable results for intermediate clients at the 6-month point. The apparent short-term advantage for intermediate care remains statistically significant (though modest in size) when controls are instituted, and it is based on a wide variety of intermediate-care facilities among the large group of 44 ATCs in the 6-month followup. However, it must be remembered that most intermediate clients were still in contact with the halfway house more than 6 months after intake. Even though the totality of the treatment data we have indicates that few of them were actually living in a halfway house at the followup point, many of them had certainly been under the influence of the facility in the very recent past. Because intermediate treatment represents such a global intervention into the client's life patterns, it seems likely that its effects might persist, at least over the short term, for a longer period of time than the effect of other treatment settings. Thus, while the 6-month results show a more favorable outcome for intermediate clients than for others, this should not be viewed as a lasting effect. On the contrary, the effect disappears over the longer term; and the short-term effect may be plausibly ascribed to the very recency and intensity of intermediate care to which these clients were exposed.

Despite these minor differences, then, the overall impression is one of uniformly high remission rates in all treatment settings. This impression is strengthened by examining the changes in daily consumption rates by treatment setting, as shown in Figure 3. The figure shows there was a major difference in drinking between clients who began treatment as inpatients and those who began as outpatients: the outpatients were drinking much less, about 5 ounces/day compared with between 8 and 10 ounces/day for inpatients. However, as indicated by the convergence of the lines approaching the followup point, clients in all five settings tended to complete treatment drinking at much lower levels, about 2 ounces/day. Thus with daily consumption, as with the remission criterion, the dominant pattern appears to be a uniform outcome—dramatic reductions in heavy drinking—despite initial differences among treatments.

The convergence pattern illustrated in Figure 3 is representative of similar patterns that appear throughout the data from both followup studies. For example, all treatment centers also show a strongly similar pattern: different groups may begin with somewhat different (but all high) consumption levels, but the groups tend to converge over the treatment period to relatively low levels of drinking and impairment. Obviously, those groups that begin with somewhat lower levels usually show slightly better outcomes, but not necessarily better rates of improvement. Though the analyses are not presented here, this pattern holds up whether the criterion used is remission, amount of drinking, amount of impairment, frequency of

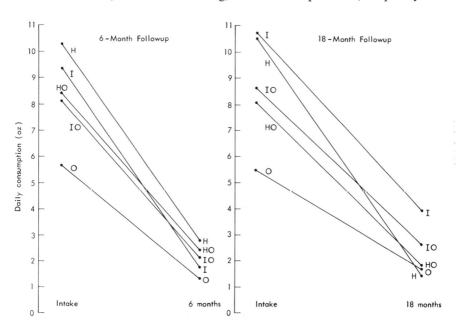

Figure 3   Changes in daily consumption.

drinking, abstention, or some combination of these. The pattern also holds whether the groups considered are types of clients, initial drinking behavior of clients, or location of treatment centers. It seems safe to say that this pattern of uniform improvement, regardless of treatment setting, is the dominant pattern among these clients.

CLIENT-TREATMENT INTERACTIONS

The convergence of both followup studies strongly suggests that no single treatment setting has more long-term effectiveness than others "across the board," for all clients in our sample. Before accepting this conclusion, however, it is necessary to take into account the effects of the client's background, including drinking history, drinking at admission to treatment, and social background. Chapter 4 explained that these background factors can have a substantial impact on the client's prognosis. In this section, we consider these "client factors"—especially the attributes that the client brings with him to treatment—in combination with the treatment setting.

The major focus of interest here is the issue of client-treatment inter-actions: the question of whether there are certain treatments that are uniquely successful with certain types of clients because the treatment is "matched" to the needs of the client. As noted before, one rationale for establishing these comprehensive treatment centers was the thesis that different clients require different styles of treatment. By examining the remission rates of many different client-treatment combinations, we should be able to estimate the benefits that may be expected from such efforts to match clients to appropriate treatments. We should also be able to deal with a second problem: the possibility that treatments may be confounded with client characteristics. If a treatment tends to receive a disproportionate number of clients with unusually good (or poor) prognoses, the outcome might appear different from other outcomes due to client characteristics, rather than because of the treatment itself. By comparing the effects of treatments within the same type of client, we will be better able to sort out client effects from treatment effects and thus to handle this methodological problem.

Types of Clients in Treatment Settings

The importance of both problems cited above is emphasized by the differ-ences in client populations among treatment settings. In Table 31 the composition of each treatment setting is tabulated according to the three most important client characteristics that we have found: definite alcohol-

Table 31. Client Background Differences Among Treatment Settings[a]

Background Characteristics	Treatment Setting				
	H	I	O	HO	IO
	Percentage with Each Characteristic				
Definitely alcoholic at intake	83	78	56	83	77
Unstable at intake	15	71	30	41	44
Low socioeconomic status at intake	27	54	42	38	55
(N)	(60)	(108)	(158)	(127)	(134)

[a] For 18-month followup sample; 6-month sample patterns (not shown) are very similar.

ism at intake, social stability, and socioeconomic status. Two sorts of differences, both probably linked to attempts to match the client to a proper treatment setting, may be seen. First, the type of client who begins treatment in an outpatient setting (the outpatient-only category) is clearly less likely to show definite alcoholism symptoms at intake. Only a little over half of outpatient clients are definitely alcoholic at this point, whereas over three-fourths of the inpatient clients show such symptoms.

Naturally, this suggests that a proper comparison of outpatient with inpatient settings ought to consider this initial difference by controlling for alcoholism symptoms. Further, it raises the important issue of possible interactions. Clients with definite and severe symptoms are much more likely to go into inpatient treatment initially than to go directly into outpatient care; this probably reflects an assumption that inpatient care is better suited to handle the problems of the severely impaired person. Yet there is also a large group of severely impaired persons in the outpatient-only treatment. If the assumption is correct, won't these outpatient clients have poorer prospects for remission than those who began with inpatient treatment? In a moment we will turn to this question, which can be answered by comparing treatment setting outcomes within groups matched for severity of alcoholic symptoms.

The second type of difference shown in Table 31 is that of social background (social stability and socioeconomic status). It appears that the intermediate-care setting receives a disproportionate share of clients of low socioeconomic status (SES) having unstable social characteristics (e.g., unstable marriage, employment, and living conditions). There is also a tendency for the hospital-only category to receive few of these disadvantaged clients. This could indicate a pattern in which relatively advantaged clients, since they have better initial prognosis, successfully complete hospital treatment and therefore discontinue contact with the treatment center.

These patterns reflect policies that attempt to match the client's social characteristics to an appropriate treatment. For example, the medical treatment (hospital) environment is sometimes advocated as properly suited for relatively advantaged persons who will accept treatment more readily if it is presented as a medical response to a disease. Intermediate care is explicitly designed to aid the unstable individual by providing a surrogate familylike environment and peer support that are not available in an outpatient clinic. Outpatient care, on the other hand, is often considered most appropriate when the client already has an intact family and a steady job to provide stability. All of these relationships between social background and the client's assignment to a treatment suggest that the remission rates ought to be higher when the proper match has been made than when a "mismatch" occurs (e.g., an unstable client in an outpatient treatment).

Interactions Involving Definite Alcoholism Symptoms

The remission rates of clients at 6- and 18-month followups, classified by treatment setting and by severity of alcoholism symptoms, are shown in Table 32. The information in Table 32 is somewhat different, in both substance and analytic method from that in previous analyses. The percentages shown here are not statistics from actual tabulations, but are rather estimates derived from an analysis of covariance model. Loosely, the percentages are those that would be expected if all 10 groups in the

Table 32. Remission Rates of Clients by Presence of Definite Alcoholic Symptoms at Intake[a] Classified by Treatment Setting

	Remission Rates (%)					
	Treatment Setting					All
Alcoholic Symptoms	H	I	O	HO	IO	Settings
6-Month Followup						
Definite alcoholism at intake	63	76	63	58	65	63
(N)	(117)	(178)	(471)	(495)	(320)	(1581)
Less definite alcoholism at intake	78	94	78	74	83	80
(N)	(16)	(71)	(316)	(128)	(105)	(636)
18-Month Followup						
Definite alcoholism at intake	69	57	61	72	61	64
(N)	(49)	(84)	(85)	(104)	(103)	(425)
Less definite alcoholism at intake	91	80	81	81	74	80
(N)	(10)	(24)	(68)	(22)	(30)	(154)

[a] Adjusted for years of heavy drinking, previous treatment, social stability, socioeconomic status, age, and race.

sample were matched at the same level on the covariates, the variables that have been statistically controlled. In this case, the controlled covariates are years of heavy drinking, social stability, previous treatment, socio-economic status, race, and age. Although it would be desirable to control for these covariates by direct partitioning of the sample, this is not possible because such a procedure would quickly exhaust the size of the cells. Instead, the covariates are used to make a linear adjustment in the percentages. In examining these adjusted tables, one can imagine that all the groups have started with the same client characteristics, i.e., with the same years of heavy drinking, social stability, socioeconomic status, and so forth.[1]

If any particular treatment were especially suited to either the definite alcoholic or to the client with less definite and severe symptoms, that treatment ought to show substantially higher remission rates for the appropriate client type. Such is not the case. Although some differences among treatments can be found, in no case is any treatment better than the general average by as much as 15 percent. In fact, neither treatment differences nor client-treatment interactions are statistically significant, despite the rather large samples involved—except, as noted earlier, for the difference between the intermediate setting and others at 6 months.

In the 18-month data, the only remarkable difference is between hospital-only and other treatments (for less-definite alcoholics), but this rests on only 10 cases—certainly an insufficient number to support any conclusion about differences. In the 6-month data, intermediate care seems to produce a moderately higher remission rate—about 14 percentage points above the average in each group. This is not, of course, an interaction, since it favors the same treatment in both client groups; and the apparent superiority of intermediate care at 6 months is not borne out by the 18-month followup results. As noted before, the inconsistency between the two followup points makes us reluctant to draw any strong conclusions about differential long-term effects of intermediate care.

Instead of showing dramatic interactions between a preferred treatment and a certain type of client, these results suggest the opposite: uniform effects of treatment across all settings. The treatment differences that do exist are not replicated between the 6-month and 18-month outcomes. By contrast, the impact of the client's symptoms at intake is substantial and consistent, *within every treatment setting and across both followup samples.* In every setting, the clients with less severe problems enjoy better remission rates, with the less-severe group averaging about 16 percent higher rates in the 18-month study and 17 percent higher in the 6-month study.

---

[1] In this mode of analysis, references to "statistical significance" mean results of standard F-tests for classifying factors or covariates.

This consistency is remarkable in comparison to the unstable variations among treatments, and even more so if the implications of the interaction hypothesis are considered. If interactions were present, the definite alcoholics should not be uniformly worse than the less-definite alcoholics in every treatment. On the contrary, the differences between client types should be small when definite alcoholics are "matched" to an appropriate treatment (e.g., hospital or intermediate). This is so because the definite alcoholics, being "matched," should have better-than-usual remission rates, whereas the less-impaired alcoholics, being "mismatched," should have worse-than-usual rates. A similar argument would predict that the difference between client types should be great for outpatient care, since then the definite alcoholics are mismatched (hence lower rates) and the less-definite alcoholics are matched (hence higher rates). Actually, the differences between the two client groups are nearly constant in every treatment category, ranging between 13 and 23 percent in every comparison but one. Thus, we find little evidence to support the claim that clients with more severe symptoms require any special treatment setting.

Interactions Involving Social Background

The arguments suggesting an interaction between treatment and social background differ, of course, from those relating to severity of alcoholism symptoms. However, as shown in Table 33, these arguments also find little confirmation in our data. For presentation purposes, we have grouped clients according to three categories: unstable, low SES (the least advantaged); unstable but high SES or stable but low SES; and stable, high SES (the most advantaged). As shown in Table 32, the treatment differences are not large, with the remission rate for any treatment never varying from the norm by more than 16 percent. Moreover, there seems to be no interpretable pattern to the differences that do exist, considering that the treatment differences are not similar across the two studies. Again, no client-treatment interactions are statistically significant.

The one systematic feature of this table is the definite advantage conferred by high socioeconomic status and social stability. The high SES, stable client shows a higher remission rate in every treatment (except the IO pattern at 6 months, where the difference is zero). The positive prognosis linked to stability and status also seems greater at 18 months than at 6 months. This again suggests that some important effects might be obscured in the 6-month data because many clients are still in contact with the center, though our analyses do not furnish any definite support for this conjecture.

Of special interest in this analysis is the comparison between interme-

Table 33.   **Remission Rates of Clients with Different Social Backgrounds[a] Classified by Treatment Setting**

	Remission Rates (%)					
	Treatment Setting					All
Social Background	H	I	O	HO	IO	Settings
6-Month Followup						
Unstable, low SES	48	79	58	51	69	63
(N)	(11)	(101)	(129)	(153)	(133)	(527)
Unstable, high SES;						
or stable, low SES	54	72	62	60	67	63
(N)	(37)	(96)	(281)	(221)	(159)	(794)
Stable, high SES	82	90	76	71	69	75
(N)	(83)	(41)	(342)	(234)	(121)	(821)
18-Month Followup						
Unstable, low SES	(b)	50	54	65	57	55
(N)	(5)	(40)	(30)	(31)	(34)	(140)
Unstable, high SES;						
or stable, low SES	74	53	58	74	61	62
(N)	(15)	(46)	(52)	(37)	(61)	(211)
Stable, high SES	86	86	77	79	69	78
(N)	(38)	(17)	(74)	(57)	(36)	(222)

[a] Adjusted for intake alcoholism symptoms, years of heavy drinking, previous treatment, age, and race.
[b] Too few cases.

diate care and outpatient care. The intermediate environment seeks to provide social support and positive surroundings that might counteract the negative influences in the outside world that originally led to the client's heavy drinking; thus it ought to prove better for the disadvantaged clients than for the relatively stable and privileged. In the 6-month data, intermediate treatment has the best record for unstable low-SES clients, but it also appears to work best for stable high-SES clients—not an interaction pattern. In the 18-month data, on the other hand, intermediate-care clients have worse records than others, except among the stable high-SES group, where intermediate care, contrary to predictions, is tied for first place among treatments. Outpatient care also shows no special relationship to type of client. Again contrary to predictions, outpatient care does not appear to work best for relatively advantaged clients, nor is it notably inferior for the disadvantaged.

The evidence thus far provides virtually no support for the interaction hypotheses. Before finally abandoning the interaction notion, one other test may be considered: the possibility of three-way interactions involving social background, definite alcoholism at intake, and treatment. It might be argued, for example, that special interaction effects or even main effects should be expected only for those who are "truly" alcoholic; according to this argument, the less-definite alcoholics might be obscuring positive effects by their presence. To assess the validity of this argument, we have examined treatment and social background interactions separately for both definite and less-definite alcoholics. The results of this analysis are shown in Table 34, which presents remission rates for definite alcoholics, classified by treatment setting and social background.[2]

If there is anything special about having severe and definite symptoms that might lead to a special need for client-treatment matching, the interactions should appear among the clients tabulated here. Again, however, there are no substantial, interpretable interactions, and none is statistically significant. In fact, the patterns for definite alcoholics are almost identical with those for the entire group. If Table 34 is compared with Table 32, it is obvious that in each cell the definite alcoholics are less likely to be in

Table 34. Remission Rates Among Definite Alcoholics with Different Social Backgrounds[a] Classified by Treatment Setting

	Remission Rates (%)					
	Treatment Setting					All
Social Background	H	I	O	HO	IO	Settings
6-Month Followup						
Unstable, low SES	46	73	55	46	63	57
(N)	(11)	(66)	(100)	(124)	(101)	(402)
Unstable, high SES;						
or stable, low SES	48	68	59	61	62	61
(N)	(29)	(71)	(176)	(172)	(115)	(563)
Stable, high SES	78	87	73	66	66	71
(N)	(75)	(31)	(161)	(182)	(93)	(542)
18-Month Followup						
Unstable, low SES	(b)	44	53	60	54	52
(N)	(5)	(32)	(21)	(25)	(29)	(112)
Unstable, high SES;						
or stable, low SES	70	50	53	69	58	59
(N)	(14)	(36)	(31)	(33)	(45)	(159)
Stable, high SES	83	85	70	80	63	76
(N)	(29)	(13)	(33)	(46)	(27)	(148)

[a] Adjusted for years of heavy drinking, previous treatment, age, and race.
[b] Too few cases.

[2] The similar table for less-definite alcoholics is not shown, because the number of cases in many cells is too small to permit any inferences.

remission, at an almost constant rate—about 3 to 6 percent. Thus the major conclusion to be drawn from Table 34 is that the treatment and client-background patterns for definite alcoholics are the same as those for all clients, except that the remission rates are uniformly lower.

Table 34 reconfirms the importance of social background factors, as noted in the previous analyses. Among definite alcoholics, as shown by the "all settings" marginals, the stable high-SES client has a definite advantage over the unstable or low-SES client. In the 6-month followup, the advantage constitutes a remission rate that is higher by 14 percent; in the 18-month followup, the advantage jumps to 24 percent. This is reflected in the high rates evident in three settings across the bottom row (stable high-SES clients at 18 months). As in previous tables, these differences for social stability and socioeconomic status are statistically significant (at the .001 level), as are the differences produced by the adjustments for other background factors. On the other hand, the 18-month treatment-setting differences do not reach a level that is statistically significant; nor, in our view, are the treatment differences of great substantive importance.

AMOUNT AND DURATION OF TREATMENT

It is frequently asserted that patients often discontinue treatment before it has had time to take effect. There is, therefore, a tendency to feel that the longer treatment progresses, the greater the chance for the client to cross the threshold of minimum care, and the greater are his/her chances for recovery. If so, then perhaps the amount of treatment might make a positive difference in outcome, even though the specific treatment does not. We have already seen that high amounts of treatment, considered overall without respect to setting, make an important difference in remission rates. Whether there might be another type of interaction here, one between treatment setting and amount of treatment, is still an open question. It might be, for example, that certain types of treatment, such as extended outpatient followup care after intensive hospital or halfway-house care, would show positive effects for additional treatment, whereas increasing amounts of hospital treatment alone might not show any improvement.

A second question involved in the concept of amount of treatment concerns the way in which a given amount of treatment is administered over time. A total of 15 outpatient visits, for example, might be concentrated in 5 weeks or spread out erratically over 10 months. Is it important to separate sheer *amount* of treatment (total number of inpatient days or outpatient visits) from *duration* of treatment? This question will be examined here.

Interactions Involving Different Amounts of Treatment

The remission rates for clients receiving low and high amounts of treatment are shown in Table 35, classified by treatment setting. Looking at the marginal for "all settings" first, we see that in both the 6- and 18-month followup studies there is a modest effect for increasing amounts of treatment. The difference between high and low amounts is somewhat greater in the 18-month followup, about 15 percentage points compared with only 9 points in the 6-month followup. These differences, however, are not constant across treatment settings. At 6 months, only the hospital, hospital-outpatient, and outpatient settings show even a modest effect for higher amounts of treatment; the intermediate settings show near-zero effects. By 18 months, in contrast, large interactions occur; for those in all three settings of outpatient care, there appears to be a substantial difference (17 to 31 percent) between low and high amounts of treatment. At the same time, clients who received only hospital care or only intermediate care (without any followup outpatient care) show near-zero or even negative effects for increasing amounts. Thus the general pattern that emerges is one of small differences at 6 months becoming large differences at 18 months, when clients receive continuing outpatient care.

Table 35. Remission Rates of Clients Receiving High and Low Amounts of Treatment[a] Classified by Treatment Setting

| | Remission Rates (%) | | | | | |
| | Treatment Setting | | | | | All |
Amount of Treatment	H	I	O	HO	IO	Settings
6-Month Followup						
Low amount of treatment[b]	61	80	62	53	71	62
(N)	(27)	(21)	(229)	(63)	(39)	(379)
High amount of treatment	68	82	69	66	70	71
(N)	(106)	(230)	(568)	(186)	(185)	(1275)
18-Month Followup						
Low amount of treatment	79	61	54	66	50	58
(N)	(14)	(47)	(56)	(26)	(41)	(184)
High amount of treatment	71	62	71	94	81	73
(N)	(45)	(61)	(101)	(24)	(41)	(272)

[a] Adjusted for intake alcoholism symptoms, years of heavy drinking, previous treatment, social stability, socioeconomic status, age, and race.
[b] Low amount of treatment is defined as 1 week or less of hospital care, 3 weeks or less of intermediate care, or 5 visits or less of outpatient care. For inpatient-outpatient combinations, a client must be below the limits on both types to qualify as "low." High amount of treatment is similarly defined as amounts above the limits.

The small difference for intermediate care and the negative differences for hospital-only care are somewhat surprising. One explanation could be that in these settings high amounts of treatment represent a more severe or intractable case of alcoholism, so that the client remains in inpatient treatment for a long period. We doubt that this can be a complete explanation, since these results have already been adjusted for several measures of the client's intake symptoms and drinking history, but it is possible that the covariance adjustments have not fully removed all the influence of the client's initial condition. If so, this would not invalidate the hypothesis that greater amounts of treatment have positive effects for the outpatient settings. It would, however, suggest that simply giving greater amounts of inpatient treatment is not likely to promote much higher remission rates.

Duration and Patterns of Treatment

It is easy to be misled by discussions of "amount" of treatment. One might assume that the total amount of treatment a client receives is concentrated over a short period of time in more or less continuous days of inpatient treatment or outpatient visits. Actually, most clients do not receive a "concentrated dose" of any treatment in such a regular fashion. This point is immediately clear if one compares the amount of treatment typically received in a setting with the duration of treatment, as shown in Table 36. In the outpatient-only setting, for example, a typical client would make approximately 9 or 10 outpatient visits to the treatment center, but the typical client makes these visits over a period of 6 months or more (180 days or more between intake and last recorded treatment). Thus, far

Table 36. Amount and Duration of Treatment Classified by Treatment Setting

Inpatient-Outpatient Days or Visits	Treatment Setting				
	H	I	O	HO	IO
6-Month Followup					
Inpatient days (median)	14	146	—	11	41
Outpatient visits (median)	—	—	10	5	6
Duration of contact (median days)[a]	31	243	215	212	244
(N)	(141)	(265)	(820)	(661)	(448)
18-Month Followup					
Inpatient days (median)	12	28	—	8	23
Outpatient visits (median)	—	—	9	3	23
Duration of contact (median) days	30	91	183	193	334
(N)	(60)	(108)	(159)	(127)	(134)

[a] Number of days between intake and last treatment.

from receiving some outpatient therapy once per week or on a regular schedule, it appears that most clients receive sporadic treatment spaced out over a long period. The same comments apply to other treatment settings. The intermediate and combination settings, for example, have a typical treatment period of 3 to 11 months; only the hospital setting has a typically short period (about 1 month).

Thus it seems that most clients go in and out of treatment and do not stay in a regular program for a definite time. This conclusion is confirmed by the pattern of actual month-by-month treatment records, as presented in Table 37. This analysis is derived from the records of each client's treatment, which are represented by a series of "checks" indicating whether or not a client received any treatment at all during each monthly reporting period. We have examined the sequence of checks from the first month after intake (month 1 in the table) through the sixth month after intake. Each client shows a pattern of treatment represented by a sequence of checks (indicating treatment during the month) or "gaps" (indicating no treatment during the month).

As can be seen from Table 37, most clients experience an "erratic"

Table 37.   Typical Patterns of Treatment

	Typical Monthly Sequences[a]						Percent in Sample[b]	
Patterns of Treatment	1	2	3	4	5	6	6-Month Followup	18-Month Followup
Short-Term Treatment	X						24	27
(during first 2 months only)	X	X						
Continuous Treatment	X	X	X				15	22
(during consecutive months	X	X	X	X				
for at least 3 months)								
Erratic Treatment	X		X				40	32
over at least a 3-month	X		X	X				
period, but with a gap of	X		X		X	X		
1 month without treatment)								
Very Erratic Treatment	X			X			21	19
(over at least a 3-month	X				X			
period, but with a gap of 2								
months without treatment)								
(N)							(8795)	(610)

[a] X indicates that some treatment was received during the month (one or more inpatient days or outpatient visits); absence of an X indicates that no treatment was received that month.
[b] Based on all male non-DWI intakes.

pattern of treatment—one that contains gaps of 1 month or more during which no treatment was given, followed by the client's reentry into treatment in later months. Indeed, about 20 percent of each followup sample left treatment for 2 months or longer and later returned. On the other hand, fewer than a quarter of these clients continued in treatment for as long as 3 consecutive months in what we have called a "continuous" pattern. It should also be remembered that this is a very weak test for continuous treatment; a client could come to the center only once each month for a 1-hour visit and be represented here as in "continuous treatment." Therefore, the patterns shown here are probably an overestimate of the number of clients who actually maintain regular weekly contact with a treatment center. Clearly, most clients do not receive a well-defined program of regular, continuing therapy. Rather, it appears that many come and go to the treatment center as external circumstances allow.

One other point should be emphasized. It is often asserted that the problem of "dropping out," or rejection of treatment is a serious one in treating alcoholic clients. From this point of view, a client who finds treatment unpleasant or burdensome is likely to sever contact with a treatment center quickly, thereby losing the benefits that might accrue if he were to continue in treatment. According to the data in Table 37, this pattern does not characterize a great number of clients at these treatment centers. The "short-term" pattern, including clients who make their last contact within the first 2 months after intake, applies to only about one-fourth of the clients in each followup sample. It seems that the "dropout" problem is not as prevalent as the problem of erratic clients who come and go in the treatment centers. Moreover, there are few differences in social background or drinking behavior among the clients who manifest these various patterns. The short-term group is not more likely to be definitely alcoholic, or unstable, or of low socioeconomic status, or to belong to a minority group, or to be otherwise different on any of the intake measures used in this report.

Effects of Duration and Amount of Treatment

Because of the wide variation in treatment patterns, it is clear that a high amount of treatment does not necessarily mean that the treatment was received over any given period of time. In fact, high amounts are often given within 2 or 3 months, whereas low amounts may be widely spaced over a period of a year or more. In short, duration of treatment is not the same as amount of treatment.

There is interest, of course, in evaluating the relative impact of amount and duration. It could be that an "intensive" treatment regimen (high amounts over a short time) is optimal, or it might happen that duration but not amount is the real causal factor, so that even low amounts over a long time produce the highest remission rates. To separate the effects of amount and duration, we have classified clients according to their duration in treatment (relative to the typical duration in their setting) as well as according to amount. The results are shown in Table 38, which distinguishes four types, based on both variables.

Descriptive names have been given to each type to convey the treatment pattern represented. The client who receives little treatment and ceases contact within a short time we have labeled a "dropout," although theoretically he could have successfully completed treatment. The client who remains in contact longer but still receives a low total amount of treatment, we have designated as "periodic," reflecting a very erratic treatment pattern with long gaps—a logical consequence if a client makes, for example, only five outpatient visits over 6 months. Both of these groups have relatively low remission rates, about 60 percent. Thus, long duration does not appear to make much difference in remission, when the total amount of treatment is low.

The third type we have called "intensive," since it reflects a high amount of treatment received within 2 months or less. The fourth type, whom we have labeled "extensive," receives a high amount of treatment administered

Table 38.   Effects of Amount and Duration of Treatment[a] on Client Remission Rates at 18-Month Followup

Typology	Amount and Duration of Treatment	Remission Rates (%)	(N)
1. Dropout	Low amount[b] Short duration[c]	60	(125)
2. Periodic	Low amount Long duration	58	(58)
3. Intensive	High amount Short duration	71	(104)
4. Extensive	High amount Long duration	74	(168)
All treated clients		67	(596)

[a] Adjusted for intake alcoholism symptoms, years of heavy drinking, previous treatment, social stability, socioeconomic status, age, and race.
[b] Low and high amounts are as defined in Table 35.
[c] Short duration is contact with treatment center for 30 days or less in hospital settings, 60 days or less in intermediate settings, or 180 days or less in outpatient or combined inpatient-outpatient settings.

over a longer period, tending to be regular but at a lower level of intensity. Both of these types show higher remission rates than the types with low amounts of treatment, with little apparent effect for the duration of treatment.

The general conclusion is clear: It is the total amount and not the duration of treatment that has an impact on the client's remission. It does not matter whether the treatment comes in a short burst or is extended over a longer time. This conclusion is also unaffected by additional controls for treatment setting or client background factors. To test for statistical significance of all of these factors simultaneously, we have replicated the analysis shown in Table 35 (amount of treatment classified by treatment setting), including duration of treatment as an additional adjusting factor. The adjusted percentages are virtually identical with those shown in Table 35, and neither the treatment-setting differences nor the adjustment produced by duration of treatment are significant. Amount of treatment, however, remains statistically significant and substantial in magnitude.

SPECIFIC THERAPIES

The results so far show no strong and consistent differences between the broad treatment categories (hospital, intermediate, outpatient). However, it is still possible that the specific kinds of therapy given within a treatment setting (e.g., group therapy as opposed to individual therapy in an outpatient setting), have differential effects upon clients' remission rates. There are two particular areas in which the kind of therapy appears especially important. The first is within the outpatient setting. From a therapeutic point of view, the hospital or intermediate setting may be regarded as an overall milieu; typically, the treatment is not so much a sequence or configuration of specific modalities as a comprehensive pattern of intensive care where the individual elements are of less importance. In outpatient treatment, on the other hand, the specific kind of therapy is of great importance and often represents the only intervention by the center in the client's life. Thus, there is intrinsic interest in comparisons among outpatient treatment modalities, which will be presented below.

The second area of interest is drug therapy. Drug treatments are used across all treatment settings, although they are most frequently found in outpatient treatment. As noted in Chapter 2, there is persistent faith in the efficacy of drug treatments, despite the weak evidence. Within these treatment centers, the most frequently administered drug is Antabuse. In the following discussion, we present an examination of Antabuse effects across treatment settings and client types.

Outpatient Therapies

A great variety of therapies may be encountered in the outpatient setting. With the data we have available, we cannot hope to examine the myriad forms of counseling, insight therapy, conditioning techniques, encounter-group therapy, or other approaches that abound in practice. Instead, we shall abstract those characteristics of therapies that seem to be measured reliably and that actually occur in sufficient numbers to support an analysis. Two distinctions can be made in these data, both of which meet these criteria: a distinction between professional therapy versus paraprofessional counseling, and a distinction between individual-session versus group-session treatment.

When a client receives outpatient care at an NIAAA treatment center, the treatment is recorded as "professional therapy" (treatment given by a person with a graduate degree in a relevant field) or "paraprofessional counseling" (treatment by a person without such a degree). The treatment is also classified as taking place in individual or group sessions. In practice, most clients receive several sessions of individual counseling, and a substantial minority receive individual therapy, group counseling, or group therapy (almost always in addition to some individual counseling). There are very few clients who receive a "pure" regimen of only one type of session, so that simple comparisons between the four types cannot be made. Instead, for analysis purposes, we have (1) a "therapy" group, clients who received most or all of their treatment from professionally trained staff members; and (2) a "counseling" group, clients who received most or all of their treatment from staff members without professional training. In a different partitioning of the same data, an "individual session" group and a "group session" group have also been defined using similar criteria. In this analysis, clients with any hospital or intermediate care are excluded; we are dealing solely with clients who received *outpatient treatment only*.

Remission rates for those clients who could be definitely classified as having a predominance of one type of therapy over another are shown in Table 39. The results must be viewed with some caution, since some of the sample sizes are exceedingly small in the 18-month followup. Overall, we conclude that there are no differences here reliable enough to warrant a serious claim of superiority for any of these therapies over another. None of these differences is statistically significant, and in our view such differences of 10 percent or less, when not even replicated across the two follow-ups, are hardly of any substantive significance. There appears to be a slight, consistent difference favoring professional therapy over counseling, but it is difficult to say much on the basis of the 2 percent difference that appears in the 18-month sample. In the comparisons of group versus

Table 39.   Remission Rates for Clients Receiving Specific Therapies[a]

	Remission Rates (%)	
Followup Period	Paraprofessional Counseling[b]	Professional Therapy
6-month followup	69	76
(N)	(572)	(103)
18-month followup	71	73
(N)	(24)	(89)

	Remission Rates (%)	
Followup Period	Group Sessions	Individual Sessions
6-month followup	80	70
(N)	(49)	(559)
18-month followup	64	73
(N)	(10)	(103)

[a] Adjusted for definite alcoholism at intake, years of heavy drinking, previous treatment, social stability, socioeconomic status, age, and race.
[b] "Counseling" is defined as treatment administered by a person without a graduate degree in a relevant field (medicine, psychology, social work, or similar field). "Therapy" is treatment administered by a person who has such a degree.

individual sessions, the two studies actually show opposite results, but this could be due simply to the sampling error to be expected in a group of only 10 cases, as in the 18-month sample for group sessions. At best, these data provide little evidence for very large differences among these types of outpatient therapy. If differences exist, they are yet to be proven.

There is also little evidence for the existence of presumed client-treatment interactions involving these specific therapies. When the groups shown in Table 39 are broken up according to our major client factors (definite alcoholism, social stability, and socioeconomic status), the patterns are essentially the same regardless of client type. This can be done effectively only with the 6-month sample, since the 18-month sample is far too small to allow further subdivision of categories. Nonetheless, such evidence as we can adduce from the 6-month data provides no support for the notion that any particular client type is best suited to any particular therapy.

We are acutely aware of the very limited nature of the data available here on therapeutic techniques. Obviously, specific information about the nature of the client-therapist relationship is lacking; our therapy categories capture only some aspects (perhaps minor ones at that) relating to the treatment process. It would be desirable to have more information on the nature of the therapy program, about the therapists and counselors, on the length and intensity of the programs involved, and in regard to many other variables not considered here. It would be desirable to have similar information on specific treatment modalities within the intermediate and hospital treatment settings. Furthermore, the definitions that we have adopted in order to obtain sufficient cases certainly do not represent a "pure" regimen of one therapy or another. Because of these qualifications, it must be admitted that this analysis can make only a preliminary statement about effectiveness of various therapies; clearly, more specific data are required. At this point we must conclude that there does not appear to be any evidence here of differential treatment effects or of significant client-treatment interactions.

Antabuse Treatment

The drug disulfiram, or Antabuse, is one of the most widely used of all drugs in the treatment of alcoholism. In the 6-month data on all NIAAA treatment centers, over 30 percent of clients received Antabuse at some time during the treatment period, most frequently in an outpatient setting. As a short-term treatment, there is ample basis for this popularity. The literature reviewed in Chapter 2 suggests that one can expect high rates of abstinence while the client is taking the drug. However, the long-term effects of Antabuse treatment are more doubtful; many practitioners do not even expect long-term effects of Antabuse per se. Frequently, Antabuse is viewed explicitly as a means of keeping the patient "dry" and available for other treatments, which in turn are expected to produce long-term effects. Thus the extent to which Antabuse facilitates the patient's long-term recovery remains an open question.

Our data, encompassing two different time periods after treatment has begun, provide a good opportunity to test the intermediate-term versus the long-term effect of Antabuse. If Antabuse works primarily as a short-term agent but does not by itself bring about long-term results, we might expect to find some moderate effects in favor of Antabuse treatment in the 6-month data but no effects in the 18-month data.

Such a pattern of initial effect declining over time is shown by the data in Table 40, which presents remission rates for clients treated with and without Antabuse. At 6 months, all treatment settings show a positive effect for Antabuse treatment, ranging from 2 percent in intermediate settings to 19 percent in the hospital-outpatient setting. Overall, Antabuse appears to have made a moderate impact, raising remission rates on the average by

Table 40. Remission Rates for Clients Treated With and Without Antabuse,[a] Classified by Treatment Setting

	Remission Rates (%)					
	Treatment Setting					All
Treatment	H	I	O	HO	IO	Settings
6-Month Followup						
Antabuse treatment	73	82	80	75	73	77
(N)	(21)	(92)	(188)	(198)	(188)	(687)
No Antabuse treatment	67	80	63	56	67	64
(N)	(112)	(159)	(609)	(429)	(238)	(1547)
18-Month Followup						
Antabuse treatment	76	68	66	74	62	68
(N)	(30)	(58)	(68)	(57)	(87)	(300)
No Antabuse treatment	69	56	64	74	67	66
(N)	(28)	(50)	(87)	(67)	(47)	(279)

[a] Adjusted for intake alcoholism symptoms, previous treatment, years of heavy drinking, social stability, age, and race.

13 percent. At the 18-month followup, however, Antabuse shows only a 2 percent effect overall, and the very settings that produced a large effect at 6 months show very small effects by 18 months. Whatever effect Antabuse may have created as short-term therapy, its effects have dissipated by 18 months.

These results seem to confirm that Antabuse has a short-term impact in some outpatient settings. The fact that the impact dies out over the long term suggests that the main reason for the effect, like that of intermediate care, may be the recency of the treatment. As time goes by, previous Antabuse treatment should not be expected to exercise a significant impact. This is consistent with the way the drug is actually used, as a supportive agent that prohibits drinking when the patient's behavior cannot be otherwise controlled. In inpatient settings such force is unnecessary, since effectice control is already exercised by the surrounding milieu (e.g., the hospital ward or the house rules and peergroup norms of the halfway house). Therefore, adding Antabuse to the other forces already acting in an inpatient setting may simply be providing additional control where none is needed. In outpatient settings, on the other hand, Antabuse may be crucial because it is the only effective force intervening in the client's motivational system. He probably continues to live in the environment that generated or sustained his alcoholism initially, and he is not likely to receive support or encouragement from that quarter. Antabuse, by operating physiologically and psychologically, does not need to change that environment; it works within the individual to bring about abstention. Of course, it only works as long as it is taken; apparently, the effects of the drug or response to it have little lasting impact.

In examining possible interactions of Antabuse with client factors, we found no significant, consistent effects. There did appear to be a strong interaction between socioeconomic status and Antabuse among outpatient settings in the 6-month results. Surprisingly, this showed that Antabuse had an effect only on clients of low socioeconomic status. Thus it appears that the positive effects shown in Table 40 for the outpatient and hospital only settings are actually present for the less-advantaged clients only. However, this interaction completely washed out in the 18-month analysis, so that we are forced to conclude that whatever short-term interactions may exist, over the long term there is little reason to suppose that Antabuse will be more effective with one type of client than with another. Briefly, the overall findings on Antabuse treatment provide further confirmation of what is by now a familiar theme: large improvements and high remission rates among all types of clients in all treatments, but no special effects due to any particular treatment type.

ASSESSING THE IMPORTANCE OF CLIENT AND TREATMENT FACTORS

All the results thus far seem to point toward a single result: The effects of differences among treatments are small, while the effects of variations in client characteristics are somewhat larger. The preceding analyses are consistent on this point, but do not allow a clear measurement of what is meant by "small" or "large." Nor do they permit us to assess the explanatory power of all the factors we have considered, taken together. One way to obtain an evaluation of the magnitude of these effects is to include all the explanatory factors—both client and treatment characteristics—in a multiple regression model predicting remission. This allows us to measure the importance of each factor by its contribution to the total variance explained by the model.

The results of such a multiple regression model, using a stepwise procedure with a predetermined order of entry for each factor, are shown in Table 41. In this analysis, the factors were entered in the order that we feel best reflects their causal status in affecting remission. Client attributes were entered first because they represent preexisting conditions that antedate treatment. Individual aspects of treatment technique were entered next, to isolate the impact of treatment technique from the impact of the actual

Table 41. Regression Estimates of Effects of Client and Treatment Factors on Remission Rates[a]

Client and Treatment Factors[b]	Increments to Variance Explained (R^2) (%)	
Client drinking[c]		
Definite alcoholism symptoms	2.9	
Alcoholism history[d]	0.3	
Total client drinking		3.2
Client social background		
Social stability	3.2	
Socioeconomic status	1.1	
Other background[e]	1.3	
Total client social background		5.6
Treatment		
Treatment setting	0.9	
Amount of treatment	2.2	
Total treatment		3.1
Treatment center		1.4
Total variance explained		13.3

[a] 18-month followup sample, 600 cases.
[b] Factors with statistically significant incremental effects are as follows: definite alcoholism symptoms ($t = 4.23$, $p < .001$); social stability ($t = 4.46$, $p < .001$); socioeconomic status ($t = 2.62$, $p < .01$); age ($t = 2.11$, $p = .05$); and amount of treatment ($t = 3.87$, $p < .001$). All others are not significant at the .05 level.
[c] At intake.
[d] Years of heavy drinking, previous alcoholism treatment, and previous AA attendance.
[e] Race, age, father's heavy drinking, and spouse's heavy drinking.

treatment center. Thus, if treatment centers differ in remission rates because of the techniques they use, those effects will appear under the "treatment setting" or "treatment amount" headings (where they logically belong) rather than under "treatment center."

With this order, the entries in Table 41 represent the increase in the model's explanatory power when each particular factor is entered after those that precede it. Thus, client drinking factors explain 3.2 percent of the total variance in remission, and client social background factors add another 5.6 percent. Treatment setting and amount of treatment add 3.1 percent in addition to the client factors, whereas treatment center adds only 1.4 percent after all the other factors have been considered. Clearly, these effects are not large even by the relaxed standards applied to models attempting to explain a dichotomous dependent variable. In fact, all factors taken together explain about 13 percent of the total variance, suggesting that there is a great deal of idiosyncratic variation in a male client's response to treatment, independent of his own characteristics or the particular type of treatment that he receives.

In general, these summary results are quite consistent with the impressions given by the preceding tabular analyses. The factors associated with the client's background—both his drinking and social environment—exercise considerably more influence than anything associated with treatment modalities. Indeed, about two-thirds of the explainable variance is due to client factors, with greater emphasis on social background than on initial drinking behavior. Among the client drinking variables, the client's drinking symptoms at intake greatly overshadow his alcoholism history; and among the social factors, social stability outweighs other characteristics. In short, much of the effect included in the 13 percent of variance that can be explained is due to two factors: alcoholism symptoms and social stability.

By contrast, treatment variables account for only about a third of the explainable variance and less than 5 percent of the total variance. Among treatment factors, only the amount of treatment shows a statistically significant effect; treatment center and the treatment setting have much smaller effects. These results argue that a great deal of emphasis should not be placed on the type or location of treatment.

Several further points about this summary analysis should be noted. First, the magnitude of these effects is not dependent on the order in which the variables are entered. Even if the treatment factors are entered before the client factors (a logically dubious procedure, but one that gives maximum impact to treatment), the pattern is essentially unchanged. Thus, the small magnitude of the treatment effects is not simply an artifact of the assumed causal order. A second point is that client-treatment interactions do not affect our estimates of these magnitudes. As we have seen in the preceding analyses, there are not substantial interactions, so that terms representing such interactions are not presented in Table 41. Additional analyses including interaction terms, moreover, produced negligible interaction effects and essentially the same results for the factors tabulated here.

One final point about treatment effectiveness deserves reemphasis. The lack of differences among treatments does not mean that treatment itself is ineffective. Alcoholism treatment is effective to a moderate extent; clients who receive treatment experience remission at higher rates than those who remain untreated. Perhaps the treatment effect would be even greater if treated clients were compared with alcoholics who never seek treatment. Moreover, a higher amount of treatment leads to higher remission rates, as though a threshold level must be passed to produce substantial benefits of treatment. On the other hand, however, the specific type of treatment is largely irrelevant to the client's prospect for remission. In fact, even for those special subgroups of clients who are frequently thought to need a certain type of treatment, the preferred treatment produces no greater remission rates than other treatment modalities. Although treatment is effective, its effectiveness does not depend in any substantial way on the specific modality employed. If anything makes a major difference in treatment effectiveness, it is the set of attributes that the client brings with him rather than what the treatment center accomplishes.

SIX

Conclusions

The variety and intricacy of the analyses presented in the preceding chapters reflect complexities inherent in the assessment of alcoholism treatment. To a large extent these complexities rest on the variations found in clinical practice. But further detail has been added by considering multiple outcomes, by evaluating a number of conceptually distinct facets of treatment, and by distinguishing several types of clients. Accordingly, a first goal of the concluding discussion will be a summarization of the major empirical findings stemming from our analyses of the NIAAA data. During the course of this discussion we will also stress where these findings either agree or disagree with recent research trends.

It has been emphasized throughout this report that treatment evaluation research can affect etiological and other issues related to the nature of alcoholism. It will be contended that some of our empirical results do in fact have a bearing on several definitional and etiological issues raised in Chapter 2. The second goal of the concluding discussion is to evaluate these issues in the light of our findings. This will lead to a tentative model of drinking behavior and of alcoholism that is compatible with our own findings as well as those of other treatment studies.

Finally, it is clear that this study has a number of implications for policy and further research. We discuss several important policy questions and suggest certain directions that might prove fruitful in future research efforts.

SUMMARY OF THE TREATMENT EVALUATION

Remission in Alcoholism Symptoms

Clients of NIAAA treatment centers show substantial improvement on a number of outcome indices. The relative rate of improvement for males is about 70 percent for those outcomes most closely tied to the alcoholism syndrome, such as consumption and behavioral impairment. Social adjustment yields a mixed outcome, with important gains in employment and hence income but almost no change in marital status. While these findings are impressive, they are not novel. Similar conclusions are offered in two recent comprehensive reviews of treatment studies that have attempted to compare outcome criteria (Emrick, 1974; Baekeland et al., 1975).

We have attempted to go beyond a simple assessment of improvement by offering a definition of remission based on combined drinking and impairment criteria. This definition recognizes three different patterns: relatively long-term abstention (6 months or more); short-term abstention (during the past month); and normal drinking in moderate amounts without serious impairment. Given this definition, both the 6-month and 18-month followup samples yielded a remission rate of nearly 70 percent, and at 18 months the remissions were about equally divided among the three patterns. Only about one-fourth of the client sample was engaging in long-term abstention at the 18-month followup. This finding is in accord with the recent literature.

The inclusion of normal drinking as a remission pattern is suggested by several considerations. First, there are now a substantial number of studies that have found varying proportions of former alcoholics drinking at moderate levels without apparent difficulties or serious impairment (Davies, 1962; Kendell, 1968; Gerard and Saenger, 1966; Pattison, 1966; Pattison et al., 1968; Pokorny et al., 1968; Kish and Hermann, 1971; Skoloda et al., 1975; Sobell and Sobell, 1973), including some studies with followup periods of 4 to 15 years (Fitzgerald et al., 1971; Hyman, 1975). Although some of these studies have found fewer normal drinkers than we have identified (and others have found more), all agree that some proportion of former alcoholics can attain moderate drinking habits. The variations among studies regarding the size of the normal drinking group is probably due to varying standards for what is a "permissible" consumption level, though most studies do not use an explicit quantitative consumption index that would allow comparisons.

A second reason for including a normal drinking group in a sample of former alcoholics is that many of these clients are drinking less than is common in the general population. Our definition of normal drinking places limits on the client's consumption (both average daily consumption and amount consumed on a typical drinking day) that are well within the range of consumption for the majority of American males. At the same time, the client must show no serious impairment symptoms in order to be classified as a "normal drinker." As a result, the typical normal drinker in our followup samples consumes an average of .7 ounce of ethanol per day and drinks on 1 out of every 3 days, at which time he consumes approximately 2.1 ounces of ethanol—which converts to roughly 4 cans of beer, 4 shots of hard liquor, or a pint of wine. Both consumption figures are lower than the comparable figures for male drinkers in general.

A third consideration that supports normal drinking as a legitimate remission pattern arises from our analysis of relapse. In general, the relapse rates over a 1-year period are low; few alcoholics who were in remission at 6 months fell back into nonremission status at 18 monhs. More importantly, the relapse rates were *just as low* among normal drinkers as among long-term abstainers. In fact, even among those clients with unequivocal signs of physical addiction, the relapse rate for normal drinkers was exactly the same as for long-term abstainers (16 percent), and lower than the rate for 1-month abstainers (22 percent). Thus the data give no reason to believe that normal drinking is a prelude to relapse. While these results are based on only one-third of the followup sample, this subgroup does not appear unduly biased according to prominent intake and 18-month followup characteristics. Therefore we consider these results tentative but suggestive that a sizable group of treated alcoholics can engage in either periodic or regular moderate drinking without relapse during a 1-year interval. For these alcoholics, normal or periodic drinking can be considered a viable mode of remission.

This is not to say that *all* alcoholics, or even a majority, are able to drink normally. There may be a subgroup of alcoholics for whom any resumption of drinking will ultimately lead to relapse. It would be desirable to have a criterion for distinguishing such a group, but unfortunately no such gauge has been established. Frequently it is argued that "loss of control" is such a criterion. That is, true alcoholics are inherently unable to control their drinking, and therefore abstention is the only solution. But since loss of control is seldom defined independently of alcoholism per se, and since experimental studies have so far been unable to document such a phenomenon (Baekeland, 1975; Lloyd and Salaberg, 1975), its utility is questionable.

It is quite possible that as a practical matter many alcoholics prefer to solve their dependency problem by total abstention rather than by monitoring and controlling their consumption. From the standpoint of conditioning theory, once alcohol addiction or dependence is well established the most important reason for continued drinking may be the prevention of withdrawal symptoms. Hence, even if normal drinking is an ultimate goal of treatment, the most effective way to eliminate withdrawal symptoms may be an initial period of total abstention. In fact, nearly 70 percent of NIAAA clients report abstention for the past month at an early followup 30 days after intake (NIAAA, 1974), in contrast to the 54 percent at 6 months and 45 percent at 18 months. Once total abstinence has been achieved and major withdrawal effects have subsided, the decision to remain abstinent may be influenced by a number of factors including a risk-aversive personality, long-held values about the morality of drinking, or perhaps a belief in the loss of control theory (which might serve as a self-fulfilling prophecy for many alcoholics). In other words, while a certain period of abstention may help eliminate dependency and withdrawal symptoms for most alcoholics, the choice of permanent abstention versus a resumption of social drinking may reflect personality or other social factors particular to some alcoholics rather than physical characteristics inherent to all. Whatever the reasons, our results and those of several other followup studies suggest that at any one time about as many alcoholics are drinking normally as are abstaining for relatively long periods. Whether these two groups can be further distinguished with regard to physical or psychological characteristics remains to be settled by further research.

There is little doubt that the results of these data concerning the overall rate of remission, as well as the proportion engaging in what we have defined as normal drinking, go against common clinical experience and beliefs. Are the data to be believed, or can clinical experience be wrong? We must reemphasize that the NIAAA data have several features that might contribute to overestimation of both the proportion of remissions and the proportion of normal drinkers. These problems include response rate, reliance on self-reports, and a relapse interval of only 12 months. Nonetheless, both our own examination of sample bias and response validity and the results of other followup studies suggest that these remission rates, although not exact, are probably not too far off the mark. The most serious question concerns the proportion of clients in the normal drinking category, since there is a possibility of underreporting true consumption. Future studies with validity controls might therefore find somewhat smaller proportions of normal drinkers.

On the other hand, there are good reasons why clinical experience can yield impressions quite different from those of controlled followup studies. The main problem has to do with sample bias inherent in clinical practice. Of every 100 clients first seen by a clinician, perhaps only 20 or 30 will be seen again by the same person. In fact we have shown that the 44 treatment centers in this study report 6-month followup interviews—meaning a client contact—for about 25 percent of intakes on the average. It is quite likely that most of these clients will either be chronic cases who return for treatment upon relapse or successful cases who are proud of their long-term abstention and maintain followup contact with the treatment facility. Thus the clinician may get the impression that alcoholics are either abstaining or in relapse, but this may be based on a very small proportion of the clients actually treated. It might be that a large proportion of the 70 or 80 percent who are never seen again are engaging in periodic or normal drinking but, given the common clinical emphasis on total abstention, they are not particularly moved to maintain contact with the treatment facility. There is no well-established organization such as AA for promoting or maintaining the visibility of alcoholics who are engaging in controlled or normal drinking.[1]

Stability of Remission

Although there is some relapse from 6 to 18 months, the overall remission rate for the 6-month followup compares quite favorably with the 18-month followup whether we use the entire 6-month and 18-month followup samples or the subsample that had both followup reports. The reason is that while some clients experienced relapse, others changed from nonremission to remission status over the 1-year period. It is therefore useful to distinguish between aggregate or *group* stability and *individual* stability. Since for clients as a group the 6-month report tends to give the same recovery picture as the 18-month one, we conclude that a followup report 6 months after intake can provide a fairly accurate assessment of remission taken at a single point in time. This stability, which also holds true for most individual treatment centers, may be explained by other research findings that most relapse occurs within a few months after treatment ends. We must, however, stress that this stability applies only to all three remission patterns combined; it does not hold, to the same degree, for abstention alone or for normal drinking alone. Between 6 months and 18 months many abstainers changed to normal drinking status, and vice-versa. Thus there is considerable net change over the 1-year period for the abstention and normal drinking categories taken separately, but not for remission when both patterns are combined.

These different patterns of stability within our sample help to clarify certain inconsistencies in conclusions about the relative instability of individual outcomes across different followup reports (Baekeland et al., 1975; Fitzgerald et al., 1971). Using the group of clients with both followup reports, we found considerable change from one remission pattern to another between 6 and 18 months, resulting in only a very small number of clients reporting long-term abstention at both followup periods. In contrast, about 63 percent fall into one of the three remission categories at both followups. This is consistent with the results of a 4-year followup of hospital-treated alcoholics, where only one-third of the clients maintained abstention or at most one drinking episode across the 4 years, but the majority maintained good adjustment either with or without drinking

---

[1] A relatively new organization called "Drink Watchers" is attempting to play such a role.

(Fitzgerald et al., 1971). Therefore, although there is a small group of clients who alternate between remission and nonremission categories, the majority of clients show a high degree of individual stability, provided remission includes both normal drinking and abstention patterns. The primary patterns of instability are alternations, occurring *within* remissions, among short-term abstention, long-term abstention, and normal drinking.

Finally, the stability of outcomes across the 6-month and 18-month followups has further implications concerning the impact of interview completion rates in followup studies. It is widely believed that the inability to locate clients for followup interviews causes biased remission rates, and this argument is sometimes used to explain why different treatment studies can obtain such widely varying levels of success (Hill and Blane, 1967; Baekeland et al., 1975). Our data do not support this view. First, both the 6-month and 18-month samples were quite well-matched with the full intake population on most intake variables—especially on those that proved to be most important for predicting treatment success—in spite of their followup completion rates of about 25 percent and 62 percent, respectively. Second, and more important, if noncompletions are more likely to be nonremissions, we would expect the substantially higher completion rate of the 18-month followup to yield a much lower remission rate than the 6-month followup, especially given its longer interval. But the nearly equal remission rates in the two groups fail to confirm this prediction. Finally, the ATC analysis in Chapter 5 showed that there is no consistent relationship between the 18-month followup completion rate for a given ATC and its remission rate. We therefore conclude that although our data do not provide a final answer, it is likely that claims of sample biases due to loss of clients at followup are exaggerated. It is more probable that inconsistent results of followup studies are due to different definitions of remission or to different types of clients entering treatment.

Client and Treatment Effects

Perhaps the most important finding of this study is that there are few noteworthy differences among remission rates for various treatment types. Regardless of the setting in which treatment occurs, remission appears quite uniform, fluctuating from the general average by 10 percent at most. In addition, those clients who received treatment in more than one setting did not show more favorable remission rates than clients who received treatment within only a single setting. Thus, for example, the evidence does not support the hypothesis that outpatient aftercare following inpatient care yields more favorable results than inpatient care alone.

The finding of uniform treatment effects is not totally new. The Emrick

(1975) and Baekeland (1975) reviews of many hundreds of treatment studies have ventured substantially the same conclusion. But these reviews were hampered by the difficult methodological problem of combining studies with different definitions of recovery. While the NIAAA data are not without their own methodological shortcomings, our conclusion of relatively uniform treatment effects is based on two similar national followup study designs, two compatible samples of clients, and standardized definitions of outcome.

The uniformity of treatment outcomes appears with equal consistency when other aspects of treatment are considered. For example, among several specific attributes of therapy that could be measured in the NIAAA data—including the group or individual context of treatment, the use of Antabuse, and the level of professional training of therapists—no significant and consistent differences in outcomes were found. Similarly, variations in the institutional context of treatment, such as the treatment center itself, showed only a few minor effects on client recovery. Remission rates appeared unrelated to any of the aggregate characteristics of the treatment center, including its client/staff ratio, the number of treatment settings available, or the average level of staff professionalization. Indeed, despite the manifest differences in philosophy, organization, and treatment procedures among the sampled centers, the most striking fact is the similarity in remission rates among them.

The minor outcome differences that do exist among centers are much better explained by the initial, pretreatment characteristics of the clients than by the particular center that provided the treatment. In Chapter 3 we showed that certain social characteristics distinguish both the problem drinker and the alcoholic from the general population, especially job and marital instability. Further, the alcoholic in treatment is distinguished from the untreated problem drinker by far more extreme alcoholism symptoms and, to a lesser extent, by lower SES levels. It is thus not surprising that the three client characteristics of symptom severity, instability, and SES are the strongest correlates of treatment success; other client background factors are relatively unimportant once these three have been taken into account. While this agrees with much other research on prognostic factors in treatment success, it would be a mistake to overemphasize the importance of these correlates. Remission is prevalent even for clients with the worst possible prognosis, and all client characteristics combined account for less than 10 percent of the variation in remission rates. Still, client background is more important than treatment variations in determining outcomes.

One plausible explanation for uniform treatment outcomes is the hypothesis of client-treatment interactions: that the client's needs are usually properly diagnosed by a treatment center, and that the client does well when properly assigned to a treatment. If so, certain types of clients should be assigned disproportionately to certain treatments. Indeed, this is the case, since the intermediate-care setting receives a high proportion of unstable and disadvantaged alcoholics, whereas the outpatient setting receives a disproportionate number of clients who do not even show definite alcoholism symptoms. However, the evidence suggests that these "matches" of client types to treatment types do not produce any substantial dividends in remission rates. Unstable, low-SES, or severely impaired alcoholics all have characteristically lower remission rates, but these rates vary only slightly from one type of setting to another. In statistical terms, there is a definite and negative main effect for all of these client factors, but there is no interaction between any of them and treatment setting. Nor is there any substantial higher way interaction; i.e., there is no specific combination of client factors and treatments (e.g., an unstable low-SES client with severe symptoms in intermediate care) that yields an especially high remission rate. Whatever the reasons for assigning certain types of clients to certain treatments, the assignment cannot be justified from these data on grounds of differential success rates.

This finding is at odds with what little research exists on client-treatment interactions (Kissen et al., 1968, 1970; Pattison et al., 1969) and with NIAAA's statement about the need for comprehensive, multimethod treatment centers (NIAAA, 1974). Of course, even though we did not find client-treatment interactions arising from a client's social condition or severity of symptoms, it is still possible that centers match treatment with other client characteristics not measured in the present study. Or, clients themselves may select treatments in which they have confidence, and it could be this confidence rather than the actual treatment modality that determines success. Such matching or self-selection possibilities can be eliminated only in a controlled study with randomized treatment assignments. Since the few existing studies that have used randomized designs have also failed to find differential treatment effects (Emrick, 1975), we have considerable confidence that the uniform success rates shown by our data are not explained away by other matching criteria or by a client self-selection phenomenon.

A different aspect of treatment that cross-cuts the type of treatment showed a significant effect on remission: the amount of treatment. It has long been recognized that a major treatment problem is simply retaining clients long enough to provide a significant amount of help. Frequently this problem is described as the "dropout" phenomenon, though it also appears as a tendency for alcoholics to evince a pattern of periodic treatment in which the client alternates between treatment and nontreatment phases. Our treatment data confirm the prominence of these patterns, which imply a low amount of treatment, and the results show that low amounts of treatment lead to significantly lower remission rates in outpatient settings. On the other hand, sheer duration of treatment, in the sense of maintaining some contact with a treatment center over a long period, does not produce a higher remission rate, if the total amount of treatment is roughly the same. Thus, there does not appear to be a payoff in delivering a high amount of treatment over a short period of time compared, for example, with delivering the same amount over a 6-month period.

We also found that low amounts of treatment do not appear to be more beneficial than no treatment at all. A more striking finding is that clients with no treatment of any kind had remission rates slightly greater than 50 percent. Thus there appears to be a substantial spontaneous remission rate, a conclusion also offered in Emrick's recent review of studies comparing treated and untreated clients (1975). The high overall remission rate among NIAAA treatment centers must therefore be interpreted in the light of a substantial remission rate among untreated clients. Formal treatment appears to add about 20 to 25 percent to overall remission rates over and above what would be expected from no treatment. For outpatient care, this increment occurs only if the amount of treatment exceeds a certain threshold on the order of five visits.

These results strongly suggest that the key ingredient in remission may be a client's decision to seek and remain in treatment rather than the specific nature of treatment received. This implication receives further support from the analysis of clients receiving other assistance after leaving the ATC, particularly AA attendance.[2] Those clients who received no treatment or low amounts of treatment from an ATC but who went on to become regular AA members showed high remission rates, although not quite so high as clients with high amounts of treatment. Moreover, irregular AA attendance is prognostic of lower remission rates, regardless of the amount of ATC treatment. At the same time, many other alcoholics are able to recover on their own, albeit at a lower rate, with no formal assistance from either a treatment center or AA. Thus, remission may not necessarily depend on formal assistance at all.

Overall, alcoholics in treatment do experience remission, but the par-

---

[2] Although AA does not profess to be a treatment program, we are using the term "treatment" here in its broadest sense to describe any type of assistance for an alcoholic.

ticular form of treatment is less important than the fact of treatment, to the point that regular AA attendance may be nearly as effective as formal treatment from an ATC. In the case of outpatient treatment, effectiveness depends on receiving a certain amount of services beyond a minimum threshold, and even then the chance of remission is only moderately better than the likelihood of remission with no assistance at all other than a single contact with an ATC. Moreover, the prognosis for remission depends more on a client's alcoholic and social condition at entry to treatment than on any particular treatment characteristic, including amount. Yet, all client and treatment factors together explain only a small portion of the variation in remission rates. This suggests a relatively uniform process in which the chances of remission are substantial for most alcoholics, regardless of those client and treatment factors identified and measured in this and many other studies.

TREATMENT AND THE NATURE OF ALCOHOLISM

Treatment evaluations are seldom conducted for the purpose of etiological inquiry; rather, it is customary to affirm whether a given therapy works or not, for whom it works, and whether it works better or worse than other therapies. But treatment regimens do not emerge full-blown from a conceptual vacuum. As indicated in Chapter 2, most treatments are predicated on a given definition of alcoholism and at least partial understanding of its causes and symptoms. For example, some psychological models assume that alcohol addiction is learned behavior that can be unlearned by conditioning techniques, and that therefore an alcoholic can be taught to drink normally. But if this etiological assumption is wrong, and in fact alcoholism is determined predominately by a physiological intolerance to alcohol, then clearly a conditioning approach teaching controlled drinking should have a higher failure rate than approaches stressing total abstention. Thus, depending on the particular treatment approach and its theoretical justification, treatment success or failure can be an implicit test of the underlying conceptual model of alcoholism.

While our treatment evaluation does not provide specific tests for all of the etiological models outlined in Chapter 2, our findings concerning normal drinking patterns, uniform treatment effects, and the high level of recovery for untreated clients do have relevance to a number of theoretical issues raised there. Moreover, these findings, taken together with the results from Chapter 3, give some support to a multistage conception of alcoholism and the recovery process.

Alcoholism and Normal Drinking

Many biological theories of alcoholism posit the existence of physical characteristics that cause a person to be particularly susceptible to alcoholism if he uses alcohol. Clearly, any such theory must necessarily conclude that once a person has demonstrated this constitutional predisposition by becoming an alcoholic, the only path to recovery is permanent abstention. Although existing biomedical research has yielded few strong and consistent physiological differences between alcoholics and nonalcoholics that are not traceable to the effects of alcohol itself, the belief that alcoholism has biological roots remains widespread, particularly among the lay public. One might conceive of other theories that require total abstention without assuming biological predisposition. One might argue, for example, that alcohol addiction will cause a permanent change in some physical or psychological processes so that a resumption of any drinking will inevitably cause a return to alcoholic drinking. This interpretation might be given to some of the "normalizing" theories reviewed by Kissin (1974).

Whatever the theoretical justification for prescribing total abstention for alcoholics, our findings suggest quite different and more complex conceptions of the addiction or dependence process. If most severely addicted alcoholics are predisposed to become addicted, or if addiction itself creates a permanent predisposition to become addicted in the future, then a return to light or moderate drinking should yield a greater chance of relapse than total abstention. Since we could not establish such a relationship in our data, even for clients with definite alcoholism symptoms, we must entertain the possibility that these theories are incorrect or that they apply only to a special subgroup of alcoholics whose characteristics have not been identified by existing research.

On the other hand, our conclusions about a return to normal drinking by some alcoholics are not necessarily an evaluation of those behavioristic theories that advocate "controlled drinking" therapies. In fact, to our knowledge, none of the ATCs in this study have an explicit controlled drinking program; most endorse abstention as their main treatment goal. Nor do we have any data about the extent to which the normal drinkers in our samples actually practice a personal policy of control; but, given their alcoholic backgrounds, it would not be surprising if many did so. Our data demonstrate only that some of the alcoholics in our samples return to moderate or normal drinking—without relapse a year later—regardless of their ATC or their treatment modality.

We want to make perfectly clear that we are not advocating a normal drinking policy in the clinical treatment of alcoholism. Existing data on this issue, including our own, are not yet complete enough for definitive proof of a normal drinking theory. More important, some alcoholics have irreversible physical impairment, such as liver disease, while other alcoholics may have attempted normal drinking repeatedly and, for whatever reasons, always failed. Abstention may be the only reasonable recourse in these instances. But it would also be scientifically imprudent to ignore the etiological implications of the fact of normal drinking among some alcoholics and the fact that permanent abstention is rare. It is conceivable that a treatment philosophy advocating total abstention may convince some alcoholics that one drink is as bad as ten. As a consequence, they might never try to stop after one or two drinks and thereby discover that such moderation is possible.

Uniform Treatment Effects and Natural Remission

Beyond the issue of normal drinking, there are a number of psychological and sociocultural theories of alcoholism according to which cause and remedy are closely intertwined. For example, such a connection exists for those psychodynamic theories holding that alcoholism is itself a symptom of a more general emotional disorder brought on by disruptive experiences in early childhood or other socialization inadequacies. From this perspective alcoholism is most effectively treated by psychotherapeutic techniques aimed at breaking through the client's defenses, releasing repressed conflicts and emotions, and achieving insight. As another example, sociocultural theories that posit alcoholism as a consequence of a general breakdown in job, marital, and residential stability generally maintain that a restoration of a stable social environment is necessary for recovery from alcoholism. This restoration is the primary therapeutic justification for many types of intermediate care, including halfway houses and recovery homes. Finally, classical medical theories that stress physical addiction as the primary definition of alcoholism might emphasize full hospitalization as the most effective treatment for alcoholics with definite signs of physical addiction, since such a setting has the best opportunity for preventing alcohol consumption until withdrawal symptoms have subsided.

If these theories are correct for sizable proportions of the treated alcoholic population, then we would expect that certain types of treatment procedures would be more effective than others, especially once we match certain types of clients with these treatments. But one type of treatment is not much more effective than another even when matched with special groups of clients. Thus hospitalization is not substantially more effective for the more severely impaired alcoholic, outpatient individual therapy is not more effective for stable, middle-class clients, and intermediate care is not more effective for unstable low-SES clients. While we cannot use treatment results alone as the basis for concluding that any of these theories is incorrect, we can assert that their validity for etiology appears unrelated to their utility for treatment.

The suggestion that recovery may be relatively independent of treatment techniques is further supported by the remission rates for persons who receive only AA assistance and for persons who receive no formal assistance at all beyond a single contact with a center. AA attendance is almost as effective as ATC treatment—provided it is regular—and clients with only a single contact with a center have a remission rate of 53 percent compared with the overall remission rate of 63 percent and the rate of 73 percent for clients with high amounts of treatment. AA is not a formal treatment method, and certainly a single contact with a center can hardly be called treatment; yet they both produce substantial remission rates. In the face of such findings it is hard not to conclude that remission and eventual recovery depend to a major extent on characteristics and behavior of the individual client rather than on treatment characteristics.

If recovery does not depend on the particular features of treatment, then what client characteristics are responsible? Again, while the severity of alcoholism symptoms and the social factors of stability and socioeconomic status affect successful remission, even the unstable, low-SES, definitely alcoholic treated clients have a remission rate of 51 percent; other background variables have little additional impact. We must therefore search elsewhere for the critical determinants of recovery. One might propose certain critical personality factors, but here again existing research has not discovered any such characteristics that affect recovery more than social instability. Given these results, the strong suggestion is that recovery depends to a large extent on the individual alcoholic's decision to stop or cut down consumption, and that this decision is only modestly related to his more permanent social and psychological profile.

By emphasizing the client's role as a decisionmaker, we are not necessarily reducing the whole problem of recovery to one of motivation, although decision-making and motivation may be difficult to separate in an empirical investigation. Motivation is a notoriously ambiguous concept, generally tied to the desire for and the acceptance of treatment per se, and is frequently assessed at the beginning of treatment (Pittman and Sterne, 1965; Baekeland et al., 1975). But our data show that a decision to stop drinking is not tied to accepting formal treatment, since in many instances remission occurs after only a single contact with a treatment center. Further, the decision may occur during the course of treatment rather than at the beginning, and it does not necessarily have to be accompanied by a great deal of verbalized enthusiasm as might be implied by most operational definitions of motivation.

In proposing a decision-making explanation, we must stress that the present study offers no data to test the hypothesis directly; indeed, such data will be hard to come by, given the difficulty of pinpointing when a decision is made and the inevitable consequence that it will be empirically entangled with the outcome criterion itself. This explanation is offered primarily because it is consistent with the relatively high and uniform remission rates of different types of clients, different types of treatment, and no treatment at all.

A Multistage Model of Alcoholism and Recovery

If, as we suggest, recovery from alcoholism is largely the result of an alcoholic's decision to stop or cut down his drinking, and this decision is not strongly related to other social and psychological factors, it follows that the causes of alcoholism are separate from its remedy. That is, while any number of factors may be responsible for heavy drinking and the onset of alcoholism, recovery from alcoholism may be largely independent of these factors. Recovery may thus be one distinct stage in a complex, multistage process of drinking, alcoholism, and remission. Combining the results of the treatment evaluation with those of Chapter 3, it is possible to offer a tentative outline of such a multistage model.

A model consistent with our findings is illustrated in Fig. 4. The model has four stages corresponding to the decision to drink, the amount of drinking, the onset of alcoholism, and the recovery process. A stage is signaled by the existence of differing causal factors associated with the outcomes of that stage.

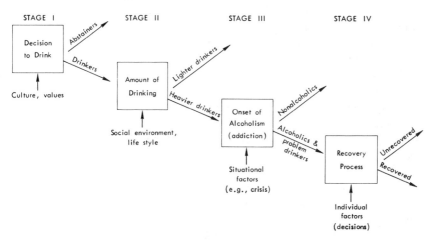

Figure 4   A multistage model of drinking, alcoholism, and recovery.

Stage I corresponds to the decision to drink or abstain. In Chapter 3 we showed that abstention is determined primarily by cultural factors, such as region (South) and religion (Protestant). Historically both of these factors have tended to be associated with the Prohibition movement and other antialcohol ideologies. Lower social class status is also associated with abstention, although in this context SES may signify basic values about alcohol rather than life style issues affecting the quantity of consumption. Finally, abstention is related to being female and being older. Age can be considered a value factor if we interpret it as a generation effect, since opposition to alcohol use was more widespread 50 years ago than it is today. Likewise, sex has a cultural and value interpretation if we acknowledge that double standards have been applied to alcohol use, with stronger prohibitions for women than for men, particularly among the older generation and in the South.

Stage II involves the amount of drinking among drinkers. Here we found that for males the cultural factors of region and religion are of little importance for predicting consumption levels among the drinking population. Rather, social environment and life style factors, such as drinking context (drinking in bars), marital status (unmarried), and race (black), are associated with heavier drinking. Higher social class status is also associated with heavier drinking, but for this relationship we would interpret SES as a life style factor. Persons in higher status occupations and in higher income brackets are more likely to experience social functions at which alcohol is served, and they are more likely to encounter regular drinking practices in their job environments. Finally, we found the interesting reversal for age; although older men are more likely to abstain, they are also more likely to drink heavily if they are in the drinking population. This finding parallels other findings that consumption tends to reach its highest levels among males in the 30 to 50 age bracket (NIAAA, 1974).

Stage III deals with the onset of alcoholism and problem drinking as signified by addiction and its physical and sociopsychological consequences. Obviously, it is difficult to draw a line between heavier or frequent drinking and alcoholism or problem drinking. This is especially true if one adopts a physical addiction model, since in this case addiction without serious impairment might occur and be maintained at moderate drinking levels well below those considered typical of alcoholics. But it is customary to distinguish alcoholics or problem drinkers from heavier users according to the consequences of alcohol. That is, the addiction must be severe enough to cause some kind of physical, psychological, or social impairment.

Given this distinction between heavier alcohol use and alcoholism or problem drinking, our results, together with those of many other studies, suggest at least two clusters of alcoholism determinants. First, we find the two most important characteristics distinguishing the alcoholic and general populations are marital breakup and unemployment; likewise, both of these characteristics are important correlates of problem drinking in the general population. Since other social factors were far less prominent correlates, particularly those reflecting more permanent background features such as SES and ethnicity, it is likely that the causal mechanisms are not marital dissolution and job loss per se but rather the psychological crises and anxiety that generally accompany them. Given persons who already drink alcohol socially and perhaps heavily, and given the tension-relieving and sedative effects of alcohol, the tensions arising from these social disruptions may cause an increase in alcohol consumption to the point where serious, impairing addiction results. Further support for this interpretation of social instability comes from our finding that many alcoholics are in remission even though they remain unemployed and unmarried. Clearly, if the status of being unmarried or unemployed is the crucial determinant of alcoholism, rather than its psychological consequences, then we would expect far lower remission rates for this group. On the other hand, the psychological stresses accompanying the disruption can subside even if the changed status persists, thereby allowing the possibility of remission.

While marital and job instability may be the most important sources of crisis leading to alcoholic drinking, they are obviously not the only ones. For example, a substantial proportion of definitely alcoholic clients in our treated population are both married and employed. Moreover, it is doubtful that psychological crisis itself is a necessary condition for alcoholism. A second and quite distinct cluster of determinants may be indicated by our findings concerning drinking context, which are substantially the same as those reported earlier by Cahalan and Room (1974). That is, persons who drink in bars or who have heavy drinking spouses or friends are more likely to be problem drinkers; in addition, the treated alcoholic is also somewhat more likely to have a spouse who drinks heavily. Thus it is quite likely that alcoholism and problem drinking can be caused by non-crisis factors, such as influence from peers and family drinking behaviors.

While the decision to drink and the amount of drinking are influenced by basic values and relatively constant normative environments, alcoholism or problem drinking itself appears to be due to less permanent situational factors of a diverse nature. This conclusion is consonant with the "multivariate" approach of Plaut (1967) cited earlier. Of course, we do not mean that situational factors are the only determinants of alcoholism; social and psychological background do play a role. Moreover, since no sociopsychological model of alcoholism tested to date explains most of the variation in consumption or problem drinking, it is quite possible there are undiscovered physiological characteristics that contribute to alcoholism. In the present study, however, the situational variables appear to be the most important of the many variables examined.

Although we found that treated alcoholics tended to be Protestant, Southern, and of lower SES compared with the general population, our interpretation is that these factors influence the decision to enter a formal treatment program and are not causes of alcoholism per se. We base this conclusion in part on the results for problem drinking where, if anything, the opposite causal prediction would be made (although the relationships are weak), and in part on the fact that these are precisely the factors associated with abstention in the general population. While alcoholism is influenced by a number of situational factors, a decision to enter treatment appears to be influenced partly by the stance toward alcohol taken by one's current social and cultural milieu. We are confident that there are many other alcoholics at large who are Northern, Catholic, and high SES who never contact a formal treatment program.

Finally, Stage IV concerns the recovery process for alcoholics or problem drinkers whether or not they make contact with or are treated in an alcoholism treatment center. The fact that remission is prevalent among alcoholics in spite of varying types and amounts of treatment, and that factors prominent in etiology—such as social instability and drinking context—are not as prominent in remission, point to the conclusion that recovery from alcoholism is a distinct stage by itself, being relatively independent of the processes that caused alcoholic behavior in the first place. Thus we agree with Bandura (1969) that the reasons for beginning to drink excessively can be quite different from the reasons for continuing excessive drinking once an addiction or dependency is established. Following addiction, a desire to avoid withdrawal symptoms—whether major or minor—may be sufficient reason for continued high consumption. This is not to say that etiological factors and treatment conditions play no role at all; actually, the chances of remission are greater for those clients with higher job or marital stability or with more treatment. Nonetheless, a majority of clients are in remission with little or no treatment at all, even if they have the worst prognostic profile. Although we did not have longitudinal data for our problem-drinking sample, recent findings by Cahalan and Room (1974) suggest substantial natural remission or changes in drinking behavior for untreated heavy and problem drinkers in the general population. Additionally, the case has been made recently that natural remission rates must be high to explain reduced consumption rates among older cohorts (Drew, 1968). We conclude that our own finding of remission among single-contact clients is likely to apply to alcoholics in general, most of whom have not had any contact at all with a regular treatment program.

It is one matter to conclude that the process of recovery from alcoholism is independent from its onset and quite another to identify the determinants of recovery. We suggest that it has to do with individual factors, among which individual decision-making might be especially prominent. Decision-making in this sense refers to what is probably a highly complex cognitive process involving at least three components: (1) experience of the "costs" of alcoholism that outweigh short-run reasons for drinking; (2) a breakdown of psychological defenses (e.g., denial) enabling a recognition of the problem; and (3) a commitment to change. Again, we note that in stressing the importance of individual decision we are not suggesting that recovery from alcoholism is reduced to a matter of sheer willpower. Such a position would take inadequate notice of the fact that alcoholism is, in part, an addictive disorder. As such, a powerful incentive arises for continued excessive drinking despite a steadfast will and removal of the original reasons for alcohol abuse, to forestall withdrawal symptoms that may persist long after the initial stages of the acute withdrawal syndrome. Since we have no direct data relevant to the decision hypothesis, it would be inappropriate to discuss this hypothesis in further detail at present. It is our intention merely to point out that, given our findings, the search for determinants of recovery must focus on individual process variables rather than on a client's general social or psychological profile.

In conclusion, the multistage model outlined here does not pretend to handle all of the complexities inherent in the causes of alcoholism and recovery. Although the particular stages and factors identified are consistent with our own findings as well as with those from a number of similar investigations, other stages and variables could certainly be added. Our most important conclusion here is that, beyond its details, a multistage approach is necessary to provide a satisfactory explanation of the many facets of drinking, alcoholism, and changes in drinking behavior.

IMPLICATIONS FOR POLICY AND RESEARCH

Evaluation research frequently raises as many new questions as it answers old ones, and the present study is no exception. Several of our major conclusions about treatment have some very important implications for current policy governing alcoholism treatment. On the other hand, the data on which these conclusions rest are by no means complete, and there is considerable need for additional information before any policy changes are contemplated.

While the NIAAA 18-Month Followup Study includes more comprehensive data than many similar studies, the data may not be adequate to assess "recovery," defined as stable remission of symptoms over time. For this reason we have distinguished the terms "remission" and "recovery" and have used the former term when describing our empirical results. Whether these findings concerning remission would also hold for such a definition of recovery is an empirical question awaiting further followup studies conducted on the same group of clients.

Keeping in mind this general caveat, the relatively uniform remission rates across different treatment modes suggest that, given no other consideration besides treatment success, less expensive forms of treatment might be substituted for more expensive forms. This could mean increased use of paraprofessional counselors (whose use is already widespread in alcoholism treatment), as well as the substitution of outpatient care for more costly inpatient treatment.

It must be emphasized, however, that there may be other considerations besides treatment success that determine treatment assignment. In particular, hospital care is obviously necessary for alcoholics with severe physical complications, and longer term inpatient care may well be advisable when an alcoholic is causing serious disruption in his family or community. In addition, intermediate care is sometimes justified on the grounds of social support over and above alcoholism recovery per se. In these cases a careful analysis must be undertaken to evaluate the goals of a particular treatment agency, the appropriateness of those goals from the point of view of a funding agency, and the success in meeting those goals. If the primary justification for treatment assignment is successful recovery from alcoholism, then more expensive settings are less cost-effective. On the other hand, if the justification for certain treatment settings is social support, medical treatment, or safety of the community, then other standards for effectiveness must be applied.

The question also arises about the amount and duration of treatment. Although we have emphasized the uniformity of treatment results, even for clients who receive no care beyond a single contact with a center, outpatient clients receiving more than a minimum amount of care do have higher remission rates. This could be explained by self-selection, whereby clients in remission remain in treatment longer, but it is also possible that the amount of treatment actually causes greater improvement. In any event, until further research settles the exact causal sequence, treatment programs should deemphasize short-term treatments, such as detoxification, and emphasize longer term treatments, especially those in outpatient settings.

Further research is also needed to settle the question of remission rates for untreated alcoholics. While our control group of single-contact clients was considered to be untreated, it is possible that even a single contact with a treatment center provides some increment of improvement beyond that experienced by alcoholics who have no contact at all. Very few studies have attempted to define such a truly untreated population and follow it longitudinally. The survey work of Cahalan and Room (1974) is relevant here but, unfortunately, subgroups of problem drinkers taken from general population surveys do not have the same levels of consumption and impairment documented for treated alcoholic populations. New methodologies need to be developed for locating alcoholics comparable to the treated alcoholic population but who have had no contact with a treatment program or AA. Once located, they should be followed longitudinally for several years to determine the rate of "natural" remission.

Finally, the findings concerning normal drinking among alcoholics raise the issue of flexible goal-setting in alcoholism treatment. This is not a new issue; many researchers faced with results similar to our own have raised questions about whether total abstention is a necessary goal for all alcoholics. Obviously, alcoholics who have suffered irreversible physical damage or who have repeatedly failed to maintain normal drinking should be advised to abstain. But our findings that some alcoholics appear to return to moderate drinking without serious impairment and without relapse, and that permanent abstention is relatively rare, suggest the possibility that normal drinking might be a realistic and effective goal for some alcoholics.

However, it would be premature to endorse or advocate a policy of normal drinking for alcoholics. The data from this study and similar studies are simply not adequate to establish, beyond question, the long-term feasibility of normal or "controlled" drinking among alcoholics; nor do the data enable us to identify those specific individuals for whom normal drinking might be appropriate. On the other hand, we have found no solid scientific evidence—only nonrigorous clinical or personal experience —for the belief that abstention is a more effective remedy than normal drinking. The conclusion, therefore, must be that existing scientific knowledge establishes neither an abstention theory nor a normal drinking theory of recovery from alcoholism. Thus, we do not make any policy recommendation at all about therapeutic goals either for alcoholics in general or for any individual alcoholic.

Clearly, before decisions can be made on policies regarding treatment goals, further research is urgently needed. First, a number of methodological issues need to be definitely resolved, including possible bias due to nonresponse, the validity of self-reports, and the effects of longer term followups. But even if more rigorous studies confirm the present findings, a second and far more difficult problem for treatment policy will be that of determining those alcoholics who might successfully adjust to normal drinking and those who cannot. Aside from such obvious criteria as physical impairment or repeated failure, there is no test at present that can distinguish these two groups; indeed, such a test may be exceedingly difficult to devise. Given the strong and often emotional positions on this issue, however, future biomedical and behavioral research must directly confront the question of possible physiological or psychological differences between alcoholics who can return to and maintain normal drinking and those who cannot.

Reliability and Validity
of Self-Reported Drinking Behavior

This report has relied heavily on measures of alcohol consumption and problem drinking or behavioral impairment assessed in the Harris general population surveys, the NIAAA Monitoring System, and the special 18-Month Followup Study. Since these measures are based on self-reports of past and present drinking behaviors, one might legitimately raise questions as to their accuracy and veracity or, to use psychometric terminology, their reliability and validity. The problem of reliability and validity of self-reports is as old as the behavioral sciences themselves. Among laymen and many professionals alike there is a common-sense assumption that information gained from personal interviews or questionnaires is not as dependable as information gathered from actual observation or official records, either because of faulty memory, intentional lying, or an unconscious desire to please an interviewer. For understandable reasons, this belief is more vigorously defended whenever self-reports involve deviant behaviors such as alcoholism.

Ironically, there is probably no issue that is debated more—and studied less—among behavioral scientists than reliability and validity. Part of the reason is that comprehensive reliability and validity studies are difficult to design, particularly in the case of alcoholism or other deviant behaviors, and their expense always seems high compared with the urgency of substantive research. Another reason may be that in certain fields self-reports have been used with remarkable precision to predict real behavior at the group or aggregate level; the success of survey organizations in forecasting presidential elections to within a percentage point or so is a major case in point (e.g., see *American Institute on Public Opinion*, 1973). Other fields may tend to generalize these results to include other types of self-reported behavior.

In general, it is probably safe to say that satisfactory reliability and validity have been established for self-reports on relatively global, objective background information. The definitive work is the "Denver Study" carried out by Parry and Crossley (1950); further confirming analyses have been reported by Cahalan (1968), and these findings have been extended to special groups such as welfare mothers (Weiss, 1968) and skid row men (Bahr and Houts, 1971). Unfortunately, these findings cannot be generalized to include alcohol use and alcoholic behavior. While there is some research in this area, there are sufficient conflicting results and opinions to make both reliability and validity unresolved problems. There is at least one study that will support whatever side one wants to take on the issue. It appears that reliability and validity tend to vary according to the type of alcoholic behavior, the type of respondent, and the type of setting.

Given this unsettled state of affairs, the purpose of this appendix is to provide an analysis of the reliability and validity of self-reported drinking behaviors with special emphasis on the consumption and impairment measures available in the NIAAA data. The analysis will include detailed definitions of these measures, definitions of the different types of reliability and validity used in the analysis, presentation of reliability and validity statistics for both the alcoholic and general population samples, and a discussion of some of the other work in this field. Although we do not expect to provide definitive answers, the NIAAA data, together with certain other data on self-reported drinking behaviors, offer a fairly clear picture of their dependability.

DEFINING RELIABILITY AND VALIDITY FOR ALCOHOLIC BEHAVIORS

Although the concepts of reliability and validity are well established in the field of psychometrics (Guilford, 1954; Cronbach, 1960), their application to alcoholic behaviors has not always been straightforward; consequently, various researchers often mean different things when they use the terms "reliable" and "valid." Therefore it is important to distinguish the several distinct types of reliability and validity and to explain the relevance of each type to various drinking behavior indices.

Reliability

The term "reliability," as used and measured in the behavioral sciences, generally refers to the amount of random measurement error generated by an instrument and to the tendency for an instrument to give *consistent* results; it does not refer to the truthfulness of those results. Yet, there are many specific definitions of reliability, each with associated coefficients and unique assumptions and meanings. Therefore, although assessment of measurement error is their common goal, it is quite possible for different reliability coefficients to give different results. This appendix will distinguish three basic types of reliability: *stability* reliability (Heise, 1969); *internal consistency* reliability (Cronbach, 1954); and *time-item* reliability (Armor, 1974). Each of these reliability methods makes assumptions that may or may not be appropriate for assessing the reliability of drinking behaviors.

Stability Reliability. Stability reliability refers to the consistency of results when the same instrument is applied to the same set of subjects at two or more time periods. That is, stability reliability is high to the extent that subjects get the same scores at different times. Traditionally, there are two ways to assess stability reliability: test-retest correlations and the simplex method.

Given measurements of some alcohol variable at two times, say x_1 and x_2, then test-retest reliability is defined simply as

$$\rho_x = r_{x1x2} , \tag{1}$$

where ρ_x is the reliability coefficient and r_{x1x2} is the product-moment correlation between the time 1 measure and the time 2 measure. Thus, if all subjects obtained exactly the same scores at two measurement periods, then $r_{x1x2} = 1$ and reliability would be "perfect." If there is random measurement error each time, however, then r_{x1x2}, and hence reliability, will vary in inverse proportion to the amount of error. This definition of reliability has a certain intuitive appeal, but it must be emphasized that the test-retest method is useful only under the assumption that the true scores of x are constant over time or, if they change, they change uniformly for *all* subjects. That is, if some subjects truly increase between time 1 and time 2, while others decrease, then even if the instrument contained no measurement error, the test-retest correlation r_{x1x2} would of necessity be less than 1. Thus the test-retest method confounds both measurement error and true but idiosyncratic changes for subjects over time.

If one has three or more measures of x at different times, say x_1, x_2, and x_3, then the test-retest reliability can be generalized by what we will call the *simplex* method (Humphries, 1960; Heise, 1969). Simplex reliability is defined as

$$\rho_x = r_{x1x2} r_{x2x3} / r_{x1x3} , \tag{2}$$

where the r is the product-moment correlation among the three measures. Like the test-retest technique, however, the simplex method makes some assumptions that may not be realistic for certain alcoholic behaviors. The most important of these assumptions is that true change must be independent from one time period to another; i.e., a given subject's change from time 2 to time 3 must not be related to his initial time 1 score or his change from time 1 to time 2. The general implication of this assumption is that $r_{x_1x_3}$ is smaller than $r_{x_1x_2}$ or $r_{x_2x_3}$; i.e., the longer the time interval between two measures, the lower the correlation. While this assumption may be reasonable for many types of behavior, it does not apply to all behavioral change. For example, clients may enter an alcoholism treatment center with varying levels of consumption (time 1). Toward the end of treatment most may be drinking no alcohol (time 2), but after discharge (time 3) many may return to their former levels, with the heavier drinkers at time 1 returning to heavier drinking at time 3. The effect of such a pattern would be a low time 1/ time 2 correlation and a higher time 1/time 3 correlation, thus violating the assumption that points more distant in time have lower correlations. We shall see such an example in a later section.[1]

In summary, the stability method of reliability assessment will confuse measurement error with certain types of true change in the behavior being studied, and when this occurs the reliability coefficient will underestimate true reliability. Specifically, if the amount of true change varies from subject to subject, and if changes in one time period are correlated with changes in a subsequent period, then neither the test-retest nor the simplex coefficients are appropriate for assessing reliability.

Internal Consistency Reliability. The problem of true change can be solved by the internal consistency method that assesses reliability at a single point in time. The internal consistency approach depends on the existence of "parallel" items or instruments having different face content but designed to tap the same underlying dimension. A good example of parallel instruments would be two tests that measure arithmetic computation skills, using different computational problems. In the case of alcoholic behaviors, a series of items measuring the frequency of various problems or symptoms caused by excessive use of alcohol might be considered parallel items for assessing overall impairment.

Given a series of n parallel items $x_1, x_2, \ldots x_n$, the usual practice is to calculate the mean or sum for each subject; this index score will have a

---

[1] See Armor (1974) for a more complete discussion of the simplex assumptions.

reliability greater than any individual item. The reliability for the mean $\bar{x}$ (or sum) can be calculated as

$$\rho_x = n\bar{r}/[1 + \bar{r}(n-1)], \tag{3}$$

where n is the number of items and $\bar{r}$ is the *average* interitem correlation. This formula is identical to Cronbach's alpha (Cronbach, 1954).[2] The average inter-item correlation is the reliability for any single item.

The advantage of the internal consistency approach is that it allows one to determine reliability at a single point in time. Its disadvantage is that it does not assess error of measurement from one time period to another using the same items. Internal consistency coefficients cannot measure random errors arising from instability of items over time.

Time-Item Reliability. Time-item reliability represents an attempt to combine the stability and internal consistency assumptions into one general model for reliability (Armor, 1974). If one has two or more parallel items measured at two or more time periods, the time-item method yields coefficients that assess errors of measurement due to inconsistency across parallel items as well as instability over time, excluding variation due to true change for individual subjects over time.

We will not give the formula for time-item reliability here, but the method yields several coefficients for assessing reliability. Two will be used for our analysis of drinking behavior. The first is δ', which assesses the average time-item reliability at a single point in time, and the second is Δ, which measures the reliability of change scores.

Validity

Although validity also has many component parts in psychometric theory, in the case of self-reported behaviors validity generally refers to the truthfulness of a given self-report. While reliability methods can assess the consistency of similar self-reports or the stability of self-reports over time, validity methods assess the agreement between self-reported behavior and actual behavior. It should be emphasized that the two procedures are quite distinct. For example, respondents in a given study could be quite consistent in reporting their educational level at two or three different times, thereby yielding high test-retest reliability; but some respondents could be

[2] The formula (3) assumes equal variances or standardized items.

consistently exaggerating their true education, so that for these persons or for the group as a whole the self-report would be biased.

As we shall use the term here, validity means the extent to which self-reported drinking behaviors correspond to the true behaviors being reported. We will further distinguish *individual* validity from *group* validity, and we shall also discuss what is known as *concurrent* validity.

Individual and Group Validity. Individual validity is the extent to which a true answer is recorded for each respondent. In the case of numeric or continuous variables, it can be assessed by calculating the correlation between self-reported scores or values and the "true" scores on the property in question, as determined by an independent masurement procedure.[3] Alternatively, in the case of a nominal variable, one might calculate the percentage of cases in exact agreement.

Group validity arises when individual self-reports are aggregated from a number of respondents to form a group characteristic, such as a mean or percentage. Group validity is the extent to which the self-reported aggregate corresponds to the true aggregate. It can be assessed by comparing a self-reported group statistic, such as a mean or percentage, with the true group statistic. For example, in a controlled experiment one might compare the mean self-reported alcohol consumption with the true mean consumption derived from observational measures.

It should be apparent that individual validity and group validity can vary independently. A measure can have low individual validity but high group validity, and the converse is also possible. For example, if persons make mistakes when estimating their age—or more realistically their alcohol consumption—then one might have a fairly low correlation between the self-report and the true scores; but if the errors (whether intentional or not) are both too high and too low in roughly equal proportions, then the group means can be very accurate. On the other hand, low group validity requires some kind of systematic bias; e.g., some subjects might consistently underestimate their alcohol consumption, a more likely outcome whenever deviant behavior is being assessed. It is also possible to have low group validity but high individual validity if there are *uniform* biases among the group of respondents, as when nearly all persons underestimate or overestimate in similar proportion.

The distinction between group- and individual-validity has important implications for treatment evaluation studies. In an evaluation of whole

---

[3] In some developments of reliability theory the correlation between an indicator and the true scores would constitute reliability, but this is not what most reliability coefficients actually measure.

programs or treatment centers, or of groups of clients receiving the same treatment, it may be that group validity is the most important type of validity to be established. High validity permits accurate statements about outcomes for a given program or treatment group as a whole even though individual validity might be quite low (or undetermined). But any research effort that is attempting to explain variation in individual criterion scores by using regression methods will require satisfactory levels of individual validity, regardless of group validity.

Concurrent Validity. Concurrent validity has to do with the extent to which an indicator is associated or correlated with other similar indicators in a systematic and theoretically expected way. Unlike the individual or group validity we have described, it has nothing to do with the relationship between observed and true scores.

An example of concurrent validity is that carried out by Jessor et al. (1968) for an alcohol consumption index. He correlated the index with other variables that were theoretically related to consumption, such as number of times drunk and drinking-related deviance. Similarly, the alcohol consumption index used in this report can be correlated with other alcohol-dependent measures, such as behavioral impairment, number of drinking days, self-rating of consumption, and so forth. Some of this analysis was presented in Chapter 4.

Concurrent validity is conceptually similar to internal consistency reliability, except that it is not necessary to make the "parallel" instrument assumption. The various indicators do not have to be measuring the same underlying property, but the properties must have some theoretically expected relationships. Satisfactory concurrent validity can be established by designing multiple indicators and demonstrating that they have reasonably high intercorrelations.

ALCOHOL CONSUMPTION

The relatively small amount of literature on the reliability or validity of alcohol consumption per se reflects the difficulties inherent in conducting research on this issue. Moreover, what little research exists is very difficult to compare because each study inevitably relies on different populations, different instruments, and different techniques of analysis. Finally, data on individual validity—perhaps the most important issue of all—are virtually nonexistent.

One of the more comprehensive studies of test-retest reliability of consumption involved two interviews about 3 months apart with 80 persons from a London suburb (Edwards et al., 1973). Recent frequency of drinking yielded a test-retest correlation of .76, whereas "usual upper quantity on 1 drinking occasion" had a very low correlation of .17, largely due to three subjects who reported very large quantities in the first interview but small quantities in the second. Internal consistency reliability of consumption has been investigated by Goldstein (1966) by comparing self-reports to peer reports. Again, this study found that frequency of drinking had a satisfactory reliability (r = .65) but amount of drinking did not (r = .34). It must be emphasized, however, that these reliability coefficients do not necessarily reflect measurement errors, since it is quite possible for persons to change their drinking behavior from one time period to another—especially in the case of heavier drinkers—or for persons to be unaware of the actual consumption of their fellow peers.

Reliability studies do not establish validity, because these coefficients do not reflect bias arising from systematic and consistent overestimates or underestimates of consumption. Although true validity studies are rare, there is some information for certain populations. It is fairly well established in Finland and Canada, for example, that self-reported consumption in national surveys accounts for only between 40 and 50 percent of total beverage sales (Makela, 1969; Pernanen, 1974). This suggests that group validity of self-reported consumption in national surveys is poor, although sample bias could also account for part of the discrepancy. Room (1971) suggests that coverage might be increased to 65 percent or so if self-report questions were designed more carefully.

As to individual validity, a recent study (Boland, 1973) investigated the relationship between self-reported and actual liquor store purchases. Surprisingly, he found that purchases were overreported. This study conflicts with an investigation (Schmidt, 1972) reported in the *Drinking and Drug Practices Surveys* by Boland and Roizen (1973). The Schmidt study showed that self-reports of alcohol purchases were quite accurate for small to moderate purchases (up to 6 or 7 bottles of wine or liquor per month), but that very heavy purchases were considerably underreported. For example, purchases of 11 bottles or more a month were underreported by about 75 percent. Obviously, the problem with alcohol-purchase studies is that they do not deal with actual consumption of alcohol, the issue of main interest.

The limited research to date suggests that reliability and validity of certain consumption behaviors may be quite satisfactory (e.g., frequency of drinking) but that other behaviors may not be (e.g., amount of drinking). More important, there are strong indications that the reliability and validity of self-reported consumption may vary according to the self-report technique used and to the population and setting under investigation.

Accordingly, we shall present new data separately for general population surveys and for alcoholic populations, and we shall be careful to specify how the self-report indices of consumption are constructed.

Reliability and Validity in the Harris Surveys

The self-reported consumption index in the Harris surveys is composed of questions asked in a self-administered form concerning the frequency and quantity of drinking. A "yes-no" question was asked first about whether beer, wine, and liquor were drunk in the past month. Each of these questions was followed first by a frequency question (which was the same for each beverage) and then by a quantity question. The frequency and quantity questions are as follows:

Question	Answer Categories	Frequency or Quantity Code
How often did you drink any [beer/wine/hard liquor]?	Every day	1
	Nearly every day	0.787
	3-4 days a week	0.5
	1-2 days a week	0.214
	Weekends only	0.143
	Less often than weekly	0.071
When drinking beer, how much did you drink in a typical day?	6 quarts or more	192
	5 quarts	160
	4 quarts	128
	3 quarts	96
	2 quarts	64
	1 quart	32
	2 or 3 glasses	20
	1 glass	8
When drinking wine, how much did you drink in a typical day?	5 fifths or more	128
	3-4 fifths	79.6
	2 fifths	51.2
	1 fifth	25.6
	2-3 water glasses or 4-6 wine glasses	20
	1 water glass or 1-2 wine glasses	8
When drinking liquor, how much did you drink in a typical day?	4 pints or more	64
	3 pints	48
	2 pints	32
	1 pint	16
	11-15 shot (ounces)	12.5
	7-10 shots (ounces)	8.5
	4-6 shots (ounces)	5.0
	1-3 shots (ounces)	2.0

The frequency code represents fractions of a day, and the quantity code represents the median ounces for that category. Consumption (quantity-frequency) indices for each beverage were derived by multiplying quantity times frequency times .04, .15, or .45 (ethanol or absolute alcohol content) for beer, wine, and liquor, respectively. A total consumption index was then derived by summing the indices for the three beverages. Thus the index represents total volume of ethanol consumed last month expressed in ounces per day. In some cases a typical quantity index is reported, which is simply the quantity times the ethanol proportion summed across the three beverages. This latter index represents the quantity of ethanol consumed on typical drinking days.

Reliability. Assessing the reliability of the quantity-frequency items in the Harris surveys is hampered by a lack of data overtime as well as specially designed parallel items. Yet, some information can be used to obtain a partial assessment of reliability, particularly for frequency of drinking.

In addition to the above frequency questions for specific beverages, respondents were asked one general question concerning the number of days they drank in the past month. The internal consistency reliability of the frequency of drinking can be estimated by correlating the overall estimate of days they drank with the projected frequency based on the most frequently consumed beverage. This second frequency measure was constructed by selecting the beverage drunk most frequently and multiplying the frequency code by 30. Thus, for example, a person drinking only beer 3 to 4 days a week would be placed in the 12- to 18-day category for frequency of drinking in the past month.

The results for males who report some drinking last month are shown in Table A-1. It is clear that the relationship between these two measures of drinking frequency is substantial, with very few persons giving inconsistent answers. No doubt, some of the inconsistency is related to the fact that we could not perfectly match the response categories of the two frequency measures. Other inconsistency may arise because the two questions are not strictly parallel measures, since we had to choose only the most frequently consumed beverage for projection purposes. Nonetheless, the correlation (and hence reliability) of nearly .8 is quite respectable for measures based on recall of fairly complex behaviors.

Reliability of the quantity items is more difficult to establish in the Harris data. In this case there are no parallel, or even similar, measures of quantity other than those listed above. The only question that comes close to being related to quantity is one that asks how many times the respondent was drunk in the past 30 days, which appeared in only one of the Harris surveys. The legal definition of intoxication in most states with drunk-

Table A-1. Reliability of Two Self-Reports of Frequency of Drinking Last Month, Male Drinkers in the General Population

Projected Frequency of Drinking Beer, Wine, or Liquor[a]	Percentage of Responses in Each Category					
	Overall Estimate of Days Drank[b]					
	No Days	1-2 Days	3-10 Days	11-20 Days	Over 20	Total
1-3 days	61	74	24	3	2	30
4-11 days	23	22	60	21	2	35
12-18 days	9	2	10	43	7	13
12-26 days	3	1	3	24	36	11
27-30 days	3	1	2	9	54	11
(N)	(64)	(478)	(903)	(320)	(344)	(2109)
Total	3	23	43	15	16	

Product-moment correlation = .78

[a] Based on the frequency items in the quantity-frequency index questions for each beverage. The beverage with the *highest frequency* was selected and projected to a 1-month base.
[b] The actual question was "On how many days did you yourself drink during the past month?" with response categories as indicated. Thus the response categories for the two questions cannot be made to correspond exactly.

driving statutes is a blood concentration of .1 percent of ethanol (absolute alcohol), which, for the average male weighing 165 pounds, corresponds to about 3 ounces of ethanol consumed within a 2- or 3-hour period. This amount of ethanol would correspond to about 6 cans (2 quarts) of beer, 1 fifth of wine, or 7 shots or ounces of hard liquor. Theoretically then, if most persons' judgments about being drunk correspond to the legal definition, we would expect the number of days on which those amounts (or more) were consumed to be similar to the number of times respondents said they were drunk.

The relationship between these two measures for males is presented in Table A-2. Although the two measures have a positive correlation, it is, unfortunately, not a very strong one. A substantial percentage of those persons reporting that they drank more than 3 ounces of ethanol for more than 5 days last month say they were not drunk at all during that same period. Since very few inconsistencies occur in the other direction (frequent reports of being drunk with infrequent drinking of more than 3 ounces), it seems fairly clear that the inconsistency arises from a discrepancy between personal perceptions of intoxication and the legal definition. For the sample as a whole, about 16 percent report 5 or more days of drinking more than

Table A-2. Relationship between "Number of Times Drunk"[a] in the Past Month and "Number of Days Drank Over 3 Ounces of Ethanol," Male Drinkers in the General Population

Number of Times Drunk	Percentage of Responses in Each Category				
	Days Drank Over 3 Ounces of Ethanol[b]				
	None	1-4	5-10	Over 10	Total
None	85	73	68	59	81
1-4	13	23	29	24	16
5-10	1	29	3	10	2
Over 10	—	3	—	7	1
(N)	(382)	(26)	(34)	(41)	(483)
Total	79	5	7	9	

Production-moment correlation = .28

[a] Data on number of times drunk were available in only one of the Harris surveys.
[b] Number of days last month on which respondent drank 2 or more quarts of beer, 1 or more fifths of wine, or 7 or more ounces of hard liquor.

3 ounces of ethanol, whereas only 3 percent report 5 days or more of intoxication. It would appear that self-reports of amount consumed might be a better indication of legal intoxication than self-reports of drunkenness, provided we can assume that the self-reported consumption took place over a 2- or 3-hour period.

Validity. While the data for assessing the reliability of the Harris consumption data are not ideal, no information exists that would enable us to establish their individual validity. The only two methods for establishing individual validity of self-reported consumption are direct observation of respondents' drinking behavior over some period of time or the use of blood alcohol tests (BACs) to validate self-reports over the past 24 hours or so. Such data are rarely available in surveys such as these.

Even though individual validity cannot be investigated, it is possible to establish group or aggregate validity by comparing mean consumption figures from the Harris surveys with mean consumption based on national beverage sales data. Systematic bias should be revealed by discrepancies between these two sources.

Information about group validity of the Harris survey self-reports is shown in Table A-3. In the first part of the table we show mean (per capita) daily ethanol consumption rates for all four of the Harris surveys,

Table A-3   Group Validity of Harris Survey Self-Reports: Comparison of Harris Survey Consumption Rates with National Beverage Sales

	Mean Daily Ethanol Consumption Rates (oz)		
Type of Beverage	Harris Surveys, 1972-1974	National Beverage Sales, 1972	Coverage (%)
Beer	.107	.364	29
Wine	.098	.097	101
Liquor	.209	.404	52
Total	.404	.915	44
(N)	(6315)	(total pop.)	
Alcoholism Rate	Harris Surveys Doubled[a]	Beverage Sales, Assuming Log Normal Distribution[b]	Revised Jellinek Formula[c]
Percent drinking 5 or more ounces per day	2.80	2.50	2.76

[a] That is, the percentage of persons drinking more than 2.5 ounces by self-report, corresponding to the assumption that persons underestimate by about 50 percent.
[b] Based on the Ledermann formulas (de Lint and Schmidt, 1971).
[c] See text for a description of the formula.

broken down by beverage type. These are compared with national beverage sales statistics for 1972 (Efron et al., 1972); coverage is simply the self-report mean taken as a percentage of the beverage sales mean. Perfect coverage—no group bias in self-reports—would be 100 percent. We note that coverage for wine is essentially perfect (101 percent), whereas coverage for beer is quite poor (29 percent). The figure for liquor is 52 percent, which suggests an underestimation factor of about one-half.

There are other possible reasons for the discrepancies over and above respondent underestimation. First, survey samples undoubtedly miss some of the heavy-drinking alcoholic population, such as persons in skid-row areas, although this is a relatively small population and probably not a serious course of bias. Second, the Harris surveys ask about *typical* quantities consumed rather than total volume; there has been some speculation (without much data so far) that typical quantity questions may underestimate the total volume of consumption (Room, 1971).

In the lower part of Table A-3 we show three different calculations for the percentage of persons drinking more than 5 ounces of ethanol per day, as determined by three different methods. This amount of ethanol is frequently used as a definition of alcoholism (de Lint and Schmidt, 1971). The first method is based on the Harris surveys and the assumption that persons underestimate their consumption by about 50 percent. The distribution of daily consumption shows 2.8 percent reporting 2.5 ounces; if persons at this and higher levels are underreporting by about half, as suggested by the data in the first part of the table, then we would estimate 2.8 percent with an actual daily consumption of 5 ounces or more.

The second method is based on national beverage sales data and the Ledermann assumption that alcohol consumption has a log normal distribution with a mean and variance in a fixed relationship. In this case the percentage of persons drinking more than 5 ounces can be determined if the mean is known (see Figure 2 in de Lint and Schmidt, 1971; the mean of .915 oz/day corresponds to about 10 liters/year). That alcohol consumption has a log normal distribution receives further support from the Harris data, as shown by the distribution of consumption among drinkers in Figure A-1. When this distribution is subjected to a log transformation, the resulting distribution is nearly normal, with a mean of -1.3 and a median of -1.5. According to the Ledermann formulas, the U.S. mean of .915 implies that approximately 2.5 percent are drinking more than 5 ounces/day.

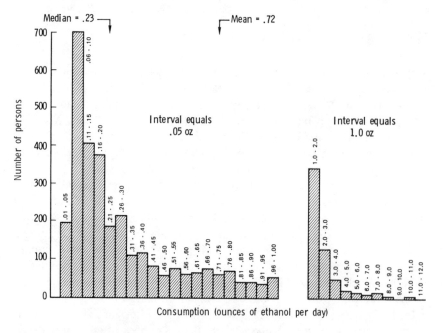

Four pooled national surveys of the adult population by Louis Harris and Associates, Inc., between 1972 and 1974; abstaining persons are eliminated.

Figure A-1   Frequency distribution of consumption for a national sample of alcohol users.

Finally, the last figure in Table A-3 represents the percentage of alcoholics among the adult population (aged 15 and older), as determined by what we propose as a revised Jellinek formula. The original Jellinek formula is

$$A = PDR/K, \qquad (4)$$

where D is the number of deaths due to cirrhosis in a given year, P is the percentage of cirrhosis deaths attributed to alcohol (different for men and women), R is ratio of all alcoholics to alcoholics with complications (or the reciprocal of the percentage of all alcoholics with complications), and K is the percentage of all alcoholics with complications who die of cirrhosis in a given year (Keller, 1962). The puzzling aspect of this formulation is the estimation of rates of alcoholism with complications—rather than with cirrhosis when, in fact, cirrhosis death rates are the ultimate criterion. It seems more straightforward, and more precise, to estimate the proportion of alcoholics with cirrhosis (P_C) and the proportion of this group that dies each year (P_D). Then we would have the formula

$$A = PD/P_C P_D, \qquad (5)$$

where the other terms are as originally defined, except that P is the proportion rather than the percentage of cirrhosis deaths due to alcohol. Generally P is given as .628 for men and .216 for women (Keller, 1962); but if D is given only for an entire population without regard to sex, one can use the overall rate of .50.[4] The range of reported cirrhosis incidence rates is between .08 and .12, so we compromise with $P_C = .10$; we further assume that the average cirrhotic alcoholic contracts the disease by age 30 and lives for 30 years after onset, so that $\frac{1}{30}$ of all cirrhotic alcoholics die in a given year. Thus, $P_D = .033$, and the number of alcoholics is thereby obtained by multiplying annual cirrhosis deaths by the factor of 150. For the year 1970, there were about 24,045 cirrhosis deaths (de Lint and Schmidt, 1971, assuming an adult population of 130,874,604), so this revised formula yields 3,606,750 alcoholics, or a rate of 2.76 percent.

Although each of these calculations is based on a number of assumptions, some not verified, it is important that they converge to similar percentages. In particular, it is interesting that the revised Jellinek formula, being tied more closely to cirrhosis incidence rates, matches the estimated percentage of alcoholics drinking more than 5 ounces/day; it is precisely

[4] The ratio of cirrhosis deaths for men compared with women is about 2 to 1, so $P = \frac{2}{3}(.628) + \frac{1}{3}(0.216)$.

this volume of alcohol consumption that yields substantial rates of cirrhosis (Feinman and Lieber, 1974). It would appear that general population surveys underestimate consumption by about 50 percent, but that when the appropriate correction is made for this bias, the proportion of alcoholics in the Harris surveys closely matches the estimates of alcoholism rates based on two other independent methods. Interestingly, these numbers are substantially below the widely cited figure of 10 million alcoholics in the United States (NIAAA, 1974).

Validity of Self-Reports in ASAP Roadside Breathtesting Survey[5]

The Harris group validity data are consistent with the conclusions of other studies that underestimation appears to occur for self-reported consumption in general population surveys by a factor of perhaps 50 percent. However, individual validity data are necessary to confirm this discrepancy, and, should it exist, to determine how the underestimation is distributed throughout the population and to what extent it is affected by the technique used for the self-report. Given the difficulty of obtaining individually validated information on alcohol consumption, some new surveys by the Alcohol Safety Action Program (ASAP) afford an opportunity for a useful, albeit preliminary, analysis of individual validity.

The ASAP surveys were conducted during 1970-1974 by individual state ASAPs, using combined highway patrol and survey teams in 25 states.[6] Randomly selected evening and nighttime drivers were stopped at various sites, interviewed, and given breath tests to determine BAC levels. The standardized data base assembled by Michigan's Highway Safety Research Institute includes interview and BAC data on 75,183 drivers and 2701 passengers from 77 different surveys. Some of the surveys included questions on self-reported consumption on the day of the survey.

The present analysis focuses on the relationship between BAC level and self-reported number of drinks on the day of the survey, information that is available for 10,487 respondents.[7] At the outset we must emphasize that the relationship between BAC and true consumption is itself extremely complex, depending on such factors as the time when alcohol is consumed, food intake, body weight, sex, and a host of other idiosyncratic factors,

---

[5] The data in this section were provided by Arthur Wolfe of the Highway Safety Research Institute at the University of Michigan.

[6] See Lehman et al. (1975) for a more complete description of these surveys.

[7] Information on the number of drinks consumed in the past 2 hours is available for a larger sample, but preliminary analysis indicated that this period is too short for the best validity test.

most of which cannot be analyzed here.[8] When we add the further complication that the self-reports are simply number of "drinks" rather than specific amounts of beverages whose alcohol contents are known, it is clear that we do not have a true validity analysis. Yet even this rough comparison is better than no information at all.

The relationship between actual BAC and self-reported drinks on the day of the survey is shown in Table A-4. Overall, the correlation of .61 may be considerably higher than what researchers would expect, particularly since the survey was conducted in a context where excessive drinking is illegal. On the other hand, much of the association is caused by the large number of persons who did not drink on the day of the test. If we remove the row of zero BACs, the correlation drops to .38, although even this is quite high given the crude drinking measure used here. It is clear that most of the discrepancy comes from the relatively large number of persons who

Table A-4. Comparison of Actual BAC[a] with Self-Reported Alcohol Consumption on Day of Survey, ASAP Roadside Breathtesting Surveys[b]

Actual BAC Level	Percentage of Responses in Each Category									Average Number of Drinks
	Self-Reported Number of Drinks on Day of Survey									
	None	1	2	3	4	5	6	7+	Total	
0	94	62	41	30	16	11	14	7	72	.7
.01–.04	5	32	42	40	39	37	32	23	17	2.2
.05–.09	1	4	12	21	28	32	28	31	6	3.9
.10–.14	—	1	4	7	12	14	16	24	3	4.6
.15+	—	1	2	3	5	6	10	15	2	4.6
	100	100	100	100	100	100	100	100	100	
(N)	(6501)	(1326)	(874)	(574)	(438)	(234)	(207)	(333)	(10,487)	
Total	62	13	8	5	4	2	2	3	100	

Overall product-moment correlation = .61
  Validity statistics with zero BACs removed
Product-moment correlation   = .38
Mean BAC level   = .055
Mean number of drinks   = 3.0

[a] Blood alcohol content expressed as the percentage concentration of absolute alcohol (ethanol) by weight. A single drink of 1¼ ounces of 86-proof spirits, 12 ounces of beer, or 4 ounces of table wine contains about .5 ounce of ethanol and, for an average male weighing 165 pounds, would yield a BAC of approximately .02 within an hour or so.
[b] Data supplied by Arthur Wolfe of the University of Michigan Highway Safety Research Institute.

[8] The ASAP data include body weight and sex; but since critical time data are missing, we do not attempt a finer analysis.

report a substantial number of drinks but whose BAC is negative or less than .05, a situation no doubt caused by the normal metabolic elimination of alcohol for persons whose drinking occurred some hours before the test.

The critical issue, from our perspective, is the amount of underestimation or "denial," given that a person reports a certain number of drinks. That is, what proportion of the BACs exceed the maximum reasonably implied by the number of drinks? If a drink is taken to be a standard bar drink with 1¼ ounces of hard liquor, a 12-ounce can of beer, or a 4-ounce glass of wine, then one drink would have the equivalence of .5 ounce of ethanol. For the average male weighing 165 pounds (the ASAP survey respondents were 80 percent male and had a medium weight of about 165 pounds), this amount of ethanol would produce a BAC of about .02 within an hour or so after intake. The line drawn in the table represents the maximum BAC under these assumptions for persons with these characteristics. In general, it is clear that extreme distortion is relatively infrequent. Of those claiming to have had no drinks on the day of the survey, 94 percent actually had a zero BAC; of those claiming 1 drink, only 6 percent had a BAC over .05; of those claiming 3 drinks only 10 percent were over .10. Taking the .10 mark as indicating fairly heavy consumption on the day of the survey, less than 10 percent of those persons claiming light or moderate drinking—from 1 to 4 drinks—had contradictory BACs over .10. In other words, if a study used self-reporting to classify persons into light or moderate drinkers versus heavy drinkers, a BAC validity check would not reclassify very many persons.

This is not to say that the underestimation is uniformly distributed. In the right-hand column of Table A-4 we have tabulated the average number of drinks reported by persons with differing BAC levels, and at the bottom of the table we show the overall mean number of drinks and mean BAC level for persons with positive BACs. For the sample as a whole, the assumption that one drink is equivalent to a BAC of about .02 appears to hold fairly well, given the mean of 3 drinks and the associated BAC mean of .055. But when the means for different BAC levels are considered, it can be seen that the correspondence diminishes as the BAC level increases. For persons with BACs in the .01 to .09 ranges, the means correspond fairly well to the assumption; but for those persons whose means are over .10, they do not. The mean number of drinks for the .10 to .14 level should be about 6, rather than 4.6; and for the .15 level, the mean should be about 10 (assuming a mean BAC of about .20 in this category) rather than 4.6. Thus for persons who have BACs at intoxicating levels, the self-reported number of drinks is not a valid measure for many persons. It is possible that the reason for the discrepancy is that the term "drink" is too ambiguous for heavy drinkers, whose average drink may contain a greater amount of beverage than we have assumed. Of course, it must be kept in mind that these persons had been stopped by the highway patrol for the test, so the circumstances may have caused persons with high BACs to intentionally underestimate.

Reliability and Validity in the ATC Data

The reliability and validity data for general population surveys are informative and useful, but it would be inappropriate to generalize them to alcoholic populations without an independent analysis. Not only do alcoholics drink far more than the average person, but the ASAP data show very clearly that the heavier drinking group—perhaps including some problem drinkers and alcoholics—may be underreporting to a greater extent that light or moderate drinkers. Therefore, in this section we present a parallel analysis for the ATC data.

The procedure for constructing the daily consumption (QF) index for the ATC data follows closely that for the Harris surveys. Questions were asked about the frequency and quantity of drinking beer, wine, and liquor for the past 30 days; the response categories were similar to those given in a previous section (see Appendix D for exact wording). Response categories were given frequency and ethanol quantity codes, multiplied to yield an index for each beverage and summed across the three beverages to yield a measure of ounces of ethanol per day. The only difference between the two sets of questions is that the ATC interview schedule has a slightly different set of response categories for the quantity questions; the quantity codes differ accordingly to reflect the number of ounces at the midpoint of the response category.

Unlike the Harris surveys, the ATC Monitoring System collects data over several time periods. It is therefore possible to assess reliability over time as well as internal consistency reliability.

Consistency Reliability. As with the Harris surveys, the ATC Monitoring System asks a question about "total number of days drank" in the past month. This can be compared with the projected number of days according to the most frequently consumed beverage to assess the internal consistency reliability of drinking frequency.

The comparison for ATC clients assessed at the 6-month followup is shown in Table A-5. It is clear that the relationship is very strong, with an overall product-moment correlation of .71. It would appear that frequency of drinking has a substantial internal consistency reliability similar to that for the general population.

Quantity of drinking has no direct parallel in the ATC Monitoring

Table A-5. Reliability of Two Self-Reports of Frequency of Drinking Last Month: ATC Male Clients Reporting Drinking at 6-Month Followup

	Percentage of Responses in Each Category					
	Overall Estimate of Days Drank					
Projected Frequency of Drinking Beer, Wine, or Liquor[a]	1-3	4-11	12-18	19-26	27-30	Total
1-3 days	69	19	—	1	—	22
4-11 days	23	46	13	1	—	24
12-18 days	4	15	42	11	2	15
19-26 days	1	3	26	60	19	17
27-30 days	3	17	18	28	79	22
(N)	(209)	(385)	(147)	(156)	(101)	(998)
Total	21	39	15	16	10	

Product-moment correlation = .71

[a] Based on the frequency items in the quantity-frequency index questions for each beverage. The beverage with the highest frequency was selected and projected to a 1-month base.

System; again, the most similar item is the self-reported number of times drunk during the past 30 days. Given the subjective nature of this question, and the alcoholics' greater tolerance to alcohol, it was felt that the number of times drunk should be compared with the number of days the client drank more than 5 ounces of ethanol. A typical male alcoholic weighing 165 pounds who drinks more than 5 ounces of ethanol during a 2- or 3-hour period would have a BAC level exceeding .20, and, according to analyses presented in a later section, should have a high likelihood of exhibiting intoxication symptoms.

The relationship between number of times drunk and days drunk more than 5 ounces of ethanol is given in Table A-6 for those male clients who reported some drinking last month at the 6-month followup. The overall correlation of .57 is substantially higher than that obtained for the Harris surveys, indicating that alcoholics are more consistent in their reports about the quantity of drinking and intoxication. The correlation is fairly large, but it does reflect considerable inconsistency, most of which stems from clients who report many days of drinking more than 5 ounces of ethanol a day but who report few or no instances of intoxication. Overall, 37 percent of the 6-month followup sample report over 10 days of drinking 5 or more ounces of ethanol, whereas only 17 percent report 10 or more instances of being drunk. In other words, there are substantial numbers of alcoholics who report high consumption without intoxication, sug-

Table A-6.   Relationship between "Number of Times Drunk" in the
Past Month and "Number of Days Drank over 5 Ounces of Ethanol":
Male Clients Reporting Drinking at 6-Month Followup

| Number of Times Drunk | Percentage of Respondents in Each Category | | | | |
| | Days Drank Over 5 Ounces of Ethanol | | | | |
	None	1-4	5-10	Over 10	Total
None	52	14	18	7	28
1-4	37	76	60	29	40
5-10	6	9	17	25	15
Over 10	6	1	5	38	17
(N)	(440)	(96)	(109)	(377)	(1022)
Total	43	9	11	37	

Product-moment correlation = .57

gesting either high levels of alcohol tolerance or an unwillingness to admit
intoxication. Results in a later section point to the former as the most likely
reason, so that this moderate correlation may be assessing a substantive
relationship rather than internal consistency reliability.

So far we have considered the consistency of responses for frequency
and quantity items taken individually. But the daily consumption index
combines both of these items into a single measure of ounces of ethanol
per day by multiplying the frequency of drinking by the quantity of drinking on drinking days. What is the reliability of this index? We cannot answer the question directly by internal consistency techniques because we
do not have two parallel methods for determining the QF score. Yet we
can get some idea of the answer by considering the relationship between
quantity and frequency of drinking. These are not strictly parallel items
but preliminary analysis suggests that they do tend to vary together for the
alcoholic population.

Table A-7 presents the relationship between frequency of drinking hard
liquor and quantity consumed, at 6-month followup; relationships are quite
similar for the other two beverages. Since persons who had not drunk
liquor in the past month were scored "none" on both items, the overall
correlation of .82 is somewhat inflated. When the no drinking category is
eliminated, the correlation drops to .38, largely due to a small minority of
"binge" drinkers, i.e., clients drinking a pint or more but less than once a
week. Nonetheless, this modest correlation means that for alcoholics as a
group more frequent drinking is associated with larger quantities.

Table A-7.   Consistency Reliability for the Daily Consumption Index (QF): Relationship between Frequency of Drinking Hard Liquor and Quantity Consumed, Male Clients at 6-Month Followup

Frequency of Drinking Hard Liquor Last Month	Percentage of Responses in Each Category									
		Typical Quantity of Hard Liquor Consumed on Drinking Days Last Month								
	None	1-3 Shots	4-6 Shots	7-10 Shots	Shots 11-15	Pint	2 Pints	3 Pints	4 Pints	Total
None	100	—	—	—	—	—	—	—	—	74
Less than weekly	—	62	43	23	33	22	18	15	10	8
Weekends only	—	8	14	7	10	9	10	15	5	2
1-2 days/week	—	13	18	23	33	27	15	—	5	5
3-4 days/week	—	9	8	14	15	13	18	22	24	4
5-6 days/week	—	6	10	23	5	14	14	15	10	3
Daily	—	3	7	11	3	14	25	33	48	4
	100	100	100	100	100	100	100	100	100	
(N)	(1718)	(103)	(72)	(44)	(39)	(183)	(126)	(27)	(21)	(2333)
Total	74	4	3	2	2	8	5	1	1	

Product-moment correlation = .82
Mean frequency   = .10 days/week   (standard deviation = .246)
Mean quantity   = 2.13 ounces ethanol   (standard deviation = 4.92)
Mean QF   = 1.04 ounces/day   (standard deviation = 3.43)

Excluding Nondrinkers

Product-moment correlation = .38
Mean frequency (F)   = .39 days/week   (standard deviation = .332)
Mean quantity (Q)   = 8.08 ounces ethanol   (standard deviation = 6.60)
Mean QF   = 3.92 ounces/day   (standard deviation = 5.77)

Stability and Time-Item Reliability. One advantage of the ATC Monitoring System is that data are collected on the same group of clients at several time periods (at intake, 30 or 60 days, and 6 months). This enables an application of reliability techniques that depend on repeated measurements over time, including the test-retest, simplex, and time-item methods described earlier.

Table A-8 shows the results of these three reliability methods applied to the QF index for daily hard liquor consumption. The three time periods used are intake (pre-treatment), 30-day followup, and 6-month followup. As we can see, the test-retest coefficients are quite low, as is the simplex coefficient. Basically, the idiosyncratic change inherent in treatment outcome measures renders these techniques relatively meaningless for assessing reliability. That is, some clients improve after treatment, some do not, and some even get worse. Since the test-retest method treats true individual change as error, it yields quite low reliabilities. The simplex method may likewise be inapplicable, since change from intake to 30 days may not be

Table A-8. Stability and Time-Item Reliability for the Hard-Liquor Consumption Index (QF)

	Reliability Coefficients for Four Time Periods			
Reliability Method	Intake to 30 Days	Intake to 6 Months	30 Days to 6 Months	Intake to 30 Days to 6 Months
Test-retest, Eq. (1)	.19	.12	.18	—
Simplex, Eq. (2)	—	—	—	.28
Time-item[a]	.85	.86	.92	.85

[a] For description, see footnote 9 in this appendix.

statistically independent from change from 30 days to 6 months. In other words, these coefficients should be interpreted as measuring not only response error but also the actual instability of liquor consumption among alcoholics in treatment.

In the lower part of Table A-8, we show reliability coefficients based on a new method that combines the logic of internal consistency and stability methods. Basically, the time-item method assumes that the quantity and frequency items are parallel items that change in the same way over time. Departures from this assumption are considered error, but, unlike stability methods, true idiosyncratic change (consistent change on both items for a given subject) is not counted as error.[9] Although the assumption that the quantity and frequency items are parallel measures is probably not strictly valid, we can see that allowing for true individual change has a substantial impact on reliability assessment.

Validity. The ATC Monitoring System does not contain information on individual validity. It is possible, however, to get a general idea about group validity by comparing the mean daily consumption at intake for the ATC population with true consumption measures determined in experimental studies of alcoholic drinking.

A number of studies have investigated the free-drinking behavior of alcoholics over an extended period in an experimental setting. We took three such studies that reported precise, detailed measures of consumption and calculated the mean ounces of ethanol consumed per day (Mello and Mendelson, 1972; Gross et al., 1971; and Nathan et al., 1971). This mean

[9] The formula is $\rho = (MS_s - MS_e) / [MS_s + MS_e(m-1)]$, where m is the number of time periods and MS_s and MS_e are mean squares from a 3-factor repeated-measures analysis of variance with subjects, items, and times as factors. MS_s is the mean square for subjects and MS_e is the pooled mean square for subject-by-item, item-by-time, and subject-by-item-by-time interactions. The mean square for subject-by-time interactions is considered true rather than error variance. See Armor (1974) for further details.

daily consumption can be taken as a true mean for severe alcoholic populations in a free-drinking environment.

The experimentally determined consumption indices are compared with ATC self-reported consumption in Table A-9. The true experimental consumption measures for the alcoholic groups are quite similar to one another, ranging from 11.4 to 12.4 ounces/day (about a fifth of hard liquor per day), even though the number of cases is quite small. The ATC national mean for male non-DWI clients based on self-reports is somewhat lower, perhaps reflecting that not all ATC clients are as severely addicted as those in the experimental studies. For this reason we have separated out two treatment centers that serve more impaired populations. In these cases the self-reported group means are extremely close to the true experimental means.

For groups of alcoholics at intake, therefore, the validity of self-reports appears to be quite reasonable, with no substantial overreporting or underreporting. It is realized, of course, that overreporting and underreporting by individual clients may be cancelling out one another, so that individual validity still needs to be established. Since the ATC Monitoring System lacks such information, we must turn to other sources.

Validity in the Orange County Data[10]

Individual validity data for the treated alcoholic populations is quite rare. As for the general population, it can be obtained only by direct observa-

Table A-9. **Daily Alcohol Consumption Rates for Males in Experimental Studies Compared with Those of ATC Clients at Intake**

Group	Mean Consumption[a]	(N)	Number of Drinking Days
Experimental Studies: True Measures			
Mello and Mendelson (1972)	11.4	(18)	8-15
Gross et al. (1971)	12.4	(5)	5
Nathan et al. (1971)			
Skid-row alcoholics	11.8	(4)	18
Skid-row nonalcoholics	9.1	(4)	18
ATC Clients at Intake: Self-Reports			
National Sample	8.4	(11,505)	30
Brooklyn ATC	12.5	(129)	30
New Orleans ATC	11.0	(619)	30

[a] Ounces of ethanol per day.

[10] The data used in this section were generously supplied by Linda Sobell.

tion methods or by the use of BAC testing, both of which present a host of methodological difficulties. New data, collected by Linda Sobell at the Orange County Alcoholism Service in California, provide an opportunity for a preliminary analysis of individual validity.

Clients entering the Orange County treatment program during 1974 underwent a standardized intake procedure that generated information relevant to the question of self-report validity. First, the intake interviewer rated the degree of intoxication based on observation of the client's behavior. This rating was scored on a 1 to 4 scale as follows:

Rating Score	Meaning
1	Sober or cannot tell difference from sober
2	No specific drunken behavior, but suspected positive BAC
3	One or two specific indicants of intoxication
4	Many specific indicants of intoxication

Second, after the behavior rating, the client was asked how much he drank in the past 24 hours (today and yesterday) and the time of his last drink; in most cases the time that drinking started was also recorded. The amounts were recorded separately for beer, wine, and liquor, using relatively standardized quantities (e.g., pints, ounces, cans, etc.). After the self-report and without forewarning, the client was escorted to a room and given a BAC test using a gas chromatograph. Acetone levels, if any, were also recorded. Thus both the observed behavior and self-report can be compared with a "true" measurement of blood alcohol concentration.

For the analysis reported here we selected all new-entry clients with valid BACs who were admitted between January and July 1974; this yielded 593 clients. Reentering clients were excluded because they were likely to remember the BAC test and hence might have adjusted their self-report accordingly.

Validity of Observer Ratings. A common assumption in clinical practice is that an observer with experience and training can make valid judgments about a patient's behavior, perhaps more valid than self-judgments by the patient himself, particularly for those behaviors that are subject to denial. In the case of alcoholism, the phenomenon of denial is legion, and many clinical personnel have come to distrust the self-reports of alcoholics regarding their drinking behavior. From this standpoint, then, it is of considerable interest to compare the trained observer's rating of intoxication with the actual BAC test of Orange County clients.

The relationship between observer rating and BAC level is shown in Table A-10. Although many overt signs of intoxication may not appear

Table A-10.   Relationship between Observer Ratings of Intoxication and Actual BAC Levels, For Orange County Clients with Positive BACs at Intake

	Percentage of Clients in Each Range						
	BAC Level						
Observer Rating[a]	Negative	.01-.04	.05-.09	.10-.14	.15-.19	.20+	Total
Sober	97	89	65	53	36	29	89
No specific signs but suspected positive BAC	2	11	26	35	36	23	7
One or two specific signs	1	—	9	12	—	16	2
Definite intoxication	—	—	—	—	29	32	2
	100	100	100	100	100	100	
(N)	(473)	(35)	(23)	(17)	(14)	(31)	(593)
Total Percent	80	6	4	3	3	5	

Product-moment correlation = .55 (excluding negative BACs)

[a] Made by staff members experienced in screening alcoholics, prior to self-reports of consumption and BAC measurement.

until the blood alcohol level attains a value of .1 or higher, some signs—such as breath odor or flushed face—can be detected by experienced observers at fairly low levels of .05 or less (Jetter, 1938). Thus, it is interesting that two-thirds of those clients in the .05 to .09 range were rated as sober with no signs of intoxication. Moreover, 53 percent of those in the .10 to .15 range were rated as sober. For this alcoholic population, signs of intoxication were not predominant for the raters until the BAC passes the .15 level. It is also interesting that there are very few false positive ratings; i.e., ratings of definite signs of intoxication in the presence of negative or very low BACs.

Even though the correlation of .55 is fairly respectable, then, the inconsistencies are not uniformly distributed, with almost all errors being caused by rater underestimation of intoxication. It is clear that what we are observing here is the phenomenon of alcohol tolerance, whereby many alcoholics can drink substantial amounts of alcohol without showing intoxicating effects. This is undoubtedly one of the reasons for the discrepancies between consumption and self-reported drunkenness discussed earlier. At the group level, the ratings yield a total of 11 percent judged as having positive BACs, whereas in fact 20 percent had positive BACs.

This result raises serious questions about the ability of experienced observers, and possibly of collateral persons such as spouses, other relatives, or friends, to judge consumption behavior of alcoholics. Clearly, the assumption that observation by clinical experts yields more valid and more reliable information than self-reports requires more extensive proof.

Self-Reported Consumption. How do self-reports of consumption fare against the BAC test? We must repeat the caution that the relationship between BAC and true consumption—not to speak of self-reported consumption—is a complex one and presents a number of hazards for a validity test. Nonetheless, the information so obtained is better than none at all.

Perhaps the easiest comparison is between a "yes-no" dichotomy of both the BAC and self-report. An alcohol quantity score was derived indicating ounces of ethanol consumed since 12:01 A.M. on the day of intake, and this was then dichotomized into the categories of "no drinking" and "some drinking." A client was considered to be drinking if the self-report score was greater than 0 ounces of ethanol. Likewise, the BAC test was dichotomized into the categories "negative" and "positive" (scores greater than 0).

The cross-tabulation of the dichotomized self-report and BAC is shown in Table A-11. There is striking agreement between the self-report and the BAC reading, with 91 percent of the clients giving accurate responses. The product-moment biserial correlation (or phi coefficient) is .70, which indicates a high degree of individual validity. Of course, part of the reason for the high validity is that the "null-null" cell is very large, encompassing three-fourths of the total sample. Another way to look at it is the proportion of drinkers underreporting, which in this case is $5/20$, or about 25 percent. On the other hand, unlike the observer ratings, the proportion overreporting (false positives) is about the same, or $4/19$.

This produces an extremely high degree of group validity, with 19 per-

Table A-11. **Cross-Tabulation of Self-Reported Alcohol Use and BAC Reading**

| Self-Report Categories[a] | Percentage Based on Total Sample | | |
| | BAC-Test Categories | | |
	Negative	Positive	Total
No drinking	76	5	81
Some drinking	4	15	19
(N)	(472)	(118)	(590)[b]
Total	80	20	100

Product-moment correlation = .70

[a] Drinking since 12:01 A.M. on intake day.
[b] Three clients had uncodeable responses on alcohol self-report.

cent reporting some drinking compared with 20 percent with positive BACs. In other words, the group validity of self-reports is considerably better than the group validity of observer ratings.

This result parallels that for the general population, suggesting that very few persons, alcoholic or not, lie about whether or not they have been drinking when asked. For the general population reporting drinking that day, however, there was some underreporting, particularly among those with high BACs. It remains for us to investigate the extent of under-reporting among Orange County clients in the recent drinking subgroup.

In order to use actual BAC level to detect underreporting or overreport-ing of consumption, we need to translate consumption into an estimated BAC level. Given that we know only the sex of the subject and the approx-imate time when drinking took place in the past 24 hours or so before the test, such an estimation requires a number of additional assumptions. First, the analysis is confined to males, each of whom is assumed to weigh 165 pounds. Second, it is assumed that 1 ounce of ethanol produces a BAC of about 0.04 for a man at this weight. Finally, it is assumed that the drinking took place uniformly during the reported time interval and that metabolic elimination of ethanol occurred at the rate of .5 ounces/ hour, starting with the onset of drinking, thereby yielding a BAC reduction of about .015 hour.[11] No correction could be made for food consumed or for any other idiosyncratic factor.

The comparison of estimated and actual BAC is shown in Table A-12 for 150 male clients who had either a positive BAC or reported such alco-hol consumption during the past 24 hours before the time of the test. The overall correlation of .50 seems quite high considering the crudeness of the estimation procedure. In particular, we note that of those clients with low estimated BACs in the 0 to .04 range, 65 percent had consistent BACs. On the other hand, 62 percent of those whose self-report yielded an esti-mated BAC of .05 to .09 had an actual BAC over .10. Note, also, that some of the inconsistency comes from overreporting; e.g., 76 percent of those with estimated BACs between .10-.19 had actual BACs less than .10.

Overall, the group validity is remarkably high for this drinking sub-group, with a mean actual BAC of .086 and a mean estimated BAC of .063. On the other hand, the means in the right-most column show that underreporting is not uniformly distributed; unrerreporting is nonexistent in the lowest BAC category but is fairly substantial in the higher categories. Overall, there are only 9 clients with estimated BACs over .10 and actual

[11] Various studies show ethanol elimination rates from .32 to .49 ounces/hour (stand-ardized to a 165-pound male), but with the higher rate applying to alcoholics (Wal-gren and Barry, 1970).

Table A-12. Estimated BAC Based on Self-Reports Compared with Actual BAC, Orange County Male Clients at Intake Who Drank in Past 24 Hours

	Percentage of Responses in Each BAC Range					Mean Estimated BAC
	Estimated BAC from Self-Reports[a]					
Actual BAC	.0-.04	.05-.09	.10-.19	.20+	Total	
.0-.04	65	19	38	15	52	.036
.05-.09	15	19	38	—	15	.030
.10-.19	13	38	12	30	18	.087
.20+	7	24	12	55	15	.140
	100	100	100	100	100	
(N)	(106)	(16)	(8)	(20)	(150)	
Total	71	11	5	13		

Product-moment correlation = .50[b]
Mean actual BAC   = .086 (standard deviation = .084)
Mean estimated BAC   = .063 (standard deviation = .079)

[a] Based on the assumptions that each male weighs 165 pounds, that 1 ounce of ethanol produces a BAC of about .04, and that metabolic elimination of ethanol will occur at the rate of about .5 oz/hr, implying a reduction in BAC level of .015/hr. Estimated BACs over .35 were recoded to .35.
[b] Based on somewhat finer gradations of BAC levels.

BACs over .10; however there are 31 clients (20 percent of the total drinking group) with estimated BACs under .1 and actual BACs over .1.

Although the mean estimated BAC is below the actual BAC in the three highest BAC categories, the fact that the mean increases progressively suggests that the estimation procedure may be partly responsible. Accordingly, Table A-13 shows the actual consumption reported for the 31 clients with serious underestimation, i.e., actual BACs over .10 but estimated BACs under .10. As we can see, even underreporting is no simple matter. Only 12 men appear to be consistently underreporting on both the day of the test and the day before (less than 3 ounces of ethanol on both days); consumption in this range should not yield BACs over .10, even for men weighing 120 pounds (all of those who reported consumption of 2 to 2.9 ounces had BACs over .15). On the other hand, 12 men reported consuming more than 7 ounces on the day *before* they come to the center, even though most reported considerably less on the day of the test; another reported consuming more than 7 ounces on the day of the test but in the early morning hours. Since consumption of 7 ounces of ethanol or more should yield BACs over .2 for the average man, and over .15 for a heavier man weighing 200 pounds, we should not classify these as cases of overall denial. They may have underreported on the day of the test,

Table A-13.   Self-Reported Consumption in the Past 24 Hours for Orange County Clients Having Actual BACs over .10 and Estimated BACs Under .10

Ounces of Ethanol Consumed Yesterday (before 12 midnight)	Number of Respondents Reporting Each Range						
	Ounces of Ethanol Consumed Today (from 12:01 A.M.)					Total (N)	Percent Total
	0-.9	1-2.9	3-4.9	5-6.9	7+		
0-.9	5	4	1	—	1	(11)	35
1-2.9	1	2	—	—	—	(3)	10
3-4.9	—	2	3	—	—	(5)	16
5-6.9	—	—	—	—	—	—	—
7+	4	2	5	—	1	(12)	41
Total (N)	(10)	(10)	(9)	—	(2)	(31)	
Total Percent	32	32	29	—	7		

but their admission of higher consumption on the day before coming to the center contradicts a conclusion of general denial for this group.[12] Combining the 6 borderline clients with the definitely underreporting group, we can conclude that of the 150 male drinking clients, only 18 (12 percent) appear to be distorting their typical true consumption by a serious amount.

These results are quite consistent with the ATC group validity analysis, and the suggestion is strong that most alcoholics entering treatment are not likely either to underestimate or overestimate their consumption by very large amounts, at least if drinking is assessed for some period before the intake day itself. But can this be generalized to followup? It is possible that clients are honest about their consumption when they are seeking treatment, but not at followup when they may want to make a good impression. We can give this hypothesis a very preliminary test with a small sample of Orange County clients interviewed and given postinterview BAC tests at various followup periods.

In order to make the analysis as comparable as possible to the ATC followup data, we have selected only clients reporting some drinking days within the past 2 months; this would correspond fairly well with those ATC clients with nonzero daily consumption score (i.e., clients reporting some drinking in the past 30 days). There were 18 such clients who contributed a total of 30 followup observations consisting of a BAC test

---

[12] The Orange County facility had a stated policy of nonadmission for clients drinking within the past 12 hours, so some clients might tend to understate their consumption on the day of intake.

preceded by a self-report of consumption on the interview day only.[13] Most interviews took place in the client's home, but some were conducted at the Orange County facility; the followup period ranged from 2 to 10 months after discharge.

The comparison of BAC and self-reported consumption is given in Table A-14. A total of 20 observations or about two-thirds of the sample were reports of low consumption (less than 2.9 ounces) with correspondingly low BACs (under .09); 14 of these were "null-null" cases with negative BACs and no drinking reported that day. Another 4 were consistently high, making a total of 24 (80 percent) valid responses. On the other hand, all of the seriously inconsistent responses occur in the underreporting category, so that 6 reports (20 percent) of the total sample appear to be denials of the true amount consumed on the followup day. Unfortunately, there is no information about amounts consumed on other days, so we cannot find out whether this denial is general or applies only to the day of the interview. Nonetheless, the data indicate that underreporting at followup does occur, although the proportion of underreporters for this nonabstaining group is fairly small.

Summary

The data presented in this section by no means offer a complete test of reliability and validity for self-reported alcohol consumption. Yet when

Table A-14. Comparison of Actual BAC and Self-Reported Consumption at Followup Test for Orange County Clients Reporting Some Drinking Days in Past Two Months

	Number of Observations in Each Range[a]						
	Self-Reported Consumption on Day of Test (ounces of ethanol)						
Actual BAC	0-.9	1-2.9	3.49	5-6.9	7+	Total (N)	Total Percent
.0-.04	17	—	—	—	—	(17)	57
.05-.09	—	3	—	—	—	(3)	10
.10-.19	1	2	—	1	—	(4)	13
.20+	—	3	—	—	3	(6)	20
Total (N)	(18)	(8)	—	(1)	(3)	(30)	
Total percent	60	27	—	3	10		

[a] The 30 observations are based on 18 clients.

[13] An analysis of the 18 first followups yielded essentially the same results as the full 30, so knowledge of the BAC test procedure did not appear to affect self-reports.

the new data here are combined with existing research reports, a fairly positive picture begins to emerge.

First, reliability and validity of the frequency of drinking—and of whether one has drunk at all—appears to be quite satisfactory for behavioral measures of this type whether we are speaking of the general or the alcoholic population. Not only is the consistency reliability high for both groups, but, when self-reports about recent drinking are compared with BAC tests, very few persons who claim no drinking are found to have positive BACs.

Second, the group validity of the amount of drinking appears to be adequate for the alcoholic population, particularly at the time of entering treatment. This means that one can probably depend on the daily consumption index to give a fairly accurate description of the amount of drinking for groups of alcoholics (e.g., for the clients of a treatment center taken as a whole).

Finally, we must contrast this positive picture with a potential trouble spot. It would appear that amount of consumption is underreported among some of the heavier drinkers in both the general and the alcoholic populations. For the general population this leads to unsatisfactory group validity, with self-reports leading to a national consumption figure that is about one-half of the figure for the national beverage sales. But we strongly suspect that the underreporting is confined to the upper one-third or one-fourth of the consumption distribution, with underestimation being on the order of 50 to 60 percent for this group. Therefore, persons in the general population who say they drink between 1 and 5 ounces of ethanol daily may in fact be drinking about twice that amount.

For alcoholic populations the underreporting appears to be confined to a smaller proportion, so that group validity is not affected to the same degree. Perhaps 10 to 15 percent of alcoholics who have been drinking recently underreport to such an extent that they might be incorrectly classified as nonalcoholic. Clearly, the size of this group is a critical issue, particularly in followup studies where one needs to assess the proportion of clients who are drinking at light or moderate levels. We encourage the broader use of BAC tests in field followup studies to establish a firmer estimate of the size and nature of this group.

BEHAVIORAL PROBLEMS AND IMPAIRMENT

Whatever the final judgment about the reliability and validity of self-reported alcohol consumption, its relevance to the reliability and validity of self-reports about alcohol-induced impairment is not obvious from a priori considerations. On the one hand, certain types of impairment behavior such as number of arrests or days absent from work may be singular events less subject to inaccurate recall; on the other hand, impairment indicators usually deal with more serious and possibly more sensitive issues and may therefore be subject to greater denial. Clearly, impairment indices such as those used in this report require an independent assessment of reliability and validity.

There is not much research on impairment validity and the little that exists does not produce complete consensus. Knupfer (1967) found underreporting of arrests among persons known to have drinking-related arrests. The underreporting rate was 27 percent, although at the group level self-reports yielded a higher total arrest rate than official records. Across-interview techniques were used by Summers (1970) to establish low reliability of various self-reported alcohol-related behaviors. On the positive side, Guze et al. (1963) used corroborating family member reports to conclude satisfactory validity of self-reported alcoholism symptoms or at least absence of underreporting; in fact, self-reports were twice as likely to yield a diagnosis of alcoholism than spouse reports, and yielded a correct diagnosis in 97 percent of the cases. A study of the same group 8 or 9 years later yielded a test-retest correlation of .41 for alcoholism diagnosis based on symptoms (Guze and Goodwin, 1972). Equal numbers shifted from a nonalcoholism to an alcoholism diagnosis, and vice versa. Although questions were asked in a "have you ever . . ." format, it is possible that much of the turnover reflects real change in alcoholism status over the 9-year period. Sobell et al. (1974) compared self-reports on drinking-related arrests with police and FBI records and found satisfactory validity. This is one of the few studies that permits determination of both individual and group validity. Individual validity was determined by a correlation coefficient between self-report and the record result; this was .65. Even though this correlation is not terribly high, it indicates considerable individual-level validity. But those making errors were about equally divided between those making overestimates and those making underestimates, so the self-reported group mean was 6.4 arrests compared with a true group mean of 7.8. The self-reported mean is still too low, but the discrepancy is not large.

The general conclusion one can reach from the existing literature is that reliability and validity of impairment symptoms are similar to consumption measures. It appears to be a lot better than might be assumed, but it is not perfect and some underreporting does occur. It remains for us to present information on our self-reported impairment and drinking problem indices.

The Drinking Problem Index for the Harris Surveys

The Harris surveys included a series of 16 items adapted from question-naires used by Cahalan (1970) to assess symptomatic drinking patterns in general populations. These items were formed into an index that was used to define problem drinkers.

The items, response categories, and frequency distributions for non-abstainers in one of the Harris surveys (January, 1974) are shown in Table A-15. The drinking problem index was formed by averaging item

Table A-15. Drinking Problem Index for Harris Surveys: Frequency Distribution for Nonabstainers[a]

		Frequency Distribution for Nonabstainers, in Four Response Categories (%)			
Items		Never	Seldom	Sometimes Not Often	Frequently
1.	Talking a lot about drinking	36	37	21	5
2.	Taking a drink at lunchtime	68	23	7	2
3.	Taking more than 2 or 3 drinks at one sitting	35	32	25	7
4.	Taking a drink to feel better	61	20	16	3
5.	Going several days without taking a drink, and then having several drinks at one time	50	20	22	8
6.	Getting morose or sad when drinking	82	12	5	1
7.	Needing a drink to have fun	75	14	10	1
8.	Gulping your drinks	82	11	5	2
9.	Showing the effects of liquor more quickly than most people	65	18	12	5
10.	Starting to drink without even thinking about it	81	11	6	2
11.	Slurring words or walking un-steadily after only a few drinks	80	12	6	2
12.	Drinking alone	59	19	15	7
13.	Getting belligerent after having a few drinks	88	9	2	1
14.	Taking a drink in the morning to relieve a hangover	95	3	1	1
15.	Forgetting what you did while drinking	83	11	4	1
16.	Keeping a bottle hidden some-where for a quick pick me-up	97	1	1	1

[a] Data shown for one survey only (January, 1974); N=922-950. Other surveys had very similar distributions.

scores (coded as 0 to 3 for "never" to "frequently," respectively). The median of this index was about .5, a score that could be obtained by answering 8 items "never" and 8 "seldom," or 12 "never" and 4 "sometimes," and so forth. A "problem drinker" was a person whose daily ethanol consumption index was greater than 1.5 and who scored above the median on the drinking problem index.

Reliability. The Harris surveys were cross-sectional in nature, and hence only internal consistency reliability can be assessed. To do so, a factor analysis was performed and appropriate reliability statistics were computed. These results are shown in Table A-16 for the January 1974 survey.

The internal consistency reliability of .85 is quite substantial, especially considering that abstainers are excluded from the analysis (i.e., they are not scored as "never" on each item). All but one of the items load over .4 on the first factor, and only a few items load heavily on the small, second

Table A-16.   Consistency Reliability Analysis for the Drinking Problem Index

Item Number[a]	Factor Loadings[b]	
	I	II
1	.39	−.15
2	.46	.41
3	.63	.28
4	.53	.41
5	.40	.06
6	.62	−.12
7	.64	.06
8	.56	−.05
9	.40	−.60
10	.57	−.06
11	.54	−.50
12	.42	.52
13	.68	−.19
14	.63	.07
15	.66	−.15
16	.54	.05
Root	4.83	1.40

Cronbach's alpha = .85[c]

[a] See Table A-15 for item wording.
[b] Principal components analysis without rotation.
[c] Approximated by the formula $n(\lambda-1)/\lambda(n-1)$ where n is the number of items and λ is the root (eigenvalue). See Armor, 1974.

factor. We conclude that the 16 drinking problem items form a single dimension with high internal consistency, so that a person who reports having one of these problems will tend to report others in this same set.

Validity. There is no information in the Harris surveys that permits a true validity assessment. The most we can do is to consider concurrent validity by taking into account the relationship between the problem index and other alcohol-related behaviors. In this respect we correlated the drinking problem index with the behavioral impairment index (available in one Harris survey) and found a correlation of only .33. Apparently these two indices are measuring different aspects of problems due to alcohol.

The ATC Behavioral Impairment Index

The behavioral impairment index was described briefly in Chapter 4. The index is composed of 12 items measuring serious physical and behavioral impairment arising from the effects of alcohol. Some of the more serious items were used in conjunction with the daily consumption index to define the remission criterion used throughout this study.

The items, categories, and frequency distribution are given in Table A-17 for all clients in the 18-month followup sample who reported some drinking in the last 30 days.[14] The collapsed categories differ for different groups of items, reflecting differing frequency distributions. For the purpose of constructing an index, the 4-category items were scored as 0 to 3 for none to the highest category; 2-category items were scored as 0 to 2, and the one 3-category item was scored as 0, 2, and 3.

Consistency Reliability. Internal consistency reliability can be established by a factor analysis of impairment items at a single time period. Factor analyses and internal consistency reliability coefficients were computed for the impairment index using the male, non-DWI sample at intake, 6 months, and 18 months. Since abstainers would, by definition, be coded "none" on each impairment item, they were excluded from the analysis to prevent spurious inflation of the correlations.

The factor loadings and reliability coefficients are shown in Table A-18 for the 18-month drinking sample consisting of 329 male, non-DWI clients.[15] All but three items have very high loadings on the first factor

---

[14] Including females, DWI, and nonintake clients (i.e., single contacts and preintakes).
[15] The factor analysis of the intake and 6-month followup data yielded very similar results.

Table A-17. ATC Behavioral Impairment Index, 18-Month Followup

Items[a]	Frequency Distribution (%), by Frequency of Occurrence in Last 30 Days[b]			
	None	1-2	3-5	Over 5
1. Number of times had difficulty sleeping	56	7	9	28
2. Number of memory lapses or "blackouts"	78	11	6	6
3. Number of times had tremors	71	10	6	13
4. Number of quarrels with others while drinking	77	10	6	6
5. Days of work missed due to drinking	82	7	5	6
	None	1-4	5-10	Over 10
6. Number of meals missed due to drinking	64	11	9	16
7. Number of times had drink on awakening	66	9	10	14
8. Number of times drunk	51	29	9	11
	12 Hours or More		Less Than 12 Hours	
9. Longest period without drinking	92		8	
	Never	Usually with Others	Usually Alone	Always
10. How often drank alone	30	38	20	13
	Under 6 Hours	6-12 Hours	12 or More Hours	
11. Longest continuous period of drinking	38	15	47	
	No	Yes		
12. Drank on the job	90	10		

[a] See Appendix D for exact wording.
[b] Number of cases ranges between 774 and 803 due to nonresponses; 537 clients had abstained for the past 30 days.

and two of these, drinking alone and drinking on the job, have moderate loadings over .2. The low loading of .06 for "time between drinks" suggests that this item is not measuring impairment as defined by the other 11 items. While the item should probably be excluded from the total impairment index, we kept it in for compatibility with ATC Monitoring System data. We note that the six items used for the "serious symptoms"

Table A-18. Consistency Reliability Analysis for the ATC Behavioral Impairment Index, 18-Month Followup

Items[a]	Factor Loadings[b]	
	I	II
1. Sleep problems	.54	−.29
2. Blackouts[c]	.67	−.25
3. Shakes[c]	.72	.05
4. Quarrels	.45	−.25
5. Missed work[c]	.63	−.07
6. Missed meals[c]	.74	.05
7. Morning drinking[c]	.79	.16
8. Drunk[c]	.79	−.03
9. Time between drinks	.06	.86
10. Drinks alone	.35	.34
11. Continuous drinking	.66	.17
12. Drinks on the job	.23	.10
Root	4.28	1.14

Cronbach's alpha = .84[d]

[a] See Appendix B for exact working.
[b] Principal components solution without rotations; N = 329 male, non-DWI clients.
[c] Items used for the "serious symptoms" index.
[a] See Appendix D for exact wording.

index all have loadings over .6 and hence form the core of the meaningful covariance among this set of items.

Stability and Time-Item Reliability. Since the behavioral impairment items are assessed several times from intake to followup, it is possible to assess reliability based on over-time measures. Given the small number of clients that had both 6-month and 18-month followup reports for this analysis, we selected a larger sample of about 1500 male, non DWI clients who had intake reports and both 30-day and 6-month followup reports from the ATC Monitoring System. Also, since many clients were seriously impaired at intake but were abstaining at followup, the analysis included abstainers scored as zero on the impairment index.

Reliability coefficients for this sample are shown in Table A-19. The test-retest correlations are quite low, reflecting considerable nonuniform change in impairment over time (i.e., some clients improved and others did not). It is especially interesting to note that the intake/30-day correlation is lower than the intake/6-month correlation, perhaps reflecting the beginning of relapse at the later period. More-impaired clients have

Table A-19.   Stability and Time-Item Reliability for the ATC Behavioral Impairment Index[a]

	Reliability Coefficients for Four Time Periods			
Reliability Method	Intake to 30 Days	Intake to 6 Months	30 Days to 6 Months	Intake to 30 Days to 6 Months
Test-retest, Eq. (1)	.21	.26	.35	—
Simplex, Eq. (2)	—	—	—	.33
Time-item[b]	.83	.86	.91	.83

[a] N = 1556 male, non-DWI clients with an intake report and both 30-days and 6-month followup reports.
[b] For descriptions, see footnote 9 in this appendix.

higher relapse rates and hence may resemble their intake profile more at 6 months than at 30 days. In any event, this pattern of correlations violates the simplex assumption that more distant time points have lower correlations, so that the simplex reliability of .33 is undoubtedly confounding true change with error.

This interpretation is bolstered further by the time-item reliabilities in the third row of the table. This method allows for true idiosyncratic change, provided the change is consistent across all items in the index. All of these reliabilities are quite high and resemble the internal consistency reliability. We conclude, then, that the behavioral impairment index has a satisfactory level of reliability.

Validity. As with the drinking problem index, we have no independent information for establishing the true validity of the impairment index. Chapter 4 presented some correlations between the impairment index and alcohol consumption measures that are useful for establishing concurrent validity. The substantial correlation of .68 between the behavioral impairment index and the daily consumption for nonabstainers at the 18-month followup (Table 13) shows a level of consistency compatible with theoretical expectations. On the other hand, the literature in this field leads us to expect that, like the consumption index, there is some denial and under-reporting of impairment in our samples. Although we cannot calculate its extent, we have no reason to believe it is any more substantial than that for the consumption index.

APPENDIX B

Reaction to the Rand Report
on "Alcoholism and Treatment"

INTRODUCTION

When this volume was published originally as a Rand report (R-1739-NIAAA) in June 1976, it generated a storm of controversy widely covered in the media. This controversy centered particularly on the finding that some alcoholics in our samples return to normal drinking. The report and its findings on normal drinking were criticized and attacked in various quarters, especially by AA-oriented treatment professionals and prominent recovered alcoholics. Support was forthcoming from other quarters, particularly from alcoholism researchers, although these voices were heard less frequently in the media. This furor is worthy of investigation in its own right since, as we have documented amply in the main text, the Rand report was by no means the first study to present such a finding.

While the reasons for the controversy and its occurrence at this particular time are intriguing, it is not our intention to investigate these issues here. We are mainly concerned about the many scientific and methodological issues raised during the debate. Controversies arising from the conflict between scientific findings and conventional wisdom frequently center on the technical validity of the research. This is especially true in the behavioral sciences, where scientists frequently disagree among themselves about the adequacies of data or analytic procedures. Thus, the bulk of the comments about the Rand report dealt with methodology, and the validity of our conclusions was often challenged because of perceived limitations of the data we used.

We disagree with those critics who claim that methodological problems invalidate most of our conclusions. While we state in the main text that the data have various limitations, numerous methodological analyses presented in Chapters 4, 5, and Appendix A suggest that our conclusions, prop-

212

erly qualified, are sound. Nonetheless, the serious student exposed to the media debate may still have questions about the seriousness of these limitations. Accordingly, the purpose of this appendix is to document some of the scientific content of the debate by presenting both comments on our work and our replies. Some of this material has been published elsewhere, but other parts are previously unpublished. We have divided this appendix into three sections: the NIAAA reviews, the National Council on Alcoholism (NCA) press conference, and the *Journal of Studies on Alcohol* (JSA) reviews.

The NIAAA Reviews

Some of the Rand report critics, particularly those from the NCA, have portrayed the study as standing universally rejected by scientists because of methodological defects. This characterization, which has also been implied by some press accounts, is incorrect. Numerous reviews from experts in the fields of alcoholism, psychiatry, and medicine have come to different conclusions. While most of these reviewers, like the authors, have pointed out the study's methodological limitations, they have generally considered it to be a careful scientific work meriting serious attention.

With the objective of providing a more balanced picture of reaction to the report, we publish three of these reviews here for the first time. They were commissioned by Dr. Ernest Noble, Director of NIAAA, shortly after the Rand report was released. These reviews are representative of many other scientific reviews, formal and informal, which the authors have received since publication of the original report.

Following these reviews is the entire text of a brief press release issued by NIAAA on June 23, 1977, in response to the broad media coverage of the normal drinking finding.

The NCA Press Conference

In the two weeks following publication of the Rand report, the National Council on Alcoholism (NCA) held two press conferences on the subject of the Rand study. At the first, the Rand report was characterized as "dangerous" and "unscientific," despite the fact that the NCA had not yet seen the report.[1] Two weeks later, the NCA held a second press conference to provide more substantive methodological criticism of the report. As the most prominent advocates of abstention, NCA spokesmen were most critical of our finding that some alcoholics returned to normal drinking.

[1] *The New York Times,* June 11, 1976, p. 1.

Indeed, the NCA even objected to public discussion of the idea of normal drinking.

Representative statements from the NCA-Rand exchange growing out of the second NCA press conference are reproduced here. Although the NCA statements are often acrimonious in tone, it is obvious that their criticisms rest upon methodological issues and hence raise serious scientific questions about the report. To illustrate both the tone and content of the exchange we are including the official press release issued by the NCA in its entirety, followed by a selection of their more specific methodological criticisms and our replies. Part of this exchange was published in the October 1, 1976, issue of *Psychiatric News.*

The JSA Studies

The *Journal of Studies on Alcohol* (JSA) received a number of comments on the Rand report from various professionals in the alcoholism field. Four of these comments were selected for publication along with our reply in the January 1977 issue of JSA. This exchange is reprinted here in its entirety.

NIAAA REVIEWS

THE UNIVERSITY OF MICHIGAN

School of Public Health

Department of Community Health Programs   Ann Arbor, Michigan 48104

June 25, 1976

Ernest P. Noble, Ph.D., M.D.
Director, NIAAA, ADAMHA
5600 Fisher's Lane
Rockville, Maryland 20852

Dear Ernie:

Thank you for the opportunity to review the Rand report on "Alcoholism and Treatment". As you know, I have been associated with NIAAA as an extra-mural research consultant since its inception as a special branch of NIMH a decade ago. In that role, I have reviewed several hundred grantee research applications and progress reports. The Rand report is the most exciting one I have seen. This is so primarily because it deals comprehensively, boldly, yet objectively with cri tical issues that have long nagged practitioners and researchers in the alcoholism field.

It is obvious, of course, that the Rand report by itself cannot resolve these critical issues. No single piece of research in this area can ever be so perfectly designed as to escape justifiable criticism in respect to some shortcomings in methodology, research design, and data analysis. In this regard, the authors of the Rand report deserve the highest commendation for their forthrightness and perceptiveness in stating clearly the major scientific constraints in their own work.

However, what the Rand report has dramatically accomplished is to invite constructive doubt about theory and practice in the alcoholism field and to pinpoint specific research questions in need of urgent answers for policymakers and service-program personnel who must make humane and rational decisions about people with drinking problems. While it is understandable (and even desirable) that there will be ideological and political-professional counter-pressures, it is to be hoped that NIAAA will remain an outspoken advocate of the constructive doubting process.

-2-

My detailed critique of the Rand report is enclosed.

Best wishes!

Cordially yours,

Len

Lenin A. Baler, Ph.D., S.D. in Hyg.
Chairman, Department of Community Health
    Programs and
Professor of Community Mental Health

Critique of "Alcoholism and Treatment"

1. Self-Report Data: Many observers of alcoholic patients have been impressed with the salience of such defenses as "denial" and sociopathic "lying". Thus they would be reluctant to accept self-reports of "consumption" and concurrent "behavioral impairment" as valid data. The validity would be most in doubt in the case of reported "normal drinking".

Self-reports on "consumption" should be checked against observational data from relatives, friends, neighbors, and other available informants in the specific case. Self-reports on "behavioral impairment" should be substantiated by clinical examinations aperiodically during the follow-up period.

2. Response-Rates (Losses to Follow-up): Most scientists would reject out-of-hand the 21% response rate for the 6-month follow-up sample as patently unacceptable as a basis for generalization about the starting cohort. Even the 62% response rate for the 18-month follow-up sample falls dramatically short of minimum standards of acceptability. The Rand report data that indicate cohort comparability on selected intake characteristics are relevant only to establishing the probability that the two cohorts can be considered "matched" initially on those parameters. There obviously can still be bias due to selective non-follow-up related to outcome. The Rand report argues that if such a bias existed there should be less favorable outcomes for the 18-month follow-up, which is not the case. The assumption is that increasing the response-rate from 21% to 62% should catch more of the lost bad-outcome group if it exists. This may not be the case if the worst bad outcomes are the hardest to follow-up and remain concentrated in the 38% losses to follow-up in the 18-month sample.

3. Research Design: Even assuming that the 6-month and 18-month samples are "matched" at intake and do not differ at outcome because of bias due to differing non-response rates, there is little reason clinically to value the aggregate comparison data. This is so, because as the Rand researchers themselves recognize, a finding of no aggregate differences could mask a huge variety of off-setting individual changes. The Rand researchers did select out a sub-sample of individuals who were in both the 6-month and the 18-month follow-ups. But this sub-sample is relatively small (N=220). Furthermore, the individuals all come from the 6-month cohort where the response-rate was only 21% at that time, and none of these individuals are obviously in the 38% of the 18-month cohort who were not located at follow-up. Few scientists would find this crucial individual relapse data acceptably free of potential bias or a reasonable basis for generalization. What is needed is a design where the same starting cohort is followed over time in such a way that losses to follow-up are minimized.

4. Data Analysis: A major finding in regard to the effects of treatment is that the total "amount" of treatment appears to be related to outcome. Since exposure to varying amounts of treatment can hardly be expected to be a randomly assigned variable, it becomes necessary to examine the relationship under sub-conditions of known or presumptive relevant variables. In terms of other Rand findings, certainly

-2-

this cross-tabulation must be done in respect to client drinking at intake, social stability, and socio-economic status. One can easily determine then whether there is client self-selection bias in the relationship between outcome and amount of treatment.

5.   Errors: Table 10, "Changes in Behavioral Impairment", is probably either mislabled or otherwise in error. This table contains critical data. If the table is correct it would be disastrous in respect to any credibility in the Rand study. For example, it implies that normal drinkers (i.e. 0-5 oz./day) actually become more behaviorally impaired from intake to follow-up in both the 6-month and 18-month samples.

WASHINGTON UNIVERSITY

SCHOOL OF MEDICINE

DEPARTMENT OF PSYCHIATRY
BARNES AND RENARD HOSPITALS
4940 AUDUBON AVENUE
ST. LOUIS, MISSOURI 63110

June 28, 1976

TO CALL WRITER DIRECT
PHONE (314) 454- 3875

Dr. Ernest Noble
Director
National Institute of
  Alcohol Abuse and Alcoholism
National Institute of Mental Health
5600 Fishers Lane
Rockville, Maryland 20852

Dear Ernie:

    Here is the report you requested.

        Sincerely yours,

        Samuel B. Guze, M.D.
        Spencer T. Olin Professor and
        Head of the Department of Psychiatry

SBG:rb
enc.

<u>Alcoholism and Treatment</u>, a Rand report, by David J. Armor,
J. Michael Polich, and Harriet B. Stambul is interesting, provocative, and
important. The authors are obviously well-informed, competent, and sophisticated.
They appear to recognize and appreciate the complex issues that their report
covers. They have done as much as possible with the data. They provide useful
analyses concerning the relative roles of social and cultural factors in abstention,
amount of drinking, and problem drinking.

Repeatedly, they explicitly describe the limitations inherent in their
study – limitations not of their doing. Their discussions of these issues are
clear and insightful. But, the overall tone of the report may cause unwary and
unsophisticated readers to draw erroneous conclusions, because the authors do
not explicitly warn their readers about such conclusions.

The authors note, on page 131, that "these results strongly suggest
that the key ingredient in remission may be a client's decision to seek and
remain in treatment rather than the specific nature of the treatment received."

On page 134, they restate their conclusion: "If recovery does not
depend on the particular features of treatment, then what client characteristics
are responsible? Again, while the severity of alcoholism symptoms and the social
factors of stability and socioeconomic status affect successful remissions, even
the unstable, low-SES, definitely alcoholic treated clients have a remission
rate of 51 percent; other background variables have little additional impact.
We must therefore search elsewhere for the critical determinants of recovery.
One might propose certain critical personality factors, but here again existing
research has not discovered any such characteristics that affect recovery more
than social instability. Given these results, the strong suggestion is that

- 2 -

recovery depends to a large extent on the individual alcoholic's decision to stop or cut down consumption, and that this decision is only modestly related to his more permanent social and psychological profile."

They continue, on page 135: "... our data show that a decision to stop drinking is not tied to accepting formal treatment, since in many instances remission occurs after only a single contact with a treatment center. Further, the decision may occur during the course of treatment rather than at the beginning, and it does not necessarily have to be accompanied by a great deal of verbalized enthusiasm as might be implied by most operational definitions of motivation."

In other words, their analyses indicate that the follow-up findings were largely unrelated to treatment. This is the authors' conclusion, but it is not the tone of their report.

What the data do demonstrate is that remission is possible for many alcoholics and that many of these are able to drink normally for extended periods. These points deserve emphasis, because they offer encouragement to patients, to their families, and to relevant professionals. The findings indicate that alcoholism is not uniformly hopeless, even if the disorder is severe and long-lasting. In addition, the findings suggest that, in time, with further research, it may be possible to facilitate remissions earlier and more readily.

As the authors know, a valid study of treatment requires adequate controls, stratified according to those variables likely to affect outcome. Even the most sophisticated statistical analyses and large samples cannot compensate satisfactorily for the absence of such controls. It is too bad the authors did not make this point explicitly in their summary and conclusions, particularly since they made it implicitly many times.

- 3 -

Finally, even though the authors indicate that they could find no differences at the initial study between alcoholics who were followed up and those lost to follow-up, it seems unreasonable to assume, as the authors do, that the rates of remission were similar for the two groups. On the contrary, it is likely that the relapse or failure rates were considerably higher for the 79 percent lost to follow-up in the six month follow-up series and for the 38 percent lost to follow-up in the 18 month follow-up series. The findings at follow-up would be noteworthy even if all subjects lost to follow-up were considered failures. The overall "success rate" would be lower, but probably closer to the true state of affairs. It is hard not to conclude that a desire to emphasize favorable outcome influenced the handling of these data.

In summary, as a sophisticated research report to professional peers, this study deserves serious consideration and thought. Its initial distribution to the news media and its tone of exaggerated optimism, however, raise misgivings that the authors could easily have avoided.

Samuel B. Guze, M.D.
Spencer T. Olin Professor and
Head of the Department of Psychiatry
Vice Chancellor for Medical Affairs
Washington University
School of Medicine
St. Louis, Missouri 63110

HARVARD MEDICAL SCHOOL   ◆   MASSACHUSETTS GENERAL HOSPITAL

GERALD L. KLERMAN, M.D.
Professor of Psychiatry

Director
Stanley Cobb Psychiatric Research Laboratories
Massachusetts General Hospital
Boston, Massachusetts 02114

13 October 1976

Ernest Noble, M.D.
Director, National Institute of
 Alcoholism and Alcohol Abuse
Parklawn Building, Room 16C03
5600 Fishers Lane
Rockville, MD 20852

Dear Ernie,

I am enclosing a copy of my report evaluating the Armor/Rand documents.

As I told Mr. Towle, I think this is a very important document. I think
the conclusions are highly justified. I understand you are under great
political pressure regarding the issue of abstinence and the finding that
no one treatment is superior. I would strongly urge you and the NIAAA
and ADAMHA to stand firm wherever possible.

It may be politically desirable for you to call a conference of scientific,
clinical, and public leadership to react to this report and to suggest
areas for further research. Sometimes such conferences allow the various
individuals with different points of view to exchange ideas and "to work
through" areas of agreement or disagreement.

In the long run, the most important strength that NIAAA can develop is to
continue high quality research on treatment assessments and the evaluation
of long-term outcomes by both naturalistic field surveys and by controlled
clinical trials. I have elaborated upon these issues in my memo.

Thank you for the opportunity to read this interesting and important document.

Sincerely yours,

Gerald L. Klerman, M.D.
GLK/hjg

HARVARD MEDICAL SCHOOL   ✦   MASSACHUSETTS GENERAL HOSPITAL

GERALD L. KLERMAN, M.D.
Professor of Psychiatry

Director
Stanley Cobb Psychiatric Research Laboratories
Massachusetts General Hospital
Boston, Massachusetts 02114

13 October 1976

MEMORANDUM

TO: Ernest Noble, M.D., Director, National Institute of Alcoholism and
Alcohol Abuse (NIAAA)

FROM: Gerald L. Klerman, M.D., Director, Stanley Cobb Psychiatric Research
Laboratories, Massachusetts General Hospital, and Professor of
Psychiatry, Harvard Medical School, Boston, Massachusetts

SUBJECT: Evaluation of Report[1] on "Alcoholism and Treatment", by D.J.
Armor, J.M. Polich, and H.B. Stambul, Rand Corporation, Santa
Monica, California

OVERVIEW

This report describes the secondary statistical analysis of three sets of
data generated by the NIAAA evaluation program in 1970-74. These three
sets of data derive from -

      1) NIAAA Alcoholism Treatment Centers (ATC) Monitoring System
         which contains data on 30,000 clients in 44 comprehensive
         centers throughout the country,

      2) the ATC 18-Month Followup Study, based on a sample of ATC data
         base, and

      3) four Public Education Campaign Surveys commissioned by NIAAA
         and conducted by L. Harris & Associates on 6,000 respondents.

Using advanced multivariate statistics, particularly multiple regression and
other correlational techniques, Armor and associates attempt to evaluate the
outcomes of current treatments and assess their relative efficacy. Based on
these analyses, they find relatively good rates of overall remission (over
70%) over an 18-month follow-up. Various indices of remission are calculated
including drinking behavior, socio-economic status, and treatment status.

---

[1]This report was prepared under a grant from NIAAA, grant no. R-1739,
June, 1976.

RE: Evaluation of Report on "Alcoholism and Treatment"   page 2

Integrating these results with review of other studies and data from public
surveys, the authors interpret their findings optimistically, but conclude
that no single treatment appears to offer greater remission rates overall,
or for unique types of alcoholics, and recommend re-assessment of complete
abstinence as the goal of treatment.

These conclusions, particularly those relating to the traditional emphases
on total abstinence, have generated moderate controversy, more so among
clinical and public groups than among researchers and public policy circles.

My comments will be divided into two aspects:

                          1)   scientific issues, and

                          2)   implications for policy

SCIENTIFIC ISSUES

Full discussion of the policy implications depends upon the reliability and
validity of the scientific procedures.   These issues need to be addressed
as forthrightly as the public policy issues.

The report is based on secondary statistical analyses of data collected by
groups other than Armor and associates at Rand.   To a certain extent, but
not completely, the validity of the statistical findings are limited by the
sampling procedures and accuracy and reliability of the data gathering and
recording.   These considerations apply particularly to the two ATC studies
which attempts to assess treatment effectiveness.   (I will not discuss the
data from the Public Education Surveys, since this area is outside my major
competence.   Moreover, these data are not being challenged and do not enter
into the controversy about abstinence and treatment effectiveness.)

There are two possible sources of limitations in the two ATC studies:
design limitations and data limitations.

          1)   As regards design - These findings do not derive from a con-
               trolled treatment trial in which the clients were randomly
               assigned to the different treatment groups or matched prior
               to treatment.   Rather, the treatment assignments were made
               in the different ATC's by clinical decisions, and statistical
               analyses were used post hoc by Armor et al to evaluate the
               comparative efficacy of the different treatments and to con-
               trol for background characteristics of the subjects.   The
               authors of the report acknowledge that this is not necessarily
               the most powerful design; controlled clinical trial design is
               far more powerful, since it approximates experimental control.
               However, the type of statistical control of naturalistic clin-
               ical treatment decisions is very acceptable.   Moreover, given
               the large sample size, there are ample opportunities for post
               hoc matching and statistical comparisons which can approximate
               some aspects of matching of samples.

2) Data limitations - The information collected on the clients,
    both at intake and at follow-up, was not designed by the
    research group, but was designed as part of the NIAAA program.
    In retrospect, it would have been desirable to have included
    more information about the clinical characteristics of the
    clients, particularly whether or not they had had episodes of
    DT's, tremor, or withdrawal. In the follow-up phase, it would
    also have been desirable to have more information about occu-
    pational performance and clinical status as regards symptoms
    such as anxiety and depression.

    These additions, however, are only possible to request after
    the completion of the study. The findings do not indicate any
    differential effects of the various treatments on subtypes of
    alcoholic clients. The clinicians still believe that different
    treatments such as AA, hospitalization, and group psychotherapy
    may be specifically indicated for certain clients, but the
    available data do not allow that conclusion.

    The main strength of the scientific aspects of the report de-
    rive from highly sophisticated statistical analysis and the
    interpretive skill used by Armor et al. They are very cautious
    in acknowledging the limitations of the data and go to great
    lengths to discuss the possible sources of unreliability.
    Other statistical techniques, such as life table method, could
    have been applied to this data, but the statistical techniques
    used here are perfectly appropriate and very powerful.

IMPLICATIONS FOR POLICY

Given these considerations, I conclude that the methods employed to analyze
the data are reliable and valid and within the limitations of the design
and information collected, the conclusions drawn are appropriate and justified. The question now arises as to what are the implications for policy.

1) Value of NIAAA evaluation effort - This report confirms the
    basic policy value of the NIAAA evaluation research efforts
    undertaken in 1970. The use of a standard intake form for
    the assessment of clients and treatment services at ATC's
    has provided a very comprehensive data base for secondary
    analysis and comparison of treatment. The leadership of
    NIAAA should be congratulated and feel proud of this basic
    policy decision. No such equivalent decision, for example,
    was made by NIMH for aspects of its community mental health
    centers' program, and that program cannot be evaluated in
    the same way as the NIAAA program. This procedure should be
    continued with a large sample of ATC's continuing to report
    to a central, independent data center using standarized forms.
    The forms should be re-evaluated and their content gradually
    expanded.

RE: Evaluation of Report on "Alcoholism and Treatment"   page 4

2) Continued support for multiple treatment approaches - The
findings here indicate that no one treatment is superior,
and NIAAA should continue to support multiple treatment approaches including AA, hospitalization, outpatient treatment,
group psychotherapy, and medication.

3) Search for new treatments - Systematic efforts are needed to
develop new treatments such as new forms of medication or
re-evaluation of medications used in other fields, new forms
of behavioral psychotherapy based on learning theory, various forms of family therapy, and other self-help groups such
as AA.

4) Continued support for policy of multiple outcomes - NIAAA
should continue to support the principle that there is no one
criteria for improvement. Clients with alcoholism should be
assessed flexibly with regard, not only to their drinking
status, but also to their occupational and vocational activities, marital and family stability, self-report of mood,
anxiety, depression, medical status, and other relevant areas
of performance.

5) Policy regarding complete abstinence - The most controversial
aspect of this report has been to challenge the traditional
emphasis on complete abstinence as the only legitimate goal
for treatment of alcoholism. I believe that the data presented
and the review of the literature provide very, very strong
support for the need to re-evaluate this traditional view and
to have a more flexible definition of the goals. The report
should not be interpreted as supporting drinking return for
all alcoholics. The report merely advocates the abandonment
of abstinence for all alcoholics. The treatment goals need
to be evaluated for individual clients, and more research is
needed as to which types of clients are capable of controlled
drinking, normal drinking, and which clients require complete
abstinence. In this respect, it is of note that almost simul-
taneous with the publication of the Armor/Rand report, E.M.
Pattison published a paper, "Nonabstinent Drinking Goals in the
Treatment of Alcoholism", in the Archives of General Psychiatry,
Volume 33: 923-930 (August, 1976). Pattison reviewed the
available literature as well as his own clinical experience
and concluded that abstinence was not the appropriate goal for
rehabilitation programs and that other treatment goals were
equally appropriate. Moreover, he indicated that in some or
even many alcoholics, the achievement of abstinence was gained
at the expense of other legitimate goals of rehabilitation.
The Pattison review confirms independently the conclusions of
the Armor/Rand report.

RE: Evaluation of Report on "Alcoholism and Treatment"   page 5

6) Needed research - I recommend that NIAAA provide more focused
   and targeted clinical research in the following three areas:

   a) Methodological - More research is needed as to the
      reliability and validity of various methods of assess-
      ment, particularly the self-report technique by clients
      and the various techniques for measuring drinking sta-
      tus, vocational status, etc.. Some of the indices
      developed by Armor need to be tested using advanced
      psychometric methods.

   b) Field studies of subsamples - The selected subsamples
      of patients from either the ATC studies or new samples
      should be evaluated by trained observers so as to as-
      certain the quality of their life in the community.
      Specific areas of evaluation should include vocational
      functioning, marital performance, financial indepen-
      dence, possible antisocial behavior, community adjust-
      ment, self-report, mood, psychological tests of intel-
      ligence, and perhaps even medical evaluation for liver
      and neurological damage, etc..

   c) Controlled trials of various treatments - The natural-
      istic design, using statistical methods for post hoc
      analysis as employed by Armor, has definite limitations.
      More powerful conclusions could be drawn from systematic
      trials in which clients were either randomly assigned
      to selected treatment (AA, group psychotherapy, medica-
      tion, etc.) or matched in advance. These techniques
      have been used in psychopharmacology of schizophrenia
      and depression and in fields of medicine such as heart
      disease.

CONCLUSIONS

This report represents a major policy advance. Traditionally held views,
as to the possible superiority of one treatment over another or the nature
of abstinence as a goal of treatment, have been challenged by a careful
analysis of data from a large sample of clients seen at a variety of ATC's.
The findings have been carefully analyzed using advanced statistical techniques, and the policy implications for NIAAA need to be reviewed carefully.

Even with the limitations fo the research design and data base and the
possible unreliability of the reports, the conclusions are internally consistent and are also consistent with other reports from the clinical and
research literature. The net conclusion of this evaluator is that the
report stands as a landmark in evaluation research in alcoholism, and credit
is due to the NIAAA leadership and to Armor and his associates.

Alcohol,

Drug Abuse,

and

Mental Health

Administration

Special Press Telephone for Information on Alcohol, Drug Abuse, and Mental Health (301) 443-3783

DEPARTMENT OF
HEALTH, EDUCATION, AND WELFARE
PUBLIC HEALTH SERVICE
ALCOHOL, DRUG ABUSE, AND
MENTAL HEALTH ADMINISTRATION
5600 FISHERS LANE
ROCKVILLE, MARYLAND 20852

OFFICIAL BUSINESS
Penalty for private use, $300

POSTAGE AND FEES PAID
U.S. DEPARTMENT OF H.E.W.
HEW 389

FIRST CLASS

NEWS RELEASE

U.S. DEPARTMENT OF HEALTH, EDUCATION, AND WELFARE

ANNOUNCEMENT   June 23, 1976

Harry C. Bell/Paul M. Garner
(301)443-3306

Ernest P. Noble, Ph.D., M.D., Director, National Institute on Alcohol Abuse and Alcoholism (NIAAA), today announced his concerns about statements being made on the report "Alcoholism and Treatment" recently released nationally by the Rand Corporation.

Of specific and major concern is the manner in which the results of this report have been isolated and construed to suggest that recovered alcoholic people can return to moderate drinking with limited risk.

"It is particularly distressing when such statements of research findings are widely reported, and these statements carry with them the potential for affecting so many lives in a negative manner."

"Until further definite scientific evidence exists to the contrary, as Director of the National Institute on Alcohol Abuse and Alcoholism, charged with the leadership responsibility for the Alcohol Abuse and Alcoholism program, I feel that abstinence must continue as the appropriate goal in the treatment of alcoholism. Furthermore, it would be extremely unwise for a recovered alcoholic to even try to experiment with controlled drinking."

The Rand Study, funded by NIAAA, "while valuable, because it raises a number of provocative questions, concerning the use of alcohol by recovered

-2-

alcoholics, is only a part of the continued search for answers to the
questions surrounding the issue of alcoholism," Dr. Noble said.

"The Institute is committed to the study of all issues related to
alcohol problems in our search for truth and understanding . . . irre-
spective of the controversy which may ensue. By the same token, it is
also crucial that all such studies receive widespread critical reviews
by the scientific community before policy is made or changed."

NCA PRESS CONFERENCE
AND
RAND RESPONSE

NCA PRESS RELEASE[1]

FROM: National Council on Alcoholism, Inc.
733 Third Avenue
New York, N.Y. 10017

FOR FURTHER INFORMATION CONTACT:
Frank A. Seixas, M.D.
or
Walter J. Murphy
(212) 986-4433

FOR RELEASE
AFTER 10:00 A.M., July 1, 1976

Washington, D.C., July 1—Research scientists who have reviewed the recently released Rand Corporation study which suggests that some alcoholics may return to "normal drinking" challenged its scientific basis during a news conference held by the National Council on Alcoholism (NCA) here today. Spokesmen for labor and management and clinical alcoholism programs also gave their views.

The group labeled the report "biased," and "dangerous" and questioned the methodology employed by Rand.

Dr. Luther A. Cloud, Vice Chairman of the Board of Directors of NCA, said: "We are compelled to respond to the Rand Report at the public level because of our grave concern that the misleading publicity generated by this study could have tragic consequences."

Dr. Cloud reported that NCA has learned that some alcoholics have resumed drinking as a result of the publicity surrounding the release of the Rand study.

"This could mean death or brain damage for these individuals unless they return to abstinence," he said.

Dr. Cloud added: "NCA favors responsible research leading to new knowledge regarding alcoholism. However, it is the position of those present today—and indeed, most scientists—that such research should be conducted with the utmost care, scrutinized by the scientific community

---

[1] Reprinted in its entirety from a statement released to the press by the National Council on Alcoholism.

and published in scientific literature before it is submitted for public consumption. This is a routine procedure which was not followed in this case."

Dr. Frank A. Seixas, Medical Director of the National Council on Alcoholism, said: "It takes little subtlety to read between the lines in this paper and see a slanted polemic advocating the return to normal drinking as a goal. . . . Any suggestion, based on this report, that an alcoholic should return to 'normal drinking' is unsupported by the data in the study itself."

Dr. David Pittman, Chairman and Professor of Sociology, Washington University, said: "We are dealing with human lives and to hold out the promise that some alcoholics can safely return to normal drinking, although the subgroup of individuals in the 'normal drinking' group are not specified in the Rand Report, is unethical, unprincipled, and playing Russian roulette with the lives of human beings."

Dr. Jokichi Takamine, Chairman, American Medical Association Committee on Alcoholism, said: "During all the years I have treated alcoholics, I have never seen an alcoholic who for any sustained period of time can go back to social drinking. In time they go back to *alcoholic* drinking. In thirteen years of practice, I have seen and consulted on thousands of alcoholics in private practice, clinics and in other contexts."

Dr. Joseph J. Zuska, Chairman, Public Policy Committee, American Medical Society on Alcoholism, said: "It is the opinion of the AMSA Public Policy Committee that the conclusions reached in the report concerning the feasibility of moderate drinking are based on insufficient data in terms of: a) duration of follow-up, and b) comparison of analysis of groups of questionable comparability."

Dr. John Wallace, Professor of Psychology, State University of New York at Purchase, and Psychologist, Hospital for Joint Diseases and Medical Center, Alcohol Treatment Center, N.Y., said: "In my work as a therapist with alcoholic clients in one of the largest urban, black ghettos—Harlem, New York—I find the Rand conclusions of no practical beneficial consequences for treatment and rehabilitation. In fact, I regard all such reports of uncontrolled experiments concerning the possibility of 'normal drinking' among recovering alcoholics as detrimental to the welfare of not only minority alcoholics who must cope with the increasingly 'chemical' environments that our large, urban centers have become, but to alcoholics everywhere."

Dr. Mary Pendery, Chairman, State Alcoholism Advisory Board, Director of Alcoholism Programs, Department of Psychiatry, University of California, San Diego Medical School, and Chief, Alcoholism Treatment Program, Veterans Administration Hospital, San Diego, said: "The information regarding a return to 'normal drinking' as possible for alcoholics was based on the most flimsy data of all, the response of actively drinking alcoholics with no objective confirming evidence whatever."

Dr. Alfonso Paredes, Professor of Psychiatry, University of Oklahoma College of Medicine and Director, Oklahoma State Department of Mental Health, Division on Alcoholism, said: "It was unfortunate (when viewed from the role of science) that they undertook to address themselves to the issues of normal drinking and etiology. It brings in an extraneous factor which strategically should not enter into a follow-up study. The difference they claim should have been tested. The well spelled-out hypothesis would have taken increased details and careful documentation to even begin to substantiate the author's claims, for which there are no controls and no reliability."

Dr. Herbert Barry III, Professor of Pharmacology, University of Pittsburgh, said: "Conclusions from this study should be viewed with particular caution because: 1) An 18-month follow-up is not sufficient time to judge potential for relapse in so-called 'normal drinkers,' 2) Conclusions by the authors which are not supported by the extremely small number of cases on which they are based, 3) The definition of remission is too loose for accurate interpretation."

Dr. John A. Ewing, Director, Center for Alcohol Studies and Professor of Psychiatry, University of North Carolina, Chapel Hill, North Carolina, author of an earlier study on controlled drinking, could not be present at the news conference, but prepared a statement which said, in part: "In my experimental attempts to inculcate controlled drinking in alcoholics the results looked promising in the first 12 to 18 months. It was only when we did a long term follow-up, ranging from 27 to 55 months since treatment ended, that we detected a universal failure to maintain controlled drinking."

Dr. Nicholas A. Pace, Medical Director, New York Executive Office, General Motors Corporation, and Leo J. Perlis, Director, Department of Community Services, AFL-CIO, released statements during the news conference.

Dr. Pace, quoting a memorandum to all General Motors physicians from Dr. Robert G. Wiencek, Associate Corporate Medical Director, General Motors, said: "The questioning alcoholic should be advised that the report is not conclusive and there are no criteria by which one may distinguish who may or who may not resume controlled drinking. All individuals should be advised to continue abstinence until conclusive evidence is compiled."

Mr. Perlis, quoting a letter which he sent to all AFL-CIO affiliates, said: "In the absence of widely accepted and scientifically based cures, it is important that we continue to cooperate with those organizations and fellowships, such as AA and NCA, that continue to take the position that 'even one drink is one too many for an alcoholic.' "

RAND RESPONSE TO NCA STATEMENTS[2]

In a recent press conference, spokesmen for the National Council on Alcoholism (NCA) have severely criticized the Rand Report, *Alcoholism and Treatment* (R-1739-NIAAA), challenging both its conclusions and the scientific methodology upon which they are based. Some of the criticisms voiced by NCA are serious issues, based either upon misconceptions about the study or, sometimes, upon genuine limitations in the data— limitations that were repeatedly pointed out in the report itself. We shall deal with eleven of the more serious issues raised by the NCA.

SCIENTIFIC REVIEW

NCA Statement. AMSA [American Medical Society on Alcoholism, Inc.] calls attention to the fact that when ethical and reputable scientists make a new discovery they defer any press notice about such a discovery until the date of publication of the research in a refereed scientific journal. The direct announcement to the press without referee review has cast doubt on the scientific validity of the report. (Joseph L. Zuska, Chairman, Public Policy Committee, American Medical Society on Alcoholism, Inc.)

We welcome research which evaluates treatment and which is carried out in a responsible fashion. We should stress . . . that it was not submitted for peer review, that the "critique" was not printed and that it was released to the press irresponsibly and even unethically. (Dr. Maxwell B. Weisman, Dept. of Health and Mental Hygiene, Baltimore, Maryland.)

Rand Response. The claim of no peer review is simply false. All Rand reports undergo a careful professional review process before publication to ensure that scientific standards are met; as was clearly stated in the Preface, this particular report was reviewed by professionals both inside Rand and outside Rand, including experts in medicine and psychiatry, psychology, sociology, alcoholism treatment, and statistics. These reviews led to extensive revisions over a period of more than a year. After such careful review and revision, it is difficult to credit the claim that publication of one's findings is irresponsible. On the contrary, we feel that the interests of science and of the public are best served by informed debate.

---

[2] The following NCA statements are excerpts from printed statements prepared by various individuals and distributed at the second NCA press conference on July 1, 1976.

CONVERGENCE WITH OTHER STUDIES

NCA Statement. The bibliography in the sense of other experiments quoted was not only incomplete, but very biased. There was no mention of major studies by highly reputable investigators which contradicted the conclusions drawn by the Report. For example, John Ewing, M.D., Director of the Center for Alcohol Studies, University of North Carolina, has conducted the longest controlled drinking study, and found that none of the patients who desperately wanted to bring his drinking under control succeeded, and that sooner or later they all drank with loss of control that is typical of alcoholism. The majority of his patients now are abstinent by taking disulfiram (Antabuse) or by joining Alcoholics Anonymous. . . . Dr. David Pittman's follow-up study was so thorough that he succeeded in contracting 99 percent of the 250 patients he was following and concluded that none of the alcoholic patients were able to resume drinking without grave consequences. (Dr. Mary Pendery, Chairman, California State Alcoholism Advisory Board.)

Rand Response. These statements are puzzling indeed. Our findings—including the one dealing with normal drinking—are consistent with literally dozens of previous studies in the scientific literature. Not only is there ample evidence that some alcoholics return to normal drinking, there is little or no systematic evidence for the belief that abstention is the only effective treatment goal.[3]

Close examination of the NCA statements on this topic yields two studies cited repeatedly as offering scientific proof of the abstention theory. One of these is the Pittman and Tate (1969) study, a field followup of one facility in St. Louis. But careful examination of the Pittman results reveals no systematic evidence in favor of the abstention theory, and in fact his findings in this regard parallel our own quite closely. At a 1 to 2-year follow-up he found about 60 percent of treated patients to have reduced their consumption (compared to our 68 percent in remission),

---

[3] See for example, the following reviews: Richard W. Lloyd and Herman C. Salzberg, "Controlled Social Drinking: An Alternative to Abstinence as a Treatment Goal for Some Alcohol Abusers," *Psychological Bulletin*, Vol. 82, 1975, pp. 815–842; E. Mansell Pattison, "A Conceptual Approach to Alcoholism Treatment Goals," *Addictive Behaviors*, Vol. 1, 1976, pp. 177–192; Chad D. Emrick, "A Review of Psychologically Oriented Treatment of Alcoholism, 1," *Quarterly Journal of Studies on Alcohol*, Vol. 35, 1974; pp. 523–549; Ovide Pomerleau, et al., "A Critical Examination of Some Current Assumptions in the Treatment of Alcoholism," *Journal of Studies on Alcohol*, Vol. 37, 1976, pp. 849–867; Melvin Kalb and Morton S. Propper, "The Future of Alcohology: Craft or Science?" *American Journal of Psychiatry*, Vol. 133, 1976, pp. 641–645.

but only 12 percent had abstained totally over the entire followup period (compared to our 9 percent long-term abstainers at both followups). The authors did state that they found no social or controlled drinkers, preferring the designation of "improved" or "reduced consumption." But since they present no quantitative data on the amount of consumption or types of impairment, it is not possible to compare their "improved" drinkers with our groups of normal or periodic drinkers.

The other study is one by Ewing, cited by several NCA critics as the definitive study of controlled drinking.[4] Again, the NCA claims for this study are highly exaggerated. We agree it is one of the longer term studies, with a 4- to 5-year followup of patients treated with a controlled drinking therapy. However, the followup data are presented for a total of only 14 patients (out of 25 in the original group) who had received a substantial amount of treatment. His conclusion that controlled drinking treatment failed is based on observing the worst drinking episode reported over the entire followup period; all patients reported "loss of control" at least once during this 4-year period and were therefore classified as failures. Such a strict definition would probably render *any* treatment procedure a failure, including AA meetings. Furthermore, no quantitative data are reported on amount of consumption or degree of impairment, so it is impossible to determine exactly what loss of control means. More important, since there is no control or comparison group of alcoholics treated with abstention goals, it is not possible to conclude from this study that abstention-oriented treatment is more effective than controlled-drinking therapy.

Interestingly, Ewing's conclusion that abstention is the preferred treatment goal appears to be based on the fact that 9 of the 14 patients were *abstaining* at the time of the 4-year followup (no data were presented on amount of drinking among nonabstainers or on the length of abstention for abstainers). In other words, most of the patients treated with controlled drinking therapy were in remission (for unknown periods) at the time of the followup. It is not clear to us that an abstention outcome—rather than an outcome of continued controlled drinking—should be interpreted as a failure of controlled-drinking therapy.

VALIDITY OF SELF-REPORTS

NCA Statement. There is not a single authenticated case of an alcoholic who has successfully resumed drinking in the entire Report. There are only

[4] John A. Ewing, and Beatrice A. Rouse, "Failure of an Experimental Program to Inculcate Controlled Drinking in Alcoholics," *British Journal of the Addictions*, Vol. 71, 1976, pp. 123–134. This article was not included in our bibliography because it was published after the Rand Report had gone to press.

statistical averages available based upon the most notoriously unreliable data possible, namely, the answers of alcoholics to questions about their own drinking. The information regarding a return to 'normal drinking' as possible for alcoholics was based on the most flimsy data of all, the response of actively drinking alcoholics, with no objective confirming evidence whatever. (Dr. Mary Pendery, Chairman, California State Alcoholism Advisory Board.)

One searches in vain throughout the pages of this report for evidence of multimethod approaches to measurement. Behavioral measures are entirely lacking. With the exception of data contributed by an independent researcher involving BACs, biochemical, physiological, and neurological measurements are unreported. Measurement consists almost entirely of self-reports gathered through the familiar method of the interview-questionnaire. . . . The data bearing on the validity of self-reported quantity consumed raise serious questions about the Rand group's inferences concerning not only 'normal drinking' but relapse and spontaneous remission as well. (Dr. John Wallace, Psychologist, Hospital for Joint Diseases and Medical Center, Alcoholism Treatment Center, New York.)

Rand Response. The implication of this criticism is that alcoholics invariably deny their true behavior, thereby making their self-reports invalid and unusable as data for scientific study. The issue of validity of self-reports is indeed a serious one for studies of alcoholic behavior. It is precisely for this reason that the Rand report includes a lengthy appendix containing empirical data comparing self-reported drinking, blood alcohol concentration determined by breath tests, and clinical assessments. Our conclusion, based on extensive analyses, is that self-reports are sufficiently valid for research purposes, and are at least as valid as other practical methods. While there is some inaccuracy of reporting in *both directions* (i.e., under- and overreporting of drinking amounts), the proportion of alcoholics who give inaccurate answers is quite small. As the report points out, these conclusions are by no means final. But the claim that self-reports are inherently invalid is a *belief* which is not supported by available empirical evidence.

Aside from the scientific problem of self-report validity, this criticism is applied selectively: it is directed solely at the normal drinking finding. If all alcoholics' self-reports are unreliable, it is difficult to account for the fact that 32 percent of the alcoholics in our two followup samples admitted to excessive drinking and severe impairment that placed them in the nonremission category. Similarly the validity argument is not used to cast doubt on the proportion of respondents who reported abstaining. In fact, self-reports of abstention by members of Alcoholics Anonymous are accepted by the NCA without any apparent demand for further verification.

SAMPLE BIAS AND FOLLOWUP RATES

NCA Statement. One sample [in the Rand Report] is composed of 11,500 alcoholism treatment center clients who were interviewed at a 6-month follow-up period. The researchers obtained self-reports from only 2,371 of these patients for a sample retrieval rate of 20.6 percent. Such a low sample retrieval rate would render any conclusions from this 6-month group as being not valid for the total sample and furthermore, not able to be generalized into any population. In the study done by Pittman and Tate, "A Comparison of Two Treatment Programs for Alcoholics," *Quarterly Journal of Studies on Alcohol*, Vol. 30, pp. 888-899, December 1969, they state, on page 891: "Of the 250 persons included in the study, follow-up information was obtained on 249. Interviews were conducted with 237 or 94.8 percent. Our data indicate that such a high followup rate is an absolute necessity due to the fact that 12 of the remaining 13 patients who were not interviewed but on whom partial information was obtained after months of intensive search by our staff, cooperating social agencies, police departments, and federal and state welfare agencies were found to be functioning poorly in the community in terms of drinking behavior, health, residence, or police involvement. Thus, we feel that considerable skepticism should be attached to any followup study with a retrieval rate of less than 90 percent." (Dr. David Pittman, Professor of Sociology, Washington University, St. Louis.)

Dr. Pittman's high retrieval rate for subjects in his study contrasts with the extremely low retrieval rates of less than 21 percent and 62 percent for Rand's 6-month and 18-month followup samples respectively. This contrast is even more significant in terms of bias in the Rand study in view of Dr. Pittman's finding that the harder a subject was to locate the more severe the impairment. (Dr. Mary Pendery, Chairman, California State Alcoholism Advisory Board.)

Rand Response. This presumption of extreme sample bias is contradicted by three separate analyses included in our report. First, the extent of sample bias was explicitly addressed (pp. 66-68) by comparing the followup and non-followup groups on a variety of measures. The conclusion was that the followup group does *not* differ materially from the original group. Second, if a low followup rate were concealing a large number of failures, then those centers with the lowest followup rates should have the highest proportion of successes. But, in fact, our analysis revealed no such relationship (Table 28). Third, the 6-month followup study had a response rate of about 25 percent, of which 68 percent were in remission; if all or most of the remaining 75 percent were treatment failures, then a second followup on a larger proportion of the sample should yield a lower remission rate. But the 18-month followup with a *62 percent* response rate yielded the almost identical remission rate of 67 percent (p. 82).

Moreover, the notion that a 90 percent rate is necessary for a valid study is an inappropriate generalization from the Pittman study. First, the Pittman sample of 250 patients was carefully selected from about 1000 consecutive admissions so as to maximize social stability and consequently the followup rate. Not surprisingly, then, he was able to locate 95 percent of this intentionally biased sample. Of the remaining 13 clients, he obtained partial (noninterview) data on 12 and "found [them] to be functioning poorly." No quantified data or systematic comparisons were presented to support this judgment. It is clearly improper to generalize a finding such as Pittman's, based on 13 cases from an intentionally biased sample, and even more improper to advance this finding as a minimum standard for the field.

SAMPLE SIZES

NCA Statement. Let us examine the major conclusion drawn by the authors and presented to the press as a new discovery. "Alcoholics who were drinking socially were no more likely to relapse than those who were abstinent." This conclusion is drawn from Table 19 on page 87. It will be seen that it relates not to 30,000 patients, nor to 10,000, nor to 1000, but to a subsample of a group of 161 patients. The numbers are so small that they appear larger when considered as percentages. I have translated these percentages back into numbers for clarity.

One can see that the relapses upon which this conclusion of paramount importance was made, were eight in number: 3 cases out of 19 people who claimed normal drinking at 6 months, and 5 out of 31 who claimed abstinence at 6 months. (Dr. Frank Seixas, Medical Director, National Council on Alcoholism.)

Rand Response. These statements reflect a mistaken idea of our samples and our use of them.

First, the figure of 30,000 is simply the number of patients treated at the 45 centers from the inception of the Monitoring System to the writing of our report (about a 3-year period); this is *not* the sample chosen for study, as is made amply clear in the report. Our major findings about the extent of remission and normal drinking are based on two different samples of 2371 and 600 patients, respectively. Contrary to the NCA allegations, these samples, the largest ever used in a study of this kind in the United States, are more than adequate to support the analysis and the conclusions drawn therefrom.

The figure of 161 comes from a single table in a special section dealing with the "relapse" analysis (pp. 82–87). Some critics may have mistaken this as our treatment outcome analysis. In our terminology a relapse is a patient who was in remission at 6 months (either abstaining or normal drinking) but who was not in remission at the 18-month followup. The fact that we had two followups on some clients offered an opportunity to test a crucial hypothesis in the alcoholism field: namely, that what might appear to be normal drinking at one followup is only a temporary stage during a patient's descent back to full alcoholic drinking. The implication would be that normal or periodic drinkers at one followup should have a higher relapse rate than abstainers at a later followup.

To test the hypothesis that normal drinkers are more prone to relapse than abstainers, we compared 18-month outcomes among patients classified by remission status at the 6-month point. For this special analysis there were 220 patients with data at both points (40 long-term abstainers, 99 short-term abstainers, 30 normal drinkers, and 51 nonremissions). The results showed clearly that these normal drinkers did *not* have higher rates of relapse than long-term or short-term abstainers. In addition, as shown in Table 19, we conducted a sensitivity analysis replicating this same finding among that subset of 161 patients (including 19 normal drinkers) who showed definite signs of physical addiction at intake. These samples, of course, were used exclusively for comparing relapse rates between abstainers and normal drinkers, not to establish rates of normal drinking. We agree, and stated in the report that the relapse sample is too small to establish definitively the relapse rates for normal drinkers. But to imply that the entire study depends upon only one table is simply wrong.

LENGTH OF FOLLOWUP PERIOD

NCA Statement. It is unfortunate that this study has been so widely publicized since it is based only on an experimental, partial followup study and contains no long-term evaluation. . . . In my experimental attempts to inculcate controlled drinking in alcoholics the results looked promising in the first 12 to 18 months. It was only when we did a long term followup, ranging from 27 to 55 months since treatment ended, that we detected a universal failure to maintain controlled drinking. (Dr. John Ewing, Professor of Psychiatry, University of North Carolina.)

The followup period 18 months to make a conclusion that an individual is a normal drinker is too short a period of time to lend any credence to that finding. (Dr. David Pittman, Professor of Sociology, Washington University, St. Louis.)

Rand Response. Even though we found most patients "in remission" at the 18-month followup point, it is indeed possible that many of them could later relapse into alcoholic drinking, as our report made clear (p. 87). It is for this very reason that we distinguished "remission" (favorable outcome at one time point) from "recovery" (a long-term, continuous favorable outcome). Although our data show that most clients in remission at 6 months remain in remission later, these data are not totally conclusive; a longer followup period with more detailed data over the patient's entire history would be desirable to assess long-term recovery. At present no such study is available; certainly this issue cannot be decided by the Ewing study, whose limitations we have already discussed. Therefore, we must regard the nature of eventual long-term outcomes as an open question.

DEFINITION OF NORMAL DRINKING GROUP

NCA Statement. A major complaint [is] use of the term "normal" drinking to describe the reduced drinking done by some of the improved clients. If this group had been designated "greatly improved, drinking less," I would have no quarrel with that aspect of the report. I can certainly identify many of my own ex-patients who are still struggling or "slipping" occasionally but doing much better after treatment.

The definition of "normal" drinking was a statistical one only. . . . Their upper limits on daily consumption (average of up to 6 shots of liquor a day) and typical quantities (not even a maximum drunk during one drinking occasion but a sort of average figure, of up to 10 shots) seem overly high. (Dr. Sheila Blume, Central Islip Psychiatric Center, New York.)

Normal drinking is not really defined anywhere in the report in such a way as to eliminate the possibility of harmful consequences. The distinction must be made since the essence of alcoholism is just that—harmful consequences of any kind related to the inability to control or predict the nature of one's drinking behavior. (Dr. Maxwell Weisman, Department of Health and Mental Hygiene, Baltimore, Maryland.)

Rand Response. There can be legitimate differences among observers about any definition, especially in the field of alcoholism. As stated in the report, our objective is not to be inclusive or exclusive, but to discriminate "normal" from "abnormal" by objective and replicable procedures. For that reason, our definitions allowed drinking in amounts that are commonly found in the general population (e.g., up to 3 ounces of ethanol per day) as long as such drinking does not lead to serious behavioral consequences or alcoholism symptoms. Actually, very few normal drinkers in our sample even approached the upper limits of the normal-drinking category; the average normal drinker, in fact, consumed about .7 ounces of ethanol per day, the equivalent of about one jigger of hard liquor or 1½ cans of beer. Moreover, no one could be classified as a normal drinker if he exhibited serious symptoms of alcoholism or evidence of physiological addiction, even if he met the alcohol consumption criteria.

RANDOM SELECTION

NCA Statement. Neither the original sample nor the Stanford sample were randomly selected. This yields what is known as a biased sample which statisticians have found gives results that are not generalizable. The eight treatment centers in the Stanford study were not randomly selected nor were the patient numbers, or characteristics similar or balanced. (Dr. Frank Seixas, Medical Director, National Council on Alcoholism.)

Rand Response. This claim reveals a misunderstanding of the utility of random sampling in studies of this kind. First, the criticism suggests that a study is of no value unless it is an experimental design with subjects randomly assigned to treatment and control groups. On the contrary, a large body of knowledge in alcoholism research, psychology, psychiatry, and other disciplines is based on nonexperimental studies which use standard statistical procedures to permit valid conclusions. Second, the fact that a sample is not *random* does not mean that it is necessarily unrepresentative or biased. Both the 18-month sample of treatment centers and the patients treated by them are representative of the full intake population, as is demonstrated by analyses in the report (p. 67). This fact makes generalization from these samples wholly appropriate.

VARIATION IN CLIENT GROUPS

NCA Statement. Client populations at these ATCs varied widely on many important characteristics and the various groups were too small to control for the variance. (Linda Gayle Hyde, former Coordinator/Planner, St. Luke's Hospital, Phoenix, Arizona.)

Rand Response. This statement, as a criticism, reveals a fundamental misunderstanding of statistical practice. The ATCs *do* vary in the population, and of course a sample of ATCs *should* vary in the same ways. Naturally, when different groups are compared for analysis, it is necessary to control for these differences, as the report does using standard statistical techniques. It is precisely the use of such procedures that allows one to take into account the effects of sample variances and sample sizes.

EXPERIMENTER BIAS

NCA Statement. [There is experimenter bias because] the staffs of the NIAAA ATCs who gathered most of the intake and outcome data were in the position of experimenters. . . . It is a commonly accepted requirement in treatment outcome research that the persons involved in delivering the treatments should not be involved in assessing the outcomes. (Dr. John Wallace, Psychologist, Hospital for Joint Diseases and Medical Center, Alcoholism Treatment Center, New York.)

Rand Response. Since the 6-month interviews were conducted by treatment center staff members, and the 18-month followup interviews were done as part of a special study conducted by an outside agency, the claim of experimenter bias can be tested by a comparison of remission rates in the 6-month and 18-month studies. If the ATCs actually affected results, surely the remission rates would be worse in the 18-month study. Yet the results of both studies are virtually identical.

INCIDENCE OF DEATH AND PHYSIOLOGICAL COMPLICATIONS

NCA Statement. Dr. Armor and his colleagues not only fail to mention the 107 known deaths in the subject cohort of their study, but neither do they allow for any other disease process associated with alcoholism. Nor do they allow for possible differences in treatment results for clients or patients who have psychiatric diseases along with alcoholism, including alcoholic brain damage. We think in these areas they are acting in a patronizing way to the public who apparently know better than they what alcoholism consists of. And they are attempting to suppress a very large dimension of the constellation of varied pathologies associated with this disease. We don't think the American public will be fooled by this sleight of hand. (Dr. Frank Seixas, Medical Director, National Council on Alcoholism.)

Rand Response. This attack upon our motives is wholly unwarranted. Of the very small proportion of deaths in our sample (about 5 percent), only a few were identified by a known cause, and there were no other outcome data available relating to deaths or pathologies of the brain or liver. Since the available information was clearly insufficient for an analysis of these factors, the Rand Report restricted itself to a study of the measured behavioral outcomes among the 95 percent who survived—a procedure that is thoroughly conventional in alcoholism research.

JSA REVIEWS

COMMENTS

THE "RAND REPORT"

Some Comments and a Response

Chad D. Emrick, Ph.D.[1] and Donald W. Stilson, Ph.D.[2]

This comment on Armor et al.'s "Rand Report" (1) follows Emrick's review (2) of the Stanford Research Institute (SRI) report by Ruggels et al. (3). The SRI and Rand reports have much in common: (*1*) they share the same major data base, (*2*) the salient findings are virtually identical, and (*3*) they have some of the same authors. Both books report on data collected through the Alcoholism Treatment Center (ATC) monitoring system which was designed to evaluate the effectiveness of the 44 ATCS funded by the National Institute on Alcohol Abuse and Alcoholism. Both SRI and Rand personnel were involved in the development of the monitoring system which evaluated ATC patients at the beginning of treatment and 6 months after intake. To acquire a longer-term evaluation, 8 of the 44 ATCS were selected for a special 18-month follow-up study. SRI conducted the follow-up, but Rand personnel helped analyze the data and report the findings. Not surprisingly, the 2 monographs draw essentially the same conclusions about the ATC treatment programs.

The Rand report is generally better written than is SRI's. In the former, an extensive review of alcoholism studies places the ATC findings in a meaningful context. Furthermore, the literature on social correlates of drinking was reviewed to develop hypotheses about the etiology and prognosis of alcoholism. Armor et al.'s Appendix A on issues involved in the validity and reliability of self-reported drinking behavior is another inter-

[1] Leader of Community Focus Team, Aurora Mental Health Center, 1646 Elmira, Aurora, CO 80010.

[2] Professor in Psychiatry and Biometrics, University of Colorado School of Medicine, 4200 East Ninth Avenue, Denver, CO 80262.

ACKNOWLEDGMENTS.—We are grateful to Jack Crawford and Myles Edwards for their helpful suggestions in the preparation of this paper. We also appreciate the assistance of Jane Shelledy and Helen Hibbard in the preparation of the typescript.

Source: Reprinted, by permission, from *Journal of Studies on Alcohol*, 1977, *38*, No. 1, pp. 152–193.

esting feature. Nevertheless, it should be noted that, as with the SRI report, the Rand volume does contain some disturbing inconsistencies between the text and tabular representations of the data as well as some troublesome inconsistencies between tables.

RESEARCH METHODOLOGY

Because they rely on the same data, both reports are subject to some of the same criticisms with respect to research methodology. A number of problems with the 6- and 18-month follow-ups were identified in the SRI review (2) and will, for the most part, not be repeated here. Ample criticism has been offered by others for some of these defects. Unfortunately, rather than being made in the spirit of scientific debate, the hidden agenda of much of this criticism appears to be that of discrediting the reports in order to throw into question their finding that some alcoholics in remission maintain normal drinking practices. Most of the criticism has been leveled by those espousing the position that "true" alcoholics can never drink normally but must pursue a total abstinence goal. This smacks of the pot calling the kettle black, since studies supporting the total abstinence position are generally no better methodologically than are the SRI and Rand projects. If data on normal drinking outcome are to be questioned because of poor methodology, so are those on total abstinence.

Perhaps the crucial issue relevant to concerns about the design problems is whether outcome results are thus invalidated. In Emrick's SRI review, he reported the results of his analysis (4) of the effects of design quality on drinking outcome rates in 265 studies of alcoholism treatment. He found that such rates appear to be unaffected by many methodological defects and, therefore, that the findings of the SRI report (and by implication, the Rand report) deserve serious attention. Further consideration has led to a more cautious position on methodological problems. There are 2 reasons for this change.

First, Emrick's analysis dealt with a large-scale review of the literature. Thus, while certain defects were observed to have little impact on outcome data for studies on the whole, this absence of influence may not hold for any one study, in this case the Rand and SRI projects.

Second, Emrick's analysis dealt with only a few design characteristics, viz., use of control groups, use of comparison groups, random assignment of patients to two or more groups, use of identical procedures for collecting pre- and posttreatment data, and collection of data of demonstrated validity (typically through interviews with collateral informants) and documented reliability. Not examined were other important characteristics such as representativeness of sampling and methods of data analysis. It is possible that defects in these areas do have substantial impact on outcome data. This possibility strikes a particularly relevant note of caution, since, as we intend to make clear, both sampling procedures and data analysis are flawed in the Rand and SRI studies.

Sampling

Among the most serious defects of the Rand and SRI reports is the apparent unrepresentativeness of the 6- and 18-month samples. One possible source of bias in the 18-month sample was the method used by Ruggels et al. to select the 8 ATCs from among the 44. Since "the ATCs' expressed willingness to participate" (3, *p. 19*) in the study was a major selection criterion, it is not unreasonable to speculate that site selection was biased. To demonstrate that the sites were representative, all patients in the 8 ATCs would have to be compared with and found comparable to all patients in the remaining 36 sites. Comparability would have to be observed particularly on those variables found to be important predictors of outcome. Since no such demonstration was reported in either study, this source of bias cannot be ruled out.

Another possible source of bias in both the 6- and 18-month samples was the failure to locate about 79% of the patients at the 6-month follow-up and about 38% of the patients at 18-month follow-up. Loss of patients at follow-up will cause bias if those who are located differ from those who are lost. A convincing demonstration of unbiasedness in a partial follow-up sample requires that there be no differences between the intake characteristics of those followed and not followed up. Armor et al. did not make this comparison. Instead, they attempted to establish lack of bias by comparing the intake characteristics of those followed up among the 44 ATCs (in the 6-month sample) and among the 8 ATCs (in the 18-month sample) with all of the patients admitted to the 44 ATCs during a 12-month period. (The 18-month sample was drawn from only a 4-month period.) These comparisons were judged to result in no large differences, and Armor et al. concluded that the samples were "not seriously biased" (1, *p. 68*), in spite of the fact that all the important differences appeared to favor the follow-up samples over the intake population. Data presented by Ruggels et al. suggest that had Armor et al. made the proper comparisons, the follow-up samples would have been found to be biased in favor of patients having better prognoses. For the 18-month sample, Ruggels et al. did compare the followed up patients with those lost to follow-up. They concluded that patients who were found "appear to underrepresent substantially those clients who have a more severe drinking problem and are less socially stable" (3, *p. 177*). These may well be important differences inasmuch as alcoholism severity and social stability are among the patient variables found by both Armor et al. and Ruggels et al. to have the strongest relationship with drinking outcome. Given that a much larger percentage of patients were lost to follow-up at 6 months than at 18 months, it is likely that at least as much bias exists in the 6-month sample.

It is important to note that Armor et al. attempted to disarm this criticism of the large percentage of lost patients by analyzing the relationship between the percentage of patients not interviewed in each ATC at 18 months and the percentage of patients in each center found to be in remission of alcoholism at follow-up (1, *p. 101*). When they found a nonsignificant rank order correlation of − .07, they concluded that differential loss of patients did not account for differential remission rates among the ATCs. The intended implication here is that group outcome data were not invalidated by loss of patients. This is a dangerous interpretation in that it has the potential of lulling outcome researchers into insouciance about losing patients. It is important to realize that there is a serious problem with the correlation Armor et al. reported. The size of the correlation may have been reduced by irrelevant variables which presumably could affect either follow-up rates or remission rates. To the extent that such random variation existed, unsystematic measurement error (or unreliability) was introduced into the correlation. Since such measurement error always reduces correlation, the correlation under discussion would be expected to be low. Thus it is possible that unsystematic measurement error, not absence of relationship between remission rates and follow-up rates, accounted for the low correlation.

Validity of Data

Another serious problem with the Rand and SRI reports is that the main treatment outcome measure used, viz., self-report of drinking behavior, is of questionable validity. Armor et al. acknowledged the possible occurrence of both underreporting and overreporting of drinking behavior by individual patients. However, they defended their group outcome rates as valid by suggesting that errors in the direction of underreporting were canceled by the same frequency and magnitude of overreporting. This is questionable inasmuch as there are no empirical data to support it, and the data Armor et al. present on self-reports of drinking behavior suggest that underreporting is much more common than overreporting (1, *Appendix A*). For example, in 4 surveys of American drinking practices conducted by Louis Harris and Associates, it is estimated that respondents underreported alcohol consumption by about 50%. Also, in surveys conducted by state Alcohol Safety Action Programs, self-reports of consumption were checked against blood alcohol concentrations (BACs). Individuals who had BACs at intoxicating levels (0.10% or higher) significantly underreported the number of drinks they had had. This finding suggests that underreporting is particularly common among heavier drinkers, perhaps including alcoholics. Even more pertinent, an outcome study by Sobell[3] checked self-reports of patients at intake against BACs. Some overreporting of consumption was observed (12%) among the 150 male alcoholics who either had a positive BAC or reported some drinking during the 24 hours before the BAC test. However, over 2½ times more underreporting was observed (32%). Of particular relevance to the ATC follow-up study is Sobell's finding that at follow-up, 20% of the 30 patients who were interviewed underreported consumption, while not a single individual gave an overreport. This suggests that underreporting is more likely to go uncanceled by overreporting at follow-up than at intake.

Clinically, one might expect that a drinking alcoholic would minimize his drinking, particularly at follow-up. Motivation for doing so would include a desire to please the interviewer and a need to justify for himself and significant others the time and money spent in treatment.

Sobell's findings regarding validity at follow-up suggest that in the ATC samples consumption levels were uniformly underreported by a sizable proportion of patients, with little or no overreporting. It seems likely, therefore, that the remission rates observed by Ruggels et al. and Armor et al. were inflated. Of note is that such inflation was probably greatest for the normal drinking rates since these rates represent alcoholics who reported some but limited amounts of drinking.

Data Analysis Issues

While sharing the same data base, the Rand and SRI reports differ in some of their data analyses. For example, the term "recovery" was used in the SRI report to refer to patients who were either drinking moderately or not at all at follow-up. Armor et al. more appropriately used the term "remission." The latter allows for the possibility that an observed outcome status is temporary.

Normal Drinking. The two reports did not use the same definition of normal drinking. Ruggels et al. included in their normal-drinking group patients who drank less than 5 oz of ethanol on a typical drinking day or who averaged less than 1 oz of ethanol per day over the 30 days before follow-up. Armor et al. used a cluster of criteria to define normal drinkers:

[3] Cited by Armor et al. (1, *pp. 159–165*).

alcoholics who in the 30 days before follow-up (*1*) consumed less than 3 oz of ethanol a day on the average, (*2*) drank less than 5 oz of ethanol on typical days of drinking, (*3*) reported no tremors, and (*4*) did not have frequent episodes of at least 3 of the following 6 symptoms: tremors, blackouts, missing meals, morning drinking, being drunk, missing work. Using these criteria, a patient could be labeled a normal drinker and have frequent episodes of any 2 of the following: blackouts, missing meals, morning drinking, being drunk, and missing work. These criteria appear overly generous.

Since publishing the Rand report, Polich[4] has imposed stricter criteria for defining normal drinking and has found a modest drop in the rates. When he excluded from the normal drinking group patients who had had any alcoholic blackouts or any drinking on awakening and who had more than twice missed work days because of drinking and who had more than four times been drunk or missed meals due to drinking, the rates dropped from 21.8 to 17.9% for all patients in the 18-month follow-up sample and from 16.6 to 13.6% for those patients having at least three serious symptoms of alcoholism at intake. Even this approach does not seem sufficiently stringent. Perhaps occasional drunkenness can be accepted so long as it does not affect nutrition or job performance, but drinking can hardly be considered normal if it causes someone to miss even one or two days of work a month or to skip several meals. A more reasonable definition would exclude from the normal drinking group patients who missed any work or meals because of drinking.

Although not sufficiently stringent, Polich's criteria bring the normal drinking rates close to what has been found in other studies of alcoholism treatment having the goal of abstinence. For nearly 20 years (*2*), researchers have been reporting that some alcoholics drink moderately after abstinence-oriented treatment. Thus, what is new about the Rand and SRI findings is not the findings per se, but rather the heated controversy about them at the level of the public media. Some hypotheses concerning the development of this controversy were considered in the SRI review (*2*).

In their definitions of normal drinking, Armor et al. and Ruggels et al. agreed on a 5-oz. limit for the amount of ethanol a patient could consume on a typical drinking day. However, the research groups differed on the upper limit for average daily consumption. Armor et al. set theirs at 3 oz, Ruggels et al. at 1 oz. In considering the cut-off points for average daily consumption and consumption on typical drinking days a distinction needs to be made between normal drinking and healthy drinking. The cut-off points used by Armor et al. and Ruggels et al. are consonant with data

[4] POLICH, J. M. [Personal communication, 6 August 1976].

on American drinking practices gathered by Louis Harris and Associates. However, they do not agree with what is generally regarded by alcoholism researchers as healthy drinking. There are not sufficient data at this time to determine precisely what the healthy drinking limit should be, but one has been suggested. Based on discussions with alcoholism researchers throughout the world, Chafetz (5, *p. 10*) stated in a recent article that "At no time should any individual wishing to remain within the safe limits consume more than 1½ ounces of absolute alcohol per day." This is not a daily average, but an upper limit for any one 24-hour period. Since this amount is well below the limits set by Ruggels et al. and Armor et al., we must consider the possibility that their limit exceeds that for healthy drinking.

A final point about normal drinking. Both Armor et al. and Ruggels et al. failed to distinguish between controlled drinking and normal drinking. It is entirely possible that some alcoholics learn to consume only limited amounts of alcohol with no negative consequences from such drinking; yet they remain alcoholics cognitively. That is, they remain preoccupied with alcohol and think of it as a major stress reliever. They must exert great effort to maintain limited drinking. These alcoholics should be considered controlled drinkers inasmuch as the cognitive component of alcoholism has not been dealt with. Very likely, some of the patients identified as normal drinkers in the Rand and SRI reports were controlled drinkers. As with the generous consumption limits Ruggels et al. and Armor et al. used to define normal drinking, failure to remove controlled drinkers from the normal drinking group probably led to exaggerated normal drinking rates.

Remission Rates. Researchers in both studies failed to identify patients who were unchanged from pre- to posttreatment. As a result, the high over-all remission rates that were observed can be misleading. The way that the data were presented is likely to leave the reader believing that about 70% of patients got better with more than minimal treatment. This was not so. According to data presented in the SRI report, the overall improvement rate was about 50 percent for the sample analyzed by Rand. This rate is substantially lower than the mean overall drinking improvement rate of 66 percent that Emrick (6) found in his large-scale review of alcoholism treatment.

Treatment Effects. Armor et al. conducted more varied analyses of treatment effects than did Ruggels et al. Differences in remission rates were analyzed by Armor et al. according to therapist type (paraprofessional vs professional) and treatment amount, duration, center, setting (hospital, intermediate, outpatient), and type (group vs individual, disulfiram vs no disulfiram, ATC vs A.A. vs other therapy). Also, interaction effects were sought between (*1*) treatment setting and social background of patients, (*2*) setting and severity of alcoholism of patients, (*3*) setting and amount of therapy, (*4*) therapist type (professional vs professional) and treatment amount, duration, center, setting type (group vs individual) and patient characteristics, and (*6*) disulfiram treatment (vs no disulfiram) and patient characteristics. Finally, to measure the size of the effects of both patient and treatment characteristics on remission rates they performed a multiple regression analysis.

The following results are among those that were observed: (*1*) outcome rates did not differ between treatment settings, between treatment centers, or between treatments of varying duration; (*2*) many patients improved with only minimal treatment, but not so many as among those who received more than a minimal amount (except patients treated in a hospital or intermediate care facility with no aftercare, in which case more treatment was associated with poorer outcome); (*3*) treatment by paraprofessionals resulted in the same remission rates as treatment by professionals; (*4*) group treatment was as effective as individual treatment; (*5*) disulfiram had no consistent effects on outcome; (*6*) A.A. resulted in more total abstinence than did ATC treatment; (*7*) there were no apparent "best fits" between patient characteristics and treatment setting, individual vs group therapy, professionally led vs paraprofessionally led treatment, or disulfiram vs no disulfiram therapy; (*8*) treatment variables accounted for almost none of the outcome rate variance; and (*9*) patient variables accounted for more rate variance, but the absolute amount was still fairly small. As is clear, very few treatment effects were observed.

While often provocative, these findings are not open to clear interpretation because of problems with the analyses. One problem common to all the analyses (with the exception of multiple regression) is that patients were not randomly assigned to the different therapist types or the various treatment categories. Thus treatment and therapist differences may have been confounded with patient differences, e.g., because patients having particular characteristics were selected for particular therapists and treatments. Apparently no attempt was made to control even statistically for patient variation in the analyses of effects due to ATC setting or due to A.A. vs ATC treatment vs other treatment.

In the remaining analyses Armor et al. did attempt to control with covariance adjustment for patient variables considered relevant to remission rates. Nevertheless, problems remain. Other patient variables which may have been important were not controlled for. Far better that proper sampling had been done and that random assignment had been made to the various treatments and therapists so that few if any statistical controls would have to have been used in the analyses. But even assuming that

Armor et al. managed to include all important covariates in their analyses, a serious concern persists: The analysis of covariance model may not have been the appropriate one to use with the data. Several weighty assumptions underlie its use, e.g., equal variance of remission scores among the treatment groups, normal distribution of scores within groups, linear regression of scores on the covariates within groups, and homogeneous regression of scores on the covariates among groups. Nowhere do the authors comment on whether any of these assumptions were met. Failure to meet at least some of them, particularly the homogeneous regression assumption, may have distorted the adjusted remission rates.

Another problem that exists with all of the analyses is that most of the categories of patients, treatments and therapists which defined the cells into which patients were entered for analysis were not restrictive enough to permit much homogeneity within categories. An example is the analysis of the interaction between treatment setting and patients' severity of alcoholism. Patients were allocated along the setting dimension according to whether they received "hospital," "outpatient," or "intermediate" care or a combination thereof. Along the alcoholism severity dimension, patients were grouped according to whether they had "definite alcoholism at intake" or "less definite alcoholism at intake." With categories so broadly defined, much variation was likely to occur within each cell. Crawford and Pell (7), in their critique of the Rand report, noted the large amount of variance certain to exist within each treatment setting category. They pointed out how the category "intermediate care," for example, included not only simple domiciliaries but also halfway and quarterway houses which offered varying degrees of counseling and other services. With the high probability of large variation within categories or groups, chances were reduced of finding significant differences between patient types, therapist types or various kinds of treatments. This imprecision may have contributed significantly to the general absence of differential treatment and therapist effects observed in this study.

Despite the problems just discussed, there are three findings which merit further attention, because they are particularly provocative (the first) or the data are open to interpretations which differ from those of Armor et al. (the second and third).

The first issue deals with the comparison of professionally and paraprofessionally administered therapy. In addition to the difficulties identified thus far, Armor et al. apparently did not attempt to control the impact of treatment variables on remission rates when making this comparison. One type of therapist, for example, may actually have been more effective than the other, but his relative success may have been masked by his systematically not seeing patients for as many sessions as the other. This additional problem should be considered when interpreting the findings on therapist type.

The second issue concerns the effectiveness of group vs individual therapy. At 6-month follow-up, the remission rate was higher for group therapy than for individual treatment (80 vs 70%). At 18-month follow-up, group therapy trailed individual treatment (64 vs 73%). Armor et al. dismissed these inconsistent findings as probably due to sampling error. While interpretation of the data is risky because of the methodological problems described above, the findings do suggest a possible interaction between treatment modality and duration of positive effects: the early success of group treatment was lost over time, whereas the positive effects of individual treatment were stable or even increased. Perhaps individual treatment is more effective over the long haul than group treatment. Of course, better designed research on the interaction between duration of effect and treatment modality will have to be done before any clear conclusion about this possibility can be drawn.

The third finding deals with differential effects across ATCs. Armor et al. interpreted their data as reflecting only minor outcome differences between centers; however, there was a 32% range in remission rates between them (49 to 81%). Perhaps, some centers were more effective than others. Individuals making ATC funding decisions may wish to pursue this possibility.

Social Correlates of Alcoholism. Unique to the Rand report is a chapter dealing with social correlates of alcoholism and problem drinking. Armor et al. compared the intake characteristics of ATC-treated alcoholics with the characteristics of drinking Americans, including a subset of problem drinkers. The drinking Americans were sampled in surveys of national drinking practices conducted by Louis Harris and Associates. Differences between the ATC and Harris samples were found and interpreted as suggesting that, compared with drinkers in general and problem drinkers in particular, treated alcoholics are more often Southern, of lower socioeconomic status, Protestant, unmarried and unemployed. This interpretation appears to be misleading insofar as the first three differences are concerned because ATCs tend to be concentrated in the South and, by association, to be skewed toward treating Protestants and lower socioeconomic groups. The Harris surveys, in contrast, were based on national probability samples. Thus the differences Armor et al. observed between ATC patients and drinkers in the Harris surveys may have been a function of noncomparable samples rather than of the correlates of treated alcoholism. Although Armor et al. mention a correction for the Southern bias in their sample, it is unclear how this was done. In any case, comparable probability samples would provide the only secure basis for such comparisons.

In addition to Southern bias, the data regarding relatively low socioeconomic status of ATC-treated alcoholics may have resulted from the fact that ATCs are federally funded agencies and presumably attract relatively poor alcoholics. As a whole, treated alcoholics may or may not be low socioeconomically relative to all American drinkers.

IMPLICATIONS FOR TREATMENT POLICY

The numerous defects of the studies by Armor et al. and Ruggels et al., particularly with respect to research design and data analysis, make it difficult to use the findings for policy decision making. We wholeheartedly agree with Armor et al., who repeatedly emphasize that alcoholism treatment policy decisions should not be made on the basis of the findings of the ATC follow-up data.

Despite this caveat, we wish to note a finding which appears to have treatment implications: Abstinence rates were found to rise with increasing amounts of ATC treatment, while normal rates remained fairly uniform as treatment amount increased. Further analysis of the data reported by Armor et al. (1, *p. 95*) reveals that 89% of the 18-percentage-point increase in remission rates between treated and untreated patients was in the two abstinence categories (Table 1). Perhaps treatment has very specific effects on drinking behavior. When the goal is abstinence, treatment raises abstinence rates but leaves normal drinking virtually unchanged. Similarly, it seems likely that treatment will need to be directed toward normal drinking if it is to have a chance of raising normal drinking rates. Results of evaluations of normal drinking programs such as the one by Sobell and Sobell (e.g., 8) are certainly consistent with this notion.

Table 1.   Remission Rates for Treated and Untreated Alcoholics, in Per Cent[a]

	Untreated Alcoholics[b] (N=425)	Treated Alcoholics (N=272)
Abstinent 6 months	17	26
Abstinent 1 month	17	21
Normal drinking 1 month	24	26
Total in remission	*55*	*73*

[a] Based on Table 24 of the Rand report (1).
[b] Alcoholics having anywhere from 1 treatment contact to 1 week or less of intermediate care or 5 visits or less of outpatient care.

SUGGESTIONS FOR RESEARCH

The findings of the Rand and SRI studies suggest many areas for future research. Three are identified here.

First, research needs to be done to improve our ability to distinguish alcoholics who can return to normal drinking from those who should become abstinent. Until this is done, clinicians, except those engaged in formal research on this issue, must be very cautious about choosing any goal other than total abstinence for alcoholics. In analyzing the normal drinking data, Armor et al. did find that patients with severe alcoholism symptoms were less likely to become normal drinkers than were those with less severe symptoms. The authors also warned that patients with severe physical problems and those who have repeatedly failed to drink moderately should not strive to become normal drinkers. These findings and position statements give direction for determining who can and who cannot return to normal drinking, but much more research is needed to develop practical guidelines for making such determinations.

Second, research is needed to assess the remission rates of truly untreated alcoholics. Too often, control groups used by alcoholism researchers have consisted of alcoholics who have had one or only a few formal treatment contacts. Remission rates for such groups have probably been affected by the albeit limited exposure to treatment the patients have had. Studies of completely untreated alcoholics would provide a more accurate baseline for assessing the effects of formal alcoholism treatment.

Third, well-designed and conducted research should investigate patient-treatment matching. Also, work needs to be done toward finding optimal patient-*therapist* matches, an area not dealt with in the Rand and SRI reports.

CONCLUSION

As with the bulk of alcoholism treatment outcome research, the SRI and Rand projects have numerous methodological flaws. Some of the results of these projects, e.g., those dealing with different treatment effects, agree with common findings of alcoholism research (9), although, as indicated earlier, at least one major finding, i.e., the size of drinking improvement rates, does not. Those findings which do agree contribute nothing new to the field. While such agreement might suggest that the results are valid, this is by no means a certainty. The findings of one methodologically flawed study may agree with those of another flawed study, neither being correct.

If we are to obtain convincing answers to any of the urgent questions regarding treatment of alcoholism, investigators must avoid the pitfalls that have waylaid so many in the past. If treatment outcome studies cannot use random assignment of patients to treatments, if follow-up samples are biased, if treatment groups are not comparable to untreated controls, if outcome measures are laden with the potential for bias—in short, if even the simpler and more rudimentary tenets of systematic empirical observation cannot be met—then the data, no matter how many of them, will tell us nothing of which we can be sure. That the execution of good studies is difficult, that it raises ethical problems, that it creates practical problems, that it annoys and inconveniences even the most tolerant administrators—none of these can be denied. But unless those studies are somehow done, our only recourse is to more or less enlightened opinion, the force of which stems primarily from the articulateness of its proponents.

REFERENCES

1. ARMOR, D. J., POLICH, J. M. and STAMBUL, H. B. Alcoholism and treatment. Prepared for the U.S. National Institute on Alcohol Abuse and Alcoholism. Santa Monica, CA; Rand Corp.; 1976.
2. EMRICK, C. D. Review of RUGGELS, W. L., ARMOR, D. J., POLICH, J. M., MOTHERSHEAD, A. and STEPHEN, M. A. follow-up study of clients at selected alcoholism treatment centers funded by NIAAA; final report. Menlo Park, CA; Stanford Research Institute; 1975. J. Stud. Alc. **37:** 1902–1907, 1976.
3. RUGGEL, W. L., ARMOR, D. J., POLICH, J. M., MOTHERSHEAD, A. and STEPHEN, M. A follow-up study of clients at selected alcoholism treatment centers funded by NIAAA; final report. Menlo Park, CA; Stanford Research Institute; 1975.
4. EMRICK, C. D. Psychological treatment of alcoholism; an analytic review. Ph.D. dissertation, Columbia University; 1973.
5. CHAFETZ, M. E. Carire Nation had a drinking problem; how to drink healthily and why so many Americans don't. Johns Hopk. Mag **27** (No. 2): 8–17, 1976.
6. EMRICK, C. D. A review of psychologically oriented treatment of alcoholism. *I.* The use and interrelationships of outcome criteria and drinking behavior following treatment. uart. J. Stud. Alc. **35:** 523–549, 1974.
7. CRAWFORD, J. J. and PELL, J. The Rand Report; a brief critique. Addictions. [In press.]
8. SOBELL, M. B. and SOBELL, L. C. Alcoholics treated by individualized behavior therapy; one year treatment outcome. Behav. Res. Ther., Oxford **11:** 599–618, 1973.
9. EMRICK, C. D. A review of psychologically oriented treatment of alcoholism.

II. The relative effectiveness of different treatment approaches and the effectiveness of teratment versus no treatment. J. Stud. Alc. **36:** 88–108, 1975.

Sheila Blume, M.D.[1]

The Rand report (1), representing as it does a tremendous investment in time, energy and financial resources, is bound to exert a considerable amount of influence on the future of alcoholism treatment in the United States. The report is a very carefully thought-out statistical analysis of data collected from 8 out of 44 treatment centers funded by the National Institute on Alcohol Abuse and Alcoholism and a series of national surveys of drinking practices. Within the confines of the data with which the authors had to work, the report's analysis was excellent. Many of the interpretations and conclusions drawn from these data, however, seem unwarranted. Even though such conclusions are stated tentatively, their effects on public policy and public opinion will be considerable (2, 3). I therefore feel moved to comment on three aspects of the Rand report from a clinician's point of view: (*1*) the conclusions about treatment drawn from the data; (*2*) the use of the terms "normal drinking" and "natural remission"; and (*3*) the implications drawn by the study concerning the disease concept or "medical model" of alcoholism.

Unwarranted Conclusions

The authors' analytic device, the input–output model for treatment evaluation (1, *pp. 38–44*), provides a useful reference point for examination of the data upon which their conclusions are based. In order to evaluate treatment, patient inputs, treatment inputs and patient–treatment interactions must be measured. The data available to them, however, failed to include many crucial variables in each of these areas, which from everyday clinical experience would be expected to have major influences on outcome.

The patient inputs measured consist mostly of demographic information

[1] Unit Chief, Charles K. Post Alcoholism Rehabilitation Unit, Central Islip Psychiatric Center, Central Islip, NY 11722.
ACKNOWLEDGEMENTS.—I acknowledge helpful discussions with Drs. Maxwell Weisman and Henry Brill.

("social background" and "social stability" on the model) with an estimate of quantity, frequency and type of alcohol consumed ("drinking history"), a limited number of alcoholism-related symptoms ("symptomatology") and some data about environmental settings ("drinking context"). Notably absent are measurements of past and concomitant drug use. None of the "psychological attributes," as indicated in the model, are included. Here the crucial omission is mental status: the presence or absence of psychosis, organic brain damage, underlying mental illness, concomitant depression, suicidal tendencies, personality disorders, etc. These factors are left out in spite of the fact that both underlying and concomitant mental disorders are not infrequently found in groups of alcoholics (4). According to a recent World Health Organization report (5, *pp. 21–22*), "clinical experience suggests that insofar as the natural history of alcohol dependence and its response to treatment are concerned, there are important interaction effects with mental pathologies. It would be virtually impossible to say anything about the degree of disability likely to result from the individual's alcohol dependence, if data were available only on the drinking behavior and the direct symptomatology of the dependence; it would be equivalent to attempting to solve a puzzle with some of the pieces missing."

Also missing under the category of "psychological attributes" are the patients' attitudes toward alcoholism and treatment, including insight, cooperativeness, preferences for types of treatment, and motivation, although the authors refer to these as probably important.

Somewhere between the categories of psychological and physical characteristics would come the sexual and psychosomatic disorders, also not reported. "Physical characteristics" included in the authors' model and referred to in the text are left out of the data entirely, although physical conditions, including withdrawal states, malnutrition, and hepatic, gastric, pancreatic, cardiac and neuropathic complications of alcoholism, are often primary factors in all kinds of clinical decisions regarding treatment. They influence decisions by the patient, family, physician and treatment program. Self-report of tremors is the only physical characteristic included in the analysis.

Environmental factors other than drinking, such as psychopathology in the family, marital adjustment and other aspects of the home environment, often important to treatment decisions and probably also to recovery, are likewise omitted.

Treatment inputs analyzed in the report also fail to measure crucial factors. Such unlike programs as "custodial" detoxication or emergency medical care and rehabilitative day or night hospitals are grouped together. Intensive therapeutic quarterway houses are grouped together with facilities offering living quarters with little or no therapy. Therapists are classified only as professional or paraprofessional, although previous studies have shown that personal characteristics of therapists are vital to the outcome of other counseling situations (6).

Conclusions concerning patient–therapy interactions would be meaningful only if one of two conditions obtained: (*1*) if patients had been randomly assigned to treatment, or (*2*) if the most important factors in treatment assignment had been measured. Neither of these were done. Assignment to treatment was quite the opposite of random. It was almost certainly a careful attempt to match the clinical condition of the patients with treatment settings and therapists. The parameters measured in the study were probably seldom, if ever, the most important factors in such decisions.

Based on these data, however, the authors state, "Perhaps the most important finding of this study is that there are few noteworthy differences among remission rates for various treatment types" (1, *p. 129*), and later, "Keeping in mind this general caveat, the relatively uniform remission rates across different treatment modes suggest that, given no other consideration besides treatment success, less expensive forms of treatment might be substituted for more expensive forms. This could mean increased use of paraprofessional counselors (whose use is already widespread in alcoholism treatment), as well as the substitution of outpatient care for more costly inpatient treatment" (1, *p. 139*). (The caveat in question refers to the "need for additional information before any policy changes are contemplated" and the lack of data on stability of remission.) The authors also conclude on the basis of their data that uniform treatment outcomes are not the result of patient–treatment matches.

In my opinion, none of the above conclusions, however tentative, is warranted, because of the absence of appropriate data. This absence is well illustrated by their own finding that all of the patient and treatment factors they measured, taken together, explain only about 13% of the variance in remission rate. This, to the authors, suggests that "there is a great deal of idiosyncratic variation in a client's response to treatment, independent of his own characteristics or the particular type of treatment that he receives" (1, *p. 122*). I submit that there are many of the patient's own characteristics and many treatment characteristics that are both measurable and crucial to recovery, but were simply not included in the study. To postulate, as the authors did, that recovery depends to a large extent on the individual's decision (also unmeasured in the study) ignores too many other important aspects of the complex condition we call alcoholism and its treatment.

Inappropriate Use of Terms

Had the authors chosen to use the term "improved," "much improved" or "reduced drinking" to describe the group of patients who had greatly decreased their alcohol intake at the time of follow-up, I would have no objection to that section of the report. It is part of common clinical experience that many patients continue to struggle with their drinking both during and after treatment. Treatment teaches such patients places to go for help, techniques for cutting short their relapses into drinking and ways of remaining well for increasing periods of time. Such patients are usually still aiming for abstinence and this goal is an important factor in their continued struggle for recovery.

The authors, however, choose to call this state of improvement "normal drinking." Their version of "normal" is a statistical one, based on comparisons with the general population, and defined by four features: daily consumption of less than 3 oz of ethanol; typical quantity on a drinking day less than 5 oz of ethanol; no tremors by self-report; and adsence of "frequent episodes" of three of a list of six symptoms—tremors, blackouts, missing meals, morning drinking, being drunk and missing work (1, *p. 80*). Given the authors' own admission that the validity of the self-report data is unestablished, and that quantity of consumption is probably considerably underreported by heavy drinkers (1, *p. 166*), these limits seem overly generous. A man can average up to five "shots" of whisky a day and drink as many as nine on a typical day (even more at times if the day is not typical), have a variety of severe consequences from his drinking, and still be considered a "normal" drinker as long as he does not report tremors. One should recall that the use of sedative drugs of the patient, either medically prescribed or illegally obtained, will suppress tremors. No question on drug use was included in the study questionnaire. An alcoholic may have been drunk, sick, arrested for drunken driving, hospitalized, detoxicated, suffered liver failure and overdosed on drugs, but as long as his relapse started gradually enough and ended abruptly enough to make a typical drinking day and average daily intake meet the study definition, he would still be judged a normal drinker.

The term "normal drinking" conjures up an image of spontaneous joyful problem-free drinking, or, at the very least, carefully controlled problem-free drinking. The study definition and data do not support either picture.

According to the authors' criteria, 25% of the patients were drinking at "normal" average daily alcohol consumption levels at the time of intake, while 11% were abstinent for at least a month before, yet they were all accepted for treatment of alcoholism. Although the authors attribute some of this effect to institutionalization prior to admission (1, *p. 70*), the instructions on the questionnaire clearly state that data should be recorded for the month prior to institutionalization (1, *p. 179*).

Use of the terms "natural remission" and "untreated clients" to refer to patients who had single contact or brief detoxication is also unjustified. As Torrey has pointed out (6, *pp. 13–28*), the intake process and the process of giving a name to the problem (in this case diagnosing alcoholism) is in itself therapeutic. We may also assume that such patients may have been encouraged to stop drinking and to look to Alcoholics Anonymous or other sources of help in their environments, such as religion, friends or family. It would be hard to imagine that the half of the "pre-intake group" that had a median stay of three days in a detoxication unit would not have had such counseling. Furthermore, the patients in this study were picked up at various points in the progression of their alcoholism and recovery. The first contact with the Alcoholism Treatment Center was arbitrarily considered "day one." Some were doubtlessly already engaged in some sort of ongoing helpful treatment. A true study of a never-treated group of alcoholics would be necessary to establish a natural remission rate. This, of course, would be of great interest to us all.

Implications of the Study Concerning the Disease Concept or "Medical Model"

The authors seem to feel that the medical model of alcoholism is "predicated on the belief that loss of control is the defining feature of the alcoholic's chronic condition, so that even one drink is thought to lead inexorably to alcoholic behavior" (1, *p. 22*). The word "inexorably" is misplaced. Everyday clinical observation shows that many alcoholics control their drinking for brief periods, and that many relapses into drinking start off slowly and gradually. Loss of control eventually takes place if the alcoholic or his or her environment does nothing to intervene and interrupt the drinking episode. Many patients consult their therapists, sober friends or A.A. groups after they have started to drink "just a little." These patients are often able with help to stop drinking far short of disaster. This in no way disproves either a physical predisposition to alcoholism or the view that it is a complex multicausal biopsychosocial disease.

A further misunderstanding of the "medical model" is expressed in the authors' conception that it causes alcoholics treated on an inpatient alcoholism unit to adopt a passive role. Nothing could be farther from accepted medical practice, which places the responsibility for taking the necessary steps to recovery squarely on the patient's shoulders. The disease concept is very helpful in removing much of the terrible burden of guilt carried by most alcoholics who, after all, never chose to become alcoholics. They are helped to see that although the illness happened to them, there are measures they can take to recover. This emphasis on patient responsibility for recovery is quite common in the management of many chronic illnesses.

I am also sorry to see that in discussing abstinence goals the authors (1, *p. 133*) repeat the idea that alcoholics may get drunk because the philosophy of their treatment programs tell them they will (the so-called self-fulfilling prophecy). This idea, blaming the disease on the treatment agency, is reminiscent of the claims a decade ago that chronic mental illness was produced by mental hospitals. Closing the hospitals was supposed to eliminate the problem. This did not turn out to be true. Neither is it true that clinicians are responsible for their patients' intemperance. Every alcoholic I have known has tried many times to reduce or control drinking without lasting success. It is because of this inability to overcome the destructive drinking that he or she seeks help, not the other way round. Thus I find the authors' statement in their summary very puzzling. They state (1, *p. vi*), "In accepting normal drinking as a form of remission, we are by no means advocating that alcoholics should attempt moderate drinking after treatment. Alcoholics who have repeatedly failed to moderate their drinking, or who have irreversible physical complications due to alcohol, should not drink at all." I know of no other kind.

As for the authors' recommendation for further studies to explore other-than-abstinence goals for therapy, I am in agreement as long as this research is done carefully. It is my own guess that the abstinence goal itself, as the treatment programs that took part in the study used it, was a therapeutic measure which spurred its patients to avoid or cut short drinking episodes. Suppose one were running an obesity clinic and prescribing 1000-calorie diets. Suppose the average rate of "cheating" among those who tried to stay on the diet was 30%, so that the average dieting patient was eating 1300 calories, but still losing weight slowly. Rather than make those who "cheat" feel guilty, someone suggests, why not aim for a 1300 calorie diet in the first place? The clinic tries this but finds the dieters now add 30% to the new diet, taking 1700 calories and not losing weight at all. The clinic might conclude that striving for the ideal was in itself a useful tool. I believe we will find the same in alcoholism.

REFERENCES

1. ARMOR, D. J., POLICH, J. M. and STAMBUL, H. B. Alcoholism and treatment. Prepared for the U.S. National Institute on Alcohol Abuse and Alcoholism. Santa Monica, CA; Rand Corp.; 1976.

2. BRODY, J. E. Study suggests alcoholic, treated, can drink safely. New York Times, 10 June 1976.
3. CASHMAN, J. And never a drop to drink? Newsday, Garden City, N.Y., 23 June 1976.
4. FREED, E. X. Alcoholism and schizophrenia; the search for perspectives; a review. J. Stud. Alc. **36:** 853–881, 1975.
5. WORLD HEALTH ORGANIZATION. Alcohol-related problems in the disability perspective. Geneva; 1975.
6. TORREY, E. F. The mind game. New York; Emerson Hall; 1972.
7. TRUAX, C. B. and CARKHUFF, R. R. Toward effective counseling and psychotherapy; training and practice. Chicago; Aldine; 1967.

Allen A. Adinolfi, Ph.D. and Bernard DiDario, A.B.[1]

Probably the most dramatic and controversial findings of the Rand report (1) are those related to later relapse from the status of remission. In particular the authors contend that an alcoholic defined as in remission on the basis of abstinence (for 6 months or 1 month prior to evaluation) is in no more danger of later relapse than an alcoholic defined as in remission on the basis of "normal drinking." They write (1, *p. 86*), "We cannot overemphasize the impact of these findings. Based on the relapse rates for a subsample of clients with followup reports a year apart, it appears that some alcoholics do return to normal drinking with no greater likelihood of relapse than alcoholics who choose permanent abstention."

These statements are based on the relapse of 3 of 19 "definitely alcoholic" normal-drinking patients, 5 of 31 long-term abstaining patients and 16 of 73 short-term abstaining patients (1, *Table 19*).

It is not our intent to dispute Armor et al.'s definitions of relapse and remission, nor to dispute the issue of "normal drinking" as a form of remission in alcoholism. Instead, we wish to point out that the relapse rate of alcoholics defined as in remission on the basis of normal drinking, which has generated so much controversy and received so much attention, is based on the sum total of only 3 of 19 patients.

The Rand Corporation researchers addressed themselves to a corpus of data on 30,000 patients in treatment at 44 alcoholism treatment centers across the nation. To suggest that any statement on outcome or relapse based on an analysis of 19 of those 30,000 patients is simply not scientific. A more accurate but essentially meaningless statement based on the data

[1] The Center for Problem Drinking, Veterans Administration Outpatient Clinic, 17 Court Street, Boston, MA 02108.

would be: Of an original, potential subject population of 30,000 alcoholics in treatment, sufficient data were available to state that 19 patients at a 6-month follow-up were found to be in remission on the basis of normal drinking and, of these 19, 7 were found at an 18-month follow-up to be in remission on the basis of normal drinking.

REFERENCE

1. ARMOR, D. J., POLICH, J. M. and STAMBUL, H. B. Alcoholism and treatment. Prepared for the U.S. National Institute on Alcohol Abuse and Alcoholism. Santa Monica, CA; Rand Corp.; 1976.

Ron Roizen[1]

Section 102 of the Public Law that created the National Institute on Alcohol Abuse and Alcoholism asked NIAAA to "submit an annual report to Congress which shall include a description of the actions taken, services provided, and funds expended under this Act, . . . an evaluation of the effectiveness of such actions, services, and expenditures of funds, and such other information as the Secretary of Health, Education, and Welfare considers appropriate" (1). Thus evaluation research of one sort or another was an integral part of NIAAA as it was conceived by the Congress. In its broadest form this evaluative effort was to be addressed to the general goals set down by Congress for the Institute: namely, to "develop and conduct comprehensive health, education, training, research, and planning programs for the prevention and treatment of alcohol abuse and alcoholism and for the rehabilitation of alcohol abusers and alcoholics" (1). In practice, a large fraction of NIAAA's resources was devoted to the treatment of "alcohol abusers and alcoholics" in a system of federally supported Alcoholism Treatment Centers, and much of the evaluation effort was directed toward this enterprise. Before too long NIAAA was busy establishing a system of alcoholism-treatment evaluation that is surely unequaled in terms of size and ambitiousness in the history of alcoholism treatment in the United States or elsewhere.

Instead of funding many little evaluation studies or a series of yearly larger studies, NIAAA created an ongoing monitoring system which could

[1] Social Research Group, School of Public Health, University of California, 1912 Bonita Ave., Berkeley, CA 94704.

produce up-to-date data in a conveniently standardized form on a regular basis. By March 1973 the system had produced a preliminary report (2) on the characteristics of treatment center patients and various cost-oriented analyses of treatment center functioning. In mid-1975 Stanford Research Institute (3) published a more complete account of the monitoring system data and of a special 18-month follow-up study in which attrition from the sample had been kept to a minimum. The data from the evaluation system also trickled out in a variety of smaller papers and news reports: *The Alcoholism Report* carried highlights of the Stanford report on one or two occasions;[2] Chafetz (4) published a slightly more detailed account of some of the major findings. Towle (5) presented summaries of the findings at NIAAA's Fourth Annual Conference on Alcoholism and at the Epidemiological Section meetings of the 21st International Institute on the Prevention and Treatment of Alcoholism in Helsinki in 1975.[3] Some of the system data were used in NIAAA's second report to the Congress (6). Until the publication of the Rand report (7), I suspect that the readership of the larger reports (2, 3) was confined to a small circle of government officials, consultants to the evaluation project, and prominent scholars with a pipeline to reports like this. The shorter papers and articles may have had a broader readership but lacked both details and the spark to ignite controversy.

The public controversy that began after the release of the Rand report in June 1976 seems to have been foreshadowed by an intense private controversy extending for over a year, about which the record is still incomplete. It is a matter of public record that both officials at Rand[4] and a United States Senator[5] were asked to delay publication of the report until its contents could be reviewed and its data, perhaps, reanalyzed. The central concern in this private controversy and in the public controversy that followed has been the report's apparent implication that at least some and perhaps a respectable fraction of alcoholics do and can return to normal, controlled or social drinking. The belief that this finding is wrong and its publication dangerous has been responsible for most of the debate, and it seems to have created the vigorous effort in many quarters to examine with a fine toothcomb the data, assumptions and implications of the report.

[2] For example, in the issue of 28 March 1975, pp. 4–5.

[3] TOWLE, L. H. Routine monitoring of alcoholism treatment services and client followup as an input to national program planning and policy. Presented at the Epidemiological Section, 21st International Institute on the Prevention and Treatment of Alcoholism, Helsinki, June 1975.

[4] PENDERY, M. NCA press conference, Shoreham Hotel, Washington, DC, 1 July 1976.

[5] The Alcoholism Report, 12 September 1976, p. 7.

Of course, neither the evaluation system nor the Rand Report was solely focused on the abstinence question. The evaluation system was designed to provide data on a number of dimensions of alcoholism treatment including management information on services rendered and their costs, on the extent to which treatment centers were meeting local demands for treatment services, and on patient change between the time of entering treatment and several follow-ups. Thus, even the "patient change" problem was only one of several that the evaluation system addressed. And "patient change" was measured in several different ways in the longer reports that concerned this subject (3, 7).

This exclusive focus on the abstinence question has caused reviewers to miss some of the other interesting findings in the report. For example:

For some years now, attempts to measure the prevalence of alcoholism with epidemiological surveys have been hampered by the absence of comparable data on clinical samples. Without clinical norms to compare them with, the findings of general population surveys alone could not indicate the prevalence of cases that were similar to or equally severe as alcoholics in treatment. As Clark (8) pointed out a decade ago, prevalence estimates could be varied from very high to very low (or zero) depending on where the cutting points were laid. And without comparable clinical data or some other method for devising them, these cutting points were left arbitrary. Armor et al. (7, *ch. 3, app. A*) analyzed problem drinkers in the general population (drawn from data collected in four Harris surveys commissioned by NIAAA) and alcoholics in alcoholism treatment centers. The findings suggested that current estimates of the prevalence of alcoholism in the U.S.A. may be much too high if what is meant by the estimate is the size of a general population group with drinking practices and alcohol-related impairments similar to those of persons entering treatment programs.

The alcoholism treatment center studies yielded comparable data on patients who were in treatment as a consequence of being arrested for driving while intoxicated (DWI) and on non-DWIS. Although the authors did not conduct a detailed analysis of these two groups, the data suggest that DWIS and non-DWIS had substantially different alcohol-related characteristics. Thus these data raise questions about the application of the concept of alcoholism to the DWI population.

The data on spontaneous remission from alcoholism have never been adequate 9, 10)[6] in spite of the fact that this subject is crucially important to a number of concerns in the alcohol problems field. The implication of the monitoring system data seems to be that a substantial fraction of untreated persons undergo improvements in their conditions without the aid of treatment.

[6] Also ROIZEN, R., CAHALAN, D. and SHANKS, P. Spontaneous remission among untreated problem drinkers. Presented at the conference on Strategies of Longitudinal Research on Drug Abuse, San Juan, Puerto Rico, April 1976.

The study found that treatment types and patient characteristics predict very little of the remission variance.

Related to this, the finding that predictors of problem drinking in the general population may not perform very well as predictors of remission in the clinical population suggests the need for a careful look at the logic of our attempts to account for and to treat drinking problems.

The Abstinence Fixation

Most of the public commentary on the Rand report has focused on the abstinence issue. This is an interesting and telling concentration of public attention. As I mentioned, the report itself was not addressed solely to the abstinence issue but was a comprehensive analysis of the data from NIAAA's monitoring system for alcoholism treatment centers. But the abstinence issue seems to burn brightly in alcohologists' campfires, so that raising the issue is likely to create a debate in which at least some participants regard the subject as a vital concern. But why does the abstinence question have this excitatory power? What are the things at stake when the question is raised? And why has a question that would seem to be quite amenable to empirical resolution nevertheless remained an unresolved matter for so long?

The abstinence issue is controversial because this question is intimately tied to a full paradigm or gestalt about alcohol-related problems. It is not the fate of the abstinence question alone that is at stake in the debate but the fate of this larger paradigm. In order to create a picture of the abstinence question it is necessary, first, to discuss a few points concerning that paradigm.

In the classical model, an alcoholic is "diseased," first and foremost, in that his drinking behavior is outside his own volitional control. His troubles with drinking, as Jellinek suggested (11), stem from the fact that he is ignorant of his own constitutional difference from other people and because he sees no reason to suspect that such a difference exists. Strong rationalizations may surround his drinking behavior, and these may serve to "explain" his drinking to himself to his own satisfaction, thereby making it more difficult for the therapist to convince him that he is different. But it is the education of the alcoholic—convincing him that he is different—that is the major element of the classical treatment ideology. Thus, this ideology does not treat "the alcoholism" in a patient, which is to say it does not attempt to affect the putative constitutional difference that makes him an alcoholic, but rather attempts to alter his conscious knowledge of his own physiology or psyche. The treatment attempts to educate him to the acceptance of the belief that he is different, and that this difference is not a piecemeal or transitory thing. In short, alcoholism treatment, as it is seen in the classical model, is largely a didactic and persuasional effort that attempts to treat an alcoholic by getting him to accept a particular theory of alcoholism, and his acceptance of that theory is itself the essence of alcoholism treatment. It is a process organized around the conscious half of the mind–body dualism that is implicit in the Alcoholics Anonymous image of man; and to that extent it is more aptly called an educational rather than a treatment program. The outcome criterion of "abstinence" is not solely a measure of the "treatment" process. The treatment is itself the inculcation of the disease conception of alcoholism, and, in this domain, the disease concept *means* that a constitutional difference in alcoholics is at the root of troubles with drinking. If the constitutional basis theory is accepted, the alcoholic may be persuaded to give up drinking. Embracing abstinence is thus a sign that the model of alcoholism has been accepted by the patient. Thus, measuring whether or not the alcoholic internalizes this theory and makes a commitment to abstinence becomes the only really important outcome criterion.

We usually think of a theory concerning a disease as "coming before" and "informing" the treatment regimen that it suggests. In the case of the classical alcoholism model, we have a theory whose acceptance-by-the-patient *is* the treatment. The close fit between theory and practice creates a number of difficulties. For one thing, it creates a confusion in the manner by which the theory should be judged and the relevant observations that should judge it. Most of us, of course, are familiar with any number of different criteria by which theories may be evaluated—we judge them by whether or not they fit the facts, whether they can be tested or falsified, whether they make sense or clear up old questions that have been nagging at us for some time, and so on. For our purposes, it is useful to distinguish two broad classes of judgmental criteria: those pertaining to the correctness of the theory, and those pertaining to its utility. While we usually think of these criteria as going together (that is to say, correct theories are more useful than incorrect ones, and useful theories are more likely to be correct than useless ones), the history of science is replete with theoretical systems in which the two criteria varied independently. The assumptions of Ptolemy's system of astronomy, in spite of being "wrong," provide a perfectly good basis for navigation of the seas—indeed teaching the use of the sextant is more simple in a Ptolemaic than a Copernican universe. Likewise some theories about which there is substantial consensus regarding their scientific correctness (e.g., Darwinian theory) seem to have few utilities either with regard to prediction or control of the things they pertain to.

In the case of the classical "alcoholism theory" it is essential that we keep separate issues of "correctness" and "utility." The classical "alcoholism" theory, as Keller has described its history (12), was adopted from A.A. ideology primarily because "it worked"—the success of A.A. was well known and impressive to the scholarly community that in the early 1940s was studying "the problem":

"At first glance it may seem surprising that much of the contemporary understanding of a disease, with which medical and allied therapeutic professionals are heavily engaged, should derive from a fellowship of laymen. Especially so when, if one re-examines the exhaustive review of the psychiatric literature published in 1941 by Karl M. Bowman and E. M. Jellinek, it is obvious what a vast amount of observation, study, theorizing and writing had been done in the effort to understand alcoholism. Why, then, in spite of all the sophisticated synthesis that came out of that review, did the medical and paramedical world, and Jellinek himself, soon after capitulate, as it were, to the lay wisdom of Alcoholics Anonymous? This problem merits a deeper consideration than I can give it in the present aside, but I would like to suggest that it was a very practical and understandable capitulation. For all the wisdom of the older medical-psychiatric writings, in the beautifully organized Bowman-and-Jellinek synthesis, made good sense in theory, but offered small help in practice. That is, in medical practice, in the practical business of successful treatment. On the other hand, at the time when that review was published, Alcoholics Anonymous began to become famous, the story of its success was then for the first time widely publicized. The medical world had to look, at first with surprise, and finally with conviction, at a way of dealing with alcoholism that worked."

Thus the theoretical stage is set by viewing the theory from a utilitarian (rather than correctness) perspective. In a sense, moreover, the utility of the theory was quite independent of its truth content. If incoming patients can be convinced that they are "alcoholics," with all of the implications that this word carries in the classical model, then by all rights they should give up drinking and commence an abstinent life. If the theory were true, all the better; but if the theory were false it would not necessarily undercut the therapeutic usefulness that it might possess—unless patients were exposed to disconfirming evidence. Thus regardless of its truth content, the classical alcoholism theory provides a basis for treating the alcoholic and providing him with a number of things we regard as benefits: it gives an "explanation" of alcoholismic behavior that avoids ladening the alcoholic with too much guilt for past drinking excesses; it wins his release from the morally based criminal justice system of social management; it provides the rationale for abstinence; it opens a route for his reintegration into conventional roles and obligations; it provides the basis for medically oriented research on the etiology of the condition; it, when an alcoholic embraces it, arrests his condition.

Of course from a purely intellectual standpoint the theory is surprisingly vacuous; it seems only to assert that alcoholics are different, without anything more than speculation regarding the source or even the evidence for that difference. What is important to recognize, however, is that the theory is ideal from a utilitarian standpoint, and thus provides social managers of alcoholism with a seeming intellectual basis for carrying out their mission. This utility is intact so long as therapists can present the theory honestly and openly without fear of contradiction. Only when a considerable body of contrary evidence is around does the theory and the entire mode of approach to alcoholism begin to weaken. Without the ability, in other words, to create a genuine conviction in the classical disease concept of alcoholism, the theory, its treatment implications, and its authority and legitimacy dissolve. Thus in a crucial sense, the utility of the alcoholism theory—which is both historically and contemporarily its best selling point —is absolutely premised on the degree of commitment or belief in the theory itself that the research and treatment communities are willing to invest. And thus the abstinence criterion is far more than a free-standing "outcome criterion"—it is at the foundation of the entire gestalt that the alcoholism theory reflects and at the foundation of its utility.

From a traditionalist's standpoint, an attack on the abstinence criterion is an attack on the classical disease concept of alcoholism. Small wonder that traditionalists balk at seeing the abstinence criterion too easily dispensed with in favor of some more eclectic or behaviorist success criteria.

One cannot report data that many or most alcoholics return to normal drinking without undercutting the fundamental "truth" that alcoholics in most treatment centers are told. And undercutting that truth is only done at great peril because the embracing of that truth proves to be the most successful treatment known for the condition. At a minimum, it cannot be undercut without supplying some other truth, either for the "telling to" of alcoholics or for the foundation of another equally efficacious treatment system.

Of course, proponents of controlled drinking have cited the ostensible social utilities of their position (e.g., 13):[7] alcoholics will be more agreeable to entering treatment if they know that permanent abstinence will not be mandatory; that treatment will become possible for patients "for whom abstinence has not been attainable" (13, *p. 820*); or that treatment will be possible for alcoholics who do not care to affiliate with groups that spe-

---

[7] It should be made clear that Lloyd and Salzberg (13), in the article from which these examples are drawn, did clearly distinguish and discussed separately the theoretical and the utilitarian advantages (and disadvantages) of "controlled drinking" as a treatment goal.

cifically reinforce nondrinking. But these sorts of arguments, again, refer to the social utilities rather than the correctness of the outcome criteria and the theoretical picture of alcoholism that they imply.

The Declining Utility of the Disease Concept

I imagine that if a report showing that a substantial fraction of alcoholics were capable of controlled drinking had been released in the mid-1940s, the impact on the alcoholism movement would have been substantial. The argument for treatment-instead-of-punishment of chronic court offenders and treatment-instead-of-hiding for earlier-stage alcoholics was closely tied to the classical disease conception of alcoholism. To find that a substantial fraction of labeled alcoholics returned to controlled drinking or that a substantial fraction of those diagnosed as alcoholics were mistakenly diagnosed would have undercut the claims to expertise that were crucial to the foundation of a transition to a medical or public health system for the management of alcoholism.

But the news falls on a different world three decades later. For instance, that 10, 20, 50 or 75% of the patients in alcoholism treatment centers return to controlled drinking is a finding that is unlikely to suggest that alcohol problems should be returned to the criminal justice system because the alcoholismic conditions are, thereby, shown to be volitional. We usually regard the disease concept as a means of softening the opprobrium toward alcoholism, but it is also possible that a declining sense of opprobrium in a society, for whatever reasons, may make the disease concept more or less superfluous. Perhaps the social history of alcohol problems will show that the ideal of medical-style social management of alcoholics survived the declining influence of the disease concept simply because no one had any interest in the punitive social controls of the past. I do not know what the sources of this diminished opprobrium are, but one can guess at several factors: Alcoholics have been upstaged, perhaps, by other-substance misusers and the larger household of social problems that attract public attention these days, and seem to pose more dramatic threats to the community. A chronically below-full-employment economy and a social structure that increasingly employs a vast sector of its population in health and social services are less likely to resent alcoholics for their absence from the labor market and perhaps will welcome their presence in one or another "target" group or "catchment population." Even the stereotypical Skid Row alcoholic's assault on public decorum has been diluted by a decade of change in hair, dress and cleanliness fashions that make the chronic court offender only one among other recognized social types about whom it has been said that "a haircut and a bath" are needed. One wonders about the extent to which the wartime circumstances of the early 1940s contributed a public sense of the need for every man and woman at some productive enterprise. This public sentiment may well have created a special animosity toward alcoholics and the special need for a vigorous means for defending them from undue rejection. But, again, the time is gone and the images are faded.

Of course, the utilities of the classical disease concept are still very alive in Alcoholics Anonymous and in other treatment enterprises where the classical model provides the basis for treatment. But where research rather than treatment (that is, where intellectual utility more than treatment efficacy) defines the situation, the abstinence issue is likely to attract attention only grudgingly.

On this broader explanatory plane, the Rand report seems to have signaled some of the serious weaknesses in conventional perspectives on alcoholism.

Writing from the perspective of a would-be science of alcohol problems, the over-all impression I get from the report is that the theoretical paradigm that is implied in the "alcoholism" concept has not served to sort out and make intelligible the realities out there. Little of the conventional wisdom seems to predict much, and that which does do a little predicting (e.g., the worse one's initial condition, the less likely that one will change to a problem-free status) does not seem to be the sort of "discovery" or "finding" that increases our knowledge over that of commonsense knowledge. We are left with the impression that an entire vocabulary drawn from theory and clinical experience does not order the world for us. The report constitutes a culmination of the alcoholism perspective as it was put into practice by NIAAA; this perspective, and its language, do not constitute a demonstrably effective way to make sense of the data that are reported. This is not to say that treatment programs do no good or do good, but merely that, as scientists, we end up knowing little about what is going on.

In summary, the public controversy over the report has been confined to the abstinence question so that several interesting findings have received little or no commentary. Thus in a sense it is not the Rand report that is the source of the furor but the abstinence question; the Rand report merely is the most recent occasion for the continuation of the abstinence debate. The debate over the abstinence question, both in the past and as it has developed around this report, has been too much narrowed to one question, namely, whether "true" alcoholics can return to controlled drinking. The intensity and the duration of the debate about this question should be clues to the fact that it is controversial because the answer to it is crucial to the coherent and complete paradigm of deviant drinking. Thus in order to make sense of the debate, and to make some progress toward its resolution, we need to examine not just the abstinence question but the paradigm that is at stake when that question is raised. I have argued that this paradigm owes its continued popularity and the allegiance of its proponents primarily to the social and therapeutic utilities that have been ascribed to it (rather than to its powers of explanation or powers to advance research in the area). And I have suggested that the social climate of opinion regarding alcoholism has changed in the last decade or so in such ways that some of the social utilities of the paradigm are no longer quite as important as they once were.

REFERENCES

1. U.S. CONGRESS. SENATE. Comprehensive alcohol abuse and alcoholism prevention treatment and rehabilitation act. S. 3835, 91st Cong. 2d sess.
2. TOWLE, L. H. Alcoholism program monitoring system development; phase II. Menlo Park, CA; Stanford Research Institute; 1972.
3. RUGGELS, W. L., ARMOR, D. J., POLICH, J. M., MOTHERSHEAD, A. and STEPHEN, M. A follow-up study of clients at selected alcoholism treatment centers funded by NIAAA. Prepared for the U.S. National Institute on Alcohol Abuse and Alcoholism. Menlo Park, CA; Stanford Research Institute; 1975.
4. CHAFETZ, M. E. Monitoring and evaluation at NIAAA. Evaluation 2 (No. 1): 49–52, 1974.
5. TOWLE, L. H. Alcoholism treatment outcomes in different populations. Proc. 4th Annu. Alcsm Conf. NIAAA, pp. 112–133, 1975.
6. U.S. NATIONAL INSTITUTE ON ALCOHOL ABU.E AND ALCOHOLISM. Second special report to the Congress. Alcohol and health; new knowledge. (DHEW Publ. No. ADM-75-212.) Washington, DC; U.S. Govt. Print. Off.; 1975.
7. ARMOR, D. J., POLICH, J. M. and STAMBUL, H. B. Alcoholism and treatment. Prepared for the U.S. National Institute on Alcohol Abuse and Alcoholism. Santa Monica, CA; Rand Corp.; 1976.
8. CLARK, W. B. Operational definitions of drinking problems and associated prevalence rates. Quart. J. Stud. Alc. 27: 648–668, 1966.
9. SMART, R. G. Spontaneous recovery in alcoholics; a review and analysis of the available research. Drug Alc. Depend., Lausanne 1: 277–285, 1975.
10. EMRICK, C. D. A review of psychologically oriented treatment of alcoholism. II. The relative effectiveness of different treatment approaches and the effectiveness of treatment versus no treatment. J. Stud. Alc. 36: 88–108, 1975.
11. JELLINEK, E. M. Phases of alcohol addiction. Quart. J. Stud. Alc. 13: 673–684, 1952.

12. KELLER, M. On the loss-of-control phenomenon in alcoholism. Brit. J. Addict. **67:** 153–166, 1972.
13. LLOYD, R. W., JR. and SALZBERG, H. C. Controlled social drinking; an alternative to abstinence as a treatment goal for some alcohol abusers. Psychol. Bull. **82:** 815–842, 1975.

A Response

D. J. Armor, Ph.D., H. B. Stambul, Ph.D. and J. M. Polich, Ph.D.[1]

We agree with Roizen that the public controversy over the Rand report (1) is due to our conclusions about the return to normal drinking by some treated alcoholics. As is common when research findings fail to support the conventional wisdom, and especially when they are contrary to the deeply held beliefs of various interest groups, there has been an intense examination of the methodological assumptions and procedures of our research to determine whether our conclusions are justified.

We are pleased that three of the four comments published here do not question our conclusion that some alcoholics return to normal drinking after treatment, although some questions have been raised about the exact size of this proportion. This distinguishes scientific discussion from much of that reported in the popular press, in which critics have proclaimed normal drinking is impossible for any alcoholic, in spite of nearly 20 years of research results to the contrary.

We also point out that, with the exception of Blume's comment, none of these authors actually claims our findings are wrong. Instead, they raise a number of technical and methodological issues that might affect our findings, stopping short of concluding that the findings are actually invalidated. This is important because we wish to state categorically that our major findings are thoroughly consistent with other outcome research. This fact alone offers strong evidence that methodological problems have not invalidated our results.

Methodological issues are important, of course, and in fact received substantial attention in the original report. But unfortunately the preceding comments have exaggerated the problems and, in a few instances, have misrepresented our data or procedures. As a result, the unwary reader may be misled and may overlook important convergences between the Rand study and other recent research. This corpus of research raises some very serious questions about common conceptions of alcoholism and its

[1] The Rand Corporation, 1700 Main Street, Santa Monica, CA 90406.

treatment; we hope that these substantive issues will not drown in a sea of technical and methodological recriminations. We strongly urge the serious reader to consult the Rand report, as well as other recent research cited there, before evaluating this exchange.

EMRICK AND STILSON

We agree with Emrick and Stilson, as stated in our report, that the methodological limitations of our data preclude any final policy actions until future research can provide more definitive answers. On the other hand, we are puzzled by Emrick's change of position on the NIAAA data since his review (2) of the Stanford (SRI) report (3). In that review Emrick stated:

"I should note that outcome data cannot be dismissed as invalid just because a study has methodological weaknesses. . . . Reality seems to be a robust thing which generally comes through at least many deficiencies. . . . Consistent with the assertion that the findings probably reflect reality to a great extent, many of them are not unusual or surprising, *being consistent with a vast body of alcoholism treatment outcome data"* [italics added].

Emrick and Stilson now take quite a different position regarding the very same data base. Because of special methodological problems, they write, the Rand results should be treated skeptically. The reasons advanced for this change of position are twofold: (1) even though Emrick previously concluded that methodological problems do not invalidate outcome studies "on the whole," such problems might affect any one study such as Rand's; and (2) Emrick previously did not examine the special problems of sample bias and data analysis, which are alleged to be unique to the Rand study.

We do not think these reasons are convincing, especially because Emrick and Stilson seem to disregard one very important fact: the Rand results are in accord with most outcome research, including the research in Emrick's major reviews (4, 5). This alone should be sufficient to allay their concerns about methodological defects. By not facing this issue squarely, Emrick and Stilson leave the reader in the ambiguous position of not knowing how serious these potential methodological problems really are.

We propose to resolve this ambiguity in two ways. First we will demonstrate the similarity between our major results and Emrick's review studies. Second, we will show that most of the methodological issues raised by Emrick and Stilson are not as serious as they claim.

Similarity of Rand and Emrick Results

The Rand study had three key conclusions that are in agreement with Emrick's reviews of over 200 outcome studies: (*1*) the majority of treated alcoholics improve with treatment, even though many continue drinking, sometimes in normal or controlled amounts, while only a relatively small fraction engage in long-term abstinence; (*2*) different types of treatment have little or no differential effects; (*3*) the only treatment variable to have a significant effect is amount of treatment.

In Table 1 we compare our over-all outcomes with Emrick's (4), which were based on a compilation of results from 265 outcome studies. Comparing Emrick's "improved" with our "remissions," which are roughly comparable categories, we see that the outcome rates are nearly identical. The different types of improvement or remissions are somewhat harder to compare, since not all studies used all of Emrick's outcome categories and our distinctions are somewhat different from Emrick's. Nonetheless, he found an average abstinence rate of 32% (for varying and unspecified follow-up periods or "windows") compared with our 24% 6-month (or more) abstainers, while all the remaining improved or remission cases engaged in some drinking episodes during the follow-up period. It is quite hard to compare our "normal drinking" with his "controlled drinking" category since we used a quantitative definition based on general population norms while Emrick had to accept the various labels used by each study with little or no quantitative information. It is possible that many patients who were in our normal-drinking category would be considered "improved" (but not "controlled") in other studies. Emrick also reported 5% controlled drinkers throughout the follow-up period, which agrees

Table 1. **Percentage of Patients Improved in Emrick's Review and In Remission in Armor et al., and Amount of Treatment Received by Improved and In-Remission Patients**[a]

Emrick		Armor et al.	
Improved	66	In remission	67
Total abstinence	32	Abstained 6 months +	24
Some drinking, including controlled or alternate controlled and absent	34	Normal drinking or short-term abstinence	43
Amount of Treatment			
No treatment	41		54
Minimal	43		58
More than minimal	65		73

[a] Data from Emrick (4, 5) and Armor et al. (1).

with our 4% in the normal-drinking category at both the 6-month and 18-month follow-up.[2]

Regarding the type of treatment, Emrick reviewed 72 studies that compared 2 or more different treatments by either randomly assigning patients to treatment groups or matching patients on outcome-relevant background characteristics. He concluded (5, *pp. 94–95*) that, "the weight of present evidence is overwhelmingly against technique variables being powerful determinants of long-term outcome. . . . A wiser expenditure of resources might be . . . to involve alcoholics in therapy, any kind of therapy, since all approaches seem generally helpful to the majority of patients." Compare this conclusion with our own (1, *p. 129*): "Perhaps the most important finding of this study is that there are few noteworthy differences among remission rates for various treatment types." These are virtually identical conclusions.

Finally, our findings on the amount of treatment also parallel those of Emrick (5). Table 1 compares our results with Emrick's for patients with no treatment, minimal treatment and more than minimal treatment. While our results show somewhat higher rates of remission, the relative effects of amount of treatment are nearly identical. The somewhat higher remission rates in our study are undoubtedly due to differing definitions of both the outcome criteria as well as the amount variable. These results led both Emrick and us to conclude that, in our respective data bases, the amount of treatment is the only treatment variable to have a significant impact on outcomes, and that improvement or remission is substantial even among patients receiving little or no treatment.

Methodological Issues

The preceding comparisons make it clear that the methodological issues raised by Emrick and Stilson do not render our findings unique when compared with the modal results of other studies. In fact, we were well aware of the limitations of the NIAAA data when we wrote the report and took considerable pains to investigate their probable effect on our results. Ironically, our conclusion that these methodological problems were not too serious was bolstered by the close agreement between many of our findings and those of Emrick's. Despite this, methodological questions continue to be raised by other critics. Therefore, it is useful to review the evidence once again.

---

[2] It is important to understand that the percentage of normal-drinking patients in the Rand report pertains to those who were doing so at follow-up, and not necessarily throughout the entire 18-month follow-up period.

Sample Bias and Response Rates. As Emrick and Stilson point out, there are 2 ways in which our 18-month follow-up sample could be biased with respect to outcomes. First, the 8 Alcoholism Treatment Centers (ATC) selected for the special 18-month follow-up could be unrepresentative of the full group of 45 ATCs. Second, the located follow-up sample of 62% could differ from the 38% not located. Emrick and Stilson err, however, when they claim that we did not properly investigate these sources of bias.

The basis of their error is a misunderstanding of how to test for sample bias. By definition sample bias is the difference between a sample statistic and its population value or parameter; in our case, the population to which we wish to generalize is the 11,500 male non-DWI patients who entered treatment at all ATCs during our target period. The proper test for sample bias, then, is a comparison between our 18-month follow-up sample and this total population. Such a comparison tests simultaneously for all potential sources of bias.

We made these comparisons on a number of patient variables at intake, including those having the greatest prognostic value for outcomes. None of the differences between the obtained sample and the total population exceeded 6 percentage points (most were within 2 or 3 points). Even though these differences tend to have the same valence, yielding a slightly better prognostic picture for the obtained sample, we fail to understand how anyone can judge such differences as serious.

Apparently, Emrick and Stilson have confused the issue of sample bias with the differences between located and unlocated portions of a follow-up sample, a confusion also prominent in the SRI report to which they refer.[3] When the population value is unknown, it is common practice to compare the located portion of a sample with the unlocated portion. While significant differences between the located and unlocated groups raise the possibility of bias, such differences are not direct measures of bias. Perhaps an example can clarify this point. Assume some characteristic is present in 50% of a total population of 10,000, and that a random sample of 1000 is drawn. Assume further that only 80% of the sample is located, and that 48% of the obtained sample have this characteristic compared with 58% of the unlocated portion. Such a difference might be statistically significant, but the bias of the obtained sample is derived by comparing the obtained rate of 48% with the total population rate of 50%; the bias is obviously trivial in this example. For a 60% response rate and a 10% difference between unlocated samples the bias would be 4% (46% compared with 50%).

---

[3] The SRI analysis of bias includes both female and DWI patients, so it is not even studying the same target groups.

Thus a follow-up sample may yield a moderate difference between the located and unlocated groups, yet still show very little bias relative to the study population. We stand on our conclusion that both the 6- and 18-month follow-up samples are not seriously biased on intake characteristics when compared with the total population of interest.

Since a sample might be unbiased on intake variables but biased on outcomes, we used a second strategy, also questioned by Emrick and Stilson, involving a comparison of remission rates and response rates in eight ATCS in the 18-month study. While the follow-up study used standardized procedures and instruments, each ATC was responsible for conducting its own follow-ups and can therefore be viewed as an independent follow-up study. Fortunately, there was substantial variation in response rates, ranging from a low of 36% to a high of 85% (five of the eight ATCS had response rates of 68% or better). If groups of unlocated patients in a single follow-up study are seriously biased by having fewer remissions, then we would naturally expect centers with higher completion rates to have lower remission rates. But since we found no such correlation, we concluded that different response rates had produced no serious bias in outcome rates.

Emrick and Stilson dismiss this analysis by stating that irrelevant (or missing) variables might be causing differences in remission rates, and this "measurement error always reduces the correlation." First of all, serious measurement error for aggregate statistics is unlikely, and, moreover, controlling for missing variables does not necessarily reduce the correlation. Adjustment for these variables could either increase or decrease the correlation—or leave it unchanged—depending upon how the adjusted remission rates change. But this is beside the point. Emrick and Stilson have ignored the fact that both patient and treatment variables were shown to have very little effect on remission rates, and particularly little effect on variation in rates from one ATC to another (1, *Table 27*). In fact, while we did not show adjusted ATC rates, they did not change by more than 1 or 2 points. Therefore, the rank-order correlation between remission rates and follow-up response rates is not affected by controls for patient and treatment variables.

By these analyses we were not trying to "lull . . . researchers into insouciance about losing patients"; rather, we were trying to estimate realistically the amount of bias in remission rates caused by less-than-ideal response rates. Some critics have insisted that outcome results are invalid unless they are based on a 90% follow-up response rate, and yet this claim is rarely backed up by adequate data and analysis. Our analyses have convinced us that these claims are exaggerated, and that response rates between 60 and 70% will not substantially bias outcome results. It is exceedingly expensive to conduct national follow-up studies with 90% response rates; after locating and interviewing 70% or so of a follow-up sample, each of the remaining cases (up to 90%) can have an average cost ranging between $500 and $1000. It is hard to justify such expenditures, given the many urgent and competing research needs in this field, unless one has solid evidence that results will be seriously affected without them.

Data Analysis. The second set of reasons Emrick and Stilson offer for questioning our results involves inadequate data analysis. This aspect of their criticism is most surprising of all; while any analysis could undoubtedly be improved, ours is far more extensive, detailed and explicit than those found in the vast majority of alcoholism research.

Their first criticism in this regard is directed at our definition of normal drinking (which is not a data analysis issue at all). We would be happy to set our cutting point for normal drinking at a level determined to be "healthy" or "safe." But in our reading of the literature such a level has not been established; assertions by experts, such as Chafetz (6), when not backed by systematic studies, are not viewed by us as scientific evidence. In the meantime it seems unreasonable to impose limits on alcoholics that are below amounts found commonly in the nonalcoholic population, providing that no serious impairment is present. Our upper limits of 3 oz of ethanol per day and 5 oz on drinking days were guided by national survey data on male drinking patterns as well as by the relationships between consumption and impairment in our alcoholic sample. Moreover, the averages in our normal-drinking group were 0.7 and 2.1 oz, respectively, and of the 129 normal drinkers at 18 months, only 5 exceeded 2 oz per day and only 16 exceeded 3 oz on drinking days.

We are not necessarily setting these limits in concrete. They seem to us the most reasonable definitions, given our data base, but we are prepared to change them when better evidence becomes available, especially with regard to amounts known to be damaging to health.

The same is true of our definition of serious symptoms, which was used as a further constraint on normal drinkers. We did not want to classify low-consuming patients as normal drinkers if they exhibited alcoholic symptoms, which for us meant either tremors or frequent episodes of three of these symptoms: morning drinking, missing meals, memory lapses, missing work, or intoxication. Some critics might argue that this permits patients with some impairment to appear in our normal-drinker group. But such an argument overlooks the fact that impairment and drinking behavior are highly correlated, so that a person with low consumption and no tremors is statistically unlikely to have even occasional episodes of impairment. Moreover there is a danger of making a definition so strict that it no longer coincides with normal behavior. Statistically speaking, occasional episodes of a serious symptom may occur in some normal drinkers without requiring a judgment of alcohol misuse.

Nonetheless we have experimented with more stringent definitions of serious impairment. Of the 129 normal drinkers by our existing definition, we could exclude 13 patients with 2 or more episodes of occasional symptoms (once or twice last month), 3 additional patients with a single memory lapse or more, and 4 additional patients with frequent episodes of a single symptom of those remaining in the list, thereby reducing the proportion of normal drinkers from 22 to 18%. This would leave 12 patients with occasional intoxication only, 5 patients with occasional missed meals only, and 1 patient with occasional morning drinking only. Even if the 6 patients missing meals or drinking in the morning were excluded, the proportion of normal drinkers would decline only to 17%. In other words, the great majority of normal drinkers have no serious symptoms at all, and our findings about normal drinking are quite robust under more restrictive definitions.

The remaining portion of the Emrick and Stilson discussion deals with points which in our opinion are incorrect or irrelevant to our main findings and conclusions:

1. *Change from pre- to posttreatment:* Table 20 in our report shows remission rates among definitely alcoholic patients at intake; all remissions in this group necessitate pre–post change by definition. Their rate of remission is 62%.

2. *No controls for patient characteristics in the ATC or A.A. versus ATC analyses:* This is an incorrect assertion; all analyses controlled for such variables, although adjusted remission rates were sometimes not shown when the effects were minimal.

3. *Analysis of covariance assumptions:* We made clear throughout the report that the study did not use randomized assignment to treatment groups, necessitating statistical controls for patient characteristics. We used two different techniques, analysis of covariance as well as multiple regression with dummy variables (the latter requires fewer assumptions than the former), and the results were identical. These methods are standard and widely used techniques in the nonexperimental behavioral and social sciences, and we are satisfied as to their assumptions and their appropriateness. We could understand questioning our control procedures if our results contradicted randomized experiments, but since they do not, we fail to comprehend the purpose of Emrick and Stilson's comment on this point.

4. *Homogeneity of treatment groups:* A valid comparison between different treatment groups does not require within-group homogeneity with respect to

other variables. On the contrary, groups can be heterogeneous provided the groups are comparable on these other variables; this is precisely the purpose of a randomized design or statistical controls.

Validity. Although in his SRI review (2) Emrick claimed that research results tended to be independent of validity measures (along with other methodological issues he studied), Emrick and Stilson nonetheless now charge that our self-report outcome measures have questionable validity. What bothers us especially about this contention is that they base it on a misunderstanding and misapplication of our own validity analysis presented in an appendix to our report.

First, we intentionally chose not to generalize findings from general population surveys to alcoholic populations, and instead presented data separately for each group. Emrick and Stilson fail to make this distinction, implying that the results of the Harris or the ASAP surveys should be applied to the alcoholic population. We disagree.

Second, their statements about the alcoholic population (the Sobell data) are incomplete and inaccurate. The most important policy issue is the degree of serious underreporting, and especially the proportion of alcoholics reporting normal drinking (by our definition) who are in fact drinking at higher levels. In the Orange County intake data, of the 122 patients reporting drinking below the normal drinking cutoff (taken as estimated blood alcohol concentrations of 0.09% or lower) on the day of the interview, 31 or 25% had actual BACs over 0.10% (1, *Table A-12*).

But Emrick and Stilson fail to mention another finding, that nearly 40% of these underreporting patients admitted drinking more than 7 oz on the day before the interview (*Table A-13*). Thus, of those patients reporting normal drinking over a 2-day period—which comes closer to our 30-day window for consumption reports—only 12% are found to have disconfirming BACs at intake to treatment.

Similarly, about 23% of a small group of patients underreported on the day of a follow-up interview, but unfortunately there were no data available for the days before the interview. Given these results, and bearing in mind that our report used a 30-day window combined with other self-reports of impairment, we concluded that our normal drinking category may include between 10 and 15% who would be disqualified if a validity check was available. If we make this assumption, then the rate of normal drinking would drop from 22 to 18% or so.

We stated that these analyses by no means settle the issue of self-report validity once and for all. On the other hand, there is little basis for Emrick and Stilson's implication that our results would change substantially given some type of validity test.

Emrick and Stilson's Conclusions about Science

Finally, we take exception to a view of scientific research expressed throughout Emrick and Stilson's comment, especially in their concluding remarks. They imply, first, that only if a study meets certain design principles, and especially the use of randomized assignment of subjects to treatment conditions, will it offer results "of which we can be sure." This is surely an oversimplified if not glorified view of experimental research. While experiments are extremely useful and often crucial for testing hypotheses, it is untrue that randomization assures certainty. The results of an experiment can be invalidated by design weaknesses as easily as a national field study, and many of these pitfalls are unique to the experimental method. Examples include artificiality, intervention effects and experimenter-expectancy effects. In fact, in his review study, Emrick (5) recognized some of these problems when he explained several significant differences between treatment and control groups as possible iatrogenic effects, whereby the control condition might "harm alcoholics by eliciting thoughts and feelings of disappointment, abuse, neglect, or rejection." Clearly, experimental designs are not without invalidating defects.

They further assert that unless one has such methodologically pure studies, "our only recourse is to more or less enlightened opinion." To relegate nonexperimental studies or studies without perfect response rates or validated self-reports to a status equivalent to opinion is, in our view, an untenable view of scientific methodology. Many branches of science, including economics, astronomy and many life sciences, are not amenable to experimental design and yet have attained a degree of "certainty" and consensus far exceeding that found among most behavioral sciences. Science is more than a particular method of collecting data, and no one method guarantees certainty of results. The essence of scientific methodology is the testing of hypotheses or prior conceptions by systematic, objective observation coupled with explicit, replicable definitions and procedures. Even in the physical sciences, the usefulness of data which meet these standards is gauged by the extent to which they fit a theory. In many other scientific fields, including alcoholism research, data are judged by their consistency with other systematic observations, thereby adding to existing knowledge and ultimately paving the way for future theoretical advances. In neither case are data judged primarily by their "certainty"; such a standard reveals a misconception of science.

BLUME

While Blume judges the quality of our data analysis to be "excellent," given the limitations of the NIAAA data base, she is concerned that our conclusions are nevertheless "unwarranted" particularly since they might reach the ears of public policy makers. This concern is especially directed toward (1) the finding of uniform treatment effects, (2) our use of such terms as "normal drinking," "natural remission" and "untreated," and (3) our interpretation of the traditional medical disease model of alcoholism. We believe Blume's critique is useful as it provides a clinician's perspective and the suggestion of some provocative, testable hypotheses for further research. We would add, however, that hypotheses and possible alternative interpretations of data are not sufficient to invalidate empirical evidence.

Treatment Effects

Blume maintains, unarguably, that many psychological and physical characteristics of patients as well as treatment variables were not measured in the NIAAA follow-up studies. She further contends that our statistical finding of no significance differences in remission rates between various treatments is simply an artifact due to the omission of measuring (presumably controlling on) "crucial" variables which she claims "from everyday clinical experience would be expected to have major influences on outcome."

We certainly favor the expansion of any data base to include some of the psychological and medical variables cited by Blume; indeed, our ongoing research efforts include measurements of many such variables. It remains, however, an empirical question whether such variables do indeed have "major influences on outcome." The issue at hand is whether the data and conclusions of the present report are invalidated by our inability to control on variables which may be masking true differences between treatment groups.

While this issue must ultimately be settled through future research, some a priori determination, at least with respect to the present data, may be made on the basis of statistical reasoning. Blume argues that essentially an undetected interaction effect exists in our data between certain unmeasured patient characteristics (e.g., mental pathology, withdrawal syndrome) and the treatment setting variable. In order for such an interaction effect to reach sufficient magnitude so as to suppress true treatment differences at least three conditions must apply: (1) the unmeasured variables must be strong correlates of outcome, (2) they must occur in the population under study with reasonable frequency so as to generate sizable enough marginal values to produce an interaction effect, and (3) the hypothetical variables must be utterly confounded with the treatment classifications in our data to create the "suspect" uniform treatment effect.

First, the patient background variables that were included in our study and used as covariates in the treatment analyses are precisely those which have consistently emerged in the research literature as the most important correlates of outcome: prior treatment, severity of symptoms, job and marital stability. The research literature indicates that few psychological variables have been demonstrated empirically to have strong prognostic significance. Thus there is no evidence to support the claim that patient variables which were unmeasured in our data would have accounted for a substantial proportion of the variance.

Second, as a statistical matter, the interaction suspected by Blume could occur only if the variables she cites are relatively common in the treated alcoholic population. As has been demonstrated in other studies, there are relatively low prevalence rates of such conditions as liver cirrhosis, organic brain syndrome and psychoses among the alcoholic population generally. These rates are probably even lower among actual patients at treatment settings such as those in the NIAAA sample, since the existence of complicating conditions often serves as the criterion for screening out and referral to other treatment facilities such as medical or psychiatric wards. With respect to less severe damage, our data and those of others show that alcohol-related impairment variables, including physical disorders and withdrawal states, are highly correlated so that much of the suspected "unmeasured" variance is probably subsumed in the impairment items that we have measured.

Third, the interaction argument is based on an assumption that important patient variables are confounded with treatment settings since, according to Blume, they "influence decisions by the patient, family, physician and treatment program." Our experience with a broad range of alcoholism treatment centers throughout the country suggests another picture of the diagnostic and treatment disposition process. Few centers have sufficient psychiatric and medical personnel to make the kinds of diagnoses Blume suggests. In fact, when the NIAAA monitoring system was designed, considerable opposition from treatment centers was voiced to the inclusion of standard psychological tests or medical history data in the intake forms. The reality is that most treatment decisions, at least in the centers sampled in our study, are based precisely on the kind of information collected in the NIAAA forms which, after all, were constructed to represent the consensus of dozens of treatment centers as to the most important information to obtain about a patient entering treatment for alcoholism. It is therefore unlikely that the kinds of variables cited by Blume are truly, especially deliberately, confounded with any one treatment setting.

Finally, the empirical question of which patient or treatment variables have prognostic significance is an important scientific issue. As a policy issue, however, it seems imperative that the effectiveness of the NIAAA centers, which cost many millions of federal dollars, be evaluated even though the information available may be incomplete from a scientific point of view. As scientists, we try to expand our conceptual models; as policy researchers, we must test and evaluate models as they exist in the field. For the latter purpose, the NIAAA data are quite adequate.

Inappropriate Terms

Blume raises a number of objections to our use of terms she views as "inappropriate." Most of her reservations and questions about normal drinking have been dealt with in our reply to Emrick and Stilson. Blume raises a particular issue with the term "normal drinking" used in our report to describe one remission category. It seems that Blume's objection is based on her feeling that "The term 'normal drinking' conjures up an image of spontaneous joyful problem-free drinking. . . ." We cannot understand this objection since we presented no such image; our definition of normal drinking is carefully specified by multiple, objective criteria. Its meaning is not left to the reader's imagination or intended for connotative interpretation.

Blume's observation that 25% of the sample were normal drinkers at intake is incorrect. This misunderstanding probably comes from Table 9 in our report which shows that 25% of the sample were below the consumption criterion at intake. By our definition, however, the consumption of less than 3 oz of alcohol per day alone is not a sufficient condition to meet the normal drinking standard; normal drinkers must also satisfy the criterion of absence of serious impairment.

Table 2 shows data not presented in the report that clarify the issue: 84% of the sample were in the nonremission category at intake, which means drinking over 3 oz per day, or drinking over 5 oz on drinking days, or having tremors or frequent episodes of serious symptoms. Only 7% of the sample were in the normal-drinking status at intake, while another 8% were 1-month abstainers. In spite of instructions to ask about consumption prior to institutionalization, we are nonetheless certain that interviewers occasionally failed to make this distinction, thereby accounting for most of these short-term abstainers at intake.

Blume raises similar objections to our use of the terms "untreated" and

Table 2.   Patient Status at 18-Month Follow-up by Status at Intake, in Per Cent

Follow-up Status	INTAKE STATUS			
	Abstained 6 Months (N=5)	Abstained 1 Month (N=46)	Normal Drinking (N=41)	Nonre- missions (N=499)
Abstained 6 months	60	37	12	23
Abstained 1 month	0	20	17	22
Normal drinking	20	15	61	19
Nonremissions	20	28	10	36
% of total (N=591)	1	8	7	84

"natural remission." We agree, and we stated in the report that patients who did contact a treatment center may not be accurately described as truly "untreated." Our terminology was influenced by the judgment that a single visit to a center with no subsequent treatment (see our Table 25) is not what professionals in the field would accept as a legitimate category of treatment.

The Medical Model

Blume is critical of our discussion concerning the implications of our data, and those from a score of other studies, which cast doubt on the validity of the traditional Jellinek model of alcoholism. Specifically, we have addressed the tenability of the belief, dominant in this field, that no "true" alcoholic can ever resume drinking of small amounts without inevitable relapse. In her discussion of the loss-of-control phenomenon, Blume reveals a conception that is partly supported by the research literature but widely discrepant from the traditional view. Blume allows that alcoholics may engage in periods of moderate drinking without relapse. In her view, it is the goal of abstinence (presumably a psychological motivation) that operates to stop such drinkers from progressing inexorably to "disaster." If the loss-of-control phenomenon were a truly physiological process, the relapse would occur despite all efforts by the therapist to set an optimal goal and thereby psychologically arrest the relapse cycle.

Blume's adherence to the abstinence goal seems to be based on a pragmatic judgment rather than on scientific evidence. Since, she argues, patients will probably resume some drinking anyway (i.e., they will cheat), the abstinence standard, while unrealistic, does keep patients headed in the right direction. Nonetheless, from a scientific point of view the goal of total abstinence for all alcoholics is simply not defensible once the loss-of-control thesis has been abandoned. Moreover, treatment approaches which demand abstinence, while covertly expecting some "slips," may suffer from lack of credibility. One must also wonder about the ultimate psychological effects on the patient of setting an unrealistic standard of total abstinence which, in all probability, will be violated and seen as a failure experience.

This is not to say that treatment personnel are responsible for the alcoholic behavior of their patients. The possibility of self-fulfilling prophecies and the relationship of beliefs to behavior must not, however, be dismissed lightly. We question the wisdom of teaching all alcoholics to believe that even one drink leads inevitably to loss of control—especially when the belief has little basis in fact.

Adinolfi and DiDario

The claim by Adinolfi and DiDario that our findings about relapse are based "on an analysis of 19 of . . . 30,000 patients" is gratuitous. On the other hand, it does give us an opportunity to explain our special analysis of relapse, the results of which have been misunderstood by many critics.

First, the number "30,000" has nothing to do with our study; that is simply the total number of patients who had entered treatment in the NIAAA centers by the time our report was being written in 1975. Obviously, it would be impossible to have completed 6- or 18-month interviews with all of them. If Adinolfi and DiDario had read the report more carefully, they would have noted that the primary study populations were 11,505 male non-DWI patients admitted to treatment at 45 ATCs from October 1972 to September 1973, of whom 2371 had 6-month follow-ups, and 960 male non-DWI patients admitted between January and April 1973 to 8 ATCs, of whom 600 had 18-month follow-up reports. Our major findings about the over-all success of treatment, the rates of abstinence and normal drinking, and differential treatment effects are therefore based on nearly 3000 patient interviews from 45 treatment centers which, contrary to the inferences drawn by Adinolfi and DiDario, make it the largest study of alcoholism treatment to date.

The relapse analysis to which they refer came about because of alternative explanations of our findings about normal drinking. One such explanation could be that many alcoholics pass through a normal drinking stage on their way back to genuine alcoholic drinking, but this is only a temporary phase and, unlike long-term abstinence, should not be considered a successful form of remission. A direct and testable hypothesis from this particular version of the abstinence thesis is that at any one follow-up a normal drinking alcoholic is more likely than the long-term abstainer to be in relapse at a later follow-up (or, in its extreme form, all such normal-drinking alcoholics will be in relapse at a later follow-up).

To test this hypothesis we used that subgroup of the 18-month follow-up sample that also had a 6-month follow-up; this amounted to 220 of the 600 18-month patients. We classified the sample by remission status at 6 months and compared rates of nonremissions (relapse) across the 3 types of remission. Since we are comparing the conditional probability of relapse at 18 months, given 3 different remission statuses at 6 months, the appropriate number for statistical tests is the 169 patients in the 3 remission categories, *not* the number in the normal-drinking category as is implied by Adinolfi and DiDario. There were no statistically significant differences, with relapse rates of 17% in 40 long-term abstainers, 19% in 99 1-month abstainers, and 13% in 30 normal drinkers. We also conducted a sensitivity analysis on a subsample of 169 definite alcoholics, on the assumption that the relapse hypothesis might hold only for those patients who are physically addicted to alcohol. The relapse rates were 16% in 31 long-term abstainers, 22% in 73 short-term abstainers and 16% in 19 normal drinkers.

Since these sample sizes are too small to detect statistical significance for any but fairly large differences (say, on the order of 20 percentage points), we avoided generalization of this finding to all alcoholics.[4] But the finding does hold for our data, and it certainly challenges the more extreme form of the hypothesis, that most "true" alcoholics cannot return to normal drinking without inevitable relapse.

ROIZEN

Roizen's comment is not really a critique of our study so much as an analysis of the reasons for the controversy. We find ourselves in considerable agreement with most of his observations.

The distinction between the utility and the correctness of a scientific paradigm is an especially useful one. We might add one further observation on this point. Roizen, quoting Keller, argues that the disease—abstinence theory was embraced because of its utility; that is, it was successful for A.A. members. Perhaps a more accurate statement is that it was *believed* to be a successful paradigm. In fact, at the time of its adoption by A.A. advocates, there was little systematic evidence—beyond

---

[4] We also pointed out that the relapse sample could be a biased subset, although it was not seriously biased with respect to 18-month outcomes.

testimonials and scattered case histories—that it worked or, especially, that it worked better than some other approach. The A.A. commitment to abstinence predated the Jellinek disease theory, and the disease theory was no doubt embraced partly because it gave prestigious scientific status to a lay belief already in vogue.

In any event, the belief in abstinence occurred without scientific verification of what Jellinek viewed as a "working hypothesis." The resistence to new scientific evidence by those who hold this belief, combined with the absence of original evidence for it, suggests that the thesis of abstinence for all alcoholics is derived from an ideological paradigm, rather than a scientific one.

CONCLUSION

The results of the Rand study are generally consistent with many smaller and usually less comprehensive studies in spite of numerous methodological differences. If the methodological limitations in our study were serious, this convergence would not occur. We have used the results of other studies to help validate our conclusions; but it is also the case that the Rand study, with its national scope, diversity of patients and treatments, and standardization of outcome measures, serves to validate previous studies. In any event, no single study of alcoholism should be expected to answer all questions with certainty. In the final analysis, our study should be judged by its ability to confirm and extend existing scientific knowledge on alcoholism and treatment.

REFERENCES

1. ARMOR, D. J., POLICH, J. M. and STAMBUL, H. B. Alcoholism and treatment. Prepared for the U.S. National Institute on Alcohol Abuse and Alcoholism. Santa Monica, CA; and Rand Corp.; 1976.
2. EMRICK, C. D. Review of RUGGELS, W. L., ARMOR, D. J., POLICH, J. M., MOTHERSHEAD, A. and STEPHEN, M. A follow-up study of clients at selected alcoholism treatment centers funded by NIAAA; final report. Menlo Park, CA; Stanford Research Institute; 1975. J. Stud. Alc. 37: 1902–1907, 1976.
3. RUGGELS, W. L., ARMOR, D. J., POLICH, J. M., MOTHERSHEAD, A. and STEPHEN, M. A follow-up study of clients at selected alcoholism treatment centers funded by NIAAA; final report. Menlo Park, CA; Stanford Research Institute; 1975.
4. EMRICK, C. D. A. A review of psychologically oriented treatment of alco-

holism. *I*. The use and interrelationships of outcome cirteria and drinking behavior following treatment. Quart. J. Stud. Alc. **35:** 523–549, 1974.

5. EMRICK, C. D. A review of psychologically oriented treatment of alcoholism. *II*. The relative effectiveness of different treatment approaches and the effectiveness of treatment versus no treatment. J. Stud. Alc. **36:** 88–108, 1975.

6. CHAFETZ, M. E. Carrie Nation had a drinking problem; how to drink healthily and why so many Americans don't. Johns Hopk. Mag. **27** (No. 2): 8–17, 1976.

APPENDIX C

Summary of the Rand Report[1]

In 1971, the National Institute on Alcohol Abuse and Alcoholism began sponsorship of a comprehensive alcoholism treatment program located in 45 community centers throughout the nation. Concurrently, NIAAA established a Monitoring System requiring routine reports on clients receiving treatment at these centers both at intake and at 6 months after intake. The information collected by the Monitoring System, together with a special 18-month followup survey in 8 treatment centers and several national surveys on drinking practices, forms the basis of this report on alcoholism and treatment.

Most studies of alcoholism treatment focus on the single issue of treatment success. The unusual richness of the NIAAA data on drinking behavior, encompassing large and heterogeneous national samples of alcoholics in treatment as well as normal drinkers in the general population, permits a broader scope for this study. Beginning with an analysis of the theories of alcoholism, the study establishes those assumptions about the nature and causes of alcoholism, which in turn shape and influence treatment goals and methods. This leads to a number of specific hypotheses about the success of different treatment modalities that can be evaluated using NIAAA data on treatment outcomes. Thus the study goes beyond a simple assessment of treatment success and examines the implications of treatment outcomes for alternative theories of alcoholism.

The alcoholics entering treatment at NIAAA centers are severely impaired from excessive use of alcohol. They drink nine times more alcohol than the average person, and they experience adverse behavioral consequences at a rate nearly 12 times that for nonalcoholic persons. They are also socially impaired, with more than half unemployed and more than half separated or divorced. These alcoholics also tend to be engaged in more blue collar occupations and to have lower income and less education than the average person.

---

[1] A summary of the original Rand report on "Alcoholism and Treatment." In the original report, this summary appeared at the beginning of the volume.

In spite of their impaired status, however, clients of these centers show substantial improvement in drinking behavior after treatment, both at 6 months and 18 months following intake. The rate of improvement is 70 percent for several different outcome indicators. Social outcomes such as employment and marital status show much less change, but this may reflect greater emphasis by the centers on the immediate problem of alcoholic behavior.

While this improvement rate is impressive, it is important to stress that the improved clients include only a relatively small number who are long-term abstainers. About one-fourth of the clients interviewed at 18 months have abstained for at least 6 months, and of those having both 6-month and 18-month followups, only 10 percent report 6 months of abstention at both interviews. The majority of improved clients are either drinking moderate amounts of alcohol—but at levels far below what could be described as alcoholic drinking—or engaging in alternating periods of drinking and abstention.

The fact that most improved clients are not abstaining for long periods of time, when considered in terms of recent research on controlled drinking, prompts a definition of remission that includes both abstention and "normal" drinking. Normal drinking means consumption in moderate quantities commonly found in the general nonalcoholic population, provided no serious signs of impairment are present. According to this definition, nearly 70 percent of the NIAAA clients are in remission after treatment; and at the 18-month followup roughly equal numbers fall into the categories of 6-month abstention, periodic drinking (abstained last month only), and normal drinking.

It is important to stress, however, that being in remission at one followup period is no guarantee that the client will be in remission at a later followup. Of those clients in remission at 6 months, approximately 15 percent experience a relapse during the following year and fall into the nonremission category at the 18-month interview. Even so, nearly two-thirds of clients with both interviews maintained their remission status throughout the period, although there was considerable shifting from one remission category to another.

The key finding of the relapse analysis is that relapse rates for normal drinkers are no higher than those for longer term abstainers, even when the analysis is confined to clients who are definitely alcoholic at intake. While the sample is small and the followup periods are relatively short, this finding suggests the possibility that for some alcoholics moderate drinking is not necessarily a prelude to full relapse, and that some alcoholics can return to moderate drinking with no greater chance of relapse than if they abstained. This finding, especially if verified for larger samples and for longer followup periods, could have major implications for theories of alcoholism. In particular, it calls into question the conception that alcoholism is caused exclusively by a physiological predisposition to addiction.

In accepting normal drinking as a form of remission, we are by no means advocating that alcoholics should attempt moderate drinking after treatment. Alcoholics who have repeatedly failed to moderate their drinking, or who have irreversible physical complications due to alcohol, should not drink at all. Beyond these cases, the current state of knowledge in this area is still inadequate to serve as a basis for recommending treatment goals for individual alcoholics. Moreover, we have no evidence whatsoever, nor is there any method at present, that enables us to identify those alcoholics who might safely return to drinking and those who cannot. We are simply reporting the fact that some alcoholics appear to have stabilized at moderate drinking levels 18 months after treatment. But since we have found no solid scientific evidence that abstainers are more likely to avoid relapse than moderate drinkers, we must entertain the possibility of normal drinking for some alcoholics.

Overall remission rates are only one part of the results of our assessment. The detailed treatment data offered by the Monitoring System, and the existence of untreated clients, made it possible for us to investigate the specific effects of treatment characteristics, including both type and amount. First, in our sample, clients who entered treatment had a slightly higher remission rate than those who had only a single contact with the center and who did not start treatment. However, when the treated sample is divided according to amount of treatment, the advantage is confined to those with higher amounts of treatment. Clients with lower amounts of treatment have remission rates only slightly higher than those who received no treatment at all.

Second, the fact that the untreated sample had remission rates on the order of 50 percent somewhat tempers the importance of the overall 70 percent remission rate. Combined with the finding that untreated clients attending Alcoholics Anonymous (AA) meetings regularly also have remission rates near 70 percent, the suggestion is strong that formal treatment may play only an incremental role in the recovery from alcoholism. The rate of "natural" remission appears to be fairly substantial, and some alcoholics can do almost as well in AA settings as in formal inpatient and outpatient settings where special counseling and therapeutic services are available.

Another major finding is that among clients with formal treatment, there are no strong and consistent differences in remission rates among different treatment settings, such as hospitalization, halfway houses, or outpatient care; nor are differences found for specific therapeutic techniques, such as group counseling, individual therapy, or Antabuse treatment. It appears that the fact of treatment is more important than the specific type of treatment, with the important proviso that to produce a remission rate exceeding that due to natural processes the treatment must be given in sufficient amounts. It is stressed, of course, that the NIAAA data are observational rather than experimental in nature, so it is possible that clients select themselves into those treatments that they prefer; it could be this match that explains the high and uniform rate of remission. Such a possibility cannot be tested with the NIAAA data, but other studies have found similar uniformity of effects even with randomized assignments to different treatments.

Some treatment theories posit that alcoholism is a multifaceted illness, and that as a consequence certain types of clients will benefit more from certain types of treatment settings. The NIAAA data were examined for various client-type/treatment-type combinations that are particularly successful, but none was found. A number of client characteristics have an important impact on the chance for remission, especially the degree of impairment at intake, and job or marital instability. But none of these characteristics interacts with specific treatment modalities in a way that suggests optimal matches.

The relatively uniform rates of remission for different treatment modes, including AA meetings, tend to contradict theories maintaining that alcoholism must be treated by dealing with deeper psychological problems, which are viewed as the source of alcoholic symptoms. Whatever the role played by psychological problems in the onset of excessive drinking— and our data do suggest they are prominent—once alcohol dependency or addiction is established it appears that nonpsychologically oriented treatments work as well as any other method. In other words, recovery from alcohol dependency may depend on mechanisms quite unrelated to the factors that led to excessive drinking in the first place.

The key findings in this study can have relevance for future policy but not without further research. First, the normal-drinking finding suggests the possibility of treatment goals other than total abstention. Before such a policy is adopted, however, more research is needed to establish whether normal-drinking clients can maintain this status for sufficiently long periods to be considered recovered rather than simply in remission. Further, even with such a longer-term finding, it must be determined whether those alcoholics who can return to, and maintain, moderate drinking habits can be distinguished prior to treatment from those who cannot. Second, the uniformity of treatment effects suggests a policy of supporting or advocating the less expensive forms of treatment. Before such a policy can be adopted, however, more research must be done on the cost-effectiveness of alternative treatments and on the role and importance of outcome criteria other than drinking behavior.

APPENDIX D

Data Collection Instruments

The most important NIAAA data collection instruments relevant to the present study are reproduced in the following pages. A brief description of each form follows:

Initial Contact Form: Records very basic demographic and referral data for all clients making contact with a center, whether or not they start treatment.

Client Intake Form: Administered to all clients starting treatment; assesses basic background information and drinking behavior. A slight modification of this form, preserving all questions about those behaviors subject to change, was administered in followup interviews at 30 days and at 6 months after intake.

Client Direct Service Report: Records treatment services received by each client treated by a center. This report is submitted monthly and summarizes a 30-day period.

ATC Followup Study Questionnaire: Used in the special 18-month followup study of clients treated by eight centers.

DEPARTMENT OF HEALTH, EDUCATION, AND WELFARE HEALTH SERVICES AND MENTAL HEALTH ADMINISTRATION NATIONAL INSTITUTE OF MENTAL HEALTH NATIONAL INSTITUTE ON ALCOHOL ABUSE AND ALCOHOLISM **INITIAL CONTACT FORM**	FORM APPROVED OMB NO. 68-R1313
	Staff Member's Name
ATC Name	Length of Interview

Name   (Last)   (First)   (MI)

Address: Number & Street   Phone
          City   Zip Code   County

ATC Code [ ] 1 ... 7   Client Code [ ] 8 ... 13   Social Security Number [ ] 14 ... 22

Census Tract, MCD, or CCD No. [ ] 23 TYPE   IDENTIFICATION NUMBER 30   County Code [ ] 31 33   Prof. Code [ ] 34   Time Code [ ] 36

1. Contact Date

38 Month Day Year 43

2. Birth Date

44 Month Day Year 49

50 **3. Sex:**   1 ☐ Male   2 ☐ Female

4. Ethnicity or race: (Check one by observation)
51
1 ☐ White   5 ☐ Puerto Rican
2 ☐ Black   6 ☐ Other Spanish-American
3 ☐ Oriental   7 ☐ American Indian/Alaskan Native
4 ☐ Mexican-American   8 ☐ Other_____
                                    (Specify)

5. Place of initial contact:
52-53
1 ☐ Detox unit   6 ☐ Traffic court
2 ☐ Central ATC alcoholism clinic   7 ☐ Non-traffic court
3 ☐ Decentralized ATC alcoholism clinic 8 ☐ Jail
4 ☐ Hospital emergency room   9 ☐ Home
5 ☐ Hospital ward   10 ☐ Other_____
                                            (Specify)

6. Your estimate of potential client's condition: (Check one)
1 ☐ Sober
2 ☐ Intoxicated, but coherent
54 3 ☐ Intoxicated, not coherent
4 ☐ Withdrawal, without DTs
5 ☐ Withdrawal, with DTs
6 ☐ Not ascertainable

**7. Person accompanying potential client at time of
initial contact.** (If more than one, determine who
was responsible for getting client there.)
1 ☐ No one (alone)
2 ☐ Spouse
3 ☐ Other family member
55 4 ☐ Friend
5 ☐ Clergy
6 ☐ Social Worker
7 ☐ Police or Court Personnel
8 ☐ Other_____
                (Specify)

COMMENTS _____

**8. What agency or who referred client
to this ATC?**_____

Agency Code [ ]
56

9. Is this referral related to drinking and driving?
58 1 ☐ Yes   2 ☐ No   3 ☐ Don't know

10. Previous alcoholism treatment
(a) How many times has client received alcoholism
treatment during the past 5 years?

Number [ ]
59

(b) Were any of these times at this ATC?
61 1 ☐ Yes   2 ☐ No

11. Disposition
(a) What was the disposition of the potential client? (Check one)
1 ☐ Waiting list for intake
62 2 ☐ No intake, ATC decision
3 ☐ Client refused intake (GO ON TO 12a)
4 ☐ Intake, Service Status _____
                (GO ON TO 12a)

Service
Status
Code [ ]
63

(b) If disposition was "waiting list for intake"
or "no intake, ATC decision": (Check reason)
1 ☐ Service required not provided at this ATC
2 ☐ Service provided at this ATC, but no space available
3 ☐ Potential client can't enter the program because
65 institutionalized (e.g., in the hospital, in jail)
4 ☐ Potential client is a client of another program for
which the ATC is providing services
5 ☐ Potential client determined to be untreatable at
this ATC

12. Referral
(a) Was the client referred elsewhere?
66 1 ☐ Yes
2 ☐ No

Agency
Code [ ]

(b) If YES: Where? _____
                (Specify)   67

MH–401-1
7-72

The information entered on these forms will be handled in the strictest confidence and no individual patient
records containing information concerning the identity of the client will be released to unauthorized personnel.

ICF

DEPARTMENT OF HEALTH, EDUCATION, AND WELFARE	FORM APPROVED
HEALTH SERVICES AND MENTAL HEALTH ADMINISTRATION	OMB NO. 68-R1313
NATIONAL INSTITUTE OF MENTAL HEALTH	
NATIONAL INSTITUTE ON ALCOHOL ABUSE AND ALCOHOLISM	Staff Member's Name
CLIENT INTAKE FORM	
ATC Name	Length of Interview

Name   (Last)   (First)   (MI)

Address: Number & Street   Phone

City   Zip Code   County

ATC Code [ ] 1 ... 7
Client Code [ ] 8 ... 13
Social Security Number [ ] 14 ... 22

Census Tract, MCD, or CCD No. [ ] 23   Type Identification Number 30
County Code [ ] 31 33
Prof. Code [ ] 34
Time Code [ ] 36

1. Date of Intake [ ] 38 Month Day Year 43
2. Date Form Filled Out [ ] 44 Month Day Year 49
3. Birth Date [ ] 50 Month Day Year 55

4. Service Status   Code [ ] 56

5. Sex:
   1 ☐ Male
   2 ☐ Female   58

6. Client resides in ATC catchment area:
   1 ☐ Yes
   2 ☐ No   59

7. Marital Status
   (a) What is client's present marital status?
      1 ☐ Never married (GO ON TO 8a)
      2 ☐ Married
      60 3 ☐ Widowed
      4 ☐ Divorced/Annulled
      5 ☐ Separated

   (b) If Separated:
      For how many years and/or months?   Years Months [ ] 61 No.

   (c) How many times has client been married? [ ] 65 Age

   (d) How old was client when he (first) married? [ ] 66

COMMENTS _____

300 Data Collection Instruments

8. Residence Information

(a) How many residences (addresses) has client
had during the past 5 years?

Number

`14`

(b) How long has client lived in the state?

Years | Months

`16` | `19`

(c) How long has client lived in his
present community or neighborhood?

Years | Months

`20` | `23`

Note to Interviewer: Obtain the following residence information
about client's permanent address.

(d) How long has client lived at his
present address?

Years | Months

`24` | `27`

(e) Does client own or rent his home?

1 ☐ Owns
28 2 ☐ Rents
3 ☐ Other _____
(Specify)

(f) What type of residence does client live in?

1 ☐ Group quarters (e.g., rooming house, dormitory,
mission) (GO ON TO 10a)
29 2 ☐ Apartment
3 ☐ House
4 ☐ Other _____
(Specify)

9. Household Composition

(a) Does client live alone or with others?

1 ☐ Alone
30 2 ☐ With others

(b) What is the total number of persons living in client's
household (including client)?

Total

`31`

10. Religion

(a) What was client's religion of upbringing?

1 ☐ Protestant
2 ☐ Catholic
33 3 ☐ Jewish
4 ☐ None
5 ☐ Other _____
(Specify)

(b) What religion does client presently practice?

1 ☐ Protestant
2 ☐ Catholic
34 3 ☐ Jewish
4 ☐ None
5 ☐ Other _____
(Specify)

11. Military

(a) Is client now in military service?

1 ☐ No
35 2 ☐ Yes, active (GO ON TO c)
3 ☐ Yes, reserves

(b) Is client a veteran of military service?

1 ☐ No
36 2 ☐ Yes

(c) If YES: How many years of active duty?

Years

`37`

12. Education

(a) What was the highest grade client completed in school?
(Check one)

1 ☐ No schooling (GO ON TO 13)
2 ☐ 1-4 grade
3 ☐ 5-6 grade
4 ☐ 7 grade
5 ☐ 8 grade
6 ☐ 9-11 grade
39-40 7 ☐ 12 grade
8 ☐ Vocational, Business, or Technical
9 ☐ 1 year College
10 ☐ 2 years College
11 ☐ 3 years College
12 ☐ 4 years College
13 ☐ Graduate School

(b) In what year did client complete this grade?

Year

`1 9`
`41`

13. What is client's principal occupational training?
(Please describe briefly: for example, civil engineer, college
teacher, elementary school teacher, draftsman, office
manager, bookkeeper, bulldozer operator, sheetmetal worker,
and so on. If none, so state.)

_____

Occupation
Code
`43`

14. What is client's current or most recent occupation?
(Please describe briefly as in the last question. If client is a
housewife or student, so state.)

_____

Occupation
Code
`45`

MH-401-2
7-72

ATC
Code `_____`

Client
Code `_____`

Date `_____`

CIF-2

15. Employment

(a) Does client have a job now?

1 ☐ No (GO ON TO c)
2 ☐ Yes full time
47 3 ☐ Yes, part time
4 ☐ Yes, odd jobs

(b) If YES: Check type of job (GO ON TO e)

1 ☐ Private wage or salary worker
2 ☐ Federal government worker
48 3 ☐ State or local government worker
4 ☐ Self-employed

(c) If NO: Has client been looking for work during the past month?

1 ☐ Yes (GO ON TO e)
49 2 ☐ No

(d) If NO: What is the main reason client was not looking for work last month? (Check one)

1 ☐ Housewife
2 ☐ Student
3 ☐ Retired/too old
4 ☐ Permanently disabled
50 5 ☐ Drinking problem
6 ☐ Institutionalized
7 ☐ Doesn't want a job
8 ☐ No job available
9 ☐ Other _____
(Specify)

(e) How many jobs has client held during the past year?

Number
51

(f) Approximately how many months was client employed during the past year?

Months
53

(g) Approximately how many days did client work last month?

Days
55

16. Financial Support

(a) What was client's major source of financial support last month? (Check one)

1 ☐ Job
2 ☐ Spouse
3 ☐ Family or friends
4 ☐ Public assistance (welfare)
57 5 ☐ Pension (include Social Security)
6 ☐ Insurance (include Workmen's Compensation, Unemployment Insurance)
7 ☐ Illegal
8 ☐ Savings /Investments
9 ☐ Other _____
(Specify)

(b) What was client's second most important source of financial support last month? (Check one)

1 ☐ Job
2 ☐ Spouse
3 ☐ Family or friends
4 ☐ Public assistance (welfare)
5 ☐ Pension (include Social Security)
59 6 ☐ Insurance (include Workmen's Compensation, Unemployment Insurance)
7 ☐ Illegal
8 ☐ Savings/Investments
9 ☐ Other _____
(Specify)

17. Income

(a) What was the gross income earned by client last month?

1 ☐ None
2 ☐ $85 or less
3 ☐ $86-$250
4 ☐ $251-$499
60 5 ☐ $500-$835
6 ☐ $836-$1,250
7 ☐ Over $1,250
8 ☐ Unwilling to state

(b) What was the shared gross income of the household in which client lived last month? (Include income from all sources)

1 ☐ None
2 ☐ $250 or less
3 ☐ $251-$499
4 ☐ $500-$835
61 5 ☐ $836-$1,250
6 ☐ Over $1,250
7 ☐ Don't know
8 ☐ Unwilling to state

(c) What was the approximate shared gross income of the household in which client lived last year? (Include income from all sources)

1 ☐ Less than $1,000
2 ☐ $1,000-$1,999
3 ☐ $2,000-$2,999
4 ☐ $3,000-$3,999
5 ☐ $4,000-$4,999
6 ☐ $5,000-$5,999
7 ☐ $6,000-$6,999
62-63 8 ☐ $7,000-$7,999
9 ☐ $8,000-$8,999
10 ☐ $9,000-$9,999
11 ☐ $10,000-$11,999
12 ☐ $12,000-$13,999
13 ☐ $14,000-$15,999
14 ☐ $16,000 or more
15 ☐ Don't know
16 ☐ Unwilling to state

The information entered on these forms will be handled in the strictest confidence and no individual patient records containing information concerning the identity of the client will be released to unauthorized personnel.

MH-401-2
7-72

ATC Code

Client Code

Date

CIF-3

18. Drinking history

   (a) At approximately what age did client first start drinking frequently or heavily?

   Age

   64

   (b) Approximately how many years has client been drinking frequently or heavily?

   Years

   66

CARD 3(Reprat 1-13)

19. Family drinking

   Determine which of the following persons were present when client was growing up, and whether anyone of them drank occasionally, frequently, or had a drinking problem.

	Not Present	Did anyone drink? No	Occ.	Freq.	Prob.
14 (a) Father	1☐	2☐	3☐	4☐	5☐
15 (b) Mother	1☐	2☐	3☐	4☐	5☐
16 (c) Brother and/or Sister	1☐	2☐	3☐	4☐	5☐
17 (d) Other persons	1☐	2☐	3☐	4☐	5☐

20. AA Meetings

   (a) Has client attended AA meetings during recent weeks?

   18 1☐ Regularly
      2☐ Occasionally
      3☐ No

   (b) Has client ever attended AA meetings?

   19 1☐ No (GO ON TO 21a)
      2☐ Yes

   (c) If YES: Over a period of how many years?

   Years

   20

21. Previous alcoholism treatment

   (a) Has client received treatment other than AA within the past 5 years?

   22 1☐ No (GO ON TO 22)
      2☐ Yes, from this ATC
      3☐ Yes, from other agencies, programs
      4☐ Yes, both from this ATC and other agencies

   (b) If YES: Specify name of agency, length of treatment, and the date of termination or dropout of the 3 most recent.
   (List this ATC first, if applicable.)

	Agency Code	Length of Treatment (Weeks)	Termination Date (Month Year)
(1)	23	25	28 31
(2)	32	34	37 40
(3)	41	43	46 49

22. Household drinking

   Determine which of the following persons are now living in client's household, and whether anyone of them drinks occasionally, frequently, or has a drinking problem. If client lives alone, check "Not Present" for all categories.

	Not Present	Does anyone drink? No	Occ.	Freq.	Prob.
50 (a) Spouse	1☐	2☐	3☐	4☐	5☐
51 (b) Children	1☐	2☐	3☐	4☐	5☐
52 (c) Father	1☐	2☐	3☐	4☐	5☐
53 (d) Mother	1☐	2☐	3☐	4☐	5☐
54 (e) Brother and/or Sister	1☐	2☐	3☐	4☐	5☐
55 (f) Other persons	1☐	2☐	3☐	4☐	5☐

   (g) Are any of these persons currently undergoing alcoholism treatment? (Check one)

      1☐ No
      2☐ Yes, from this ATC
   56 3☐ Yes, from other agencies, programs
      4☐ Yes, both from this ATC and other agencies

23. Motor vehicle driving and arrests

   (a) Does client drive a car, truck, or other motor vehicle?

   57 1☐ No (GO ON TO 24)
      2☐ Yes

   (b) If YES: How many times has client been arrested for drinking and driving during the past year?

   Number

   58

24. Other arrests

   How many times has client been arrested for drinking, not related to driving, during the past year?

   Number

   60

25. How many times has client been in jail for any reason?

   Number

   62

26. Hospitalization

   (a) How many times has client been hospitalized during the past year?

   Number

   64

   (b) How many of these times were alcohol related?

   Number

   66

27. How many days has client been institutionalized (e.g., in the hospital, in jail) during the past month?

   Days

   68

The information entered on these forms will be handled in the strictest confidence and no individual patient records containing information concerning the identity of the client will be released to unauthorized personnel.

ATC Code ⎿⎯⎯⎯⎯⎯⎯⎯⏌   Client Code ⎿⎯⎯⎯⎯⎯⏌   Date ⎿⎯⎯⎯⏌   CIF-4

28. Drinking status

(a) How long has it been since client's last drink?

14
1 ☐ 1-6 days
2 ☐ 7-29 days
3 ☐ 1-5 months
4 ☐ 6-11 months
5 ☐ 1-2 years
6 ☐ Over 2 years

(b) What was client's longest "dry" period (abstinence)
during the past 3 months?

15
1 ☐ None
2 ☐ 1-2 days
3 ☐ 3-6 days
4 ☐ 1-2 weeks
5 ☐ 3-4 weeks
6 ☐ 5-8 weeks
7 ☐ Over 2 months

(c) How many days did client drink
during the past month?

16 ☐☐ Days

(d) How many days was client's most
recent drinking bout?

18 ☐☐ Days

Note to Interviewer: _If the client has been institutionalized
during the past month, obtain the information requested
in questions 29-32 for the month before he was
institutionalized._

29. Drinking quantity and frequency—Beer

(a) Did client drink beer during the past month?

20
1 ☐ No (GO ON TO 30a)
2 ☐ Yes

(b) If YES: About how often did client drink any beer?

21
1 ☐ Constantly
2 ☐ Every day
3 ☐ Nearly every day
4 ☐ 3-4 days a week
5 ☐ 1-2 days a week
6 ☐ Weekends only
7 ☐ Less often than weekly

(c) About how much did client drink in a typical day?

Note to Interviewer: _1 quart = three 11 oz. bottles
(cans) or four 8 oz. glasses._

22
1 ☐ 6 quarts or more
2 ☐ 5 quarts
3 ☐ 4 quarts
4 ☐ 3 quarts
5 ☐ 1-2 quarts
6 ☐ 1-3 glasses

30. Drinking quantity and frequency—Wine

(a) Did client drink wine during the past month?

23
1 ☐ No (GO ON TO 31a)
2 ☐ Yes

(b) If YES: About how often did client drink any wine?

24
1 ☐ Constantly
2 ☐ Every day
3 ☐ Nearly every day
4 ☐ 3-4 days a week
5 ☐ 1-2 days a week
6 ☐ Weekends only
7 ☐ Less often than weekly

(c) About how much did client drink in a typical day?

Note to Interviewer: _1 fifth is a standard size bottle and is
equal to about three 8 oz. water or six 4 oz. wine
glasses. There are 5 fifths to a gallon or 2½ fifths to a
half gallon._

25
1 ☐ 5 fifths or more
2 ☐ 3-4 fifths
3 ☐ 2 fifths
4 ☐ 1 fifth
5 ☐ 2 or 3 water glasses or 4-6 wine glasses
6 ☐ 1 water glass or 1 or 2 wine glasses

31. Drinking quantity and frequency—Liquor

(a) Did client drink whiskey, gin, or other hard liquor during
the past month?

26
1 ☐ No (GO ON TO 32a)
2 ☐ Yes

(b) If YES: About how often did client drink any hard liquor?

27
1 ☐ Constantly
2 ☐ Every day
3 ☐ Nearly every day
4 ☐ 3-4 days a week
5 ☐ 1-2 days a week
6 ☐ Weekends only
7 ☐ Less than weekly

(c) About how much did client drink in a typical day?

Note to Interviewer: _1 pint = 16 oz. or sixteen 1 oz. shots.
There are 2 pints in 1 quart and a little over 1½ pints in a fifth._

28
1 ☐ 4 pints or more
2 ☐ 3 pints
3 ☐ 2 pints
4 ☐ 1 pint
5 ☐ 11-14 shots
6 ☐ 7-10 shots
7 ☐ 4-6 shots
8 ☐ 1-3 shots

MH-401-2
7-72

ATC
Code ☐☐☐☐☐☐☐

Client
Code ☐☐☐☐☐☐☐

Date ☐☐☐☐☐

CIF-5

32.   Behavioral aspects of drinking

Note to Interviewer: Determine the following for client during past month.

29	(a)	Number of times drunk	1☐ None	2☐ 1-4	1☐ 5-10	4☐ More than 10
30	(b)	Longest period between drinks	1☐ 12 hours or more		2☐ Less than 12 hours	
31	(c)	Longest period of continued drinking	1☐ Less than 6 hours	2☐ 6-12 hours	3☐ More than 12 hrs	
32	(d)	Number of days had drink upon awaking	1☐ None	2☐ 1-4	1☐ 5-10	4☐ More than 10
33	(e)	Meals missed because of drinking	1☐ None	2☐ 1-4	1☐ 5-10	4☐ More than 10
34	(f)	Percent of time drinking alone	1☐ 0-9%	2☐ 10-25%	3☐ 26-50%	4☐ More than 50%
35	(g)	Number of memory lapses or "blackouts"	1☐ None	2☐ 1-2	3☐ 3-5	4☐ More than 5
36	(h)	Number of times had the "shakes"	1☐ None	2☐ 1-2	3☐ 3-5	4☐ More than 5
37	(i)	Number of nights had difficulty sleeping	1☐ None	2☐ 1-2	3☐ 3-5	5☐ More than 5
38	(j)	Number of quarrels with others while drinking	1☐ None	2☐ 1-2	3☐ 3-5	4☐ More than 5
39	(k)	Drinking while on job/during daily activities	1☐ No	2☐ Yes		
40	(l)	Days of work missed/days of inactivity because of drinking	1☐ None	2☐ 1-2	3☐ 3-5	4☐ More than 5

33.   Client self-perception

Note to Interviewer: *Question 33 is to determine client's perception of his own drinking problem. Do not give your opinion. Please read the questions exactly as they are worded below, do not reword them.*

(a)   How would you, yourself, describe your drinking problem at the present time—would you say none, social drinking, problem drinking on sprees, or steady problem drinking?

41
1☐ None (no drinking at all)
2☐ Social drinking
3☐ Problem drinking on sprees
4☐ Steady problem drinking

(b)   At the moment, how serious a problem do you feel your drinking is—is it no problem at all, a slight problem, a moderate problem, or a very serious problem?

42
1☐ No problem at all
2☐ A slight problem
3☐ A moderate problem
4☐ A very serious problem

(c)   During the past month would you say that your drinking problem has improved, stayed about the same, or worsened?

43
1☐ Improved
2☐ Stayed about the same
3☐ Worsened

(d)   What do you think you will be able to do in the next few months about your drinking? Do you intend to stop altogether, cut down, stay the same, or drink more?

44
1☐ Stop altogether
2☐ Cut down
3☐ Stay the same
4☐ Drink more

(e)   Do you worry about any of these things?

45	(1)	Getting and keeping a job you like?	1☐ Yes	2☐ No
46	(2)	Finding friends that don't drink?	1☐ Yes	2☐ No
47	(3)	Getting along with people?	1☐ Yes	2☐ No
48	(4)	Getting along with your family?	1☐ Yes	2☐ No
49	(5)	Finding a good place to live?	1☐ Yes	2☐ No
50	(6)	Your health?	1☐ Yes	2☐ No
51	(7)	Having enough money to live on?	1☐ Yes	2☐ No
52	(8)	Finding things to do in your spare time?	1☐ Yes	2☐ No

Note to Interviewer: *Ask question (f) only if client has been in the program for at least 24 hours.*

(f)   In general, how do you feel about the way you are being treated at this center—are you very satisfied, somewhat satisfied, somewhat dissatisfied, very dissatisfied, or just neutral?

1☐ Very satisfied
2☐ Somewhat satisfied
53   1☐ Somewhat dissatisfied
4☐ Very dissatisfied
5☐ Just neutral

34.   Medical questions

(a)   Was a medical examination given on intake (or at the time of initial contact)?

54   1☐ Yes   2☐ No

(b)   Is client currently under medical care?

55   1☐ Yes   2☐ No

(c)   **If NO:** Are treatment and medical management needed?

56   1☐ Yes   2☐ No

(d)   If treatment and medical management are needed, was client referred for treatment?

57   1☐ Yes   2☐ No

MH-401-2
7-72

ATC Code ⎣_ _ _ _ _ _⎦   Client Code ⎣_ _ _ _ _ _⎦   Date ⎣_ _ _ _⎦   CIF-6

DEPARTMENT OF HEALTH, EDUCATION, AND WELFARE
HEALTH SERVICES AND MENTAL HEALTH ADMINISTRATION
NATIONAL INSTITUTE OF MENTAL HEALTH
NATIONAL INSTITUTE ON ALCOHOL ABUSE AND ALCOHOLISM

CLIENT DIRECT SERVICES REPORT

FORM APPROVED
OMB NO. 68-R1313

ATC Name

Name	(Last)	(First)	(MI)

Address:
Number & Street   Phone
City   Zip Code   County

ATC Code 1 ___ 7   Client Code 8 ___ 13   Date 14 Month Day Year 19

	CPF 30	CPF 90	CPF 180	CPF 1 yr
1. Circle appropriate 20-1 reporting period	1 2 3 4	5 6 7 8	9 10 11 12	13

2. Client Status (Check one)
1 ☐ Preintake
22 2 ☐ Active
3 ☐ Inactive (no direct services provided this reporting period)

3. Did the client terminate or drop out during this reporting period? (Check one)
1 ☐ No
2 ☐ Yes, treatment plan completed
3 ☐ Yes, voluntarily, e.g., client left because dissatisfied with program, client left against medical advice (AMA)
23
4 ☐ Yes, inaccessible, e.g., client left area, client in prison
5 ☐ Yes, client died
6 ☐ Yes, client inactive for 3 months

4. Outpatient Activities   Number*
Appointments made 24
Appointments kept 26
Unscheduled visits 28

5. Inpatient Activities   Number of Days*
Inpatient (hospital) 30
Intermediate care (partial hospitalization) 32
Intermediate care (quarterway house) 34
Intermediate care (halfway house) 36
Residential care 38
(Record "0" if none)

CARD 2 (Repeat 1-13)

6. Direct Services Provided   No. of Times*   Total Hours*
Emergency/detox care 14 ___ 18
Individual counseling 19 ___ 23
Individual therapy 24 ___ 28
Group counseling 29 ___ 33
Group therapy 34 ___ 38
Family counseling/therapy 39 ___ 43
Vocational rehabilitation 44 ___ 48
Social, occupational and recreational therapy 49 ___ 53
(Record "0" if none)

7. Is this client currently taking antabuse?
54 1 ☐ Yes   2 ☐ No

CARD 1 (Repeat 1-13)

8. Supplemental Information
(a) Drug Code 14 ___ 25
(b) Referral (Agency Code) 26 ___ 33
(c) Type Charge 34
(d) Payors 36 ___ 38

COMMENTS

MH-401-3
7-72

The information entered on these forms will be handled in the strictest confidence and no individual patient records containing information concerning the identity of the client will be released to unauthorized personnel.

CDSR

DEPARTMENT OF HEALTH, EDUCATION, AND WELFARE
PUBLIC HEALTH SERVICE
ALCOHOL, DRUG ABUSE, AND MENTAL HEALTH ADMINISTRATION
NATIONAL INSTITUTE ON ALCOHOL ABUSE AND ALCOHOLISM

OMB NO. 68-S73155
APPROVAL EXPIRES: 12-31-74
BEGIN CARD 02
NO.

ATC FOLLOW-UP STUDY QUESTIONNAIRE

TIME STARTED: _____ AM _____ PM

1. Do you think of the place in which you live <u>now</u> as your regular place of residence, or is it a temporary residence?

   Regular place of residence . . 1
   Temporary residence . . . 2   10

2. How long have you lived in this place of residence?

   No. of Years _____ 11-12
   No. of Months _____ 13-14

3. And how long have you lived in your community or neighborhood?

   No. of Years _____ 15-16
   No. of Months _____ 17-18

4. <u>Including yourself</u>, how many people live in your household?

   No. of People _____ 10-20

5. Do you own or rent your home?

   Own 1
   Rent 2   21
   Other (SPECIFY) 3

6. CIRCLE ONE CODE: ASK IF NECESSARY:

   In what type of residence do you live . . .

   Hotel or rooming house . . 1
   Apartment 2
   Private house 3   22
   Mobile home (trailer) . . . 4
   Other (SPECIFY) 5

7. In how many different places have you lived during the past 12 months?
   (PROBE FOR NUMBER OF DIFFERENT <u>RESIDENCES</u>)

   No. of Places _____ 23-24

8. And now, I would like to know your date of birth.

   Month _____ 25-26
   Day _____ 27-28
   Year _____ 29-30

9. How tall are you?   (PROBE FOR BEST ESTIMATE)

   Feet _____ 31
   Inches _____ 32-33

10. And how much do you weigh?   (PROBE FOR BEST ESTIMATE)

    Lbs. _____ 34-36

11. In regard to military service, are you . . .
    (CODE ALL THAT APPLY)

    On active duty (ASK A) . . 01   37-38
    In the reserves 02
    Formerly in the reserves . . 04
    A veteran (ASK A) 08
    Or, have you never been in the service 16

    IF ON ACTIVE DUTY OR VETERAN

    A. How many years of active duty have you served?

    No. of Years _____ 39-40

12. A. What was the highest grade you completed in school?

No schooling	01
1st - 4th grades	02
5th - 6th grades	03
7th grade	04
8th grade	05
9th - 11th grades	06
12th grade or GED	07
1 year of college	08
2 years of college	09
3 years of college → (ASK B)	10
4 years of college	11
Some graduate school	12
Graduate school	13

41-42

B. Have you ever received any diploma or degree?

Yes (ASK C)	1
No	2

43

C. What is your highest diploma or degree?

High school diploma or equivalent	1
Associate degree (Junior College)	2
Bachelor's degree	3
Master's degree	4
Doctor's degree	5
Other (SPECIFY)	6

44

13. Have you completed any vocational, business, or technical school?

Yes	1
No	2

45

14. Are you now married, widowed, divorced, separated, or have you never been married?

Married (ASK A–C)	1
Widowed (ASK A–D)	2
Divorced (ASK A–D)	3
Separated (ASK A–D)	4
Never married (GO TO Q. 15)	5

46

IF EVER MARRIED:

A. How many times have you been married? No. of times ____ 47

B. How old were you when you were (first) married? Age ____ 48-49

C. In what month and year did you get married (the last time)?

Month ____ 50-51
Year ____ 52-53

IF CURRENTLY WIDOWED, DIVORCED, OR SEPARATED:

D. How long have you been (widowed/divorced/separated)?

No. of years ____ 54-55
No. of months ____ 56-57

ADM-T20
6-74

15. At the present time do you have a full time job, part time job, do you work at odd jobs or are you not employed?

Full time job 1	58
Part time job . . ➔ (ASK D-G) 2	
Work at odd jobs 3	
Not employed (ASK A) . . . 4	

A. Have you been looking for work during the past 30 days?

Yes (GO TO C) 1	59
No (ASK B) 2	

B. What is the main reason you haven't been looking for work?
RECORD VERBATIM AND CODE

Housewife 01	60-61
Student 02	
Retired/too old 03	
Ill or disabled 04	
Drinking problem 05	
Institutionalized 06	
Don't want a job 07	
No job available 08	
In this location only temporarily/ intend to move on 09	
Have independent income/no need to work 10	
Seasonal worker 11	
Other (SPECIFY) 12	

C. Have you worked in the past 12 months?

Yes (ASK D-G) 1	62
No (SKIP TO Q. 19) 2	

IF CURRENTLY NOT WORKING, USE ALTERNATE WORDING:

D. What kind of work (do/did) you do (most recently in the past 12 months)?
(PROBE: What (is/was) your job called?)

_____ OCCUPATION	63-64/R 65-66

IF NOT ALREADY ANSWERED, ASK:

E. What (do/did) you actually do in that job?
(PROBE: What (are/were) some of your main duties?)

F. What kind of place (do/did) you work for?
(PROBE: What do they make or do?)

_____ INDUSTRY	

CIRCLE ONE CODE, ASK IF NECESSARY:

G. Which of these best describes the type of job you (have/had) . . .

Private wage or salary worker . . 1	67
Federal government worker . . 2	
State or local government worker 3	
Self-employed 4	

16. How many jobs have you had during the past 12 months (including your present job)?

No. of Jobs _____   68-69

17. How many months were you employed during the past 12 months?

No. of Months _____   70-71

18. How many days did you work last month?

No. of Days Worked _____   72-73

ASK EVERYONE

And now some questions that have to do with drinking habits in families. First of all . . .

BEGIN
CARD 03

19. While you were growing up, until the age of about 16, did you live mostly with your father and mother?

Yes, both (ASK A & B)	1	10
Father only (ASK A ONLY)	2	
Mother only (ASK B ONLY)	3	
No, neither	4	

IF LIVED WITH FATHER, ASK:

A. Looking back on the days when you were growing up, do you think your father drank occasionally, drank frequently, had a drinking problem, or didn't he drink?

Drank occasionally	1	11
Drank frequently	2	
Had a drinking problem	3	
Didn't drink	4	

IF LIVED WITH MOTHER, ASK:

B. Looking back on the days when you were growing up, do you think your mother drank occasionally, drank frequently, had a drinking problem, or didn't she drink?

Drank occasionally	1	12
Drank frequently	2	
Had a drinking problem	3	
Didn't drink	4	

20. And what about your drinking behavior, would you say you . . .

Now drink either frequently or heavily. . . .	1	13
Used to drink either frequently or heavily. . .	2	
Or, did you almost never drink frequently or heavily (SKIP TO Q. 23)	3	

21. About how old were you when you started drinking frequently or heavily?

Age _____   14-15

22. Altogether about how many years would you say you (drank/have been drinking) frequently or heavily?

No. of Years _____   16-17

IF CURRENTLY MARRIED, ASK:

23. Do you think of your (wife/husband) as drinking occasionally, drinking frequently, having a drinking problem, or doesn't (he/she) drink?

Drinks occasionally	1	18
Drinks frequently	2	
Has a drinking problem	3	
Doesn't drink	4	

ADM-T20
6-74

24 A.   How did you happen to contact the (ENTER NAME OF ATC _____)
         a year or so ago –– was it . . .
         (CODE ALL THAT APPLY)

HAND RESP CARD AND READ	Your own idea 1	19
	Your (husband/wife)'s idea 2	20
	Another family member's idea 3	21
	A friend's idea 4	22
	Your employer's idea 5	23
	Your doctor's idea 6	24
	Your clergyman's idea 7	25
	A social worker's idea 8	26
	At the suggestion or order of the police 9	27
	At the suggestion or order of a court 10	28
	Someone else's idea (SPECIFY): _____ 11	29

   B.   Was this in any way related to driving?

         Yes 1   30
         No 2

25. How did you feel about going the first time –– would you say you . . .

         Felt that it was a good idea 1   31
         Didn't care much about the idea one way or the other . . 2
         Or, did you resent the idea 3

         IF VOLUNTEERED:
         You really didn't know what you were getting into . . . 4

26. Did you ever stay at (NAME OF ATC) overnight?

         Yes (ASK A–C) 1   32
         No 2

   A.   How many different <u>times</u> did you stay there overnight?   No. of Times _____ 33-34

   B.   How many <u>days</u> did you stay there the last time?   No. of Days _____ 35-37

   C.   Altogether how many <u>days</u> did you stay there overnight?   No. of Days _____ 38-40

27. About how many different <u>times</u> have you visited (NAME OF ATC) altogether?

         No. of Times _____ 41-42

ADM-T20
6-74

28. Are you still going to (NAME OF ATC)?

Yes 1   43

No (ASK A & B) 2

A. When was the last time that you went?

Month _____   44-45

Year _____   46-47

B. What was the main reason that you stopped going?

48-49

50-51

29. What are some of the things that you don't like about (NAME OF ATC)?

52

53

54

55

30. And what are the things that you do like about (NAME OF ATC)?

56

57

58

59

31. In general, how do you feel about the program at (NAME OF ATC) —— do you think it is . . .

Excellent 1   60

Very good 2

Good 3

Fair 4

Or, poor 5

32. And how do you feel about the staff at (NAME OF ATC) -- do you think they are . . .

Excellent	1	61
Very good	2	
Good	3	
Fair	4	
Or, poor	5	

33. Regardless of any medical insurance you may have, what do you think of the fees that are charged by (NAME OF ATC) -- do you think they are . . .

Too high (ASK A)	1	62
About right (ASK A)	2	
Too low (ASK A)	3	
Or, is there no fee	4	

A. (Is/was) any part, or all of your fee covered by medical insurance?

Yes	1	63
No	2	

34. How about transportation -- (is/was) that a problem for you?

Yes	1	64
No	2	
Stayed as in-patient only	3	

35. (Are/were) the hours convenient for you?

Yes	1	65
No	2	
Stayed as in-patient only	3	

36. Have you ever attended any AA meetings?

Yes (ASK A & B)	1	66
No	2	

A. About how long ago did you last attend an AA meeting?

Days _____		67-68
Weeks_____		69-70
Months_____		71-72
Years _____		73-74

IF 6 WEEKS OR LESS, ASK B

B. How often have you attended AA meetings during the past 6 weeks -- would you say . . .

Regularly	1	75
Or, occasionally	2	

37. Have you ever taken antabuse?

		BEGIN CARD 04
Yes (ASK A)	1	10
No (GO TO Q. 38)	2	

IF YES:

A. Are you now taking antabuse?

Yes	1	11
No (ASK B)	2	

B. When did you stop taking it?

Month_____		12-13
Year _____		14-15

38. During the past 30 days did you stay overnight in any institution such
as a hospital, nursing home, other treatment center, or jail?

Yes (ASK A)	1	16
No	2	

A. In the past 30 days how many days altogether did
you spend there?   No. of Days _____ | 17-18

39. Have you driven a car, truck, or other motor vehicle during
the past 12 months?

Yes (ASK A)	1	19
No	2	

IF YES:
A. Have you been arrested for drinking and driving during
the past 12 months?

Yes [ASK (1)]	1	20
No	2	

(1) How many times?   No. of Times _____ | 21-22

40. How long has it been since you had an alcoholic drink?

RECORD VERBATIM AND CODE

1 – 6 days (ASK A)	1	23
7 – 29 days (ASK A)	2	
1 – 5 months	3	
6 – 11 months	4	
1 – 2 years ➡ (SKIP TO Q. 49)	5	
Over 2 years	6	

IF DRANK DURING PAST MONTH:

A. On how many days would you say you drank during the past 30 days?   No. of Days _____ | 24-25

41. Did you drink any beer during the past 30 days?

Yes (ASK A & B)	1	26
No	2	

IF YES:
A. About how often —— would you say . . .

Every day	1	27
5 – 6 days a week	2	
3 – 4 days a week	3	
1 – 2 days a week	4	
Or, less often than weekly	5	

B. About how much beer do you drink on a typical day when you drink beer?

6 quarts/ 3 six packs or more . . .	1	28
5 quarts	2	
4 quarts/ 2 six packs	3	
3 quarts	4	
1 – 2 quarts		
3 – 6 bottles or cans/ 1 six pack ➡	5	
4 – 8 water glasses		
1 – 2 bottles or cans		
1 – 3 water glasses ➡	6	

42. Did you drink any wine during the past 30 days?

Yes (ASK A & B)	1	29
No	2	

IF YES:

A. About how often –– would you say . . .

Every day	1	30
5 – 6 days a week	2	
3 – 4 days a week	3	
1 – 2 days a week	4	
Or, less often than weekly	5	

B. About how much wine do you drink on a typical day when you drink wine?

5 fifths or more	1	31
3 – 4 fifths	2	
2 fifths / 2 quarts ➡ . . .	3	
1 fifth / 1 quart / 3 water glasses / 6 wine glasses ➡ . . .	4	
2 water glasses / 3 – 5 wine glasses ➡ . . .	5	
1 water glass / 1 or 2 wine glasses ➡ . . .	6	

43. Did you drink any whiskey, gin, or other hard liquor during the past 30 days?	Yes (ASK A & B)	1	32
	No	2	
IF YES:			
A. About how often — would you say . . .	Every day	1	33
	5 – 6 days a week	2	
	3 – 4 days a week	3	
	1 – 2 days a week	4	
	Or, less often than weekly	5	
B. About how much hard liquor do you drink on a typical day when you drink hard liquor?	4 pints or more 2 quarts or more 3 fifths or more →	01	34-35
	3 pints 2 fifths →	02	
	2 pints 1 quart 1 fifth →	03	
	1 pint 15 – 16 shots →	04	
	11 – 14 shots	05	
	7 – 10 shots / ½ pint	06	
	4 – 6 shots	07	
	1 – 3 shots	08	
	11 – 14 drinks	09	
	7 – 10 drinks	10	
	4 – 6 drinks	11	
	1 – 3 drinks	12	
44. These next few questions have to do with things that may have happened to you during the past 30 days.			
A. First, during the past 30 days, how many times did you have difficulty sleeping at night?	No. of Times ______		36-37
B. During the past 30 days, how many times did you have lapses or "blackouts"?	No. of Times ______		38-39
C. How many times did you have the "shakes"?	No. of Times ______		40-41
D. What was the longest period you went without a drink?	No. of Hours ______		42-43
	No. of Days ______		44-45

ADM-T20
6-74

E. When you drank during the past 30 days, did you . . .

Always drink with others . . .	1	46
Usually drink with others . . .	2	
Usually drink alone	3	
Or, always drink alone	4	

F. How many times did you miss a meal because of drinking? . . . . . No. of Times_____ | 47-48

During the past 30 days . . .

G. How many times did you have a drink as soon as you woke up? . . . . No. of Times_____ | 49-50

H. How many times did you have quarrels with others while drinking? . . No. of Times_____ | 51-52

I. During the past 30 days, how many times have you been drunk? . . . No. of Times_____ | 53-54

J. What was your longest continuous period of drinking during
the past 30 days? . . . . No. of Hours _____ | 55-56
OR
No. of Days _____ | 57-58

K. How many times did you drink while on the job? . . . . No. of Times_____ | 59-60
Not working 00

L. During the past 30 days, how many times did you miss work or
other activities because of drinking? . . . . No. of Times_____ | 61-62

45. How would you describe your drinking problem at the present
time——would you say you do . . .

None (no drinking at all) . . .	1	63
Social drinking	2	
Problem drinking on sprees . .	3	
Or, steady problem drinking . .	4	

46. At the moment, how serious a problem do you feel
your drinking is, is it . . .

No problem at all	1	64
A slight problem	2	
A moderate problem	3	
Or, a very serious problem . . .	4	

47. During the past 30 days, would you say that your
drinking problem has . . .

Improved	1	65
Stayed about the same	2	
Or, worsened	3	

48. What do you think you will do in the next few months
about your drinking——do you intend to . . .

Stop altogether	1	66
Cut down	2	
Drink the same amount . . .	3	
Or, drink more	4	

ADM-T20
6-74

ASK EVERYONE

Here are some things that people worry about. Tell me whether you worry about these.

49. Do you worry about getting or keeping a job you like?

Yes 1	67
No 2	
Retired 3	

50. Do you worry about finding friends that don't drink?

Yes 1	68
No 2	

51. Do you worry about getting along with people?

Yes 1	69
No 2	

52. Do you worry about getting along with your family?

Yes 1	70
No 2	
Have no family . . . 3	

53. Do you worry about finding a good place to live?

Yes 1	71
No 2	

54. Do you worry about your health?

Yes 1	72
No 2	

55. Do you worry about having enough money to live on?

Yes 1	73
No 2	

56. Do you worry about finding things to do in your spare time?

Yes 1	74
No 2	

ADM-T20
6-74

57. During the past 12 months have you received any help for drinking problems other than from (NAME OF ATC) or AA?

Yes 1   10

No (SKIP TO Q. 64) 2   11

58. What are the names of the agencies or persons from whom you received this help? ENTER EACH AGENCY OR PERSON IN COL. A BELOW. FOR EACH PERSON ASK B-D. FOR EACH AGENCY ASK B-E.

A NAME OF PERSON OR AGENCY (PROBE: Any other?)	B How many different times altogether have you visited (AGENCY/PERSON)	C Are you still going to (AGENCY/PERSON)?	D When was the last time you went?	E Did you ever stay at (AGENCY) overnight? IF YES: ASK F, G, H	F How many different times did you stay there overnight?	G How many days did you stay there the last time?	H Altogether how many days did you stay there overnight?
(1) _____	No. of Times 12-13	YES 1 | NO 2 14	Mo. / Yr. 15-16 17-18	YES 1 | NO 2 19	No. of Times DK . . 00 20-21	No. of Days DK . . . 00 22-24	No. of Days DK . . . 00 25-27
(2) _____	No. of Times 28-29	1 | 2 30	Mo. / Yr. 31-32 33-34	1 | 2 35	No. of Times DK . . 00 36-37	No. of Days DK . . . 00 38-40	No. of Days DK . . . 00 41-43
(3) _____	No. of Times 44-45	1 | 2 46	Mo. / Yr. 47-48 49-50	1 | 2 51	No. of Times DK . . 00 52-53	No. of Days DK . . . 00 54-56	No. of Days DK . . . 00 57-59
(4) _____	No. of Times 60-61	1 | 2 62	Mo. / Yr. 63-64 65-66	1 | 2 67	No. of Times DK . . 00 68-69	No. of Days DK . . . 00 70-72	No. of Days DK . . . 00 73-75

ADM-T20

318

IF RECEIVED ANY HELP FOR DRINKING PROBLEMS FROM AGENCIES OR PERSONS <u>OTHER</u> THAN ATC OR AA —— "YES" TO Q. 57 —— ASK Q. 59-63.		BEGIN CARD 06
59. When you went to (this/these) [agency(ies)/person(s)] did you go to any group meetings?	Yes (ASK A) . . . . 1 No (GO TO Q. 60) . 2	10
IF YES, ASK: A. About how many meetings did you go to?	No. of Meetings _____	11-12
IF MORE THAN ONE MEETING, ASK: B. Were any of the group meetings led by a counselor?	Yes ASK C) . . . . 1 No 2	13
IF YES, ASK: C. Were they led by the same counselor . . .	Usually . . . . . . 1 Sometimes . . . . . 2 Or, never 3	14
60. Did you talk with a counselor <u>alone</u> about your problems?	Yes (ASK A) . . . . 1 No 2	15
IF YES, ASK: A. About how many times did you talk with a counselor?	No. of Times _____	16-17
IF MORE THAN ONE TIME, ASK: B. Did you talk with the same counselor about your problems more than once?	Yes . . . . 1 No 2	18
61. Did you talk with a counselor about your problems with members of your family present?	Yes (ASK A) . . . . 1 No 2	19
IF YES, ASK: A. How many times did you talk with a counselor with members of your family present?	No. of Times _____	20-21
IF MORE THAN ONE TIME, ASK: B. Did you talk to the same counselor more than once with members of your family present?	Yes . . . . 1 No 2	22
62. Did you go through detox, or "drying out"?	Yes . . . . 1 No 2	23
63. Besides what you have just told me, what else did you do there? (PROBE: And what else?)		24 25 26 27

320   Data Collection Instruments

ASK EVERYONE

64. What is your religious preference?

Protestant	1	28
Catholic	2	
Jewish	3	
None	4	
Other (SPECIFY)_____	5	

65. How often do you attend religious services — would you say . . .

Regularly	1	29
Occasionally	2	
Rarely	3	
Or, never	4	

66. What was your major source of financial support last month?

RECORD VERBATIM AND CODE

Job(s)	1	30
Spouse	2	
Family or friends	3	
Public assistance (welfare)	4	
Pension (include Social Security)	5	
Insurance (include Workmen's Compensation, Unemployment Insurance)	6	
Savings/Investments	7	
Other (SPECIFY)_____	8	

67. What was your second most important source of financial support last month?

RECORD VERBATIM AND CODE

No second source	0	31
Job	1	
Spouse	2	
Family or friends	3	
Public assistance (welfare)	4	
Pension (include Social Security)	5	
Insurance (include Workmen's Compensation, Unemployment Insurance)	6	
Savings/Investments	7	
Other (SPECIFY)_____	8	

68. Which letter on this card indicates the total income before taxes that you earned last month?

```
HAND
RESP
CARD
A
```

A.	None	1	32
B.	$85 or less	2	
C.	$86–$250	3	
D.	$251–$499	4	
E.	$500–$835	5	
F.	$836–$1,250	6	
G.	$1,251–$1,699	7	
H.	$1,700–$2,500	8	
I.	$2,501 or more	9	

69. What was the approximate total income of your household in 1973 before taxes?
(INCLUDE INCOME FROM ALL SOURCES)

```
HAND
RESP
CARD
B
```

A.	Less than $1,000	1	33-34
B.	$1,000–$1,999	2	
C.	$2,000–$2,999	3	
D.	$3,000–$3,999	4	
E.	$4,000–$4,999	5	
F.	$5,000–$5,999	6	
G.	$6,000–$6,999	7	
H.	$7,000–$7,999	8	
I.	$8,000–$8,999	9	
J.	$9,000–$9,999	10	
K.	$10,000–$11,999	11	
L.	$12,000–$13,999	12	
M.	$14,000–$15,999	13	
N.	$16,000–$18,999	14	
O.	$19,000–$25,999	15	
P.	$26,000–$50,000	16	
Q.	Over $50,000	17	

70. RECORD TIME INTERVIEW ENDED AND CLOSE QUESTIONNAIRE.

TAKE OUT AND COMPLETE THE LOCATING INFORMATION PAGE.

TIME ENDED: _____A.M. _____P.M.

Thank you very much for your time.

I

INTERVIEWER OBSERVATIONS
FILL IN ITEMS BELOW AFTER YOU LEAVE THE HOUSEHOLD

---

a.	Length of interview in minutes . . .	No. of Minutes _____	35-37

---

b.	Number of <u>telephone</u> contacts required with respondent and others to complete this case . . .	No. of Telephone Contacts _____	38-39

---

c.	Number of <u>personal</u> visits with respondents and others . . .	No. of Personal Visits _____	40

---

d.	Total time spent in locating and arranging interview, excluding travel time . . . (TRY TO ESTIMATE SEPARATELY FOR THE CASE)	No. of Hours _____ No. of Minutes _____	41-42 43-44

---

e.	Sex of respondent:	Male . . . . 1 Female 2	45

---

f.	Respondent is:	White 1	46
		Black 2	
		Asian-American 3	
		Mexican-American 4	
		Puerto Rican 5	
		Other Spanish-American 6	
		American Indian/Alaskan Native . 7	
		Other (SPECIFY)_____ 8	

---

g.	Did the respondent show any signs of being under the influence of alcohol during the interview?	Yes, definitely 1	47
		Yes, possibly 2	
		No, probably not 3	
		No, definitely not 4	

---

h.	Any drinking during interview? (CIRCLE ALL THAT APPLY)	None 1	48
		Soft Drinks 2	49
		Tea––Coffee 3	50
		Beer 4	51
		Wine 5	52
		Whiskey/Other hard liquor . . . 6	53
		Water 7	54
		Other (SPECIFY)_____ 8	55

---

i.	To what extent did R start on the subject of a question but wander off the subject?	None 1	56
		Some 2	
		Moderately 3	
		A lot 4	

ADM-T20
6-74

j.	To what extent did R have trouble grasping the sense of a question?	No trouble	1	57
		Some trouble	2	
		Moderate trouble	3	
		A lot of trouble	4	
k.	Impression of hands . . .	Steady	1	58
		Fine tremor	2	
		Gross tremor	3	
l.	Did respondent seem upset in any way that you knew (he/she) had been to an ATC?	Yes (ANSWER A)	1	59
		No	2	
	A. How upset would you say respondent was?	Very upset	1	60
		Fairly upset	2	
		Slightly upset	3	

INTERVIEWER NUMBER _____ 61-65

INTERVIEWER'S SIGNATURE _____ 66-67

DATE OF INTERVIEW _____ 68-69

ADM-T20
6-74

As you know, all the information you have contributed to this study is completely confidential.

We may wish to speak with you again about a year from now. In order to help us get in touch with you, we should like you to give us the name of a relative or friend outside this household who would be likely to know where you'll be at that time.

This information -- along with your own name and present address -- will be kept on file at the (NAME OF ATC) here in (SITE), and will continue to be kept completely confidential.

What is the name of the relative or friend who would usually know where you'll be?

NAME

ADDRESS | TELEPHONE

RELATIONSHIP

What is the person's relationship to you?

And where do you expect to be living about a year from now?

(IF OTHER THAN PRESENT ADDRESS, OBTAIN AS DETAILED INFORMATION AS POSSIBLE)

RECORD BELOW:

RESPONDENT'S NAME

RESPONDENT'S PRESENT ADDRESS

RESPONDENT'S PRESENT TELEPHONE NUMBER

Bibliography

Aharan, C. H., R. D. Oqiluie, and J. T. Pastington, "Clinical Indicators of Motivation in Alcoholic Patients," *Quarterly Journal of Studies on Alcohol,* 1967, *28,* pp. 486–492.

American Institute of Public Opinion, *The Gallup Opinion Index,* Report No. 93, Princeton, N. J., March 1973.

Anant, S. S., "A Note on the Treatment of Alcoholics by a Verbal Aversion Technique," *Canadian Psychologist,* 1967, *8,* pp. 19–22.

Armor, D. J., "Toward a Unified Theory of Reliability for Social Measurement," The Rand Corporation, P-5264, July 1974.

Armstrong, J. D., "The Search for the Alcoholic Personality," *Annals of the American Academy of Political and Social Science,* 1958, *315,* pp. 40–47.

Ausubel, D. P., *Drug Addiction: Physiological, Psychological and Sociological Aspects,* (New York: Random House Inc., 1958).

Baekeland, F., L. Lundwall, and B. Kissin, "Methods for the Treatment of Chronic Alcoholism: A Critical Appraisal," in Y. Israel (ed.), *Research Advances in Alcohol and Drug Problems,* Vol. II (New York: John Wiley & Sons Inc., 1975), pp. 247–328.

Baekeland, F., L. Lundwall, B. Kissin, and T. Shanahan, "Correlates of Outcome in Disulfiram Treatment of Alcoholism," *Journal of Nervous and Mental Disorders,* 1971, *153,* pp. 1–9.

Baekeland, F., L. Lundwall, and T. Shanahan, "Correlates of Patient Attrition in the Outpatient Treatment of Alcoholism," *Journal of Nervous and Mental Disorders,* 1973, *157,* pp. 99–107.

Bahr, H. M., and K. C. Houts, "Can You Trust a Homeless Man? A Comparison of Official Records and Interview Responses by Bowery Men," *Public Opinion Quarterly,* Fall 1971, pp. 374–382.

Bales, R. F., "Cultural Differences in Rates of Alcoholism," *Quarterly Journal of Studies on Alcohol,* 1946, *6,* pp. 480–499.

Bandura, A., *Principles of Behavior Modification* (New York: Holt, Rinehart & Winston, Inc., 1969).

Barry, H., Jr., H. Barry III., and H. T. Blane, "Birth Order of Delinquent Boys with Alcohol Involvement," *Quarterly Journal of Studies on Alcohol,* 1969, *30,* pp. 408–413.

Barry, H., III., "Psychological Factors in Alcoholism," in B. Kissin and H. Begleiter (eds.), *The Biology of Alcoholism,* Vol. 3, *Clinical Pathology* (New York: Plenum Publishing Corporation, 1974), pp. 53–108.

Bateman, N. I., and D. M. Petersen, "Factors Related to Outcome of Treatment for Hospitalized White Male and Female Alcoholics," *Journal of Drug Issues,* 1972, *2,* pp. 66–74.

Belfer, M. L., R. I. Shader, M. Carroll, and J. S. Harmatz, "Alcoholism in Women," *Archives of General Psychiatry,* 1971, *25,* pp. 540–544.

Benor, D., and K. S. Ditman, "Tranquilizers in the Management of Alcoholics: A Review of the Literature to 1964, Part I," *Journal of New Drugs,* 1964, *6,* pp. 319–337.

Benor, D., and K. S. Ditman, "Tranquilizers in the Management of Alcoholics. A Review of the Literature to 1964, Part II," *Journal of Clinical Pharmacology,* 1967, 7, pp. 17–25.

Blake, B. G., "A Follow-Up of Alcoholics Treated by Behavior Therapy," *Behavior Research and Therapy,* 1967, *5,* pp. 89–94.

Blake, B. G., "The Application of Behavior Therapy to the Treatment of Alcoholism," *Behavior Research and Therapy,* 1965, *3,* pp. 75–85.

Blane, H. T., *The Personality of the Alcoholic: Guises of Dependency* (New York: Harper & Row, Publishers, 1968).

Blane, H. T., and M. E. Chafetz, "Dependency Conflict and Sex-Role Identity in Drinking Delinquents," *Quarterly Journal of Studies on Alcohol,* 1971, *32,* pp. 1025–1039.

Blane, H. T., and W. R. Meyers, "Behavioral Dependence and Length of Stay in Psychotherapy Among Alcoholics," *Quarterly Journal of Studies on Alcohol,* 1963, *24,* pp. 503–510.

Blane, H. T., and W. R. Meyers, "Social Class and Establishment of Treatment Relations by Alcoholics," *Journal of Clinical Psychology,* 1964, *20,* pp. 287–290.

Boland, B., "A Test of the Validity of Questionnaire Reports of Alcohol Purchasing," Draft Report, unpublished, 1973.

Boland, B., and R. Roizen, "Sales Slips and Survey Responses: New Data on the Reliability of Survey Consumption Measures," *The Drinking and Drug Practices Surveyor,* No. 8, Social Research Group, Berkeley, California, August 1973, pp. 5–10.

Bourne, P. G., J. A. Alford, and I. Z. Bowcock, "Treatment of Skid Row Alcoholics with Disulfiram," *Quarterly Journal Studies on Alcohol,* 1966, *27,* pp. 42–48.

Bowen, W. T., and L. Androes, "A Follow-Up Study of 79 Alcoholic Patients: 1963–1965," *Bulletin of the Menninger Clinic,* 1968, *32,* pp. 26–34.

Bowman, K. M., and E. M. Jellinek, "Alcohol Addiction and Its Treatment," *Quarterly Journal of Studies on Alcohol,* 1941, 2 pp. 98–176.

Bowman, K. M., A. Simon, C. H. Hine, E. A. Macklin, G. H. Crook, N. Burbridge, and K. Hanson, "A Clinical Evaluation of Tetraethyl Thiuram Disulphide (Antabuse) in the Treatment of Problem Drinkers," *American Journal of Psychiatry,* 1951, *107,* pp. 832–838.

Brown, C. T., and E. C. Knoblock, "Antabuse Therapy in the Army" (A Preliminary Report of Fifty Cases), *U.S. Armed Forces Medical Journal,* 1951, *2,* pp. 191–202.

Brun-Gulbrandsen, S., and O. Irgens-Jensen, "Abuse of Alcohol Among Seamen," *British Journal of the Addictions,* 1967, *62,* pp. 19–27.

Cahalan, D., "Correlates of Respondent Accuracy in the Denver Validity Survey," *Public Opinion Quarterly,* Winter 1968–1969, pp. 607–621.

Cahalan, D., *Problem Drinkers* (San Francisco: Jossey-Bass, 1970).

Cahalan, D., and R. Room, *Problem Drinking Among American Men* (New Brunswick, N. J.: Rutgers Center of Alcohol Studies, 1974).

Cahalan, D., I. H. Cisin, and H. M. Crossley *American Drinking Practices: A National Survey of Behavior and Attitudes,* Monograph No. 6 New Brunswick, N.J.: Rutgers Center of Alcohol Studies, 1969).

Camps, F. E., and B. E. Dodd, "Increase in the Incidence of Nonsecretors of ABH Blood Group Substance Among Alcoholic Patients," *British Journal of Medicine,* January 1967, *1,* pp. 30–31.

Cappell, H., and C. P. Herman, "Alcohol and Tension Reduction: A Review," *Quarterly Journal of Studies on Alcohol,* 1972, *33,* pp. 33–64.

Chafetz, M. E., "Alcohol Excess," *Annals of the New York Academy of Sciences,* 1966a, *133,* Art. 3, pp. 808–813.

Chafetz, M. E., "A Procedure for Establishing Therapeutic Contact with the Alcoholic," *Quarterly Journal of Studies on Alcohol,* 1961, *22,* pp. 325–328.

Chafetz, M. E., "Management of the Alcoholic Patient in an Acute Treatment Facility," in J. H. Mendelson (ed.), *Alcoholism* (Boston: Little, Brown & Co. Inc., 1966b).

Chafetz, M. E., and H. W. Demone, Jr., *Alcoholism and Society* (New York: Oxford University Press, 1962).

Chafetz, M. E., H. T. Blane, H. S. Abrams, E. Clark, J. H. Golner, E. L. Hastie, and W. F. McCourt, "Establishing Treatment Relations with Alcoholics: A Supplementary Report," *Journal of Nervous and Mental Disease,* 1964, *138,* pp. 390–393.

Chafetz, M. E., H. T. Blane, H. S. Abrams, J. Golner, E. Lacy, W. F. McCourt, E. Clark, and W. Meyers, "Establishing Treatment Relations with Alcoholics," *Journal of Nervous and Mental Disease,* 1962, *134,* pp. 395–409.

Child, G. P., W. Osinski, R. E. Bennett, and E. Davidoff, "Therapeutic Results and Clinical Manifestations Following the Use of Tetraethyl Thiuram Disulfide," *American Journal of Psychiatry,* 1951, *107,* pp. 774–780.

Chwelos, N., D. B. Blewett, C. M. Smith, and A. Hoffer, "Use of D-lysergic and Diethylamide in the Treatment of Alcoholism," *Quarterly Journal of Studies on Alcohol,* 1959, *20,* pp. 577–590.

Cicero, T. J., R. D. Meyers, and W. C. Black, "Increase in Volitional Ethanol

Consumption Following Interference with a Learned Avoidance Response," *Physiology and Behavior,* 1968, *3,* pp. 657–660.

Clark, R., and E. Polish, "Avoidance Conditioning and Alcoholic Consumption in Rheses Monkeys," *Science,* 1960, *132,* pp. 223–224.

Coleman, J., *Abnormal Psychology and Modern Life,* 4th Ed. (Glenview, Ill: Scott, Foresman & Company, 1972).

Conger, J. J., "The Effects of Alcohol on Conflict Behavior in the Albino Rat," *Quarterly Journal of Studies on Alcohol,* 1951, *12,* pp. 1–29.

Corder, B. F., R. F. Corder, and N. D. Laidlaw, "An Intensive Treatment Program for Alcoholics and Their Wives," *Quarterly Journal of Studies on Alcohol,* 1972, *33,* pp. 1144–1146.

Cowen, J., "A Six-Year Follow-Up of a Series of Committed Alcoholics," *Quarterly Journal of Studies on Alcohol,* 1954, *15,* pp. 413–423.

Cronbach, L. J., "Coefficient Alpha and the Internal Structure of Tests," *Psychometrika,* 16 (3), 1954, pp. 297–334.

Cronbach, L. J., *Essentials of Psychological Testing* (New York: Harper & Row, Publishers, 1960).

Cruz-Coke, R., "Colour Blindness and Cirrhosis of the Liver," *Lancet,* November 1964, *2,* pp. 1064–1065.

Curlee, J., "Alcoholism and the 'Empty Nest,' " *Bulletin of the Menninger Clinic,* 1969, *33* (3), pp. 165–171.

Cutter, H. S. G., J. C. Key, E. Rothstein, and W. C. Jones, "Alcohol, Power and Inhibition," *Quarterly Journal of Studies on Alcohol,* 1973, *34,* pp. 381–389.

Davies, D. L., "Normal Drinking in Recovered Alcohol Addicts," *Quarterly Journal of Studies on Alcohol,* 1962, *23,* pp. 94–104.

Davis, H. F., *Variables Associated with Recovery in Male and Female Alcoholics Following Hospitalization,* Doctoral Dissertation, Texas Technological College, 1966.

de Lint, J., and W. Schmidt, "The Epidemiology of Alcoholism," in Y. Israel and J. Mardones (eds.), *Biological Basis of Alcoholism* (New York: John Wiley & Sons Inc., 1971).

Ditman, K. S., "Evaluation of Drugs in the Treatment of Alcoholics," *Quarterly Journal of Studies on Alcohol,* 1961, Supplement No. 1, pp. 107–116.

Ditman, K. S., "Review and Evaluation of Current Drug Therapies in Alcoholism," *International Journal of Psychiatry,* 1967, *3,* pp. 248–258.

Ditman, K. S., M. Hayman, and J. R. B. Whittiesay, "Nature and Frequency of Claims Following LSD," *Journal of Nervous and Mental Disorders,* 1962, *134,* pp. 346–352.

Drew, L. R. H., "Alcoholism as a Self-Limiting Disease," *Quarterly Journal of Studies on Alcohol,* 1968, *29,* pp. 956–967.

Dubourg, G. O. "After-Care for Alcoholics—A Follow-Up Study," *British Journal of the Addictions,* 1969, *64,* pp. 155–163.

Edlin, J. V., R. H. Johnson, P. Hletko, and G. Heilbrunn, "The Conditioned Aversion Treatment of Chronic Alcoholism" (Preliminary Report), *Archives of Neurology and Psychiatry,* 1945, *53,* pp. 85–87.

Edwards, G., and S. Guthrie, "A Comparison of Inpatient and Outpatient Treatment of Alcohol Dependence," *Lancet,* 1966, *1,* pp. 467–468.

Edwards, G., C. Hensman, and J. Peto, "Drinking in a London Suburb," *Quarterly Journal of Studies on Alcohol, 34,* 1973, pp. 1244–1254.

Efron, V., M. Keller, and C. Gurioli, *Statistics on Consumption of Alcohol and on Alcoholism,* (New Brunswick, N. J.: Rutgers Center of Alcohol Studies, 1972).

Egan, W. P., and R. Goetz, "Effects of Metronidazole on Drinking by Alcoholics," *Quarterly Journal of Studies of Alcohol,* 1968, *29,* pp. 899–902.

Ellis, A. S., and J. Krupinski, "The Evaluation of a Treatment Program for Alcoholics: A Follow-Up Study," *Medical Journal Aus.,* 1964, *1,* pp. 8–13.

Emerson, H., *Alcohol: Its Effects* on Man (New York: Appleton-Century-Crofts Inc., 1934).

Emrick, C. D., "A Review of Psychologically Oriented Treatment of Alcoholism: I. The Use and Interrelationship of Outcome Criteria and Drinking Behavior Following Treatment," *Quarterly Journal of Studies on Alcohol,* 1974, *35,* pp. 523–549.

Emrick, C. D., "A Review of Psychologically Oriented Treatment of Alcoholism: II. The Relative Effectiveness of Different Treatment Approaches and the Effectiveness of Treatment versus No Treatment," *Journal of Studies on Alcohol,* 1975, *36,* pp. 88–108.

Ends, E. J., and C. W. Page, "A Study of Three Types of Group Psychotherapy with Hospitalized Male Inebriates," *Quarterly Journal of Studies on Alcohol,* 1957, *18,* pp. 263–277.

Ends, E. J., and C. W. Page, "Group Psychotherapy and Concomitant Psychological Change," *Psychological Monographs,* 1959, *73,* No. 480.

Erikson, E. H., *Childhood and Society* (New York: Norton & Company Inc., 1950).

Esser, P. H., "Conjoint Family Therapy with Alcoholics—A New Approach," *British Journal of the Addictions,* 1970, *64,* pp. 275–286.

Farrar, C. H., B. J. Powell, and L. K. Martin, "Punishment of Alcohol Consumption by Apneic Paralysis," *Behavior Research and Therapy,* 1968, *6,* pp. 13–16.

Feinman, L., and C. S. Lieber, "Liver Disease in Alcoholism," in B. Kissin and H. Begleiter (eds.), *The Biology of Alcoholism,* Vol. 3, *Clinical Pathology* (New York: Plenum Press, 1974).

Fisher, A., "How Much Drinking Is Dangerous?" *New York Times Magazine,* The New York Times Co., May 18, 1975.

Fitzgerald, B. J., R. A. Pasewark, and R. Clark, "Four-Year Follow-Up of

Alcoholics Treated at a Rural State Hospital," *Quarterly Journal of Studies of Alcohol,* 1971, *32,* pp. 636–642.

Fort, T., and A. L. Porterfield, "Some Backgrounds and Types of Alcoholism Among Women," *Journal of Health and Human Behavior,* 1961, *2,* pp. 283–292.

Foster, F. M., J. L. Horn, and K. W. Wanberg, "Dimensions of Treatment Outcome: A Factor-Analytic Study of Alcoholics' Responses to a Follow-Up Questionnaire," *Quarterly Journal of Studies on Alcohol,* 1972, *33,* pp. 1079–1098.

Fox, V., and M. A. Smith, "Evaluation of a Chemopsy-chotherapeutic Program for the Rehabilitation of Alcoholics: Observations Over a Two-Year Period," *Quarterly Journal of Studies on Alcohol, 20,* pp. 767–780.

Franks, C. M. "Conditioning and Conditioned Aversion Therapies in the Treatment of the Alcoholic," *International Journal of Addiction,* 1966, *1,* pp. 61–98.

Freed, E. X., "Effects of Alcohol on Conflict Behaviors," *Psychological Reports,* 1968, *23,* pp. 151–159.

Freud, S., *The Standard Edition of the Complete Psychological Works of Sigmund Freud,* I. Starchey (ed.) (London: Hogarth Press Ltd., 1955).

Gerard, D. L., and G. Saenger, *Out-Patient Treatment of Alcoholism: A Study of Outcome and Its Determinants* (Toronto, Canada: University of Toronto Press, 1966).

Gerard, D. L., G. Saenger, and R. Wile, "The Abstinent Alcoholic," *Archives of General Psychiatry,* 1962, *6,* pp. 83–95.

Gerrein, J. R., C. M. Rosenberg, and V. Manohar, "Disulfiram Maintenance in Outpatient Treatment of Alcoholism," *Archives of General Psychiatry,* 1973, *28,* pp. 798–802.

Gillis, L. S., and M. Keet, "Prognostic Factors and Treatment Results in Hospitalized Alcoholics," *Quarterly Journal of Studies on Alcohol,* 1969, *30,* pp. 426–437.

Glasscote, R. M., T. F. A. Plant, D. W. Hammersley, F. J. O'Neill, M. E. Chafetz, and E. Cuming, *The Treatment of Programs and Problems,* (Washington, D.C.: Joint Information Service, 1967).

Goldfried, M. R., "Prediction of Improvement in an Alcoholism Outpatient Clinic," *Quarterly Journal of Studies on Alcohol,* 1969, *30* pp. 129–139.

Goldstein, K. M., "Note. A Comparison of Self and Peer Reports of Smoking and Drinking Behavior," *Psychological Reports,* 1966, *18,* p. 702.

Goodwin, D. W., and S. B. Guze, "Heredity and Alcoholism," in B. Kissin and H. Begleister (eds.), *The Biology of Alcoholism,* Vol. 3, *Clinical Pathology* (New York: Plenum Publishing Corporation, 1974), pp. 37–52.

Goodwin, D. W., F. Schulisinger, L. Hermansen, S. B. Guze, and G. Winokur, "Alcohol Problems in Adoptees Raised Apart from Alcoholic Biological Parents," *Archives of General Psychiatry,* 1973, *28,* pp. 238–243.

Gross, M., "The Relation of the Pituitary Gland to Some Symptoms of Alcoholic Intoxication and Chronic Alcoholism," *Quarterly Journal of Studies on Alcohol,* 1945, *6,* pp. 25–35.

Gross, M. M., D. R. Goodenough, J. M. Hastey, S. M. Rosenblatt, and E. Lewis, "Sleep Disturbances in Alcohol Intoxication and Withdrawal: Section II, Physiological Research," in *Recent Advances in Studies of Alcoholism,* National Institute of Mental Health, National Institute on Alcohol Abuse and Alcoholism, Washington, D. C., June 25–27, 1970.

Guilford, J. P., *Psychometric Methods* (New York: McGraw-Hill Book Company Inc., 1954).

Guze, S. B., and D. W. Goodwin, "Consistency of Drinking History and Diagnosis of Alcoholics," *Quarterly Journal of Studies on Alcohol,* 1972, *33,* pp. 111–116.

Guze, S. B., V. A. Tuason, M. A. Stewart, and B. Picken, "The Drinking History: A Comparison of Reports by Subjects and Their Relatives," *Quarterly Journal of Studies on Alcohol,* June 1963, *24,* pp. 249–260.

Harrington, C. C., *Errors in Sex-Role Behavior in Teen-Age Boys* (New York: Teachers College Press, Teachers College, Columbia University, 1970).

Harris, L., and Associates Inc., *Public Awareness of the NIAAA Advertising Campaign and Public Attitudes Toward Drinking and Alcohol Abuse,* February 1974.

Hayman, M., "Current Attitudes to Alcoholism of Psychiatrists in Southern California," *American Journal of Psychiatry,* 1956, *112,* pp. 484–493.

Heise, D. R., "Separating Reliability and Stability in Test-Retest Correlation," *American Sociological Review,* February 1969, *34,* pp. 93–101.

Hilgard, J. R., and M. F. Newman, "Parental Loss by Death in Childhood as an Etiological Factor Among Schizophrenic Alcoholic Patients Compared with a Non-Patient Community Sample," *Journal of Nervous and Mental Diseases,* 1963, *137,* pp. 14–28.

Hill, M. I., and H. T. Blane, "Evaluation of Psychotherapy with Alcoholics: A Critical Review," *Quarterly Journal of Studies on Alcohol,* 1967, *28,* pp. 76–104.

Hoff, E. C., *The Alcoholisms,* Paper presented at the 28th International Congress on Alcohol and Alcoholism, Washington, D. C., September 15–20, 1968.

Hoff, E. C., "The Use of Pharmacological Adjuncts in the Psychotherapy of Alcoholics," *Quarterly Journal of Studies on Alcohol,* 1961, Supplement 1, pp. 138–150.

Hollister, L. E., J. Shelton, and G. Krelger, "A Controlled Comparison of Lysergic Acid Diethylamide (LSD) and Dextroamphetamine in Alcoholics," *American Journal of Psychiatry,* 1969, *125,* pp. 1352–1357.

Horton, D., "The Functions of Alcohol in Primitive Societies: A Cross-Cultural Study," *Quarterly Journal of Studies on Alcohol,* 1943, *4,* pp. 199–320.

Hsu, J. J., "Electroconditioning Therapy of Alcoholics: A Preliminary Report," *Quarterly Journal of Studies on Alcohol*, 1965, *26*, pp. 449–459.

Humphreys, L. G., "Investigations of the Simplex," *Psychometrika*, 1960, *25*(4), pp. 313–323.

Hunt, G. M., and N. H. Azrin, "A Community Reinforcement Approach to Alcoholism," *Behavior Research and Therapy*, 1973, *11*, pp. 91–104.

Hyman, M. M., "Alcoholics 15 Years Later," Unpublished paper presented at the 6th Annual Medical-Scientific Session, National Council on Alcoholism, April 28–29, 1975, Milwaukee, Wisconsin.

Irwin, T., "Attacking Alcohol as a Disease," *Today's Health*, 1968, *46*, pp. 21–23, 72–74.

Jacobsen, E., "Biochemical Methods in the Treatment of Alcoholism, with Special Reference to Antabuse," *Proceedings of the Royal Society of Medicine*, 1950, *43*, pp. 519–526.

Jellinek, E. M., "Heredity of the Alcoholic," *Quarterly Journal of Studies on Alcohol*, 1945, *6*, p. 105.

Jellinek, E. M., "Phases of Alcohol Addiction," *Quarterly Journal of Studies on Alcohol*, 1952, *13*, pp. 673–684.

Jellinek, E. M., *The Disease Concept of Alcoholism* (New Brunswick, N. J.: Hillhouse Press, 1960).

Jensen, S. E., "A Treatment Program for Alcoholics in a Mental Hospital," *Quarterly Journal of Studies on Alcohol*, 1962, *23*, pp. 315–320.

Jessor, R., T. D. Graves, R. C. Hanson, and S. L. Jessor *Society, Personality, and Deviant Behavior* (New York: Holt, Rinehart & Winston Inc., 1968).

Jetter, W. W., "Studies in Alcohol: I. The Diagnosis of Acute Alcoholic Intoxication by a Correlation of Clinical and Chemical Findings," *The American Journal of the Medical Sciences*, October 1938, *196*(4), pp. 475–487.

Johnson, F. G., "LSD in the Treatment of Alcoholism," *American Journal of Psychiatry*, 1969, *126*, pp. 481–487.

Johnson, L. C., "Sleep Patterns in Chronic Alcoholics," in N. K. Mello and J. H. Mendelson (eds.), *Recent Advances in Studies of Alcoholism*, 1971, pp. 288–316.

Jones, M. C., "Personality Correlates and Antecedents of Drinking Patterns in Adult Males," *Journal of Consulting Clinical Psychology*, 1968, *32*, pp. 2–12.

Kant, F., "The Use of Conditioned Reflex in the Treatment of Alcohol Addicts," *Wisconsin Medical Journal*, 1945, *44*, pp. 217–221.

Karolus, H. E., "Alcoholism and Food Allergy," *Illustrated Medical Journal*, 1961, *119*, pp. 151–152.

Keller, M., "Definition of Alcoholism," *Quarterly Journal of Studies on Alcohol*, 1960, *21*, pp. 125–134.

Keller, M., "The Definition of Alcoholism and the Estimation of Its Prevalence," in D. J. Pittman and C. R. Snyder (eds.), *Society, Culture and*

Drinking Patterns (New York: John Wiley & Sons Inc., 1962), pp. 310–329.

Keller, M., and M. McCormick, *A Dictionary of Words About Alcohol* (New Brunswick, N.J.: Rutgers Center of Alcohol Studies, 1968).

Kendell, R. E., "Normal Drinking by Former Alcohol Addicts," *Quarterly Journal of Studies on Alcohol*, 1968, *24*, pp. 44–60.

Kish, G. B., and H. T. Hermann, "The Fort Meade Alcoholism Treatment Program: A Follow-Up Study," *Quarterly Journal of Studies on Alcohol*, 1971, *32*, pp. 628–635.

Kissin, B., "The Pharmacodynamics and Natural History of Alcoholism," in B. Kissin and H. Begleiter (eds.), *The Biology of Alcoholism*, Vol. 3, *Clinical Pathology*, (New York: Plenum Press, 1974); pp. 1–36.

Kissin, B., and M. M. Gross, "Drug Therapy in Alcoholism," *American Journal of Psychiatry*, 1968, *125*, pp. 31–41.

Kissin, B., and A. Platz, "The Use of Drugs in the Long Term Rehabilitation of Chronic Alcoholics," in D. E. Efron (ed.), *Psychopharmacology: A Review of Progress*, Public Health Service Publication No. 1836, Washington, D. C., 1968.

Kissin, B., M. M. Gross, and I. Schutz, "Correlation of Urinary Biogenic Amines with Sleep Stages in Chronic Alcoholization and Withdrawal," in M. M. Gross (ed.), *Experimental Studies of Alcohol Intoxication and Withdrawal* (New York: Plenum Press, 1973).

Kissin, B., A. Platz, and W. H. Su, "Selective Factors In Treatment Choice and Outcome in Alcoholics," in N. K. Mello and J. H. Mendelson (eds.), *Recent Advances in Studies of Alcoholism*, Publication No. (HSM) 71-9045 (Washington, D.C.: U.S. Government Printing Office, 1971), pp. 781–802.

Kissin, B., A. Platz, and W. H. Su, "Social and Psychological Factors in the Treatment of Chronic Alcoholism," *Journal of Psychiatric Research*, 1970, *8*, pp. 13–27.

Kissin, B., S. M. Rosenblatt, and S. Machover, "Prognostic Factors in Alcoholism," *Psychiatric Research Reports*, 1968, *24*, pp. 22–43.

Kissing, B., V. J. Schenker, and A. C. Schenker, "The Acute Effects of Ethyl Alcohol and Chlorpromazine on Certain Physiological Functions in Alcoholics," *Quarterly Journal of Studies on Alcohol*, 1959, *20*, pp. 480–492.

Kline, N. S., *Evaluation of Lithium Therapy in Chronic Alcoholism*, Paper presented at the Third Annual Alcoholism Conference, National Institute on Alcohol Abuse and Alcoholism, June 1973.

Knight, R. P., "The Psychoanalytic Treatment in a Sanatorium of Chronic Addiction to Alcohol," *Journal of the American Medical Association*, 1938, *111*, pp. 1443–1448.

Knupfer, G., *The Validity of Survey Data on Drinking Problems: A Comparison Between Respondent's Self Reports and Outside Sources of Information*, Unpublished transcript, University of California, Berkeley, 1967.

Kraft, T., and I. Al-Issa, "Alcoholism Treated by Desensitization: A Case Report," *Behavioral Research and Therapy*, 1967, *5*, pp. 69–70.

Laverty, S. G., "Aversion Therapies in the Treatment of Alcoholism," *Psychosomatic Medicine*, 1966, *28*, pp. 651–666.

Ledermann, S., "Alcool-alcoolisme-alcoolisation; donn$_e$es scientifiques de carac$_e$tre physiologique, $_e$conomique et social," Institute National d'Etudes Demographiques, Travaux et Documents, Cahier No. 29, Presses Universitaires de France, 1956.

Lehman, R. J., A. C. Wolfe, and R. D. Kay, *A Computer Archive of ASAP Roadside Breathtesting Surveys, 1970–1974*, prepared for the Department of Transportation by the Highway Safety Research Institute, The University of Michigan, January 1975.

Lemere, F., "What Happens to Alcoholics," *American Journal of Psychiatry*, 1953, *109*, pp. 674–676.

Lemere, F., W. L. Voegtlin, W. B. Broz, P. O'Hollaren, and W. E. Tupper, "Conditioned Reflex Treatment of Chronic Alcoholism: VII Technic," *Diseases of the Nervous System*, 1942, *3*, pp. 243–247.

Lester, D., "A Biological Approach to the Etiology of Alcoholism," *Quarterly Journal of Studies on Alcohol*, 1960, *21*, pp. 701–703.

Lester, D., "Self-Selection of Alcohol by Animals, Human Variation, and the Etiology of Alcoholism: A Critical Review," *Quarterly Journals of Studies on Alcohol*, 1966, *27*, pp. 395–438.

Levinson, T., and G. Sereny, "An Experimental Evaluation of 'Insight Therapy' for the Chronic Alcoholic," *Canadian Psychiatric Association Journal*, 1969, *14*, pp. 143–145.

Linksy, A. S., "The Changing Public Views on Alcoholism," *Quarterly Journal of Studies on Alcohol*, 1970, *31*, pp. 692–704.

Linton, P. H., and J. D. Hain, "Metronidazole in the Treatment of Alcoholism," *Quarterly Journal of Studies on Alcohol*, 1967, *28*, pp. 544–546.

Lisansky, E. S., "The Etiology of Alcoholism: The Role of Psychological Predisposition," *Quarterly Journal of Studies on Alcohol*, 1960, *21*, pp. 314–343.

Lisansky-Gomberg, E. S., "Etiology of Alcoholism," *Journal of Consulting Clinical Psychology*, 1968, *32*, pp. 18–20.

Lloyd, R. W., Jr. and Salzberg, H. C. "Controlled Social Drinking: An Alternative to Abstinence as a Treatment Goal for Some Alcohol Abusers." *Psychological Bulletin*, 1975, *82*, pp. 815–842.

Lovell, H. W., and J. W. Tintera, "Hypoadvenocorticism in Alcoholism and Drug Addiction," *Geriatrics*, 1951, *6*, pp. 1–11.

Lovibond, S. H., and G. Caddy, "Discriminated Aversive Control in the Moderation of Alcoholics' Drinking Behavior," *Behavior Therapy*, 1970, NY1, pp. 437–444.

Ludwig, A., J. Levine, L. Stark, and R. Lazer, "A Clinical Study of LSD

Treatment in Alcoholism," *American Journal of Psychiatry,* 1969, *126,* pp. 59–69.

Lundwall, L., and F. Baekeland, "Disulfiram Treatment of Alcoholism: A Review," *Journal of Nervous and Mental Diseases,* 1971, *153,* pp. 381–392.

MacKay, J. R., "Clinical Observations on Adolescent Problem Drinkers," *Quarterly Journal of Studies on Alcohol,* 1961, *22,* pp. 124–134.

Makela, K., "Alkoholinkulutuksen Mittaaminen," *Alkoholipolittisen Tutkimuslaitoksen Tutkimusseloste,* March 1969, *36.*

Mardones, J., "On the Relationship Between Deficiency of B Vitamins and Alcohol Intake in Rats," *Quarterly Journal of Studies on Alcohol,* 1951, *12,* pp. 563–575.

Martensen-Larsen, O., "Five Years' Experience with Disulfiram in the Treatment of Alcoholics," *Quarterly Journal of Studies on Alcohol,* 1953, *14,* pp. 406–418.

Masserman, J. H., and K. S. Yum, "An Analysis of the Influence of Alcohol on Experimental Neuroses in Cats," *Psychosomatic Medicine,* 1946, *8,* pp. 36–52.

Maters, W., "The Quarter-Way House: An Innovative Alcoholism Treatment Program," *Maryland State Medical Journal,* 1972, *21* (No. 2), pp. 40–43.

Mayer, J., and D. J. Myerson, "Outpatient Treatment of Alcoholics: Effects of Status, Stability and Nature of Treatment," *Quarterly Journal of Studies on Alcohol,* 1971, *32,* pp. 620–627.

McClearn, G. E., and D. A. Rodgers, "Differences in Alcohol Preference Among Inbred Stains of Mice," *Quarterly Journal of Studies on Alcoholism,* 1959, *20,* pp. 691–695.

McClearn, G. E., and D. A. Rodgers, "Genetic Factors in Alcohol Preference of Laboratory Mice," *Journal of Comparative Physiological Psychology,* 1961, *54,* pp. 116–119.

McClelland, D. C., W. N. Davis, R. Kalin, and E. Wanner, *The Drinking Man* (New York: The Free Press, 1972).

McCord, W., J. McCord, and J. Gudeman, *Origins of Alcoholism* (Stanford, Calif.: Stanford University Press, 1960).

Mello, N. K., and J. H. Mendelson, "Drinking Patterns During Work-Contingent and Noncontingent Alcohol Acquisition," *Psychosomatic Medicine,* March-April 1972, *34*(2), pp. 139–164.

Miller, M. M., "Treatment of Chronic Alcoholism by Hypnotic Aversion," *Journal of the American Medical Association,* 1959, *171,* pp. 1492–1495.

Milmore, S., R. Rosenthal, H. T. Blane, M. E. Chafetz, and I. Folf, "The Doctor's Voice. Postdictor of Successful Referral of Alcoholic Patients," *Journal of Abnormal Psychology,* 1967, *72,* pp. 78–84.

Mindlin, D. F., "Evaluation of Therapy for Alcoholics in a Workhouse Setting," *Quarterly Journal of Studies on Alcohol,* 1960, *21,* pp. 90–112.

Mindlin, D. F., "The Characteristics of Alcoholics as Related to Prediction of

Therapeutic Outcome," *Quarterly Journal of Studies on Alcohol,* 1959, *20,* pp. 604–619.

Mindlin, D. F., and E. Belden, "Attitude Changes with Alcoholics in Group Therapy," *California Mental Health Research Digest,* 1965, *3,* pp. 102–103.

Moore, R. A., and F. Ramseur, "Effects of Psychotherapy in an Open-Ward Hospital in Patients with Alcoholism," *Quarterly Journal of Studies on Alcohol,* 1960, *21,* pp. 233–252.

Moore, R. A., and T. C. Murphy, "Denial of Alcoholism as an Obstacle to Recovery," *Quarterly Journal of Studies on Alcohol,* 1961, *22,* pp. 597–609.

Mottin, J. L., "Drug-Induced Attenuation of Alcohol Consumption: A Review and Evaluation of Claimed, Potential or Current Therapies," *Quarterly Journal of Studies of Alcohol,* 1973, *34,* pp. 444–472.

Mulford, H. A., *Meeting the Problems of Alcohol Abuse: A Testable Action Plan for Iowa* (Cedar Rapids, Iowa: Iowa Alcoholism Foundation, 1970).

Muzekari, L. H., "The MMPI in Predicting Treatment Outcome in Alcoholism," *Journal of Consulting Psychology,* June 1965, *29,* p. 281.

Naitoh, P., and R. F. Docter, "Electroencephalographic and Behavioral Correlates of Experimentally Induced Intoxication with Alcoholic Subjects," Twenty-Eighth International Congress on Alcohol and Alcoholism, Washington, D. C., 1968.

Narrol, H. G., "Experimental Application of Reinforcement Principles to the Analysis and Treatment of Hospitalized Alcoholics," *Quarterly Journal of Studies on Alcohol,* 1967, *28,* pp. 105–115.

Nathan, P. E., M. A. O'Brien, and D. Norton, "Comparative Studies of the Interpersonal and Affective Behavior of Alcoholics and Nonalcoholics During Prolonged Experimental Drinking," in N. K. Mello and J. H. Mendelson (eds.), *Recent Advances in Studies of Alcoholism,* National Institute on Alcohol Abuse and Alcoholism (Washington, D. C.: U. S. Government Printing Office, 1970).

National Council on Alcoholism, "Criteria for the Diagnosis of Alcoholism," *Annals of Internal Medicine,* 1972, *77,* pp. 249–258.

NIAAA, *Alcohol and Health,* 2d Report (Rockville, Maryland: U. S. Department of Health, Education, and Welfare, 1974.)

O'Reilly, P. O., and A. Funk, "LSD in Chronic Alcoholism," *Canadian Psychiatric Association Journal,* 1964, *9,* pp. 258–261.

Parker, F. B., "Sex-Role Adjustment in Women Alcoholics," *Quarterly Journal of Studies on Alcohol,* 1972, *33,* pp. 647–657.

Parry, H. J., and H. M. Crossley, "Validity of Responses to Survey Questions," *Public Opinion Quarterly,* Spring 1950, *14*(1), pp. 61–80.

Partanen, J., K. Bruun, and T. Markkanen, *Inheritance of Drinking Behavior: A Study on Intelligence, Personality, and Use of Alcohol of Adult Twins* (Helsinki: Finnish Foundation for Alcohol Studies, 1966).

Pattison, E. M., "A Critique of Alcoholism Treatment Concepts; With Special

Reference to Abstinence," *Quarterly Journal of Studies on Alcohol,* 1966, *27,* pp. 49–71.

Pattison, E. M., "Rehabilitation of the Chronic Alcoholic," in B. Kissin and H. Begleiter (eds.), *The Biology of Alcoholism,* Vol. 3, *Clinical Pathology,* (New York: Plenum Press, 1974), pp. 587–658.

Pattison, E. M., L. A. Bishop, and A. S. Linsky, "Changes in Public Attitudes on Narcotic Addiction," *American Journal of Psychiatry,* 1968, *125,* pp. 160–167.

Pattison, E. M., R. Coe and R. I. Rhodes, "Evaluation of Alcoholism Treatment: A Comparison of Three Facilities," *Archives of General Psychiatry,* 1969, *20,* pp. 478–488.

Pemberton, D. A. "A Comparison of the Outcome of Treatment in Female and Male Alcoholics," *British Journal of Psychiatry,* 1967, *113,* pp. 367–373.

Penick, S. B., R. N. Carrier, and J. B. Sheldon, "Metronidazole in the Treatment of Alcoholism," *American Journal of Psychiatry,* 1969, *125,* pp. 1063–1066.

Pernanen, Kai, "Validity of Survey Data on Alcohol Use," in Y. Israel (ed.), *Research Advances in Alcohol and Drug Problems,* Vol. 1 (New York: John Wiley & Sons Inc., 1974).

Petrie, A., *Individuality in Pain and Suffering* (Chicago: University of Chicago Press, 1967).

Pfeffer, A. Z., and S. Berger, "A Follow-Up Study of Treated Alcohol," *Quarterly Journal of Studies on Alcohol,* 1957, *18,* pp. 624–648.

Pittman, D. J., and C. W. Gordon, *Revolving Door: A Study of the Chronic Police Case Inebriate* (Glencoe, Ill.: Free Press, 1958).

Pittman, D.J., and M. Sterne, "Concept of Motivation: Sources of Institutional and Professional Blockage in the Treatment of Alcoholics," *Quarterly Journal of Studies on Alcohol,* 1965, *26,* pp. 41–57.

Pittman, D. J., and R. L. Tate, "A Comparison of Two Treatment Programs for Alcoholics," *Quarterly Journal of Studies on Alcohol,* December 1969, *30,* pp. 888–899.

Pittman, D. J., and R. L. Tate, "A Comparison of Two Treatment Programs for Alcoholics," *International Journal of Social Psychiatry,* Autumn 1973, *18,* pp. 183–193.

Plaut, T. F., *Alcohol Problems: A Report to the Nation by the Cooperative Commission on the Study of Alcoholism* (New York: Oxford University Press, 1967).

Pokorny, A. D., B. A. Miller, and S. E. Cleveland," Response to Treatment of Alcoholism: A Follow-Up Study," *Quarterly Journal of Studies on Alcohol,* 1968, *29,* pp. 364–381.

Popham, R. E., "A Critique of the Genotrophic Theory of the Etiology of Alcoholism," *Quarterly Journal of Studies of Alcohol,* 1953, *14,* pp. 228–237.

Proctor, R. C., and T. H. Tooley, "Antabuse in Chronic Alcoholism," *North Carolina Medical Journal,* 1950, *11,* pp. 323–327.

Randolph, T. G., "The Descriptive Features of Food Addiction: Addictive Eating and Drinking," *Quarterly Journal of Studies on Alcohol,* 1956, *17,* pp. 198–224.

Rathod, N. H., E. Gregory, D. Blows, and G. H. Thomas, "A Two-Year Follow-Up Study of Alcoholic Patients," *British Journal of Psychiatry,* 1966, *112,* pp. 683–692.

Reinert, R. E., "The Concept of Alcoholism as a Disease," *Bulletin of the Menninger Clinic,* 1968, *32,* pp. 21–25.

Richter, C. P., "Loss of Appetite for Alcohol and Alcoholic Beverages Produced in Rats by Treatment with Thyroid Preparations," *Endocrinology,* 1956, *59,* pp. 472–478.

Ritson, B., "Involvement in Treatment and Its Relation to Outcome Amongst Alcoholics," *British Journal of the Addictions,* 1969, *64,* pp. 23–29.

Ritson, B., "Personality and Prognosis in Alcoholism," *British Journal of Psychiatry,* 1971, *118,* pp. 79–82.

Robins, L. N., *Deviant Children Grow Up: A Sociological and Psychological Study of Sociopathic Personality* (Baltimore: Williams & Wilkins Company, 1966).

Robins, L. N., W. M. Bates, and P. O'Neal, "Adult Drinking Patterns of Former Problem Children," in D. I. Pittman and C. R. Snyder (eds.), *Society, Culture and Drinking Patterns* (New York: John Wiley & Sons Inc., 1962).

Rodgers, D. A., "Factors Underlying Differences in Alcohol Preference Among Inbred Strains of Mice," *Psychosomatic Medicine,* 1966, *28*(4), pp. 498–513.

Roman, P. M., *Constructive Coercion and the "Alcoholic": A Critique of Assumptions,* Paper presented at the 28th International Congress on Alcohol and Alcoholism, Washington, D.C., September 15–20, 1968.

Roman, P. M., and H. M. Trice, *Alcoholism and Porblem Drinking as Social Roles: The Effects of Constructive Coercion,* Paper presented at the 17th Annual Meeting of the Society for the Study of Social Problems, San Francisco, Calif., August 27, 1967.

Room, R., *Assumptions and Implications of Disease Concepts of Alcoholism,* Paper presented at the 29th International Congress on Alcoholism and Drug Dependence, Sydney, Australia, February 1970.

Room, R., "Survey vs. Sales Data for the U.S.," *Drinking and Drug Practices Surveyor,* Social Research Group, Berkeley, California, January 1971, *3,* pp. 15–16.

Rosen, A. C., "A Comparative Study of Alcoholic and Psychiatric Patients with the MMPI," *Quarterly Journal of Studies on Alcohol,* 1960, *21,* pp. 253–266.

Rosenblatt, S. M., M. M. Gross, B. Malenowski, M. Broman, and E. Lewis, "Marital Status and Multiple Psychiatric Admissions for Alcoholism," *Quarterly Journal of Studies on Alcohol,* 1971, *32,* pp. 1092–1096.

Rosenthal, R., and L. Jacobson, *Pygmalian in the Classroom* (New York: Holt, Rinehart & Winston Inc., 1968).

Rossi, J. J., "A Holistic Treatment for Alcoholism Rehabilitation," *Medical Ecological Clinical Research,* 1970, *3,* pp. 6–16.

Rossi, J. J., A. Stach, and N. J. Bradley, "Effects of Treatment of Male Alcoholics in a Mental Hospital," *Quarterly Journal of Studies on Alcohol,* 1963, *24,* pp. 91–108.

Rubington, E., "The Future of the Halfway House," *Quarterly Journal of Studies on Alcohol,* 1970, *31,* pp. 167–174.

Rudfeld, K., "Recovery from Alcoholism by Treatment with Antabuse Combined with Social and Personal Counseling: A Statistical Calculation of the Prognosis in Different Social Groups," *Danish Medical Bulletin,* 1958, *5,* pp. 212–216.

Ruggels, W. L., et al., *A Follow-Up Study of Clients at Selected Alcoholism Treatment Centers Funded by NIAAA,* Stanford Research Institute, May 1975.

Sampson, E. E., "The Study of Ordinal Position: Antecedents and Outcomes," in B. A. Maher (ed.), *Progress in Experimental Personality Research,* Vol. 2 (New York: Academic Press Inc., 1965), pp. 175–228.

Sanderson, R. E., D. Campbell, and S. G. Laverty, "An Investigation of a New Oversize Conditioning Treatment for Alcoholism," *Quarterly Journal of Studies on Alcohol,* 1963, *24,* pp. 261–275.

Sarett, M., F. Cheek, and H. Osmond, "Reports of Wives of Alcoholics of Effects of LSD-25 Treatment of Their Husbands," *Archives of General Psychiatry,* 1966, *14,* pp. 171–178.

Schaefer, H. H., M. B. Sobell, and K. C. Mills, "Some Sobering Data on the Use of Self Confrontation with Alcoholics," *Behavior Therapy,* 1971, *2,* pp. 28–39.

Schmidt, W., "Analysis of Alcohol Consumption Data: The Use of Consumption Data for Research Purposes," *The Epidemiology of Drug Dependence: Report on a Conference: London, 25–29 September, 1972,* Regional Office for Europe, World Health Organization, Copenhagen, 1973.

Schukit, M. A., D. A. Goodwin, and G. Winokur, "A Study of Alcoholism in Half Siblings," *American Journal of Psychiatry,* March 1972, *128*(9), pp. 1132–1136.

Scott, P. D., "Offenders, Drunkenness and Murder," *The British Journal of Addiction,* 1968, *63,* pp. 221–226.

Selzer, M. L., "Problems Encountered in the Treatment of Alcoholism," *University of Michigan Medical Center Journal,* 1967, *33,* pp. 58–63.

Selzer, M. L., and W. H. Holloway, "A Follow-Up of Alcoholics Committed to a State Hospital," *Quarterly Journal of Studies on Alcohol,* 1957, *18,* pp. 98–120.

Sereny, G., and M. Fryatt, "A Follow-Up Evaluation of the Treatment of Chronic Alcoholics," *Canadian Medical Association Journal,* 1966, *94,* pp. 8–12.

Skoloda, T. E., A. I. Alterman, F. S. Cornelison, Jr., and E. Gottheil, "Treatment Outcome in a Drinking-Decisions Program," *Journal of Studies on Alcohol, 36,* March 1975, pp. 365–380.

Smart, R. G., "Effects of Alcohol on Conflict and Avoidance Behavior," *Quarterly Journal of Studies on Alcohol,* 1965, *26,* pp. 187–205.

Smart, R. G., and T. Storm, "The Efficacy of LSD in the Treatment of Alcoholism," *Quarterly Journal of Studies on Alcohol,* 1964, *25,* pp. 333–338.

Smart, R. G., T. Storm, E. F. W. Baker, and L. Solursh, "A Controlled Study of Lysergide in the Treatment of Alcoholism, I. The Effects on Drinking Behavior," *Quarterly Journal of Studies on Alcohol,* 1966, *27,* pp. 469–482.

Smatr, R. G., T. Storm, E. F. W. Baker, and L. Solursh, *Lysergic Acid Diethylamide (LSD) in the Treatment of Alcoholism: An Investigation of Its Effects on Drinking Behavior, Personality Structure and Social Functioning* (Toronto: University of Toronto Press, 1967).

Smith, C. G., "Alcoholics: Their Treatment and Their Wives," *British Journal of Psychiatry,* 1969, *115,* pp. 1039–1042.

Smith, C. M., "A New Adjunct to the Treatment of Alcoholism: The Hallucinogenic Drugs," *Quarterly Journal of Studies on Alcohol,* 1958, *19,* pp. 406–417.

Smith, J. J., "A Medical Approach to Problem Drinking," Preliminary Report, *Quarterly Journal of Studies on Alcohol,* 1949, *10,* pp. 251–257.

Sobell, M. B., and L. C. Sobell, "Alcoholics Treated by Individualized Behavior Therapy: One-Year Treatment Outcome," *Behavior Research and Therapy,* 1973, *11,* pp. 599–618.

Sobell, M. B., and L. C. Sobell, "Individualized Behavior Therapy for Alcoholics: Rationale, Procedures, Preliminary Results and Appendix," *California Mental Health Research Monograph No. 13,* Department of Mental Hygiene, Sacramento, California, 1972.

Sobell, M. B., L. C. Sobell, and F. H. Samuels, "Validity of Self-Reports of Alcohol-Related Arrests by Alcoholics," *Quarterly Journal of Studies on Alcohol,* 1974, *35,* pp. 276–280.

Stein, L. I., D. Niles, and A. M. Ludwig, "The Loss of Control Phenomenon in Alcoholics," *Quarterly Journal of Studies on Alcohol,* 1968, *29,* 598–602.

Sterne, M. W., D. J. Pittman, "The Concept of Motivation: A Source of Institutional and Professional Blockage in the Treatment of Alcoholics," *Quarterly Journal of Studies on Alcohol,* 1965, *26,* pp. 41–57.

Sullivan, H. S., *The Interpersonal Theory of Psychiatry* (New York: Norton & Company Inc., 1953).

Summers, T., "Validity of Alcoholics' Self-Reported Drinking History," *Quarterly Journal of Studies on Alcohol,* 1970, *31,* pp. 972–974.

Sutherland, E. H., H. G. Schroeder, and C. L. Tordella, "Personality Traits and the Alcoholic: A Critique of Existing Studies," *Quarterly Journal of Studies on Alcohol,* 1950, *11,* pp. 547–561.

Syme, L., "Personality Characteristics and the Alcoholic," *Quarterly Journal of Studies on Alcohol,* 1957, *18,* pp. 288–302.

Tarnower, S. M., and H. M. Toole, "Evaluation of Patients in an Alcoholism Clinic for More Than 10 Years," *Diseases of the Nervous System,* 1968, *29,* pp. 28–31.

Thimann, J., "Conditioned Reflex Treatment of Alcoholism: II. The Risks of Its Application, Its Indications, Contra-indications and Psychotherapeutic Aspects," *New England Journal of Medicine,* 1949, *241,* pp. 406–410.

Tomsovic, M., and R. V. Edwards, "Cerebral Electrotherapy for Tension-Related Symptoms in Alcoholics," *Quarterly Journal of Studies on Alcohol,* 1973, *34,* pp. 1352–1355.

Towle, L. H., et al., *Alcoholism Program Monitoring System Development: Evaluation of the ATC Program,* Stanford Research Institute, March 1973.

Trice, H. M., "Alcoholism: Group Factors in Etiology and Therapy," *Human Organization,* 1956, *15,* pp. 33–40.

Trice, H. M., "A Study of the Process of Affiliation with Alcoholics Anonymous," *Quarterly Journal of Studies on Alcohol,* 1957, *18,* pp. 39–54.

Trice, H. M., and P. M. Roman, "Sociopsychological Predictors of Affiliation with Alcoholics Anonymous: A Longitudinal Study of 'Treatment Success,' " *Social Psychiatry,* 1970, *5,* pp. 51–59.

Trice, H. M., P. M. Roman, and J. A. Belasco, "Selection for Treatment: A Predictive Evaluation of an Alcoholism Treatment Regimen," *International Journal of the Addictions,* 1969, *4,* pp. 303–317.

Van Dusen, W., W. Wilson, W. Miners, and H. Hook, "Treatment of Alcoholism with Lysergide," *Quarterly Journal of Studies on Alcohol,* 1967, *28,* pp. 295–304.

Voegtlin, W. L., and W. R. Broz, "The Conditioned Reflex Treatment of Chronic Alcoholism: X. An Analysis of 3125 Admissions Over a Period of Ten and a Half Years," *Annals of Internal Medicine,* 1949, *30,* pp. 580–597.

Voegtlin, W. L., and F. Lemere, "The Treatment of Alcohol Addiction: A Review of the Literature," *Quarterly Journal of Studies on Alcohol,* 1942, *2,* pp. 717–798.

Voegtlin, W. L., F. Lemere, W. R. Broz, and P. O'Hollaren, "Conditioned Reflex Therapy of Chronic Alcoholism: IV. A Preliminary Report on the Value of Reinforcement," *Quarterly Journal of Studies on Alcohol,* 1942, *2,* pp. 505–511.

Vogel, M. D., "The Relation of Personality Factors to GSR Conditioning of

Alcoholics: An Exploratory Study," *Canadian Journal of Psychology,* 1960, *14,* pp. 275–280.

Vogel, M. D., "The Relationship of Personality Factors to Drinking Patterns of Alcoholics: An Exploratory Study," *Quarterly Journal of Studies on Alcohol,* 1961, *22,* pp. 394–400.

Vogel-Sprott, M., "Alcoholism and Learning," in B. Kissin and H. Begleiter (eds.), *The Biology of Alcoholism,* Vol. 2, *Physiology and Behavior* (New York: Plenum Press, 1972), pp. 485–507.

Vogler, R. E., R. Ferstl, and S. Kraemer, "Problems in Aversive Training in Alcoholics Related to Social Situation," *Stud. Psychol. Bratisl.,* 1971, *13,* pp. 211–213.

Vogler, R. E., S. E. Lunde, G. R. Johnson, and P. L. Marten, "Adversion Conditioning with Chronic Alcoholics," *Journal Consulting and Clinical Psychology,* 1970, *34,* pp. 302–307.

von Wright, J. M., L. Pekanmaki, and S. Malin, "Effects of Conflict and Stress on Alcohol Intake in Rats," *uarterly Journal of Studies on Alcohol,* 1971, *32,* pp. 420–433.

Wall, J. H., "A Study of Alcoholism in Men," *American Journal of Psychiatry,* 1936, *92,* pp. 1389–1401.

Wall, J. H., and E. B. Allen, "Results of Hospital Treatment of Alcoholism," *American Journal of Psychiatry,* 1944, *100,* pp. 474–479.

Wallerstein, R. S., "Comparative Study of Treatment Methods for Chronic Alcoholism: The Alcoholism Research Project at Winter VA Hospital," *American Journal of Psychiatry,* 1956, *113,* pp. 228–233.

Wallerstein, R. S., *Hospital Treatment of Alcoholism: A Comparative Experimental Study,* Menninger Clinic Monograph Series No. 11 (New York: Basic Books Inc., 1957).

Wallgren, H., and H. Barry, *Actions of Alcohol,* Vol. II (Amsterdam: Elsevier, 1970).

Walton, H. J., E. B. Ritson, and R. I. Kennedy, "Response of Alcoholics to Clinic Treatment," *British Medical Journal,* 1966, *2,* pp. 1171–1174.

Wanberg, K. W., "Prevalence of Symptoms Found Among Excessive Drinkers," *International Journal of Addiction,* 1969, *4,* pp. 169–185.

Wanberg, K. W., and J. L. Horn, "Alcoholism Symptom Patterns of Men and Women," *Quarterly Journal of Studies on Alcohol,* 1970, *31,* pp. 40–61.

Weingartner, H., and L. A. Faillace, "Verbal Learning in Alcoholic Patients," *Journal of Nervous and Mental Diseases,* 1971, *153,* pp. 407–416.

Weingold, H., J. M. Lachin, A. H. Bell, and C. Coxe, "Depression as a Symptom of Alcoholism: Search for a Phenomenon," *Journal of Abnormal Psychology,* 1968, *73,* pp. 195–197.

Weiss, C. H., "Validity of Welfare Mothers' Interview Responses, *Public Opinion Quarterly, Winter* 1968-1969, *32,* pp. 622–633.

Wexberg, L. E., "A Critique of Physiopathological Theories of the Etiology of

Alcoholism," *Quarterly Journal of Studies on Alcohol,* 1950, *11,* pp. 113–118.

Williams, R. J., "The Etiology of Alcoholism: A Working Hypothesis Involving the Interplay of Hereditary and Environmental Factors," *Quarterly Journal of Studies on Alcohol,* 1947, *7,* pp. 567–587.

Williams, R. J., *Alcoholism: The Nutritional Approach* (Austin: University of Texas Press, 1959).

Williems, P. J. A., F. J. J. Letemendia, and F. Arroyave, "A Categorization for the Assessment of Prognosis and Outcome in the Treatment of Alcoholism," *British Journal of Psychiatry,* 1973, *122,* pp. 649–654.

Wilsnack, S. C., *Psychological Factors in Female Drinking,* Ph.D. Dissertation, Harvard University, 1972.

Winokur, G., T. Reich, J. Rimmer, and F. Pitts, "Alcoholism: III. Diagnosis and Familial Psychiatric Illness in 259 Alcoholic Probands," *Archives of General Psychiatry* (Chicago), August 1970, *23,* pp. 104–111.

Winship, G. M., "Antabuse Treatment," in R. S. Wallerstein (ed.), *Hospital Treatment of Alcoholism: A Comparative, Experimental Study,* Menninger Clinic Monograph Series 11, 1957, pp. 23–51.

Witkin, H. A., S. A. Karp, and D. R. Goodenough, "Dependence in Alcoholics," *Quarterly Journal of Studies on Alcohol,* 1959, *20,* pp. 493–504.

Wolff, K., "Hospitalized Alcoholic Patients: III. Motivating Alcoholics Through Group Psychotherapy," *Hospital and Community Psychiatry,* 1968, *19,* pp. 206–209.

Wolff, S., and L. Holland, "A Questionnaire Follow-Up of Alcoholic Patients," *Quarterly Journal of Studies on Alcohol,* 1964, *25,* pp. 108–118.

Wolpe, J., *Psychotherapy of Recipiocal Inhibition* (Stanford, Calif.: Stanford University Press, 1958).

Wood, H. P., and E. L. Duffy, "Psychological Factors in Alcoholic Women," *American Journal of Psychiatry,* 1966, *123,* pp. 341–345.

World Health Organization, "Expert Committee on Mental Health Alcoholism Subcommittee," *Second Report,* W.H.O. Technical Report Series, No. 48, August, 1952.

Yanushevskii, I. K., "Effektivnost' Protwoolykogol' Nogo Techeniya Po Dannym Katamnexa" ["The Effectiveness of Antialcohol Treatment According to Follow-Up Data"], *Zhurnal Nevro-Patologii I Psikhiatrii,* 1959, *59,* pp. 693–696.

Zucker, R. A., "Sex-Role Identity Patterns and Drinking Behavior of Adolescents," *Quarterly Journal of Studies on Alcohol,* 1968, *29,* pp. 868–884.

Index

Selected Rand Books

Bagdikian, Ben H., *The Information Machines: Their Impact on Men and the Media* (New York: Harper and Row, 1971).

Downs, Anthony, *Inside Bureaucracy* (Boston, Mass.: Little, Brown and Company, 1967).

Fisher, Gene H., *Cost Considerations in Systems Analysis* (New York: American Elsevier Publishing Company, Inc., 1971).

Greenwood, Peter W., Jan Chaiken, and Joan Petersilia, *The Criminal Investigation Process* (Lexington, Mass.: D. C. Heath and Company, 1977).

Kakalik, James S., and Sorrel Wildhorn, *The Private Police: Security and Danger* (New York: Crane, Russak and Company, 1977).

Quade, E. S., *Analysis for Public Decisions* (New York: American Elsevier Publishing Company, Inc., 1975).

The Rand Corporation, *A Million Random Digits with 100,000 Normal Deviates* (Glencoe, Ill.: The Free Press, 1955).

Turn, Rein, *Computers in the 1980s* (New York: Columbia University Press, 1974).

Williams, John D., *The Compleat Strategyst: Being a Primer on the Theory of Games of Strategy* (New York: McGraw-Hill Book Company, Inc., 1954).

Yin, Robert K., Karen A. Heald, and Mary E. Vogel, *Tinkering with the System: Technological Innovations in State and Local Services* (Lexington, Mass.: D. C. Heath and Company, 1977).